INSIGHTS ON LEADERSHIP

ALSO EDITED BY LARRY C. SPEARS

On Becoming a Servant-Leader (with Don M. Frick), 1996

Seeker and Servant (with Anne T. Fraker), 1996

Reflections on Leadership: How Robert K. Greenleaf's Theory of Servant-Leadership Influenced Today's Top Management Thinkers, 1995

INSIGHTS ON LEADERSHIP

Service, Stewardship, Spirit, and Servant-Leadership

Edited by Larry C. Spears

John Wiley & Sons, Inc.

New York • Chichester • Weinheim • Brisbane • Singapore • Toronto

This text is printed on acid-free paper.

Copyright © 1998 by The Greenleaf Center.

Published by John Wiley & Sons, Inc.

All rights reserved. Published simultaneously in Canada.

This publication is designed to provide accurate and authoritative information in regard to the subject matter covered. It is sold with the understanding that the publisher is not engaged in rendering legal, accounting, or other professional services. If legal advice or other expert assistance is required, the services of a competent professional person should be sought.

Library of Congress Cataloging-in-Publication Data:

Insights on leadership : service, stewardship, spirit, and servant-leadership/edited
  by Larry C. Spears.
      p. cm.
    Includes index.
  ISBN 0-471-17634-6 (cloth : alk. paper)
    1. Leadership. 2. Organizational effectiveness. I. Spears,
  Larry C., 1955-
  HD57.7.I57   1998
  658.4'092—dc21   97-23165
                                          CIP

Printed in the United States of America
10 9 8 7 6 5 4 3 2 1

CONTENTS

PART FOUR   SERVANT-LEADERSHIP

PREFACE

This book owes much to the favorable public response that has followed the 1995 publication of *Reflections on Leadership: How Robert K. Greenleaf's Theory of Servant-Leadership Influenced Today's Top Management Thinkers*. That book, also published by John Wiley & Sons, is currently in its fourth printing and has piqued the interest of thousands of readers who are now exploring and implementing servant-leadership in many and varied ways.

As a result of the publication of *Reflections on Leadership*, many articles and essays have been written in the past two years on servant-leadership. This current collection of 30 essays brings together into one volume some of the most current and significant pieces on servant-leadership and the growing influence of Robert Greenleaf. Most of these essays have been specially written for inclusion in this book.

Insights on Leadership represents an even more significant companion volume to *Reflections on Leadership*. These essays, organized around the closely related themes of *service, stewardship, spirit* and *servant-leadership* have been written by some of the leading thinkers, writers, and practitioners of servant-leadership today.

If you are intrigued, inspired, or moved by what you are about to discover, I invite you to contact me for more information concerning the wide array of servant-leadership programs and resources at:

The Greenleaf Center for Servant-Leadership
921 E. 86th St., Suite 200
Indianapolis, IN 46240
(317) 259-1241 (phone)
(317) 259-0560 (fax)

—Larry C. Spears
Indianapolis, Indiana
September 1997

FOREWORD

Servant-Leadership from the Inside Out

Stephen R. Covey

The deepest part of human nature is that which urges people—each one of us—to rise above our present circumstances and to transcend our nature. If you can appeal to it, you tap into a whole new source of human motivation. Perhaps this is why I have found Robert Greenleaf's teaching on servant-leadership to be so enormously inspiring, so uplifting, so ennobling.

A great movement is taking place throughout the world today. Its roots, I believe, are to be found in two powerful forces. One is the dramatic globalization of markets and technology. And in a very pragmatic way, this tidal wave of change is fueling the impact of the second force: timeless, universal principles that have governed, and always will govern, all enduring success, especially those principles that give "air" and "life" and creative power to the human spirit that *produces* value in markets, organizations, families, and, most significantly, individual's lives.

Servant-Leadership Will Continue to Increase in Relevance

One of these fundamental, timeless principles is the idea of servant-leadership, and I am convinced that it will continue to dramatically increase in its relevance. There is a growing awareness and consciousness around it in the world. One of the things that is driving it, as I have mentioned, is the global economy, which absolutely insists on quality at low cost. You've got to produce more for less, and with greater speed than you've ever done before. The only way you can do that in a sustained way is through the empowerment of people. And the only way you get empowerment is through high-trust cultures and through an empowerment philosophy that turns bosses into servants and coaches.

When you've got a low-trust culture that is characterized by high-control management, political posturing, protectionism, cynicism, and internal competition and adversarialism, you simply cannot compete with the speed, quality, and innovation of those organizations around the world that *do* empower people. You may be able to buy someone's hand and back, but you cannot buy their heart, mind, and spirit. And in the competitive reality of today's global marketplace, it will be only those organizations whose people not only willingly volunteer their tremendous creative talent, commitment, and loyalty, but whose organizations align their structures, systems, and management style to support the empowerment of their people that will survive and thrive as market leaders.

Leaders are learning that this kind of empowerment, which is what servant-leadership represents, is one of *the* key principles that, based on practice, not talk, will be the deciding point between an organization's enduring success or its eventual extinction.

The "Strange Attractor"

I love the statement made by business author Stan Davis: "When the infrastructure shifts, everything rumbles." Well, everything is rumbling because the old rules of traditional, hierarchical, high-external-control, top-down management are being dismantled—they simply aren't working any longer. They are being replaced by a new form of control that the chaos theory people call the "strange attractor"—a sense of vision that people are drawn to, and united in, that enables them to be driven by *inner* motivation toward achieving a common purpose. This has changed the role of manager from one who has driven results and motivation from the outside in to one who is a servant-leader—one who seeks to draw out, inspire, and develop the best and highest within people from the inside out. The leader does this by engaging the entire team or organization in a process that creates a shared vision that inspires each to stretch and reach deeper within themselves and to use their unique talents in whatever way is necessary to independently and interdependently achieve that shared vision.

Point North

To illustrate this in my teaching, I often ask everyone in the audience to close their eyes and point north. I then ask them to open their eyes and see where everyone is pointing. Without exception, people are literally pointing in every possible direction. The rest of the dialogue goes something like this:

> "Now, let's go to the experts. All those who are absolutely confident you know which way north is, raise your hands." [About 10 percent usually respond.] "Those with their hands up, please stand up. Those standing, close your eyes and point north. Now open your eyes." [Again, people are pointing every possible direction.] "These are people who are *absolutely sure* they know which way is north. Now, you realize that if you are off only one degree between here and Jerusalem, you'll end up in

Moscow. Does this shake any of you 'nonexperts' up to see such disagreement among the 'experts'—people who are absolutely confident?"

If you want to have an interesting experience that is just about the equivalent of the one that I just mentioned, when you're done reading this foreword, go to people one-on-one in your organization and say something to this effect: "In one sentence, what is our mission?" Have them write it down, and then ask them one additional question: "What is our strategy to accomplish that mission?" Have them write it down. I do this all the time with executive cabinets of Fortune 100 companies—the biggest, largest, most progressive companies—and guess what? It's just about like our Point North exercise—their answers are pointing all over the place, and they honestly cannot believe it! They say to each other, "How can you possibly think that is our strategy? I mean, no wonder you're so off base!"

One time I worked with the executives of an organization in Dallas. I asked them if they would share their mission statement with me. They replied a little sheepishly, "Well, we don't normally share it openly. It's kind of private. But since this is a small group, I guess we can." They pulled out of a desk a statement that read: "Our mission is to increase the asset base of the owners."

I said, "Well, do you put that on the wall to inspire all of your customers and employees?"

He said, "Come on, Stephen, this is just kind of a small group here. You don't have to try and impress us. You're not in front of some big audience. Come on. You and I know what life is all about. It's what business is—to make money, right?"

I said, "That's one of four needs, no question about it—the economic need. If there is no margin, there will be no mission. But I'll tell you what your culture is like. You have an unbelievably messed-up culture, and I haven't even studied it. If your industry is unionized, you got one right up to your bottom lip. It's giving you fits. Your organization is filled with interpersonal conflicts and interdepartmental rivalries. Most of your people who have eight cylinders are running on about four—and there is nothing you can do about it. There are great power plays going on between formal leaders and informal leaders. And the list goes on."

Amazed, he replied, "How could you know so much about us?"

I continued, "Furthermore, after this meeting is over, half of you will be bad-mouthing and talking about the other half behind their backs."

I went on to explain that they are dealing with only one need of one stakeholder (someone who has a stake in the success of the organization).

"Are there no other stakeholders involved? Are there no other needs? What about the relationship need between people? What about the need to develop and use talent, the mind? What about the need for meaning, for purpose, for contribution, for service, for adding value, for making a difference? Those are three other needs, and there are many other stakeholders."

They replied, "What can we do? How long will it take?"

I asked, "How bad are you hurting?"

"Not too bad."

"I wouldn't get started yet then if I were you, because you're not sincere; there is no conviction here."

"How long will it take?" they inquired.

"Well, the way you described the level of pain and awareness of that, my guess is that you might get the beginning in a couple of years."

"You don't understand, Stephen; you seem to understand all this, but really, we can whip this baby out this weekend."

"Really?" I asked.

You see, they thought they were going to go off-site to some resort and have one of these visionary workshop retreats to come up with which way is "True North" for their company.

Well, within two years they got real momentum going, and within five, they were an entirely new organization. And they did the kind of things that Greenleaf talked about. They focused on helping people become responsible to care, not to caretake—to help people grow as individuals. Then they went to work on the institution.

To get the kind of trust in a culture that enables an empowerment approach to thrive, you must not only have individuals who are trustworthy and whose vision is shared with the organization, you must also have a trustworthy organization—one that fosters and supports empowerment. Principles based on "True North" must be institutionalized, or there will be no reinforcement. That was the basic message of Edwards Deming to this country—that, arguably, more than 90 percent of the problems are due to bad systems, not bad people. However, Greenleaf correctly points out that people are the programmers. They are the ones who write the systems. Ultimately, however, you must work with people to give them a new concept of their stewardship and redefine leadership as service and stewardship.

My study of 200 years of success literature in the United States taught me that we shifted away from the principled approach when we moved away from the agricultural age. We pulled away from a value system focused on character and principles and moved toward one focusing more on techniques and technology. We lost our moral bearings. Take the compass, for example. The needle always points north. True North always stays the same. There's also a movable arrow on a compass called the direction of travel arrow. That could represent our social value system, our habits. The key is to align our social values and personal habits with these natural laws or principles. This would represent true alignment.

Servant-Leadership Is a Natural Law

The servant-leadership concept is a principle, a natural law, and getting our social value systems and personal habits aligned with this ennobling principle is one of the great challenges of our lives. Let me give you an illustration of this that I think many of us relate to. How many of us crammed in school? How many got good at it? Now how many have worked on a farm? How many crammed on the farm—you know, forgot to plant in the spring, goofed around all summer, and then worked extra hard in the fall to sow and reap the harvest? Interesting. We cram in school but not on a farm. Yet it works in school. Why? It's because the social system is governed by social laws. But with the farm, which is a natural system governed by natural laws, cramming doesn't work. And yet does it really work in school? Wouldn't we agree that you can get a degree or credential, pass tests, get credit, and yet not get a real education? What about the body—farm or school? Farm. What about marriage and family? Major farm. What about raising teenagers? It's called rock farming. What about business? Farm. It's self-evident. You see, everything is an ecosystem. Servant-leadership emphasizes increased service to others, a holistic ecological approach to work, promoting a sense of community, of togetherness, of connection. That is what the whole future is going to be. It's interdependency, it's connection, and it's the sharing of power in decision making.

Changeless Principles at the Core

There has to be something at the soul of an organization that does not change that will enable people to live *with* change. This unchanging core is natural principles. I certainly didn't invent them. Greenleaf didn't invent them. These are natural laws that are self-evident and universal. We all inwardly know them. They are common sense. As T. S. Eliot so beautifully put it, "We must not cease from exploration. And the end of all our exploring will be to arrive where we began and to know the place for the first time."[1]

I find it both interesting and profound that as hundreds of my colleagues and I go around the world working with organizations, we find that if you can get enough people interacting freely and synergistically to develop a value system that will inform and guide their decisions, they always come up with the same value system. They may use different words, but if you study them carefully, they always come up with the same basic value system. They deal with four areas: our bodies (to live), our hearts (to love), our minds (to learn), and our spirit (to leave a legacy). If you study the sacred literature of the six great religions of the world, basically they all deal with the same four areas, the same basic underlying principles.

Synergy comes from the balance and integration of the four basic needs of life—physical, social, mental, and spiritual:

> *To live* is simple physical and financial survival, fairness, and security.
>
> *To love* has to do with quality of relationships. No one on their deathbed ever wished they'd spent more time at the office.
>
> *To learn* is the development of the mind and of our talents. I estimate that one-fifth of our workforce is obsolete. We've moved out of the

industrialized age, and the high-wage, low-skilled jobs are gone. Organizations are downsizing and outsourcing. In my opinion, it's only just starting. And Europe is behind the United States in this trend.

This is causing deep disillusionment because people feel like the social compact has been violated. We are all at risk now. Every organization is at risk. There is no safety net. The global economy makes every competitor, every option that can meet your needs, a buyable choice for a consumer. There is an absolute need for constant lifelong education. Education is a process, not a place. I know that I have to literally discipline myself, on average, to a minimum of two hours a day, and two full days a month to reading and development in my field, just to stay current. The half-life of many professions is only four years. I mention so much about this area because, of the four areas, this tends universally to be the most neglected by both individuals and organizations.

To leave a legacy is to be involved in ways that contribute and truly make a difference—in every area of life—in our work, our communities, our churches, our neighborhoods, and, most of all, in our families.

An Organization without Principles

Now, how do organizations operate in the absence of a core of principles? In other words, what if you are working in a culture without the trust that flows from personal and organizational trustworthiness? What is the leadership approach going to be? What do you do when trust is low and you have to get jobs done? You give orders, threaten, and instill fear. If you have this kind of heavy-control approach, what are the structures and systems going to look like? Rigid. The organizational structure will be hierarchical, with many layers. What about the procedure manuals? They'll be huge. Now with the dynamism of today's marketplace with all of its new technology and economic, political, and social forces, how is this organization with all of its rigidity, bureaucracy, and structure going to maintain its viability in the long run? It can't.

What if you try to introduce the concept of servant-leadership in such an organization? What will happen? How will those concepts be received? People will probably see you as "holier than thou," trying to push your spiritual, moral approach as a solution to my needs. There is no trust. They'll be looking for your hidden agenda with all the cynicism that comes from perpetual "programs of the month"—reengineering, restructuring, reinvention, empowerment, the self-directed work team, the whole vocabulary of what's happening in the world of management and leadership—including servant-leadership. You see, people get beat up. They get fatigued. They become cynical. They don't believe the rhetoric anymore. So where do they find their satisfactions? Off the job. Then what's the job? A pure means to an end—not an end in itself.

Leader *and* Organization as Servant: An Ecosystem

If you really want to get servant-leadership, then you've got to have institutionalization of the principles at the organizational level and foster trust through individual character and competence at the personal level. Once you have high trust, then you lead people by coaching, empowerment, persuasion, example, modeling. That is servant-leadership. The Greenleaf concept is that not only is the leader a servant, but the organization also is a servant.

An Inside-Out Approach

In the last analysis, the power to cultivate servant-leadership comes from the individual. It's an inside-out approach. The more I study and try to apply the principle of servant-leadership, the more I am inspired by the power of the individual as the programmer. A trim tab is the small rudder that moves the big rudder that moves the whole ship. If a person can become a trim tab, he or she can move an entire organization. It comes from *your* modeling, *your* example. It comes from your mentoring; that's relationship—you care, and I can feel it. Then it comes from your teaching. I'm open to your teaching and influence. It's like the saying, "I don't care how much you know until I know how much you care." You are then in a position to truly make a difference with me. "Give a man a fish, you feed him for the day, teach him how to fish and you feed him for a lifetime." You want to make me independent of you, you don't want to be a caretaker, you want to be caregiver, and help me grow in the ability to live with a new dynamic role—with risk and responsibility.

Illustration: Olivet College

One of the most inspiring examples of the living of the principle of servant-leadership that I know of is Olivet College in Michigan. Michael Bassis, president of Olivet College, is bringing in a total ecological approach that puts the college in alignment with its mission. The whole mission of the institution is geared toward individual and social responsibility, which means to serve, contribute, and make a difference. The way he is accomplishing it is as a servant and model. By deeply involving all the academic and administrative areas and with patience, more than 85 percent of the people have accepted this mission and have developed learning objectives that are congruent with it. Once they had the learning objectives, then everything in student and academic life was geared and structured so that systems and processes would accomplish those learning objectives.

I have worked with many universities, and this is one of the most unusual and inspirational examples of an ecological approach. Bassis has been there for only a few years but has an unusual awareness of ecology, of the larger systems, and of the need for patience.

It's like the *Chinese bamboo tree*. You plant it and see nothing but a small shoot above the ground for four years. During those four years the root structure is developing deep inside the soil—yet you see nothing. You work diligently all the while. In the fifth year the Chinese bamboo tree grows 80 feet!

Islands of Excellence in a Sea of Mediocrity

What if we could get model communities in this country, and model institutions, schools, businesses, and government units, that would become islands of excellence in a sea of mediocrity? What if they could become models and then transport what they learn and become mentors to others so that this whole spirit of stewardship, of servant-leadership, of working at the empowerment process through structures and systems could take root and flourish? I honestly think we could heal our country. I believe that the overwhelming majority of the people of this country, with the right kind of servant-leadership at all levels, most importantly at the family level, could heal our country. Otherwise, our social problems will worsen and deepen until eventually they will overwhelm the economic machinery—and this would discombobulate everything.

I have hope and confidence that we can. I have the same hope of people in every nation, for the principles of servant-leadership are universal. I believe that hope is a moral imperative, and that as we keep our flame of hope burning by our own efforts, we become a big part of the solution.

Stephen R. Covey is founder and chairman of the Covey Leadership Center, an international firm that has worked with thousands of organizations in implementing principle-centered leadership. He is also founder of the nonprofit Institute for Principle-Centered Leadership. Dr. Covey has been the recipient of numerous awards, including the first Thomas More College Medallion for continued service to humanity and the McFeely Award from the International Management Council for significant contributions to management and education. Dr. Covey received the National Entrepreneur of the Year Lifetime Achievement Award for Entrepreneurial Leadership and is also the recipient of three honorary doctorate degrees. He is the author of a half-dozen books including The Seven Habits of Highly Effective People, *which has sold more than ten million copies. Covey was a keynote speaker at The Greenleaf Center's 1996 conference.*

INTRODUCTION

Tracing the Growing Impact of Servant-Leadership

Larry C. Spears

The servant-leader is servant first. It begins with the natural feeling that one wants to serve. Then conscious choice brings one to aspire to lead. The best test is: do those served grow as persons; do they, while being served, become healthier, wiser, freer, more autonomous, more likely themselves to become servants?

—Robert K. Greenleaf

The mightiest of rivers are first fed by many small trickles of water. This observation is also an apt way of conveying my belief that the growing number of practitioners of servant-leadership has increased from a trickle to a river. On a global scale it is not yet a mighty river. However, it is an expanding river, and one with a deep current.

The servant-leader concept continues to grow in its influence and impact. In fact, we have witnessed an unparalleled explosion of interest and practice of servant-leadership in the 1990s. In many ways, it can truly be said that the times are only now beginning to catch up with Robert Greenleaf's visionary call to servant-leadership.

Servant-leadership, now in its third decade as a specific leadership and management concept, continues to create a quiet revolution in workplaces around the world. Both this book and this introduction are intended to provide a broad overview of the growing influence this unique concept of servant-leadership is having on people and their workplaces.

As we near the end of the twentieth century, we are beginning to see that traditional, autocratic, and hierarchical modes of leadership are yielding to a newer model—one based on teamwork and community, one that seeks to involve others in decision making, one strongly based in ethical and caring behavior, and one that is attempting to enhance the personal growth of workers while improving the caring and quality of our many institutions. This emerging approach to leadership and service is called *servant-leadership*.

The words *servant* and *leader* are usually thought of as being opposites. When two opposites are brought together in a creative and meaningful way, a paradox emerges. And so the words *servant* and *leader* have been brought together to create the paradoxical idea of servant-leadership. The basic idea of servant-leadership is both logical and sensible. Since the time of the industrial revolution, managers have tended to view people as objects; institutions have considered workers as cogs within a machine. In the past few decades we have witnessed a shift in that long-held view. Standard practices are rapidly shifting toward the ideas put forward by Robert Greenleaf, Stephen Covey, Peter Senge, Max DePree, and many others who suggest that there is a better way to manage our organizations in the twenty-first century.

Today there is a much greater recognition of the need for a more team-oriented approach to leadership and management. Robert Greenleaf's writings on the subject of servant-leadership helped to get this movement started, and his views have had a profound and growing effect on many.

Robert K. Greenleaf

Despite all the buzz about modern leadership techniques, no one knows better than Greenleaf what really matters.

—*Working Woman* magazine

The term *servant-leadership* was first coined in a 1970 essay by Robert K. Greenleaf (1904–1990), entitled *The Servant as Leader.* Greenleaf, born in Terre Haute, Indiana, spent most of his organizational life in the field of management research, development, and education at AT&T. Following a 40-year career at AT&T, Greenleaf enjoyed a second career that lasted 25 years, during which time he served as an influential consultant to a number of major institutions, including Ohio University, MIT, Ford Foundation, R. K. Mellon Foundation, the Mead Corporation, the American Foundation for Management Research, and Lilly Endowment Inc. In 1964 Greenleaf also founded the Center for Applied Ethics, which was renamed the Robert K. Greenleaf Center in 1985 and is now headquartered in Indianapolis.

As a lifelong student of how things get done in organizations, Greenleaf distilled his observations in a series of essays and books on the theme of "The Servant as Leader"—the objective of which was to stimulate thought and action for building a better, more caring society.

The Servant-as-Leader Idea

The idea of the servant as leader came partly out of Greenleaf's half century of experience in working to shape large institutions. However, the event that crystallized Greenleaf's thinking came in the 1960s, when he read Hermann Hesse's short novel *Journey to the East*—an account of a mythical journey by a group of people on a spiritual quest.

After reading this story, Greenleaf concluded that the central meaning of it was that the great leader is first experienced as a servant to others, and that this simple fact is central to his or her greatness. True leadership emerges from those whose primary motivation is a deep desire to help others.

In 1970, at the age of 66, Greenleaf published *The Servant as Leader*, the first of a dozen essays and books on servant-leadership.[1] Since that time, more than 500,000 copies of his books and essays have been sold worldwide. Slowly but surely, Greenleaf's servant-leadership writings have made a deep, lasting impression on leaders, educators, and many others who are concerned with issues of leadership, management, service, and personal growth.

What Is Servant-Leadership?

In all of his works, Greenleaf discusses the need for a new kind of leadership model, a model that puts serving others—including employees, customers, and community—as the number one priority. Servant-leadership emphasizes increased service to others, a holistic approach to work, promoting a sense of community, and the sharing of power in decision making.

Who *is* a servant-leader? Greenleaf said that the servant-leader is one who is a servant first. In *The Servant as Leader* he wrote, "It begins with the natural feeling that one wants to serve, to serve first. Then conscious choice brings one to aspire to lead. The difference manifests itself in the care taken by the servant—first to make sure that other people's highest priority needs are being served. The best test is: Do those served grow as persons; do they, while being served, become healthier, wiser, freer, more autonomous, more likely themselves to become servants?"[2]

It is important to stress that servant-leadership is *not* a "quick-fix" approach. Nor is it something that can be quickly instilled within an institution. At its core, servant-leadership is a long-term, transformational approach to life and work—in essence, a way of being—that has the potential for creating positive change throughout our society.

Ten Characteristics of the Servant-Leader

Servant leadership deals with the reality of power in everyday life—its legitimacy, the ethical restraints upon it and the beneficial results that can be attained through the appropriate use of power.
—*The New York Times*

After some years of carefully considering Greenleaf's original writings, I have identified a set of 10 characteristics of the servant-leader that I view as being of critical importance. The following characteristics are central to the development of servant-leaders:

1. *Listening:* Leaders have traditionally been valued for their communication and decision-making skills. While these are also important skills for the servant-leader, they need to be reinforced by a deep commitment to listening intently to others. The servant-leader seeks to identify the will of a group and helps clarify that will. He or she seeks to listen receptively to what is being said (and not said!). Listening also encompasses getting in touch with one's own inner voice and seeking to understand what one's body, spirit, and mind are communicating. Listening, coupled with regular periods of reflection, is essential to the growth of the servant-leader.

2. *Empathy:* The servant-leader strives to understand and empathize with others. People need to be accepted and recognized for their special and unique spirits. One assumes the good intentions of coworkers and does not reject them as people, even while refusing to accept their behavior or performance. The most successful servant-leaders are those who have become skilled empathetic listeners. It is interesting to note that Robert Greenleaf developed a course in "receptive listening" in the 1950s for the Wainwright House in New York. This course continues to be offered to the present day.

3. *Healing:* Learning to heal is a powerful force for transformation and integration. One of the great strengths of servant-leadership is the potential for healing one's self and others. Many people have broken spirits and have suffered from a variety of emotional hurts. Although this is a part of being human, servant-leaders recognize that they have an opportunity to "help make whole" those with whom they come in contact. In *The Servant as Leader* Greenleaf writes: "There is something subtle communicated to one who is being served and led if, implicit in the compact between servant-leader and led, is the understanding that the search for wholeness is something they share."[3]

4. *Awareness:* General awareness, and especially self-awareness, strengthens the servant-leader. Making a commitment to foster awareness can be scary—you never know what you may discover!
    Awareness also aids one in understanding issues involving ethics and values. It lends itself to being able to view most situations from a more integrated, holistic position. As Greenleaf observed: "Awareness is not a giver of solace—it is just the opposite. It is a disturber and an awakener. Able leaders are usually sharply awake and reasonably disturbed. They are not seekers after solace. They have their own inner serenity."[4]

5. *Persuasion:* Another characteristic of servant-leaders is a reliance on persuasion, rather than using one's positional authority, in making decisions within an organization. The servant-leader seeks to convince others, rather than coerce compliance. This particular element

offers one of the clearest distinctions between the traditional author-itarian model and that of servant-leadership. The servant-leader is ef-fective at building consensus within groups. This emphasis on per-suasion over coercion probably has its roots within the beliefs of The Religious Society of Friends (Quakers), the denomination with which Robert Greenleaf himself was most closely allied.

6. *Conceptualization:* Servant-leaders seek to nurture their abilities to "dream great dreams." The ability to look at a problem (or an or-ganization) from a conceptualizing perspective means that one must think beyond day-to-day realities. For many managers this is a characteristic that requires discipline and practice. The traditional manager is consumed by the need to achieve short-term opera-tional goals. The manager who wishes to also be a servant-leader must stretch his or her thinking to encompass broader-based con-ceptual thinking. Within organizations, conceptualization is, by its very nature, the proper role of boards of trustees or directors. Un-fortunately, boards can sometimes become involved in the day-to-day operations (something that should always be discouraged!) and fail to provide the visionary concept for an institution. Trustees need to be mostly conceptual in their orientation, staffs need to be mostly operational in their perspective, and the most ef-fective CEOs and managers probably need to develop both per-spectives. Servant-leaders are called to seek a delicate balance be-tween conceptual thinking and a day-to-day focused approach.

7. *Foresight:* Closely related to conceptualization, the ability to fore-see the likely outcome of a situation is hard to define, but easy to identify. One knows it when one sees it. Foresight is a characteris-tic that enables the servant-leader to understand the lessons from the past, the realities of the present, and the likely consequence of a decision for the future. It is also deeply rooted within the intu-itive mind. As such, one can conjecture that foresight is the one servant-leader characteristic with which one may be born. All other characteristics can be consciously developed. There hasn't been a great deal written on foresight. It remains a largely unex-plored area in leadership studies, but one most deserving of careful attention.

8. *Stewardship:* Peter Block (author of *Stewardship* and *The Empow-ered Manager*) has defined stewardship as "holding something in trust for another."[5] Robert Greenleaf's view of all institutions was one in which CEOs, staffs, and trustees all played significant roles in holding their institutions in trust for the greater good of society. Servant-leadership, like stewardship, assumes first and foremost a commitment to serving the needs of others. It also emphasizes the use of openness and persuasion rather than control.

9. *Commitment to the growth of people:* Servant-leaders believe that people have an intrinsic value beyond their tangible contributions as workers. As such, the servant-leader is deeply committed to the growth of each and every individual within his or her institution. The servant-leader recognizes the tremendous responsibility to do everything within his or her power to nurture the personal, professional, and spiritual growth of employees. In practice, this can include (but is not limited to) concrete actions such as making available funds for personal and professional development, taking a personal interest in the ideas and suggestions from everyone, encouraging worker involvement in decision making, and actively assisting laid-off workers to find other employment.

10. *Building community:* The servant-leader senses that much has been lost in recent human history as a result of the shift from local communities to large institutions as the primary shaper of human lives. This awareness causes the servant-leader to seek to identify some means for building community among those who work within a given institution. Servant-leadership suggests that true community can be created among those who work in businesses and other institutions. Greenleaf said: "All that is needed to rebuild community as a viable life form for large numbers of people is for enough servant-leaders to show the way, not by mass movements, but by each servant-leader demonstrating his own unlimited liability for a quite specific community-related group."[6]

These 10 characteristics of servant-leadership are by no means exhaustive. However, I believe that the ones listed serve to communicate the power and promise that this concept offers to those who are open to its invitation and challenge.

Tracing the Growing Impact of Servant-Leadership

Servant leadership has emerged as one of the dominant philosophies being discussed in the world today.
                                                    —*Indianapolis Business Journal*

Servant-Leadership as an Institutional Model

Servant-leadership principles are being applied in significant ways in a half-dozen major areas. The first area has to do with servant-leadership as an institutional philosophy and model. Servant-leadership crosses all boundaries and is being applied by a wide variety of people working with for-profit businesses; not-for-profit corporations; and churches, universities, health care, and foundations.

In recent years, a number of institutions have jettisoned their old hierarchical models and replaced them with a servant-leader approach. Servant-leadership advocates a group-oriented approach to analysis and decision making as a means of strengthening institutions and improving society. It also emphasizes the power of persuasion and seeking consensus, over the old top-down form of leadership. Some people have likened this to turning the hierarchical pyramid upside down. Servant-leadership holds that the primary purpose of a business should be to create a positive impact on its employees and community, rather than using profit as the sole motive.

Many individuals within institutions have adopted servant-leadership as a guiding philosophy. An increasing number of companies have adopted servant-leadership as part of their corporate philosophy or as a foundation for their mission statement. Among these are the Sisters of St. Joseph's Health System (Ann Arbor, Michigan), The Toro Company (Minneapolis, Minnesota), Schneider Engineering Company (Indianapolis, Indiana), Townsend & Bottum Family of Companies (Ann Arbor, Michigan), and TDIndustries (Dallas, Texas).

TDIndustries, one of the earliest practitioners of servant-leadership in the corporate setting, is a Dallas-based heating and plumbing contracting firm that was recently profiled in Robert Levering and Milton Moskowitz's best-selling book, *The 100 Best Companies to Work for in America*. In their profile of TDIndustries, the authors discuss the longtime influence that servant-leadership has had on the company. TDI's founder, Jack Lowe Sr. stumbled upon *The Servant as Leader* essay in the early 1970s and began to distribute copies of it to his employees. They were invited to read through the essay and then to gather in small groups to discuss its meaning. The belief that managers should serve their employees became an important value for TDIndustries.

Twenty-five years later, Jack Lowe Jr. continues to use servant-leadership as the guiding philosophy for TDI. Levering and Moskowitz note: "Even today, any TDPartner who supervises at least one person must go through training in servant-leadership."[7] In addition, all new employees continue to receive a copy of *The Servant as Leader* essay.

Some businesses have begun to view servant-leadership as an important framework that is helpful (and necessary) for ensuring the long-term effects of related management and leadership approaches such as continuous quality improvement and systems thinking. Several of the authors represented in this book suggest that institutions which want to create meaningful change may be best served in starting with servant-leadership as the foundational understanding and then building on it through any number of related approaches.

Servant-leadership has influenced many noted writers, thinkers, and leaders. Max DePree, chairman of the Herman Miller Company and author of *Leadership Is an Art* and *Leadership Jazz* has said, "The servanthood of leadership needs to be felt, understood, believed, and practiced."[8] And Peter Senge, author of *The Fifth Discipline,* has said that he tells people "not to bother reading any other book about leadership until you first read Robert Greenleaf's book, *Servant-Leadership*. I believe it is the most singular and useful statement on leadership I've come across."[9] In recent years, a growing number of leaders and readers have "rediscovered" Robert Greenleaf's own writings through DePree and Senge's books.

Education and Training of Not-for-Profit Trustees

A second major application of servant-leadership is its pivotal role as the theoretical and ethical basis for "trustee education." Greenleaf wrote extensively on servant-leadership as it applies to the roles of boards of directors and trustees within institutions. His essays on these applications are widely distributed among directors of for-profit and nonprofit organizations. In his essay *Trustees as Servants* Greenleaf urged trustees to ask themselves two central questions: "Whom do you serve?" and "For what purpose?"[10]

Servant-leadership suggests that boards of trustees need to undergo a radical shift in how they approach their roles. Trustees who seek to act as servant-leaders can help to create institutions of great depth and quality. Over the past decade, two of America's largest grant-making foundations (Lilly Endowment Inc. and the W. K. Kellogg Foundation) have sought to encourage the development of programs designed to educate and train not-for-profit boards of trustees to function as servant-leaders.

Community Leadership Programs

The third application of servant-leadership concerns its deepening role in community leadership organizations across the country. A growing number of community leadership groups are using Greenleaf Center resources as part of their own education and training efforts. Some have been doing so for more than 15 years.

The National Association for Community Leadership (NACL) has adopted servant-leadership as a special focus. Recently, NACL named Robert Greenleaf as the posthumous recipient of its National Community Leadership Award. This award is given annually to honor an individual whose work has made a significant impact on the development of community leadership worldwide.

M. Scott Peck, who has written about the importance of building true community, says the following in *A World Waiting to Be Born:* "In his work on servant-leadership, Greenleaf posited that the world will be saved if it can develop just three truly well-managed, large institutions—one in the private sector, one in the public sector, and one in the nonprofit sector. He believed—and I know—that such excellence in management will be achieved through an organizational culture of civility routinely utilizing the mode of community."[11]

Service-Learning Programs

The fourth application involves servant-leadership and experiential education. During the past 20 years experiential education programs of all sorts have sprung up in virtually every college and university—and, increasingly, in secondary schools, too. Experiential education, or "learning by doing," is now a part of most students' educational experience.

Around 1980, a number of educators began to write about the linkage between the servant-leader concept and experiential learning under a new term called "service-learning." It is service-learning that has become a major focus for experiential education programs in the past few years.

The National Society for Experiential Education (NSEE) has adopted service-learning as one of its major program areas. NSEE has published a massive three-volume work called *Combining Service and Learning,* which brings together many articles and papers about service-learning—several dozen of which discuss servant-leadership as the philosophical basis for experiential learning programs.

Leadership Education

The fifth application of servant-leadership concerns its use in both formal and informal education and training programs. This is taking place through leadership and management courses in colleges and universities, as well as through corporate training programs. A number of undergraduate and graduate courses on management and leadership incorporate servant-leadership within their course curricula. Several colleges and universities now offer specific courses on servant-leadership. Also, a number of noted leadership authors, including Peter Block, Ken Blanchard, Max DePree, and Peter Senge, have all acclaimed the servant-leader concept as an overarching framework that is compatible with, and enhancing of, other leadership and management models such as total quality management, learning organizations, and community-building.

In the area of corporate education and training programs, dozens of management and leadership consultants now utilize servant-leadership materials as part of their ongoing work with corporations. Some of these companies have included AT&T, the Mead Corporation, Arthur Andersen, and Gulf Oil of Canada. A number of consultants and educators are now touting the benefits to be gained in building a total quality management approach upon a servant-leadership foundation. Through internal training and education, institutions are discovering that servant-leadership can truly improve how business is developed and conducted, while still successfully turning a profit.

Personal Transformation

The sixth application of servant-leadership involves its use in programs relating to personal growth and transformation. Servant-leadership operates at both the institutional and personal levels. For individuals it offers a means to personal growth—spiritually, professionally, emotionally, and intellectually. It has ties to the ideas of M. Scott Peck (*The Road Less Traveled*), Parker Palmer (*The Active Life*), Ann McGee-Cooper (*You Don't Have to Go Home from*

Work Exhausted!), and others who have written on expanding human potential. A particular strength of servant-leadership is that it encourages everyone
to actively seek opportunities to both serve and lead others, thereby setting
up the potential for raising the quality of life throughout society. A number
of individuals are working to integrate the servant-leader concept into various programs involving both men's and women's self-awareness groups and
12-step programs like Alcoholics Anonymous. There is also a fledgling examination under way of the servant-leader as a previously unidentified Jungian archetype.

Servant-Leadership and Multiculturalism

For some people, the word *servant* prompts an immediate negative connota-
tion, due to the oppression that many workers—particularly women and
people of color—have historically endured. For some, it may take a while to
accept the positive usage of this word *servant*. However, those who are willing to dig a little deeper come to understand the inherent spiritual nature of
what is intended by the pairing of *servant* and *leader*. The startling paradox
of the term *servant-leadership* serves to prompt new insights.

In an article titled, "Pluralistic Reflections on Servant-Leadership,"
Juana Bordas has written: "Many women, minorities and people of
color have long traditions of servant-leadership in their cultures. Servant-
leadership has very old roots in many of the indigenous cultures. Cultures
that were holistic, cooperative, communal, intuitive and spiritual. These cultures centered on being guardians of the future and respecting the ancestors
who walked before."[12]

Women leaders and authors are now writing and speaking about servant-
leadership as a twenty-first century leadership philosophy that is most appropriate for both women and men to embrace. Patsy Sampson, who is former
president of Stephens College in Columbia, Missouri, is one such person. In
an essay on women and servant-leadership she writes: "So-called (service-
oriented) feminine characteristics are exactly those which are consonant with
the very best qualities of servant-leadership."[13]

A Growing Movement

*Servant-leadership works like the consensus building that the Japanese are
famous for. Yes, it takes a while on the front end; everyone's view is solicited,
though everyone also understands that his view may not ultimately prevail.
But once the consensus is forged, watch out: With everybody on board, your
so called implementation proceeds wham-bam.*

—Fortune magazine

Interest in the philosophy and practice of servant-leadership is now at an all-time high. Hundreds of articles on servant-leadership have appeared in various magazines, journals, and newspapers over the past few years. Many books on the general subject of leadership have been published that have referenced servant-leadership as the preeminent leadership model for the twenty-first century.

The Greenleaf Center for Servant-Leadership is an international, not-for-profit educational organization that seeks to encourage the understanding and practice of servant-leadership. The Center's mission is to fundamentally improve the caring and quality of all institutions through a new approach to leadership, structure, and decision making.

In recent years, the Greenleaf Center has experienced tremendous growth and expansion. Its growing programs include the following: the worldwide sales of more than 80 books, essays, and videotapes on servant-leadership; a membership program; workshops, retreats, institutes, and seminars; the Greenleaf Biography Project; a Reading-and-Dialogue Program; a Speakers Bureau; and an annual International Conference on Servant-Leadership. A number of notable Greenleaf Center members have spoken at our annual conferences, including: James Autry, Peter Block, Max DePree, Stephen Covey, Meg Wheatley, Ann McGee-Cooper, M. Scott Peck, Peter Senge, and Peter Vaill, to name but a few. These and other conference speakers have spoken of the tremendous impact that the servant-leader concept has played in the development of his or her own understanding of what it means to be a leader.

Paradox and Pathway

The Greenleaf Center's logo is a variation on the geometrical figure called a "mobius strip." A mobius strip, pictured here, is a one-sided surface constructed from a rectangle by holding one end fixed, rotating the opposite

end through 180 degrees, and applying it to the first end—thereby giving the appearance of a two-sided figure. It thus appears to have a front side that merges into a back side, and then back again into the front.

The mobius strip symbolizes, in visual terms, the servant-leader concept—a merging of servanthood into leadership and back into servanthood again, in a fluid and continuous pattern. It also reflects the Greenleaf Center's own role as an institution seeking to both serve and lead others who are interested in leadership and service issues.

Life is full of curious and meaningful paradoxes. Servant-leadership is one such paradox that has slowly but surely gained hundreds of thousands of adherents over the past quarter century. The seeds that have been planted have begun to sprout in many institutions, as well as in the hearts of many who long to improve the human condition. Servant-leadership is providing a framework from which many thousands of known and unknown individuals are helping to improve how we treat those who do the work within our many institutions. Servant-leadership truly offers hope and guidance for a new era in human development, and for the creation of better, more caring institutions.

PART ONE

Service

The idea of servant is deep in our Judeo-Christian heritage. Servant (along with serve and service) appears in the Bible more than thirteen hundred times. Part of the human dilemma is that the meaning of serve, in practical behavioral terms for both persons and institutions, is never completely clear. Thus one who would be servant is a life-long seeker, groping for light but never finding ultimate clarity. One constantly probes and listens, both to the promptings from one's own inner resources and to the communications of those who are also seeking. Then one cautiously experiments, questions, and listens again. Thus the servant-seeker is constantly growing in self-assurance through experience, but never having the solace of certainty.

Robert K. Greenleaf
Seeker and Servant

The past two decades have witnessed a growing interest in service of various kinds—customer service, public service, and service-learning are just three examples. An awareness of the need to serve one another in an increasingly interdependent world has emerged in our collective understanding of what is needed as we enter the twenty-first century.

Robert Greenleaf's writings on the nature of serving, and of its relationship to leadership, have helped to inspire a whole generation of people who are blazing new paths for meaningful service in our lives. The essays in this section offer a good look at the emergence of new thinking around service and servant-leadership.

1

Servant-Leadership

Robert K. Greenleaf

Robert K. Greenleaf coined the term servant-leadership *in his seminal 1970 essay, "The Servant as Leader." The servant-leader concept has had a deep and lasting influence over the past three decades, on many modern leadership theories and theorists. Greenleaf spent his first career of 40 years at AT&T, retiring as director of management research in 1964. That same year Greenleaf founded The Center for Applied Ethics (later renamed The Greenleaf Center for Servant-Leadership). He went on to have an illustrious second career that lasted another 25 years as an author, teacher, and consultant. Greenleaf, who died in 1990, was the author of numerous books and essays on the theme of the servant as leader. His books include two posthumous collections:* On Becoming a Servant-Leader *(1996) and* Seeker and Servant *(1996). During his lifetime he published two other books:* Teacher as Servant *(1979) and* Servant-Leadership *(1977), along with many other separately published essays that are available through The Greenleaf Center.*

This short excerpt from Greenleaf's essay, "The Servant as Leader," contains an essential understanding of the origin and definition of servant-leadership. Here Greenleaf relates how his reading of Hermann Hesse's Journey to the East *led to his developing the servant-as-leader terminology.*

Servant and leader—can these two roles be fused in one real person, in all levels of status or calling? If so, can that person live and be productive in the real world of the present? My sense of the present leads me to say yes to both questions. This chapter is an attempt to explain why and to suggest how.

The idea of the servant as leader came out of reading Hermann Hesse's *Journey to the East*. In this story we see a band of men on a mythical journey, probably also Hesse's own journey. The central figure of the story is Leo, who accompanies the party as the servant who does their menial chores, but who also sustains them with his spirit and his song. He is a person of extraordinary presence. All goes well until Leo disappears. Then the group falls into disarray and the journey is abandoned. They cannot make it without the servant Leo. The narrator, one of the party, after some years of wandering, finds Leo and is taken into the Order that had sponsored the journey. There he discovers that Leo, whom he had known first as servant, was in fact the titular head of the Order, its guiding spirit, a great and noble leader.

One can muse on what Hesse was trying to say when he wrote this story. We know that most of his fiction was autobiographical, that he led a tortured life, and that *Journey to the East* suggests a turn toward the serenity he achieved in his old age. There has been much speculation by critics on Hesse's life and work, some of it centering on this story, which they find the most puzzling. But to me, this story clearly says that the great leader is seen as servant first, and that simple fact is the key to his greatness. Leo was actually the leader all of the time, but he was servant first because that was what he was, deep down inside. Leadership was bestowed on a man who was by nature a servant. It was something given, or assumed, that could be taken away. His servant nature was the real man, not bestowed, not assumed, and not to be taken away. He was servant first.

I mention Hesse and *Journey to the East* for two reasons. First, I want to acknowledge the source of the idea of *the servant as leader.* Then I want to use this reference as an introduction to a brief discussion of prophecy.

In 1958 when I first read about Leo, if I had been listening to contemporary prophecy as intently as I do now, the first draft of this piece might have been written then. As it was, the idea lay dormant for 11 years during which I came to believe that we in this country were in a leadership crisis and that I should do what I could about it. I became painfully aware of how dull my sense of contemporary prophecy had been. And I have reflected much on why we do not hear and heed the prophetic voices in our midst (not a new question in our times, nor more critical than heretofore).

I now embrace the theory of prophecy which holds that prophetic voices of great clarity, and with a quality of insight equal to that of any age, are speaking cogently all of the time. Men and women of a stature equal to the greatest prophets of the past are with us now, addressing the problems of the day and pointing to a better way to live fully and serenely in these times.

The variable that marks some periods as barren and some as rich in prophetic vision is in the interest, the level of seeking, the responsiveness of the bearers. The variable is not in the presence or absence or the relative quality and force of the prophetic voices. Prophets grow in stature as people respond to their message. If their early attempts are ignored or spurned, their talent may wither away.

It is seekers, then, who make prophets, and the initiative of any one of us in searching for and responding to the voice of contemporary prophets may mark the turning point in their growth and service. But since we are the product of our own history, we see current prophecy within the context of past wisdom. We listen to as wide a range of contemporary thought as we can attend to. Then we choose those we elect to heed as prophets—both old and new—and meld their advice with our own leadings. This we test in real-life experiences to establish our own position.

One does not, of course, ignore the great voices of the past. One does not awaken each morning with the compulsion to reinvent the wheel. But if one is servant, either leader or follower, one is always searching, listening, expecting that a better wheel for these times is in the making. It may emerge any day. Any one of us may discover it from personal experience. I am hopeful.

I am hopeful for these times, despite the tension and conflict, because more natural servants are trying to see clearly the world as it is and are listening carefully to prophetic voices that are speaking now. They are challenging the pervasive injustice with greater force, and they are taking sharper issue with the wide disparity between the quality of society they know is reasonable and possible with available resources and the actual performance of the institutions that exist to serve society.

A fresh, critical look is being taken at the issues of power and authority, and people are beginning to learn, however haltingly, to relate to one another in less coercive and more creatively supporting ways. A new moral principle is emerging, which holds that the only authority deserving one's allegiance is that which is freely and knowingly granted by the led to the leader in response to, and in proportion to, the clearly evident servant stature of the leader. Those who choose to follow this principle will not casually accept the authority of existing institutions. *Rather, they will freely respond only to individuals who are chosen as leaders because they are proven and trusted as servants.* To the extent that this principle prevails in the future, the only truly viable institutions will be those that are predominantly servant-led.

I am mindful of the long road ahead before these trends, which I see so clearly, become a major society-shaping force. We are not there yet. But I see encouraging movement on the horizon.

What direction will the movement take? Much depends on whether those who stir the ferment will come to grips with the age-old problem of how to live in a human society. I say this because so many, having made their awesome decision for autonomy and independence from tradition, and having taken their firm stand against injustice and hypocrisy, find it hard to convert themselves into *affirmative builders* of a better society. How many of them will seek their personal fulfillment by making the hard choices, and by undertaking the rigorous preparation that building a better society requires? It all depends on what kind of leaders emerge and how they—we—respond to them.

My thesis, that more servants should emerge as leaders, or should follow only servant-leaders, is not a popular one. It is much more comfortable to go with a less-demanding point of view about what is expected of one now. There are several undemanding, plausibly argued alternatives from which to choose. One, since society seems corrupt, is to seek to avoid the center of it by retreating to an idyllic existence that minimizes involvement with the "system" (with the system that makes such withdrawal possible). Then there is the assumption that since the effort to reform existing institutions has not brought instant perfection, the remedy is to destroy them completely so that fresh, new, perfect ones can grow. Not much thought seems to be given to the problem of where the new seed will come from or who the gardener to tend them will be. The concept of the servant-leader stands in sharp contrast to this kind of thinking.

Yet it is understandable that the easier alternatives would be chosen, especially by young people. By extending education for so many so far into the adult years, normal participation in society is effectively denied when young people are ready for it. With education that is preponderantly abstract and analytical it is no wonder that a preoccupation with criticism exists and that not much thought is given to "What can I do about it?"

Criticism has its place, but as a total preoccupation it is sterile. In a time of crisis, like the leadership crisis we are now in, if too many potential builders are completely absorbed with dissecting the wrong and striving for instant perfection, then the movement so many of us want to see will be set back. The danger, perhaps, is to hear the analyst too much and the artist too little.

Albert Camus stands apart from other great artists of his time, in my view, and deserves the title of prophet, because of his unrelenting demand that each of us confront the exacting terms of our own existence, and, like Sisyphus, accept our rock and find our happiness by dealing with it. Camus sums up the relevance of his position to our concern for the servant as leader in the last paragraph of his last published lecture, entitled *Create Dangerously:*

> One may long, as I do, for a gentler flame, a respite, a pause for musing. But perhaps there is no other peace for the artist than what he finds in the heat of combat. "Every wall is a door," Emerson correctly said. Let us not look for the door, and the way out, anywhere but in the wall against which we are living. Instead, let us seek the respite where it is— in the very thick of battle. For in my opinion, and this is where I shall close, it is there. Great ideas, it has been said, come into the world as gently as doves. Perhaps, then, if we listen attentively, we shall hear, amid the uproar of empires and nations, a faint flutter of wings, the gentle stirring of life and hope. Some will say that this hope lies in a nation, others, in a man. I believe rather that it is awakened, revived, nourished by millions of solitary individuals whose deeds and works every day negate frontiers and the crudest implications of history. As a result, there shines forth fleetingly the ever-threatened truth that each and every man, on the foundations of his own sufferings and joys, builds for them all.[1]

Who Is the Servant-Leader?

The servant-leader is servant first—as Leo was portrayed. Becoming a servant-leader begins with the natural feeling that one wants to serve, to serve first. Then conscious choice brings one to aspire to lead. That person is sharply different from one who is leader first, perhaps because of the need to assuage an unusual power drive or to acquire material possessions. For such people, it will be a later choice to serve—after leadership is established. The leader-first and the servant-first are two extreme types. Between them are the shadings and blends that are part of the infinite variety of human nature.

The difference manifests itself in the care taken by the servant first to make sure that other people's highest priority needs are being served. The best test, and most difficult to administer, is this: Do those served grow as persons? Do they, while being served, become healthier, wiser, freer, more autonomous, more likely themselves to become servants? And what is the effect on the least privileged in society; will they benefit, or, at least, not be further deprived?

All of this rests on the assumption that the only way to change a society (or just make it go) is to produce people, enough people, who will change it (or make it go). The urgent problems of our day—the disposition to venture into immoral and senseless wars, destruction of the environment, poverty, alienation, discrimination, overpopulation—exist because of human failures, individual failures, one-person-at-a-time, one-action-at-a-time failures.

If we make it out of all of this (and this is written in the belief that we will), the system will be whatever works best. The builders will find the useful pieces wherever they are, and invent new ones when needed, all without reference to ideological coloration. "How do we get the right things done?" will be the watchword of the day, every day. And the context of those who bring it on will be: All men and women who are touched by the effort grow taller, and become healthier, stronger, more autonomous, and more disposed to serve.

Leo the servant, and the exemplar of the servant-leader, has one further portent for us. If we assume that Hermann Hesse is the narrator in *Journey to the East* (not a difficult assumption to make), at the end of the story he establishes his identity. His final confrontation at the close of his initiation into the Order is with a small transparent sculpture: two figures joined together. One is Leo, the other is the narrator. The narrator notes that a movement of substance is taking place within the transparent sculpture.

> I perceived that my image was in the process of adding to and flowing into Leo's, nourishing and strengthening it. It seemed that, in time . . . only one would remain: Leo. He must grow, I must disappear. As I stood there and looked and tried to understand what I saw, I recalled a short conversation that I had once had with Leo during the festive days at Bremgarten. We had talked about the creations of poetry being more vivid and real than the poets themselves.[2]

What Hesse may be telling us here is that Leo is the symbolic personification of Hesse's aspiration to serve through his literary creations—creations that are greater than Hesse himself—and that his work, for which he was but the channel, will carry on and serve and lead in a way that he, a twisted and tormented man, could not—except as he created.

Does not Hesse dramatize, in extreme form, the dilemma of us all? Except as we venture to create, we cannot project ourselves beyond ourselves to serve and lead.

To which Camus would add: *create dangerously*!

2

Servant-Leadership Revisited

Ken Blanchard

Dr. Ken Blanchard is the coauthor of the best-selling book, The One Minute Manager, *which sold more than 9 million copies worldwide. He coauthored* The Power of Ethical Management *with Dr. Norman Vincent Peale. Blanchard is chairman of Blanchard Training and Development Inc., a management training and consulting company that he and his wife, Dr. Marjorie Blanchard, founded in 1979. He has received many awards and honors for his contributions to the field of leadership and management. Blanchard is a recipient of the Golden Gavel Award from Toastmasters International, and in 1992 he was inducted into the HRD Hall of Fame by* Training *magazine.*

In this essay, Blanchard directly addresses the misconception that servant-leadership is somehow leadership without direction. He makes an important contribution to the understanding of servant-leadership as both a visionary and implementation role.

For a long time, students of leadership like myself, have been talking about servant-leadership. I first heard about the concept from Robert K. Greenleaf when I was a young assistant professor of management at Ohio University in the late 1960s. Bob had come to campus to talk to the student leaders. I was fascinated by his thinking and began to include a discussion of servant-leadership in my teaching.

My aim in talking about servant-leadership has always been to encourage managers to move from the traditional direct, control, and supervise approach to the roles of cheerleader, encourager, listener, and facilitator. In the past, managers have emphasized judgment, criticism, and evaluation rather than providing the support and encouragement that people need to be their best.

The Past Will Not Work in the Future

The past approach to management worked when companies had no competition for customers or for good employees. Today, mistreated customers go next door, followed shortly by the best employees. I have always loved the quote attributed to Benjamin Franklin, "You can't expect an empty bag to stand up straight." That translates in this context into an important concept. If your managers don't support and take care of their people, you can't expect them to stand up with integrity and serve your customers well.

Too many companies inappropriately use "bicycle leadership." The visual picture implied in bicycle leadership is that managers bend their back to those above while they trample those below. Somebody criticizes the top manager. Then that person attacks one of his or her managers, which motivates the latest victim to hit someone below him or her. This negative chain reaction eventually moves down the hierarchy to a frontline/customer-contact person who has only one person to kick—your customer. Norman Rockwell illustrated this beautifully in one of his classic *Saturday Evening Post* covers. The first frame showed a man being reprimanded by his boss, the second frame had the disciplined manager yelling at his wife, the next frame showed her screaming at their young child, and the final frame showed the young boy backing the cat into the corner so he could kick the helpless animal. Bicycle leadership is a relic of the past while servant-leadership is the way to manage people today and in the future.

A Misconception about Servant-Leadership

In talking about servant-leadership at a recent conference of corporation presidents, I sensed some real resistance to the concept. In talking with these managers, I found a misconception about servant-leadership that needs to be cleared up. Their assumption when they heard the term was that managers should be working for their people, who would be deciding what to do, when to do it, where to do it, and how to do it. If that was what servant-leadership was all about, it didn't sound like leadership to them at all. It sounded more like the inmates were running the prison.

I think it's important for us to correct this misconception. Leadership has two aspects—a visionary part and an implementation part. Some people say that leadership is really the visionary role (doing the right thing), and management is the implementation role (doing things right). Rather than getting caught in the leadership versus management debate, let's think of these *both* as leadership roles.

Leadership is an influence process in which you try to help people accomplish goals. All good leadership starts with a visionary role. This involves not only goal setting but also establishing a clear picture of perfection—what the operation would look like when it was running effectively. In other words, leadership starts with a sense of direction. In the book I coauthored with John Carlos and Alan Randolph, *Empowerment Takes More Than a Minute,* we said, "A river without banks is a large puddle."[1] The banks permit the river to flow; they give direction to the river. Leadership is all about going somewhere; it's not about wandering around aimlessly. Even Alice in Wonderland learned that concept when she came to a fork in the road and asked the Cheshire cat which road she should take. He replied by asking her, "Where are you going?" She essentially said, "I don't know." His response was quick: "Then it doesn't matter what road you take." If you aren't sure where you are going, your leadership style won't really matter, either.

I want to make it clear that when we're talking about servant-leadership, we aren't talking about lack of direction. Although emphasis in most servant-leader discussions is on implementation, I think servant-leadership involves both a visionary role and an implementation role.

The Hierarchical Paradox

Most organizations are typically pyramidal in nature. Who is at the top of the organization? The chief executive officer, the chairman, the board of directors. Who is at the bottom? All the employees—the people who do all the work. The people who make the products, sell the products, service the products, and the like. Now there is nothing wrong with having a traditional pyramid for certain tasks or roles. The paradox is that the pyramid needs to be right side up or upside down depending on the task or role.

It's absolutely essential that the pyramid stay upright when it comes to vision, mission, values, and setting major goals. Moses did not go up on the mountain with a committee. People look to leaders for direction, so the traditional hierarchy isn't bad for this aspect of leadership. While the vision and direction might start with the leader, if you're dealing with experienced people, you want to get them involved in shaping and refining that direction. Some companies, such as W. L. Gore & Associates, do not even have appointed leaders. They think leadership is a follower-driven concept. Therefore, leadership should emerge rather than be appointed. But no matter how the leadership is determined, providing direction is an important aspect of servant-leadership.

The Problem Occurs with Implementation

Most organizations and managers get in trouble in the implementation phase of the leadership process. The traditional pyramid is kept alive and well. When that happens, who do people think they work for? The person above them. The minute you think you work for the person above you for implementation, you are assuming that person—your boss—is *responsible,* and your job is being *responsive* to that boss and to his or her whims or wishes. As a result, all the energy in the organization is moving up the hierarchy, away from customers and the frontline folks who are closest to the action.

People tell me all the time that the worst thing that can happen to you is to lose a boss, particularly one you have just figured out. Because now you have to figure out a new boss and what he or she wants. People think their career depends solely on the quality of their relationship with their boss. As a result, the most important people in your organization—those individuals who have contact with your customers—spend all their time looking over their shoulder trying to figure out what their boss wants rather than focusing on the needs of the customer. They respond to customer requests by saying things like, "I'm sorry. We can't do that. It's against our policy." And the customer says, "What do you mean it's against your policy? It's a stupid policy." And the reply: "I'm sorry. I just work here. I don't make the policies." These people end up defending policies rather than serving customers. Why? Because they think that's what the boss wants them to do. After all, they're not paid to think. Sad, isn't it?

To put this situation in perspective, consider how Seeing Eye dogs are trained to work with the visually impaired. Trainers take two kinds of dogs out of the program—the completely disobedient and the completely obedient. You'd expect the first group to be dismissed, but why the second? Because the only dogs trainers keep are the ones that will do whatever the master says *unless* it doesn't make sense. Imagine letting dogs think! And yet, it would be a disaster if a Seeing Eye dog and his or her master were waiting on the corner and the master said, "Forward." The dog, seeing a car speeding in their direction, shrugs his shoulders and thinks to himself, "This is a real bummer" as he leads his master into the middle of the street. Frontline/customer-contact people are asked to do that all the time—do what they're told, follow policy, even if it doesn't make sense for the particular situation.

My wife, Margie, and I experienced a perfect example of this during a trip to Australia. We arrived early on a Sunday morning and were picked up by our Australian partners, Trevor and Leonie Keighley. As we left the airport, they told us it was a holiday weekend in Australia and all the hotels overlooking the Sydney harbor were booked. Therefore, we wouldn't be able to get into our room until after 2:00 P.M. They suggested we stop by the hotel anyway to check in and drop off our bags. They had put us on the 32nd floor—the concierge level, where the best service was provided. When we arrived at the hotel, we were told to check in on the 32nd floor. There we were greeted by an energetic, enthusiastic customer-service person. She said, "Welcome to the concierge floor. You are very important customers." Then she gave us a letter from the general manager reiterating how important we were.

After we checked in, we asked her if she could watch our bags as we were going to wander around the harbor and have brunch. We would return after 2:00 when we could check into our room.

She said, "No problem." And then she asked, "Is there anything else I can do for you?" I said, "Yes. Could you cash a traveler's check?"

She put her head down and sa␣   I don't have your room number yet."

"Room number?" I echoed.

"Yes. I have to write your room nu␣   oack of the traveler's check."

"But you have our bags," I responded.

"I know," said the woman. "But I need your room number. It's our policy."

"I think it's a good policy," I said, "but not when you have people's bags. This is ridiculous."

She said, "I'm sorry. I just work here. I don't set the policies."

The Solution: Invert the Pyramid

How do you correct this situation? One way is by turning the pyramid upside down when it comes to implementation and giving your customer-contact people responsibility. Remember, the word *responsible* means "able to respond."

When you turn the pyramid upside down, who is at the top of the organization? The customer-contact people. Who is *really* at the top of the organization? The customers. Who's at the bottom now? The "top" management. When you turn a pyramid upside down philosophically, who works for whom when it comes to implementation? You work for your people. This one change, although it seems minor, makes a major difference. The difference is between who is *responsible* and who is *responsive*. With the traditional pyramid, the boss is always responsible, and the staff are supposed to be responsive to the boss. When you turn the pyramid upside down those roles get reversed. Your people become responsible and the job of management is to be responsive to their people. That creates a very different environment for implementation. If you work for your people, what is the purpose of being a manager? *To help them accomplish their goals.* Your job is to help them win. Wonderful examples of this kind of management abound in legendary service organizations like Nordstrom. This Seattle-based retail store chain is wiping out competition wherever there is a Nordstrom department store. Why? Because they are beating everybody to the punch when it comes to customer service.

My daughter Debbie worked as a sales cashier for Nordstrom in San Diego when she was in college. After about a week on the job, I had dinner with her and asked, "What is it like to work at Nordstrom? Tom Peters and everyone is talking about Nordstrom and their tremendous service." She said, "It's very different." I asked, "What's different about it?" She said, "Well, the first thing that is different is their orientation program. Every employee has to go through an orientation program before they can start work. The whole emphasis in the first part of the program is to teach everyone, all the employees, how to say 'No problem.' The number one thing they want coming out of your mouth is 'No problem.' "

To give you an example of this philosophy in action, a friend of ours wanted to buy some perfume for his wife's birthday as she was running low on her favorite brand. He went to Nordstrom to purchase this gift.

The woman behind the perfume counter said, "I'm sorry. We don't carry that brand. I know where I can get it, though, in the mall. How much longer will you be in the store?"

He replied, "Another half hour."

She said, "Fine. Stop by here on your way out of the store and I will have your perfume gift wrapped."

This woman left the Nordstrom store, went out into the mall, bought the perfume her customer wanted, brought it back, gift wrapped it, and charged him the same price she had paid at the other store. In other words, Nordstrom did not make a cent on this sale. But what did they make—a raving fan customer.

At Nordstrom, they will take back anything that you have a problem with. One of Debbie's jobs as a cashier was taking back merchandise. She said, "You wouldn't believe some of the junk people bring back." At Nordstrom the assumption is that the customer is always right. In most cases, Nordstrom gives cash back for returns. The company doesn't want its customers to go through all kinds of paperwork. The assumption of Nordstrom's top management is that 90 percent of the people in America are honest and want good service for being a customer. The other 10 percent will rip you off. The problem is that most organizations are set up to stop the 10 percent minority rather than serve the 90 percent majority of honest customers.

I asked Debbie, "What else is different about working at Nordstrom?" She said, "My boss. About three or four times a day he comes up to me and says, 'Debbie, is there anything I can do for you?' He acts like he works for me." The reality in the Nordstrom philosophy is that he does. Every manager works for his or her people. It's in relation to this responsive, serving role that the effective manager now encourages, supports, coaches, facilitates, and does everything possible to help his or her people be successful. This is where servant-leadership really takes over.

Jesus as an Example of Servant-Leadership

A few years ago I followed best-selling Christian author Charles Colson on a leadership program for Christian leaders sponsored by Bob Buford and The Foundation. Colson ended his speech by saying "All the kings in history sent their people out to die for them. There is only one king I know who decided to die for his people."

That closing remark set up my talk on leadership because what Jesus did struck me as the ultimate in turning the pyramid upside down. In fact, when people talk about servant-leadership, Jesus is often a model, without even referring to his ultimate sacrifice. So let me talk about him as an example of servant-leadership.

Regardless of your religious background you'll have to admit that Jesus was a leader. In fact, he's the only religious leader I know of who built a management team. And yet he went out and "hired" inexperienced people. He could have recruited good preachers. None of the disciples he chose had the kind of background that you would have expected him to need. And yet he built them into quite a team. For a long time I've been saying the important thing about being a leader is not what happens when you are there; it's what happens when you're not there. You can usually get people to do what you want when you are there; the real test is what do they do on their own. When Jesus was gone, his disciples carried on quite successfully. How did he make that happen?

Jesus was continually asked questions like, "How do I become first?" or "Who is the greatest?" His responses were consistent "If anyone wants to be first, he must be the very last, and the servant of all" (Mark 9:35). "Whoever welcomes this little child in my name welcomes me; and whoever welcomes me welcomes the one who sent me. For he who is the least among you all—he is the greatest" (Luke 9:48).

It was important to Jesus that his answers be clear to his disciples in both word and act. How many of you have been invited to your boss's house recently and the first thing he or she did was ask you to take off your shoes and socks so he or she could wash your feet? When Jesus washed the feet of the disciples, he was symbolically telling them about servant-leadership.

> *You call me Teacher and Lord, and rightly so, for that is what I am. Now that I, your Lord and Teacher, have washed your feet, you also should wash one another's feet. I have set you an example that you should do as I have done for you. I tell you the truth, no servant is greater than his master, nor is a messenger greater than the one who sent him. Now that you know these things, you will be blessed if you do them.*
>
> —John 13:13–17

Jesus wanted his disciples to get this important message. And yet, while Jesus wanted his disciples to be servants of all, was he sending them out to serve without clear direction? Absolutely not. He got his direction literally from the top of the hierarchy. Once the vision, and how people could be "saved," was clear he wanted his disciples to go out and support, encourage, coach, and facilitate other people, making the necessary commitment to get that same salvation. In other words, the essence of Jesus' servant-leadership symbolized in his washing of the disciples feet only began once the vision and direction were clear.

Leaders Need Their People

When I talk about being a servant-leader in organizations, I'm not suggesting you die for your people. But you might want to listen to them once in a while or praise them, encourage them, and help them win. But remember, the servant aspect of leadership only begins when vision, direction, and goals are clear. It emphasizes that leaders cannot accomplish goals all by themselves. They need their people. When I wrote *Everyone's a Coach* with Don Shula, the winningest coach in National Football League history, he made it clear that as a coach he couldn't throw one pass, he couldn't make one tackle, he couldn't throw a single block; therefore, his goal accomplishment as a coach depended on his effectiveness in helping his people to be their very best.

The year before Don retired in 1996 he tore his Achilles tendon and missed his first practice in 25 years as a Dolphin coach. When I asked him why he felt he needed to be at practice all the time, his reply was, "You can't coach from the press box."[2] You want to be where the action is, so you can observe what's happening and respond in a way that helps people be their very best. Servant-leaders are ones who move among their people in a way that helps them be as responsible as they can in doing their job. The hierarchy can help set the direction, but effective servant-leaders in the future, when it comes to implementation, will figuratively and literally turn the pyramid upside down and work side by side with their people in a supportive way. Their eventual goal is to help their people increase their skills to the point that they will be able to perform just as well when their leader is not there as when he or she is there.

That, to me, is what servant-leadership is all about: making goals clear and then rolling your sleeves up and doing whatever it takes to help your people win. In that situation, they don't work for you—you work for them.

3

Work as a Calling

Elizabeth Jeffries

Elizabeth Jeffries, RN, CSP, works with health care organizations that want their people to work together better and with people who want to grow as servant-leaders. She is the author of The Heart of Leadership: How to Inspire, Encourage and Motivate People to Follow You. *A professional speaker and consultant, Jeffries is a partner with her husband, Stephen Tweed, in the firm Tweed Jeffries, LLC, based in Louisville, Kentucky. The four cornerstones of her work are servant-leadership, change strategies, team alignment, and communication.*

In this essay, Jeffries relates the idea of vocation to Greenleaf's belief that servant-leadership begins with the "feeling that one wants to serve." She describes several methods for clarifying one's own calling in life and challenges each of us to serve one another through our work.

It was a sunny, warm June day in New England and I had just finished speaking to a group of health care executives at a leadership conference in Sturbridge, Massachusetts. Having a bonus of a few hours before my flight home, I decided to walk down the hill to enjoy the sights and sounds of this quaint Victorian village.

Scores of shops lined the old streets. I wandered past the bakery with its aroma of freshly baked bread, past an antique furniture store with history captured in old chairs and tables, and past a boutique where cherished linens had been preserved for generations.

My initial intent was to aimlessly wander the streets for a while. That is, until I came to a shop that seemed to call me inside. I opened the door of *The Hour Glass* and felt as though I were entering another era.

The small shop was completely vacant of human energy and the only sounds I heard were from a collection of old clocks, the most beautiful I had ever seen! There were grandfather clocks, grandmother clocks, mantel clocks, table clocks, and even alarm clocks from ages past. Just as my enthusiasm was about to bubble over, I heard the tinkling of a bell and noticed the parting of the curtains in the corner. An elderly, rather frail gentleman in his

80s with slightly stooped shoulders and a shuffling gait slowly made his way toward me. He wore a pinstriped shirt with the sleeves rolled up, wide navy suspenders, and bifocals with a jeweler's loop off to the side. Mainly he wore a loving, gentle face with lots of life lines and a big warm smile! Assuming he was the clock repair person, I approached him with enthusiasm and a sense of respect for his work and said, "These are magnificent! You must repair these clocks, right?" Acknowledging my comment, he paused for a moment, stood just a little taller, smiled gently at my apparent naïveté, and softly but firmly said, "Oh no, my dear. I don't repair clocks. I restore history!"

I met Louis Cormier many years ago, and yet I can still see his bright eyes and impish smile, recall the title on his business card—"Clock Surgeon Since 1922"—and hear his poignant words, *"I don't repair clocks. I restore history!"*

Although Louis Cormier didn't use the exact words, his work with clocks was his calling. How else could he devote nearly 70 years to a career and be as peaceful and centered as he was? How else could he see beyond the process of his work to repair clocks to the meaning of his work to restore history?

The Clock Surgeon, the Calling, and Robert Greenleaf

In describing servant-leadership, Robert Greenleaf says that "the servant-leader is servant first. It begins with the natural feeling that one wants to serve, to serve first. Then conscious choice brings one to aspire to lead."[1] As I've pondered Greenleaf's work over the last 10 years, I've often wondered where this "feeling that one wants to serve" comes from. My conclusion is that it comes to us as a calling and often manifests itself in our work.

Greenleaf seemed to refer to this idea of calling when he said "everything begins with the initiative of an individual. The forces for good and evil in the world are propelled by the thoughts, attitudes, and actions of individual beings. What happens to our values and therefore to the quality of our civilization in the future, will be shaped by the conceptions of individuals that are born of inspiration."[2]

According to *Webster's New World Dictionary,* the word *inspire* means "to breathe life into." It also means "to cause, communicate or motivate as by divine influence." It's a powerful word that paints a picture of someone or something beyond ourselves infusing us with a purpose or a mission and calling us to action.

I love the word *inspire*. It has such a ring of hope to it! Greenleaf captured this in his 1984 commencement talk at Alverno College in Milwaukee when he said, "When I started to write on the servant-leader theme, I was trying to communicate a basis for hope . . . with the intent that the combined influence (of teachers, students, trustees, churches, and administrators) might give a greater basis for hope than is now generally available to young people, and make for a better society."[3]

When I think of "calling," I can't help but think of Sister Mary Norbert, my second-grade teacher at Presentation School on the west side of Chicago. She constantly talked to us about our vocation, and of course she meant a religious vocation. She encouraged us to be open and listen to God to see if we had a vocation to serve as a sister. (I admit I considered it for a brief time in high school. I actually investigated the cloistered community, the Order of the Poor Claire's, and was quite serious about it until I understood what a cloistered order was. Since I now make my living speaking, you can see why that didn't work for me.)

Later I also found out that the word *vocation* comes from the Latin word *voca,* which means "to call." I now believe that we all have a vocation, that we are all called to a unique purpose and certainly some even to a religious vocation. I have a picture of that calling in my mind that looks like this.

Before our spirit enters our body, we're having this conversation with God about what we'll contribute when we come to earth in our human form. We discuss and discard many possibilities and finally hit on "it." We're very excited (God, too, because God wants us to love our work), and we're bursting with enthusiasm and shouting, "This is awesome! Send me, God. I'll go. I know I can do this! You can count on me!" So we come to an agreement with God about our unique assignment, we promise to do a great job, and our spirit goes off to enter our tiny body. On the way, however, it seems we forget what we agreed to do, and so we spend the rest of our lives trying to remember what it was we told God we would do here on earth.

Why Are We Here, Anyway?

Today, more and more organization executives and boards are crafting or revisiting their mission statements. I hope it's more than management by bestseller and that they truly see that a clearly articulated, shared organizational mission statement gives people a reason to do their work with pride and integrity. And yet while all this crafting is going on, few bring in the idea of personal mission or talk about their own calling or that of their people.

When my partner and I work with organizations on their mission, we are compelled to discuss the next step, which is how to bring the organizational mission and the personal mission of the people who work there in alignment. I'm still surprised at how few managers and executives have consciously contemplated this at all, let alone have articulated their own personal reason for working or what drives them to do their specific job. Yet it is also a paradox that when we discuss the concept of calling, I see lightbulbs go on and the door of awareness opening. Is intuition involved here? Do we know on some deep level exactly what it is we are called to do? I believe so. This also gives some credibility to the "assignment from God" concept mentioned previously.

Greenleaf himself states that he did not get his notion of the servant as leader from conscious logic. It came to him as an "intuitive insight" as he contemplated Leo in Hermann Hesse's novel, *A Journey to the East.*

Last year, I decided to be more bold in my discussion on calling, and I began asking my audiences, "How many of you feel the work you are doing is something that you are called to do?" I wasn't sure what to expect and I certainly didn't want to embarrass the people who hated their work or create a situation where people felt they had to say yes because their boss was in the room. But I truly believe that if we want to change the world, as Greenleaf says, "we must first know who we are and where we stand."[4] I've now asked more than 50 different groups of people numbering from 25 to 2,500, and about 80 percent of the audience raise their hands that they do indeed feel some sort of calling to the work they are doing.

Perhaps I need to clarify here that, as a professional speaker and an author, I work primarily with health care organizations and that it makes sense that most of these managers would see their work this way. After all, health care is a service, an ennobling cause, considered a ministry to many, and a spiritual practice to some. The interesting response is the one I've gotten from business audiences. Recently I addressed a group of 80 managers from a large successful franchise management company on the servant-leadership ideas and personal calling. I asked them the same question and nearly everyone in the group responded that they, too, felt called to do their work.

Amazing, you say. Yes, with the ridicule piled on business leaders today, with CEOs routinely portrayed in movies and on television as crooked, greedy, and overpaid boors, even business magazines dare to raise the question "Is there no more to business than the bottom line?" Well, apparently there is for some businesses.

In *Business as a Calling: Work and the Examined Life,* Michael Novak says that not only is business a morally serious vocation, it is a morally noble one in that "it creates social connections, lifts its participants out of poverty, and builds the foundations for democracy."[5] So why shouldn't salespeople, manufacturing managers, and retail store clerks think of their work as a calling, too? It serves as a motivator and helps to initiate, focus, benchmark, and refine all our activities.

How Do I Know It's a Calling?

Here are some ways you can uncover or clarify your calling.

Listen and be attentive to your surroundings. One of Greenleaf's tenets of servant-leadership is listening. He says that "a true, natural servant automatically responds to any problem by listening first."[6] If you want to discover, clarify, or refine your calling, start by listening. This may entail finding quiet time—being still, and getting out of the constant state of busyness most of us live in.

Since we're talking about being called, it stands to reason that someone is doing the calling. Therefore, we need to listen for and to the caller. Sounds like Sister Mary Norbert's advice again. God speaks to us in many ways and gives us directives, information, and guidance. It may be through other people, through prayer, through writing, through meditation, and through simply hearing the right thing at the right moment. In his talk at Alverno College, Greenleaf shared with the graduating class how he came to his decision of his life's work in business:

> I went to college with a clear vocational aim that I would become an astronomer, like a favorite uncle who encouraged me. I quickly concluded that, although I had the aptitude for science and mathematics that qualified, I did not have the temperament for an astronomer: I was not cut out for it.[7]

Greenleaf goes on to say that he had a professor in his last term in college who spoke of the United States as a nation of large institutions that were not serving us well. The professor challenged the students to get inside those organizations and change things for the better. Greenleaf continues:

> My doors of perception must have been open a bit wider than usual that day because that message came through loud and clear. My career aim was settled. I would get inside the largest business that would hire me and stay there if I could.[8]

Answering his call, Greenleaf chose AT&T for that very reason.

Get your ego out of the way. In *Wishful Thinking: A Theological ABC*, Frederick Buechner says, "There are all different kinds of voices calling you to all different kinds of work. The challenge is to find which is the voice of God rather than society, ego or self interest. . . . The place God calls you to is where your deep gladness and the world's deep hunger meet."[9]

Richard Bolles in *How to Find Your Mission in Life* says: "You will never know your career mission without having an understanding of your personal mission (calling). The two are inextricably linked."[10] He says that our mission here on earth is one that we share with the rest of the human race; that is, to do what we can, moment by moment, day by day, to make the world a better place—following the guidance from within and the needs around us.

Bolles says there is also a mission that is uniquely your own, and no one else can have it, simply because they are not you! It is

- to exercise the talent you came here to use—your greatest gift that you most love to use,
- in the place or environment which most appeals to you,
- for the purposes that are most apparent in the world.

Richard Bolles believes that a personal calling is spiritual and that we can't deal with a career mission without understanding the spiritual aspects of it.

Stephen Covey says in *The Seven Habits of Highly Effective People* that until you can stand in front of others and talk about your mission in life, you can't hope to be an effective leader.[11]

Be open to ideas all the time. Greenleaf cites five specific ideas he received from others up to and including the servant-leader idea from Hermann Hesse. He says, ". . . in retrospect, responding to each of these ideas when it was offered was the ticket of admission for receiving the next one."[12] Our challenge is to be so consciously connected to our spiritual self that we can discern when something is right for us.

Four Power Points of a Calling

According to Michael Novak a calling has four characteristics:[13]

1. *Each calling is unique to each individual.* Not everyone wants to be a psychiatrist (as Dr. Scott Peck discovered when he was trying to persuade a young man to go into psychiatry who wanted to go into business). A calling causes a desire and, oftentimes, a passion for doing something that you simply can't say no to.

2. *A calling requires certain preconditions. One is talent.* You may love opera, ballet, or running a big business, but a desire in itself does not make it a calling. "For a calling to be right, it must fit our abilities." Another precondition, says Novak, is *love*, "Not just of the final product, but as essayist Logan Pearsall Smith said, 'love of the drudgery it involves.' "[14] Along with desire and talent, will you put in the hours and have the commitment to be an Olympic class athlete? You have the desire and talent to write a book. Do you love the drudgery and discipline of writing, editing, and rewriting enough to birth it?

3. *A true calling reveals its presence by the enjoyment and sense of renewed energies its practice yields us.* We are willing, without complaint, to shoulder the burdens of the calling because we know it is our duty—part of what we are meant to do—to go on. "Enjoying what we do is not always enjoyment."

4. *Callings are not usually easy to discover.* Many false paths may be taken before the fulfilling path is uncovered. "Experiments, painful setbacks, false hopes, discernment, prayer, and much patience are often required before the light goes on."

But oh, when the light goes on! Some people know very early on what their life's work is. One is our computer consultant. A twenty-something young man with a cheery countenance and a passion for his work, Lee Pfieffer attacks each computer problem with a sense of excitement, confidence, and determination. One day as I was marveling at his expertise in solving a networking problem at our company, I commented to Lee that he seems to have found his calling. Without hesitation, he gave a full-bellied laugh and a resounding "Yes!" Questioning further, he told me he knew when he was five years old that he had an aptitude for fixing things. It seems he took apart his mother's hair dryer and returned it to perfect order! Lee has a desire, coupled with talent, loves what he does, and is willing to spend hours every week studying the changes in technology to be the best at his craft. Although he may not have had the language at his fingertips until I asked the question, Lee has uncovered and is living out his calling. He is a servant-leader at its best because as he functions from his calling, people follow him (in this case, they buy from him).

A Calling Is Not Always Comfortable

If we only did what felt comfortable, the work of the world would never be accomplished. I've been telling a story in my seminars for some time now because when I first heard it as an adult, it changed my life. Its message gave me the courage to listen to my own call and start my business, even when I had no idea how I was going to do it. It's at the core of what servant-leadership and calling is all about. It's the story of Jonah, the biblical character who was swallowed by a big fish.

The story goes like this. Jonah was asked by God to go to Nineveh and preach. You can almost hear Jonah saying, "Who me? You've got to be kidding. Who's going to listen to me? I don't really know what to say! Nineveh is so far away, and I already have so much to do. Thanks for asking, but I don't think I'm the person for the job. Might be a good idea if you asked someone else."

To make sure that he is not selected for this assignment, Jonah goes down to the pier and hops aboard the first passing ship and sails off, hoping that God will eventually choose someone else for the job. After setting sail, the ship heads into a big storm. Jonah takes it personally, sure that God is trying to punish him for not accepting the Nineveh post. Rather than have everyone on the ship incur God's wrath, Jonah jumps overboard.

Jonah is then swallowed by a big fish and for three days and three nights Jonah sits in silence in its belly. Jonah now has plenty of time to think about his life and all that's happened. It's cold, damp, smelly, and so dark inside the fish that Jonah can't even see his hand in front of his face. It's so lonely and Jonah just wants out. Pretty soon Nineveh doesn't sound so bad after all!

In time, God in His mercy has the fish cough Jonah out onto the shore. You can almost see Jonah dusting himself off, looking down the beach, and saying, "Okay, God, which way is it to Nineveh?"

When God Says Go

A few years ago I discovered that famed psychologist Dr. Abraham Maslow coined the phrase "the Jonah Complex" to describe a documented psychological group of symptoms found in people who run away from their real calling in life. Jonah's story demonstrates, as Maslow concluded, that you can't run away from your calling. Maslow says, "If you deliberately set out to be less than you are capable of, you will never truly be happy."[15] The Jonah Complex, as Maslow describes it, is that tendency within each of us to try to run away from our greatness, to not accept the challenge we hear calling us from within. It's a refusal to face up to our capacities for tremendous achievement for changing the world. That's a pretty strong statement from Maslow, but Greenleaf was no less subtle when he answered his call and challenged all of us to build a better society as servant-leaders.

We've all had times when we were in the belly of the whale. No doubt some of you have an awareness of being in that uncomfortable spot right now. As Greenleaf observed, "Awareness is not a giver of solace—it is just the opposite. It is a disturber and an awakener. Able leaders are usually sharply awake and reasonably disturbed."[16] I must admit I still find myself in the belly of the whale sometimes. It's not because I don't know my calling, it's because I get into my own ego and control needs. But the state of being disturbed now and then does keep me sharply awake.

Roadblocks to Hearing and Answering the Call

We don't hear and answer God's call for some fairly common reasons. *Negative self-talk*—such as "I'm not worthy." "I can't do this." "I must not be hearing right." "It must be someone else who should do this. Not me." "Surely you jest!"—is one reason. *We have fears.* "I don't know how." "I'll mess it up." "I'm not smart enough." *Laziness is another* roadblock. Following our calling can be very hard work. We may think, "I'm pretty comfortable. If I start this, then I have to give up some of my creature comforts."

Lack of faith is still another roadblock to hearing and answering our call. The Jonah story is really a story of faith. It's about stepping out and taking action without having all the answers. We get into the details of "how on earth am I going to do this?," not accepting in faith that we are never given an assignment without being given the tools somehow to carry it out. Whether it's Kennedy and the space program, Disney and a theme park, or Moses and the people of Egypt, God always shows us the way when we answer the call in faith. If we come from a place of service, surrender to our inevitable inadequacies, stay focused on the mission we were sent to do, and simply get our ego out of the way, we can change our world, or as author Peter Block says, *the room we are in.*[17]

An Urgent Time to Hear the Call

In a world that seems upside down, where change is so rapid and continuous, where there is no job security for any of us, we need and are hungry for meaning in our lives and our work. The word *work* comes from the Greek, meaning "to worship." No, it doesn't mean to worship our work. It is a means of worshiping God. It does mean that each of us has been given unique talents, skills, abilities, and gifts. We don't own them. We are called to uncover our gifts, develop them, and use them to serve others. The answer to how and where we serve is clear, if we but ask, listen, and take action in faith. That is what servant-leaders do.

4

Servant-Leadership: A Passion to Serve

Joe Batten

Joe Batten is chairman and CEO of the consulting firm of Joe Batten Associates, based in Des Moines, Iowa. His clients have included McDonald's, Xerox, Marriott, and IBM. One of his books, Tough-Minded Management, *has been translated into 21 languages. Ross Perot called* Tough-Minded Management *"the greatest management book in the world." A noted lecturer, Batten was one of the first people inducted into the Speakers Hall of Fame. His latest book is* The Leadership Principle of Jesus. *He gave the U.S. Army the phrase* Be All You Can Be.

In this essay, Batten describes a number of tools that can be used to prepare us for servant-leadership. Batten offers as one of these tools a "Values Manifesto for Tough-Minded Servant-Leaders." He closes with a powerful reflection on his belief that "work is love made visible."

The pursuit of, development of, and recognition of servant-leaders is going to be one of the most powerful movements and trends in the coming decade.

My colleagues and I have taught for many years that go-getters ultimately get got. Go-givers ultimately become rich in every way. The more we serve and build others, the better our own lives become. Three of the most key and crucial ingredients involved in passionate serving are caring, sharing, and forgiving. To care, share, and forgive is to live at life's cutting edge. As we care, we reach out beyond ourselves. Caring suffuses all superior leadership and full functioning. If we do not care much about others, we will ultimately not care much about ourselves in the real sense of the word.

To share is to serve and express caring tangibly. It is a further expression of emotional vulnerability, wonder, faith, hope, love, and gratitude. It is the here-and-now, hands-on, practical way to enrich the human condition. An excellent and appropriate expectation is one of the finest things we can share.

Forgiveness is a requisite for happiness and peace of mind, for a liberated and energizing approach to life. The all-too-rare ability to forgive is best developed as part of an overall lifestyle. We never truly forget; we simply tuck the "forgotten" feelings into our subconscious. We must *remember* in order to truly forgive. As we develop a lifestyle based on being forgiving we become capable of forgiving. Passion is powerful stuff and must be used by pivotal leaders in a disciplined, focused, and mentally tough way. The real servant-leader of tomorrow is, above all, a thinker who acts with passion.

Leaders who learn from, teach, serve, and empower others—particularly their customers, clients, and others—are tomorrow. "Leaders" who are simply getters are yesterday! The company philosophy, principles, policies, procedures, processes, programs, and people must reflect this awareness in action at all times. Everyone on the payroll is a potential servant-leader. Great leaders who are committed to total service and total quality will place a premium on serving the members of their team, and thus the customer.

Specifically how do we prepare ourselves for servant-leadership?

Applied Thought: Servant-leaders believe this is the most practical form of labor.

Generate Enthusiasm: Servant-leaders do not look to others to charge their battery but take the necessary action to internalize perpetuating values, inspiration, and intellectual enrichment.

Not Deterred by Small People: Servant-leaders secure maximum participation from their key people and move resolutely toward the actual practice of management by integrity.

Build on Strengths: Although servant-leaders recognize that they as well as all people have weaknesses, their primary concerns are the strengths of people, because it will be strengths—not weaknesses—that will make their organizations thrive. A weakness is only a missing strength or an insufficiently developed strength.

High Expectations: Servant-leaders stretch themselves and their people. Although they never expect more from a person than that person is capable of performing, they often expect more than that person believes he or she can accomplish. This is their key for developing the confidence and ability in individuals and helping them to obtain a maximum feeling of accomplishment.

Goal-Oriented: Since a straight line is the shortest distance between two points, servant-leaders know we must have some future point clearly in mind to stretch toward.

Significance: Servant-leaders know people can truly live and grow only if they feel real, if they can experience faith, hope, love, and gratitude.

Team Synergy: This occurs when the effort of two or more people adds up to a whole that is greater than the sum of its parts.

Enrich Lives of Others: Servant-leaders are proud of their lives and seek to enrich the lives of others by the richness of their own.

Live Integrity: Servant-leaders know that management by integrity is realistic and workable; that, in reality, there is no fit substitute for it.

Emphasize Results, Not Activity: Tough-minded servant-leaders measure the performance of their team members by results and their contribution to company objectives.

Define Their Philosophies: Servant-leaders take steps to ensure that their organization's and families' philosophy, objectives, and standards are researched, developed, and clearly communicated.

Define Results Expected: Servant-leaders know that people are more efficient and happy when they understand clearly what results are expected.

Age of the Mind: Servant-leaders define management or leadership as "an ever-changing, ever-dynamic system of interacting minds."

Manage Change: Servant-leaders require and encourage a climate conducive to innovation and creativity in all facets of the business.

Relate Compensation to Performance: Servant-leaders believe that providing rewards solely for seniority, long hours, education, and old school ties denies the dignity and worth of the individual.

Understand People: Servant-leaders continually strive to attain a better understanding of people and their differences—to determine what it takes to impel each person to produce and create. They recognize that many people need to be stretched, helped, encouraged, and sometimes pressured to reach out and grasp the opportunities all around them.

Need for Respect: Servant-leaders believe it is possible to be both respected and liked, but realize that respect is primary. Expectations stretch, pull, open, strengthen, motivate, and "turn on." Insistence, or "driving," pushes, compresses, represses, and depresses.

Grace: Grace is a special warmth felt and expressed toward all other human beings; an absence of pettiness and self-concern.

Tough-Minded: Servant-leaders are flexible, pliant, lasting, durable, high quality, difficult to break—expanding and strengthening with experience. The tough-minded personality has an infinite capacity for growth and change. Toughness and hardness are totally different.

Dare to live, love, and lead passionately. Dare to take some quantum leaps toward becoming all you can be. When I first gave the phrase *Be All You Can Be* to the U.S. Army a number of years ago, I had no idea it would become a household word throughout the United States, Canada, and other parts of the world. Be All You Can Be was the boiled-down statement of intent or vision that helped launch our company, now known as Joe Batten Associates, 39 years ago. Most people who have some real understanding of passionate living would like to live and work that way but don't know how. To truly live at the leading or cutting edge of our possibilities . . . to expect the best . . . and get it requires mental, physical, emotional, and spiritual tools. At the center, the core, of all achievements are strengths. Our strengths profile and define us—they are who we *are*. Again, our weaknesses are only missing strengths or insufficiently developed strengths. They're only what we *aren't*.

Our self is the sum of our strengths and values, and our esteem is our awareness and understanding of our strengths. I submit that the greatest need throughout the world is for greater self-esteem. Insufficient self-confidence and esteem is at the core of all criminal, bestial, perverted, violent, warlike, and sick behavior. So targeting greater self-esteem for all— starting with the person in the mirror—is probably the greatest challenge and opportunity in the world today. Are you ready for the challenge? In my audiotape, *The Greatest Secret,* the "Greatest Secret" is at the top of a mythical stairway consisting of 36 steps. As the listener climbs each step, he or she learns that every step is a key component in successful passionate living. Each step is discussed, and then the listener arrives at the top where, behind a door, is the greatest secret. The listener learns that the greatest secret of all is the great commandment to love your God, your fellow person, and yourself. If you want to reap the rewards that justice dictates must always fall to the victor, you have the privilege of making a fundamental decision: to expand and empower people, not compress, repress, suppress, or depress them; to build on their strengths, not focus on their weaknesses.

Again, we cannot "understand" a weakness, because a weakness is only an absence, a fault, a zero, a vacuum, a nothing. We can understand and acquire only strengths. Once this is fully perceived and understood, once we realize that the only tools we possess are our present and potential strengths, we can begin to focus on:

What is rather than what isn't
What can rather than what can't
What will rather than what won't
What does rather than what doesn't
What has rather than what hasn't

Please begin an all-out quest for greater awareness and use of all your current and potential strengths. *The kind of life you live tomorrow begins in your mind today.*

Warren Bennis and Burt Nanus wrote in their book *Leaders* that recognition and appreciation of self-worth is the most crucial requirement for leadership: "People without self-respect choke on self-reproach. Every unanswered letter becomes a monument to their own sloth, an epitaph to their guilt. Without self-respect, we give ourselves away and make the ultimate sacrifice. We sell ourselves out. The first step in achieving positive self-regard is recognizing strengths and compensating for weaknesses."[1]

When you reach the rare condition of searching for, knowing, and relishing your strengths, you then find it relatively easy to look for, identify, and fulfill and unleash the strengths of others. We recommend that people create and establish their own personal strengths notebooks.

As your strengths acquisition program moves forward and you begin to discover and delight in how special and unique you are—and how enormous your possibilities are—it is crucial to begin to feel and express your gratitude to your conception of God, your fellow person, and you. The passionate growth process becomes exponential. The more strengths you discover, the greater your gratitude. And the more you express gratitude in every dimension of your life, the more your search for new strengths grows and accelerates. Many people write or call me to say that they've continued to add one strength a week to their strength notebook for years. Power, purpose, poise, passion, and enrichment can be yours.

Remember: We are imprisoned by our weaknesses—we are liberated and empowered by our strengths. This core belief fuels and sustains servant-leaders.

Dare to Dream and Stretch

A dream is a deeply felt and yearned-for hope of the possible.

Unless you have thought or will think through your dream, there is no way you can achieve it. Taking the time, thoughts, and effort to do this will provide a thousand subtle benefits—every thought and action will be influenced consciously, subconsciously, or unconsciously by your dream. It can lift you, pull you, and enrich you. Without purpose and direction, we are like the person who jumped on a horse and rode 10 ways at once. Not only is it unproductive but it's painful. It is important to let ourselves dream freely and soaringly, or we will not know how to use our mental, physical, and spiritual muscles with any degree of purpose, discipline, and system. One goal of this essay is to provide you with insights, concepts, principles, values, and techniques for putting muscle into your dreams. But how do we go about defining a dream? Our perception of how we should behave to *believe* and *become* is best served by a dream, a transcendent vision of expectancy. To help put some meaningful sequence into the process, please study Figure 4.1, "Continuum of Actualization: The Possible Dream."

What you imagine is what will transpire. What you believe is what you will achieve.

We all need dreams, transcendent hopes, and expectations that subliminally flavor, season, and nourish all that we say and do. If that dream is made of happy expectations, it comes back to us like a boomerang. To be able to

Figure 4.1
Continuum of actualization: the possible dream.

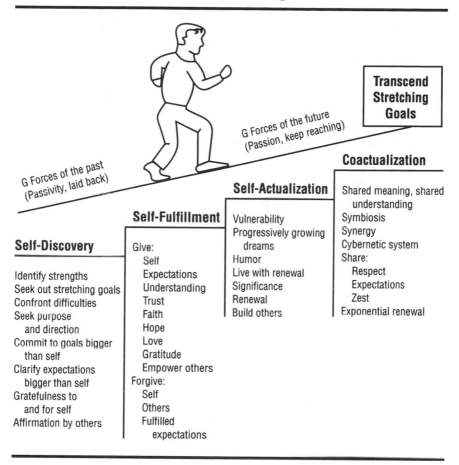

move from one point on life's continuum to the next in a fairly organized and purposeful way is important to vibrant, productive living. I have found in my own life that the moments of greatest productivity and accomplishment, although often hectic and frenetic, are those in which I felt a rhythm and cadence. Rhythm and cadence can only flow out of a daily sense of purpose and direction. Servant-leaders are fueled and pulled in purpose and direction.

What is your dream? Please take the time to begin to formulate it. Write it down and carry it around with you. This will begin to add the emotional muscle needed for full expective living. In a recent study, the American Psychiatric Association concluded that the principal cause of fatigue in the world today, and most particularly in the United States, is the failure of people to have something that seems bigger and more important than themselves to live for. Stated positively, having something bigger and more important to live for than ourselves is the finest kind of stretching we can have. It is the stuff of servant-leadership! What, then, would you conclude is the most fatiguing way to live? Pulled and stretched? Or pushed and pressed? Here are some stretching challenges.

Do you care enough to:

Define yourself?
Confront your hopes?
Ask much from life?
Build "forgiving" relationships?
Seek strength in all things?
Replace cynicism with wonder?
Share the real you with others?
Distinguish between tranquility and real happiness?
Lead?

As you dare to dream and stretch, here are a few affirmations. I will:

Exemplify a passion for excellence.
Ask, listen, and hear—to determine the wants, needs, and possibilities of my customers and my team.
Provide an example of accountability, commitment, and integrity.
Follow a path of continual empowerment for myself and others.
Consistently look for a focus on the strengths rather than the weaknesses of all with whom I come in contact.
Cultivate optimum physical, mental, and spiritual fitness.
Lead as I would like to be led.
Savor the flavor of each passing moment.
Infuse every thought and relationship with faith, hope, love, and gratitude.
Dare to be all I can be.

Making Quality Possibilities Come True

The times cry out for people who are committed to making all quality possibilities come true. You can be a person whose expectations and possibilities can become realities. All great people and great nations become or became great because of great expectations.

Let life in and let you out. We let life in by relating our expectations to the world around us and the future as we anticipate it. We let ourselves out—

to become—as we focus on many other-directed things. Such things include humor and laughter, reinforcing strengths of self; warm, reciprocal relationships; good food and drink; eagerness for change; good books and conversation; the joy of discovery; and so much more.

Remember: *A stretching and transcendent goal etches out and confirms the reality and identity of you.*

G Forces of the Future

The very essence of living passionately is change. Life without change would soon result in death. Change is something to embrace, to invite, to zestfully seek.

Rosabeth Moss Kanter says, "The individuals who will succeed and flourish will also be masters of change: adept at reorienting their own and others' activities in untried directions to bring about higher levels of achievement. They will be able to acquire and use power to produce innovation."[2]

There are basically two kinds of psychological, intellectual, and emotional G forces in our lives. Understanding them and committing to the right one is absolutely crucial to a life of passionate and successful living, serving, and leading.

What is a *G force*, anyway? "G" stands for gravity and is a term scientists use as a unit of measure to describe the amount of the force exerted by gravity. I use the term figuratively, and in this figurative sense there are both negative and positive G forces. Negative G forces are the self-defeating habits of the past—passivity, focus on weaknesses, "driving" attitudes—which only pull us down. Positive G forces of the future are the passionate attitudes and practices that energize and pull us. In a sense these G forces pull us up (even though we all know that literal gravity cannot). Let's talk about how to release yourself from the negative G forces of the past and plug into the positive G forces of the future. Like a compass, positive G forces guide, lift, and pull. Significant changes must occur in the value systems of leaders, changes that bring a greatly heightened interest in the positive potential of other people. The final goal is to achieve abundance of the human spirit. From this spirit flows all innovation, all creativity, all positive change, and all else that is renewing. From this spirit comes the motivating power. The future cries out for passionate commitment to strong, tough, and stretching values and ideals. As new leaders seek to mine the riches of the human spirit, they must strive always to free themselves from the negative pull—the deadly and self-defeating pull—of the negative G forces of the past.

Remember: *A quality inner life leads to a rich and abundant total life.*

The search for full functioning of the self promises to be the most fruitful endeavor the modern and relevant leader can undertake. The potential yield from nonhuman resources, from money, material, time, and space, will continue to be limited until new breakthroughs are made in the understanding of people. A brand-new look at the nature of objectives as expectives is an important early step. Objectives will need to be formulated and stated in qualitative terms, with more-sophisticated use of quantitative measurement.

Attitude is everything. Our attitudes are, of course, a product of our experience, the information we ingest, the thoughts we think, the words we use, and the ways other people respond to us. In global terms, we must raise our sights, loosen our biases, and let our minds go forth. Great goals are never reached until you decide to dare to fail.

I'm going to challenge all potential servant-leaders to the most challenging changes of all—the quality of your relationships with others.

There are certainly all kinds of relationships: courageous, cowardly, selfish and greedy, caring and sharing, hateful, loving, warm and cold. Perhaps the most crucial ingredient in the creating of wholesome, productive, and satisfying relationships is courage. The great philosophers have stated in various ways that courage is not the absence of despair. Rather, it is the capacity to move ahead despite despair. Relationships crumble and degenerate into various forms of destructiveness, anger, and negativism when we begin to give up, ever so slightly, on a relationship—a form of despair. As we examine change in relation to expectations and possibilities—expective living—it is important to recognize some key elements that induce this kind of despair and some ways to overcome it.

Have you ever been rebuffed or ignored by a sales clerk or a waitress? Felt the indifference of a doctor, lawyer, teacher, or dentist? Do you ever find yourself thinking people just don't care anymore? Why do people manifest these indications of insufficient caring? I submit that they do it primarily as a defensive reaction to feelings of insignificance that beset them. Their own self-concept, self-confidence, and self-esteem lack quality; their failure is to understand real servant-leadership.

The Leader Is In, the Driver Is Out

Never before in history has the need for strong, excellent leadership been so great. Yet, there is an incredible lack of understanding of what a real servant-leader is.

Real servant-leaders are committed to the growth and renewal of all with whom they come into contact. I once met with a group of CEOs for a seminar entitled "Tough-Minded Leadership." I asked, "How many of you are leaders in your company?" Every hand went up. I then said, "I'll ask you the same question after I've shared a true story with you." The story went like this: In the Middle East, there are two countries (separated only by a border) with large sheep and mutton industries. The cultures of the two countries are radically different and hostile to each other. In one country, the shepherds walk behind their flocks. In the other, the shepherds walk in front of their flocks.

In the country where the shepherds always walk behind their flocks, the quality of the mutton and the wool is poor, and it is not a profitable industry. In the country where the shepherds walk in front of their flocks, the quality of the mutton and wool is excellent and the profit high. Why? In the flocks where the shepherd walks behind and pushes, drives, corrects, and is always in charge, the young sheep grow up afraid to stray from the flock for fear of being tapped on the head by the shepherd's staff. They have no opportunity to explore for better grass and water or to play with other young lambs. They simply become obedient, passive, apathetic, and unhealthy. In the country where the shepherds walk in front of their flocks, the young lambs have plenty of opportunity to stray, play, experiment, and then catch up to the flock. Instead of feeling overcontrolled and compressed, repressed, depressed, and suppressed, they feel free, empowered, enhanced, stretched, and healthy. They eat more, sleep better, and grow up large and healthy. *They are truly led.*

When I had finished the story and assured the executives that it was utterly true, I asked again, "How many of you truly lead in your company?" Not a hand was raised. I then asked, "Would you like to truly lead?" The response was loud and enthusiastic.

Leadership in every phase of your life can happen only if others like what they see in you, respect you, and want to achieve what you are asking them to be and do. When I say "follow," I mean this figuratively, symbolically, and sometimes literally. Pushers and drivers are a dime a dozen. Pullers, stretchers, askers—and real leaders—are still in short supply. If you're committed to really living a life of passionate growth and success, it is vital to realize that we not only become what we *think*, we also become what we *say!* Most of us would benefit enormously by thoughtfully and thoroughly overhauling our vocabulary. All achievements are stimulated, created, implemented, and understood by words. Get rid of outdated oxymorons like *vision-driven, value-driven, customer-driven.* Instead, begin to understand the significant difference in using words like *vision-led, value-led, customer-led.* Please think about this deeply.

I have built a "Values Manifesto for Tough-Minded Servant-Leaders" around 37 values that real leaders believe in and practice every day of their lives. This manifesto consists of the following:

1. *Openness and emotional vulnerability.* Servant-leaders let other people in and let themselves out. They believe that the absence of defensiveness is an indication of strength and management maturity.
2. *Warmth.* Servant-leaders reach out to people; they do not simply sit back and wait.
3. *Consistency.* Servant-leaders meet commitments, keep their word, and can be relied upon. They expect the same from others.

4. *Unity.* Servant-leaders have a fused and focused oneness of purpose, effort, and direction.

5. *Caring.* Servant-leaders want others to grow and benefit.

6. *Positive listening.* Servant-leaders are positive listeners. They keep an open and flexible mind.

7. Un*satisfaction*—not dis*satisfaction*. Servant-leaders are hungry for improvement, growth, and a better way.

8. *Flexibility.* Servant-leaders abhor rigidity in all forms. Their minds are resilient and supple. This is crucial to real growth.

9. *Giving.* Servant-leaders believe, in fact they know, that the more people put into—or give—to life and their work, the more they receive.

10. *Involvement.* Servant-leaders seek the involvement of their people in developing their goals and plans, not only because they want to use all the talents within their organization but also because they know that people will be more committed to meeting these objectives if they have a part in determining them. Involvement must precede commitment if it is to be carried out with conviction.

11. *Tolerance of mistakes.* Servant-leaders have the courage to let people make mistakes. They recognize that people learn by doing; so if they do anything, they are going to make mistakes.

12. *Values.* Servant-leaders realize values should be precision instruments that inspire, unify, and stretch. True leaders are value-led. The value of a person is the sum of their values.

13. *Psychological wages.* Servant-leaders provide for a psychic as well as a real wage for their people because they recognize psychological and spiritual as well as physical needs.

14. *Simplicity.* Servant-leaders constantly strive to make the complex simple.

15. *Time.* Servant-leaders guard their time preciously and allot it to key areas where it will produce the greatest impact.

16. *The winning formula. Integrity* plus *quality* plus *service* says it all.

17. *An open mind.* An open mind can grow. A closed mind dies.

18. *Development of people.* Servant-leaders believe and live the concept that the development of people, as a whole and in depth, pays real dividends to both the organization and the individual.

19. *Self-discipline.* Servant-leaders practice self-discipline in every dimension of their lives.

20. *Physical fitness.* Servant-leaders recognize that developing optimum physical fitness is an important requisite of mental health and acuity.

21. *Enjoyment of life.* Servant-leaders enjoy life—and people know it. They radiate their feelings.

22. *Broad perspective.* Servant-leaders' interests and activities may range globally. Truly broad-gauge leaders read widely and have their own personal development program. They believe that a broad and eclectic fund of knowledge makes for not only a better generalist but also a better specialist.

23. *Faith in self and others.* Servant-leaders believe we are the sum of our strengths and that the only real things to search for and believe in are the strengths of ourselves and others.

24. *Vision.* Vision provides the basic energy, lift, and stretch for pulling the organization toward the future.

25. *Positive thinking.* Servant-leaders believe negativism is never justified. They know that there are plus and minus elements in many situations, but that the minus areas can be made into pluses.

26. *Desire to learn.* Servant-leaders cultivate a curiosity for new dimensions of knowledge and resist efforts to predicate plans on past and present knowledge only.

27. *Enjoyment of work.* Servant-leaders know that life without work is a shortcut to deterioration, that hard and positive work is one of life's great renewing agents.

28. *Enrichment of others.* Servant-leaders are proud of the free enterprise way of life and seek to enrich the lives of others by the richness of their own.

29. *Integrity.* Servant-leaders live integrity, instead of relying on preachments and pointing fingers. They expect the best of others.

30. *Results, not activity.* Excellent leaders believe that people are on the payroll for only one reason—to make a significant contribution to company objectives and to grow.

31. *Candor.* Servant-leaders practice truth rigorously and reflect a true warmth of feeling toward their associates.

32. *Management by example.* Servant-leaders know that the actions of a responsible leader are contagious, and that there is virtually no limit to potential accomplishment if leaders set the example of consistently looking for strengths and expecting the best.

33. *A clear philosophy.* Servant-leaders make sure their organization's philosophy and objectives are researched, developed, clearly communicated, and practiced.

34. *Accountability.* Servant-leaders believe people are more efficient and happy when they understand clearly what results are expected of them and when they are involved in determining these results.

35. *Purpose and direction.* Servant-leaders are visionaries. They know that all team members will contribute and receive more if they are helped to develop clear feelings of purpose, direction, dignity, and expectations. They provide direction, not directions.

36. *Expectations of excellence.* Servant-leaders know that perhaps the finest gift you can give another person is the gift of a stretching expectation based on a never-ending search for that person's strengths.

37. *Laserlike focus.* Servant-leaders compare the average group of people on one hand and their untapped possibilities on the other to the difference between an ordinary room full of diffused particles of light and the laser beam with its mind-boggling propensities and possibilities. They know the answer is: Vision + Focus + Action = The G Forces of the Future.

When I presented these 37 tough-minded principles to 375 top executives of Nissan in Sendai, Japan, the response was stunning. When the seminar ended, a line formed and *every single one* said variations of the following: "Mr. Batten, tomorrow (or this evening) I will *start* to do these things."

How about you? Will you dare to discover the unmined potential in this greatest of all leadership styles?

Work Is Love Made Visible

Love has probably been discussed more than any other word in history. And yet, it is so little understood. Love is a powerful, healing, renewing, and fulfilling emotion. People who live passionately—at the cutting edge—know that love has infinite possibilities when harnessed, focused, and lived. It is an outgrowing of care, service, and commitment to the needs and desires of others. It is a common denominator in the toolkit of the passionate leadership artist. Love is the toughest-minded emotion in the world and the finest mental and spiritual nutrient you can possess for a total life of fulfillment and actualization. It is truly the nutrient that grows winners.

Leadership is an example. Effective leaders set an example of what they expect and want from team members. If quality and service are truly important to you, exemplify quality and service in all you say, do, and are. I believe we may be at a watershed in the evolution of a new tough-minded breed of leaders who not only won't shy away from love but also will perceive the intrinsic power in it.

Among the excellent examples of success as a product of unconditional love and service are Ross Perot, Vince Lombardi, Jim Autry, and others. When Ross Perot, a master motivator, was asked the secret of the fabulous success of Electronic Data Systems, EDS, the company he started from scratch, he smiled broadly, threw his arms wide, and said, "I don't just like the people at EDS, I love them." He meant it (*Fortune* magazine, February, 1987).

What do I mean by "unconditional"? I mean that the other person's inadequacies, disfigurements, racial and ethnic differences, the stereotyped stigmata are of no importance. Rather, we look for strengths, for that central spark of God that reposes (although sometimes difficult to find or see) in all people.

Faith is incomplete without hope, love, and gratitude. Hope is incomplete without faith and love. Above all, faith without passion is like soda water without the sparkle. Without these renewing feelings—faith, hope, love, and gratitude—our behavior in the home, on the job, and in the community can be marred by insecurity, defensiveness, cynicism, and other feelings that corrode our possibilities. The sheer practicality of faith—enriched by love—on a deep and pervasive level is enormous. Faith and belief, after all, mean the same. And there is practically no limit to what you and I can do if our belief in ourselves, our fellow person, and our own perception of a higher power are strong and constant. Socrates said this: "Human nature will not easily find a helper better than love." We take a giant step toward confirming that work is love made visible when we invest in generous portions of faith, hope, love, and gratitude.

Faith

To believe in people, events, relationships, in life itself, is to really live with every fiber of your being. A life of doubt and cynicism curdles, reduces, and sours.

Hope

Hope is the living 24-hour-a-day evidence that we count, we are real, there is good in life. Expectations are usable instruments in each of our hope chests. Without hope, we have no motivation to live, to work, to grow.

Love

Love is the healing, unifying, integrating, stimulating, renewing, reassuring, and constructive life force at the core of all good things. Without it, we have violence, destruction, confusion, and more.

Gratitude

Gratitude puts it all together. It provides us with specific ways of expressing faith, hope, praise and love and, perhaps more important, sets in motion a reciprocity that further nourishes and increases the amounts of faith, hope, and love in one's life.

Diligently practice the principles, values, and techniques in this essay. Specific techniques and tools are provided to help you mine the mother lode of talent within you:

1. You find out how to itemize your strengths and dissolve your weaknesses.
2. You discover how to develop that elusive and vital something, the spirit that enlightens and energizes the ordinary individual so that he or she may accomplish extraordinary things.

3. You can move from segmented, sterile habits and attitudes to explosive living as a whole and unified person.
4. You can set into motion a lifetime of youth and excitement.
5. You can learn to:

Understand yourself. Develop glowing self-confidence. Formulate your personal blueprint.

Use tension as an asset. Create the winning edge—self-discipline.

Take the Herculean leap from blandness and passivity to a life of zest and passionate enthusiasm.

Build on your strengths and strengthen your total value system.

I challenge you to:

- Dream big and put timetables in that dream.
- Become all you can be and do all you can do.
- Shun rigidity by keeping an open and tough mind.
- Expect the best from yourself and others.
- Find something to love in every person.
- Set big goals and stretch to meet them.
- Fill your battery with faith, hope, love, and gratitude.
- Build (not destroy) with everything you think, say, and do.
- Confront life openly and vulnerably with courage, faith, commitment, and confidence.
- Displace "loser" attitudes by writing down 200 victories in your life since you were born.
- Be an inspiring go-giver.

Our great and wonderful opportunity is to chart a course of the possible dream and dare to keep our sight and senses on it. Setbacks and failures may occur, but we will almost certainly have a higher level of accomplishment and actualization than if we have no dream at all. The sheer practicality of aspiring and expecting yourself and others to work harder and smarter in a cause greater than self has been tested through the centuries.

- Will you dare to serve in every dimension of your life?
- Will you dare to dream?
- Will you dare to articulate high hopes?
- Will you dare to put muscle into those dreams?
- Will you constantly confront your possibilities?
- Will you expect the best?
- Will you dare to become all you can be?

For love to deliver its full payload, to chart a course that will make that possible dream a living reality, it is important that it be at the heart of your vision, your values, your vitality, and your voltage.

Robert Schuller said, in one of his sermons, "The world of tomorrow belongs to the person who has the vision today"[3]—something to reach for and to stretch. A vision remains pretty much a tempting and pleasant generality unless fortified by values.

Values—you can't see them, touch them, taste them, or smell them. They are critical, intangible essentials that bring continuity and meaning to life.

The Value-Led Visioneer

In my book *Building a Total Quality Culture,* I have listed 23 values and beliefs that are crucial in preparing for a future of boundless achievement and joy.[4] They include power tools for passionate living such as:

- The leader is in; the driver is out.
- Visioneers stop telling, commanding, and coercing; instead, they ask, listen, and hear.
- Tough-minded people thrive on quality nutrients such as confidence, self-respect, courage, commitment, integrity, stretch, moral values, resiliency, tenacity, mental agility, sensitivity to change, openness, emotional vulnerability, and a belief in something or someone greater than the self.
- The most practical thing in the world is applied thought.
- The epigram "work is love made visible" will take on a new meaning. Work is truly one of the best ways to illustrate love in action.

The happiest and most fulfilled people will consistently illustrate and practice the power of love and service at work as well as in every corner of their life. Will you do it?

5

On the Path
to Servant-Leadership

Lawrence J. Lad and David Luechauer

Lawrence J. Lad and David Luechauer are both associate professors of management at Butler University in Indianapolis. Lad, who has received numerous teaching awards and writes about business, community and social issues, is also the author of the book Current Principles and Practices of Association Self-Regulation. *Luechauer, an award-winning teacher and creative speaker, writes in the area of leadership and spirituality.*

Lad and Luechauer's essay examines five separate "pathways" to servant-leadership, including the cognitive, experiential, spiritual, organizational, and community. They offer many practical suggestions for addressing the barriers and paradoxes associated with practicing servant-leadership.

> *A journey of a thousand miles begins with the first step.*
> —Chinese Proverb

> *If you seek enlightenment for yourself simply to enhance yourself and your position, you miss the purpose; if you seek enlightenment for yourself to enable you to serve others, you are with purpose.*
> —Dalai Lama

The Context

A casual review of the academic and business press on leadership in the last decade reveals two interesting patterns. One is the attention to organizational-level, even systems-level, changes and the challenge of leading through the maze of technology, globalization, and expectations of a knowledge-based workforce. Representative works by Hammer and Champy, *Re-engineering the Corporation;* Moore, *The Death of Competition;* Toffler, *Powershift;* Osborne and Gaebler, *Reinventing Government;* and Etzioni, *The*

Moral Dimension: Towards a New Economics illustrate the scope of change in industries and systems. Moreover, they confirm the dramatic undercurrents of change in the 1990s—it is rapid, deep, faster, and multisector. There is no turning back.

Another profound pattern in the literature is the reexamination of the roles of the individual in the change process. As we move to globalization while struggling to hold communities together, as we learn new technologies and new lessons of collaboration, and as we search for balance in our work and personal lives, the emerging literature offers some guideposts. Work by Covey *(The Seven Habits of Highly Effective People)*, Senge *(The Fifth Discipline)*, Moore *(Care of the Soul)*, Bly *(Iron John)*, Cowan *(Small Decencies)*, and Novak *(Business as a Calling)* have focused on the individual and the tools for proactively addressing the change around us. Like Greenleaf's *Servant Leadership*, these works lend credence to the search for meaning and self-discovery and legitimacy to expressing our humanity in organizations.

This essay focuses on the latter pattern—the process of individual discovery and pathwork. It suggests a set of alternative paths for exploring who we are and where we are called to serve. The search or inquiry into service is a personal one; no one way or route fits everyone. We note that, although each pathway requires commitment, discipline, and ultimately a relationship to others, different tools and processes work better for different people. We explore common themes and paradoxes within these paths and share some of our stories from the classroom, consulting, and personal life. Consider this a toolkit for self-discovery. Use it in a way that works for you on your journey.

Pathways

Consider for a moment a great biography. What makes it special? Is it the story of triumph or the story of tragedy? Is it the story of challenge or the story of getting up after defeat? Or is it the story of a person in a moment in time standing up against circumstances and making something happen? Beyond the quality of the author's research and the way of capturing the moment, it is likely that many elements play a role in bringing the individual to life, and our subsequent appreciation of the work. Like Joseph Campbell who studied heroes throughout history, we connect with those ordinary individuals who display extraordinary courage or perseverance in their lives. They go beyond their "individual" selves, they discover, they evolve, and they struggle. In "pressing through," in being mindful, in telling the truth to power, they contribute and they serve.

As we read about servant-leadership, we may see the possibility in our own lives. Yet we may question, where to start? We offer five pathways. They are presented individually in Table 5.1. It presents the pathways, notes representative authors, discusses key themes, suggests activities that may be part of the pathway, and offers the link to servant-leadership.

Table 5.1
Pathways to Servant-Leadership

Pathway	Representative Author	Themes/Key Message	Actions/Representative Activities	Link to Servant-Leadership
Cognitive: Concept/ Knowledge/ Insight	Wheatley Senge Peck Gardner Kegan	Frames, maps, mental models New learning Integration Wonder, curiosity Connection to ideas, consciousness	Read broadly/join a reading group Take a class/study a new discipline Self-assessment/career development Get (be) a "coach"/mentor Left brain/right brain learning	New mind-set Cross-disciplinary Lifelong learning and self-discovery
Experiential: Doing/Action	Covey de Bono Hall and Joiner	Learn from doing Engage multisensory Connection to self	Do a workshop Start therapy Keep a journal Take risks Take nature walks/exercise	Action Proactivity Risk taking
Spiritual: Search for Meaning	Moore Chopra Palmer Redfield Silverstein Ram Dass Hawley	Search/inquiry into purpose Ascension and transformation Connection to higher power	Practice religion/engage in solitude Meditate/take reflective moments Read poetry, study art or music Practice voluntary simplicity	Reflection Values Ethics

Organization: External	Drucker Peters Kanter Autry	Connection to customer, employees, and other stockholders	Reengineer/restructure Start dialogue groups Customize, personalize customer connections Use GE "Workout" sessions (solve problems)	Vision Purpose Mindfulness
Organization: Internal	Bennis Block DePree Bolman and Deal	Connection to sub-ordinates, peers Search for new work configurations	Use 360° feedback for managers Mentor, coach Create and support teams Support progressive HR practices: child and elder care, paid sabbaticals, etc. Do creative "executive development"	Self-awareness Create teams
Community: Connectedness	Peck Bellah Fuller	Connection to others, community creation Building bridges Integration Think global	Volunteer for a cause Raise money/donate money Travel to different country Explore various "causes"/find one that moves you	Service Discovery Local issues addressed

Cognitive Path

This is the thinking and inquiring approach to discovery. It begins with the notion that more knowledge will create more insight. While it may be "left brain" (i.e., logical, deductive, analytical) rather than intuitive and relational, inductive leaps and insights are captured here. The conscious process here is the deliberate choice to find self and meaning via an intellectual pathway. Yet the path could show up in a variety of ways. Some might choose graduate school or the pursuit of a professional credential. Others might create or join a reading group to explore works of fiction or nonfiction. Still others might do a structural assessment of personality to match with career goals, or enter short-term therapy to address what's blocking them from moving on in their lives. Regardless the type of activity, the distinction of the cognitive path is the intellectual exploration and the reflection into how this adds meaning and defines self.

Experiential Path

In this simplest form, this path is about trying new things. It could be about physical risk such as rock climbing or training for marathons, but it might include learning music, being in a stage play, taking an art class, or volunteering for a challenging project at work. The distinction here is to learn by doing that which allows you to see yourself as capable when you are at risk and vulnerable. The deliberate choice is to put oneself outside the usual "comfort zone," and to experience self at risk and in the moment. Powerful experiential learning typically involves some element of risk, a support system, and time for reflection. For some, the risk could be a physical challenge. In others, simply doing a presentation in front of an audience or running a committee may be significant. As with any new learning experiential activities (rock climbing, training for a marathon, taking a cooking class), we are enhanced by thoughtful coaching. Beyond the task or skill being addressed, reflecting on what is being learned, what we feel, what we notice about ourselves is critical.

Spiritual Path

This path is characterized by reflective action around the broader question of meaning and purpose. It might entail patterned prayer, meditation, reading, or dialogue. While not focused on finding the "right" belief system, it could be a search for more thoughtful practice within a framework or belief system that works for the individual.

This path also allows reflection on the shadow side of our nature. It enables forgiveness and awe; it defuses self-righteousness and self-importance. For servant-leaders, it might involve the questioning along a broad spectrum, from "Where am I called to serve?" to "How can I do a better job in the place I currently serve?"

Organizational Path

Beyond individual acts of self-discovery and one-on-one Samaritanship, serving others happens most often in the context of organizations—families, businesses, churches, government agencies, voluntary groups, professional associations, and not-for-profits. This path reflects the leverage institutions have in making a difference in society, and the roles individuals play in enabling their organizations to serve and being enabled to serve. Two layers of paths are suggested here—one addresses the big picture and broader questions of organizational purpose; the other focuses on where people lead, manage, and follow every day. For the former, the path is about questioning organizational purpose, culture, status quo, and values. It entails challenging the prevailing order and moving to a new order in relating to workforce, customers, and communities. It's a proactive stance on issues of environment and workplace safety. It's diversity training before the lawsuit. It's GE's workout sessions where real customer service questions are addressed in real time. And for the latter, the path to servant-leadership is found in looking at daily work—meetings, memos, plans, conversations, and so on—and asking the basic questions: Are we growing, are we learning, are people better off as a result of what we do?

Community Path

This is the action path of service and discovery in community. It is a pathway of being connected. Some may see the obvious parallels to the organizational, spiritual, or experiential paths, but this route also has some unique elements. Community service and volunteer opportunities allow discovery and contribution. Service-learning in high schools and universities provides students a structured way of doing service and reflecting on its meaning back in the classroom. Its uniqueness is in its exploratory nature, in its creative possibility, and in the leverage it creates for others. Community nourishes. Community connects. Community breaks down barriers. We have suggested a range of ways to use this path beyond the typical volunteer experience at Habitat for Humanity or a soup kitchen. Find opportunities to bring diverse groups together. Create a community where none exists. Mobilize around a cause, build a cause-related foundation, create a yearly neighborhood event. This path extends our view of "separate self" to one of self embedded in community.

Common Themes

Table 5.1 clearly indicates that there are numerous paths toward servant-leadership. We barely scratched the surface. Nonetheless, a quick review of authors/approaches listed in the table reveals a few common themes.

First, the approaches appear to take a systems or holistic perspective. Each individual path can be seen as complete and whole. One could discover self and the call to service in any one of these. Yet as a group, the paths represent a variety of dimensions of learning and life. They are mind, body, and spirit in the major arenas of life—work and community/family. They might cause us to see what's needed close to home or where we can contribute beyond our current community.

Second, the paths might loosely reflect life stages and thereby be seen as having an order or flow. Possibly! Within each path, a flow of inquiry, search, reflection, vulnerability, sharing, and discovery should take place. Each path is an ongoing process marked by milestones, discoveries, and new questions. Life stages or life events might highlight a step on a path (e.g., we ask the spiritual questions after the loss of a loved one or a personal health crisis). Perhaps the most important process issue is the connection to others—as mentors, coaches, or companions in the dialogue. Could it be that we discover and learn to serve by being of service and by being served just like we learn to lead by following?

Third, each of the approaches recognizes the importance of moving self, others, relationships, and structures from their present states of "disease" to more enlightened states of existence. Thus, following the paths they suggest requires a transformation from mind-sets and systems that promote excessive independence/dependence to states or conditions of interdependence. The transformation may be achieved by reframing such areas as self-image/esteem (e.g., Silverstein), values (e.g., Covey), organizational culture (Peters), or mental maps (Senge), but such reframing is encouraged in the hope of overcoming the dysfunctions and limitations associated with the excessive independence/dependence to which we have become accustomed.

Fourth, each of the approaches is inherently paradoxical. For example, Parker Palmer encourages leaders to become in touch with their lighter or better side by confronting and living in their shadow side. Senge invites groups to risk failure even though they are eager to succeed. Lee Bolman and Terrence Deal espouse the benefits of going nowhere to leaders who are focused on moving ahead. In short, the approaches recognize that there is a little bit of good in the worst of us and a little bit of bad in the best of us. Fortunately, accepting and coping with paradox is one of the skills at the heart of the journey toward servant-leadership. The special role of paradox will be explored in more depth later in this essay.

Fifth is the notion that servant-leadership is an active process that requires both engagement and reflection. Each of the approaches listed in the table encourages passionate commitment, action, and a sense of urgency on behalf of the leader. Paradoxically, however, each approach requires and suggests that leaders should frequently engage in significant periods of silence, solitude, and reflection. The essence of the message appears to be simple—action without thought is pointless, and thought without action is dead. Thus, your journey will likely be characterized by periods of intense action followed by periods of slowing down to smell the roses.

The sixth common theme is balance. Life goes on while we walk the path and search. The journey needs deliberate action, but not at the sacrifice of job or family. There are times for intense focus and work. There are times for mindfulness in the basic routines of living.

Finally, each of the approaches is focused on the journey not the destination. In this regard, the approaches may best be summed up by that famous T-shirt saying, "I am in the process of becoming." To take a process orientation on your journey toward servant-leadership is to recognize that 90 percent of the joy stems from the work, not the outcome or results attained. Certainly, the authors clearly discuss the gains or results to be generated from following their approaches. However, the gains to be garnered lie more in the *process* of becoming than in the actual becoming of what it is you are hoping to attain.

Barriers, Paradoxes, and Downsides to Servant-Leadership

The journey toward becoming a leader who seeks to serve rather than be served is worthy, commendable, and, unfortunately, filled with many personal, organizational, and environmental barriers, paradoxes, and downsides. This section describes a few of the many roadblocks you might expect to encounter along the path toward servant-leadership.

Barriers

A number of factors may prevent or at least delay the process of becoming a servant-leader. It is important to note that these barriers are both perceived and legitimate. They exist in our minds, in our firms, and in the minds of those with whom we work. The good news, however, is that the barriers you encounter will provide both an opportunity to test your skills and a focal point toward which to direct your energies. Thus, naming, claiming, and reframing the barriers you encounter are necessary and important steps in your journey.

Our personal experience as well as our research and consulting efforts with people and firms who are on the path to servant-leadership indicate five barriers you are likely to encounter. The following brief explanations of the barriers and the source of resistance inherent in each barrier are offered in the hope that you will gain insight regarding the efforts you might take to reduce the forces against your change:

1. *This is just another "management fad."* This phrase has been uttered since the invention of the first organizational development efforts. Unfortunately, we live in an age that propels leaders/firms to frequently jump from program to program, guru to guru, and philosophy to philosophy in search of immediate results. Typically, they

make such moves without taking the time to fully understand or implement the ideas to which they have been exposed. Hence, employees become conditioned to believe that each week will bring a new emphasis. Worse, they expect little if anything in the way of substantive change or results. This is, perhaps, the most real of all the barriers you are likely to encounter. It is based on the inherent distrust that has emerged from the many times leaders/firms have violated the psychological contracts created with employees who seriously desire real change.

2. *I'm too busy keeping my job and fighting fires to practice servant-leadership.* This position is taken by the leaders/firms who probably have the most pressing need for becoming more servantlike in their leadership. This barrier is based on the functional atheistic philosophy that is best stated by the phrases "if it is going to be . . . it is up to me" and "someday when I have more _____ (fill in the blank with whatever excuse you need) I'll get started on practicing servant-leadership." Thus, servant-leadership seems to be an "add on" to a calendar that is already jam-packed with events, meetings, deadlines, and obligations. It is viewed as something we should do, but it is not seen as something we have to do to be successful, secure, or competitive. Therefore, since the need for practicing servant-leadership does not appear to be pressing we become trapped in a whirlwind of other events and concerns that demand our time, attention, and energy.

3. *My boss/company just isn't into this stuff.* This is the battle cry of the unempowered, apathetic, and alienated! This is fear and dependence in disguise. It is the fuel that fires bureaucracy. It fosters a mind-set of myopic self-interest that drives literally millions of employees to believe that their primary concern is to look out for number one. It is based on the misguided assumption that we have no voice and no control over our organizations. It propels those who are caught in its web to lead what Thoreau has called, "lives of quiet desperation."

4. *If it ain't broke, don't fix it.* This mentality is based on the belief that organizations exist to survive. This approach tends to focus our attention on quantitative outcomes such as ROI, profits, and market share. Leaders/firms who operate from this base see the bottom line as the only criteria by which to measure their effectiveness. Unfortunately, what people/firms caught in this trap fail to recognize is that generally a high price must be paid for the successes generated from this orientation. As a result, they frequently overlook the hidden costs (e.g., low morale, lack of trust, anxiety/stress) associated with their success. More importantly, they often fail to recognize that what works today may be outdated or nonexistent tomorrow.

5. *Sounds great in theory . . . but . . . it will never work in practice.* This argument is most often presented by those who know how to talk the talk but don't know how or don't want to walk the talk. This form of resistance is based on the belief that the world is a dangerous, harsh, and inherently evil place filled with people who can't and shouldn't be trusted or empowered. Leaders/firms who adopt this orientation see organizational life as a battleground with nothing less than personal/organizational survival at stake. They are smart enough to keep abreast of current thinking in leadership/organization theory, but they are fundamentally uncomfortable with what they must change in themselves. Hence, they spend a great deal of energy telling you why servant-leadership is a great concept, but why this approach will not work. Their organization is too unique; the theory doesn't apply.

Barriers, however, are your opportunity in disguise. They allow you to assess where you, others, and the organization stand in regard to servant-leadership. Barriers are good news for those who are willing to see the blessing in the storm clouds.

Paradoxes

Servant-leadership, in our opinion, is paradoxical. In this regard, it is a lot like the popular Al-Anon approach known as "tough love." The journey toward becoming a servant-leader will require you to become comfortable with the many paradoxes embedded in its principles. The following discussion outlines a few of the paradoxes both we and our clients have had to confront.

There are many paths but one destination is based on the systems theory tenet known as equifinality. The paradox in servant-leadership is that there is no singular best technique, model, or path to follow in your journey even though you are trying to get to the same destination as many others. This is unlike virtually any other form of travel, where there clearly are best routes given time, money, and other constraints. Hence, though two people may have very different characteristics, personalities, and managerial styles, they both may be servant-leaders. Furthermore, people who are the same age, race, gender, or level in the organization may be at different points in their journey. Thus, both may be implementing servant-leadership as they understand it, even though it may appear to peers, subordinates, and superiors that they are doing fundamentally different things. In short, the paradox of servant-leadership is that it may take different and ever-changing forms. One must be comfortable with such variation in the process and realize the commandment that "thou is not the only servant in the organization."

Tough standards with soft processes is another way of saying excellence is not sacrificed in the process of practicing servant-leadership. High performance standards, as attained by such servant-oriented firms as Schneider Engineering and TDIndustries, emanate from employee commitment, involvement, and empowerment that is cultivated from below rather than enforced and dictated from the top. In short, commanding quality is no way to achieve quality, and servant-leaders recognize this. As one servant-leader told us, "If I set the rules, they are my rules . . . but . . . when the people in this firm set the rules—they own them!"

Leadership at the top and leadership at the bottom is a way of confronting the myth that servant-leadership means no rules, no hierarchy, and no structure. There is nothing in the concept of servant-leadership that implies that rules, hierarchy, or structure should be abolished. What does change, however, is the role these functions perform. They are created to educate, facilitate, and support rather than dictate, suffocate, and control. Servant-leaders still lead . . . they just do so from a different base.

Commitment to vision, is perhaps, the most common paradox of servant-leadership. Servant-leaders typically have a passionate zeal for creating a preferred future. Then again, Hitler, Mussolini, and Jim Jones all had visions! What differentiates servant-leaders from maniacal dictators is their deep desire to pursue this vision from a base of humility, empathy, compassion, and commitment to ethical behavior. In short, they articulate a vision and then enable, ennoble, and empower those around them to work for the attainment of that vision. In essence, servant-leadership represents a pull rather than a push model of vision attainment.

In "In Praise of Paradox," Mary Morrison wrote that, "we stand in a turmoil of contradictions without having the faintest idea how to handle them. . . . Paradox is the art of balancing opposites in such a way that they do not cancel each other out but shoot sparks of light across their points of polarity. . . . Paradox looks at our desperate either/ors and tells us they are really both/ands. . . ."[1] Morrison offers sage advice for all those who seek to practice servant-leadership. We should embrace the paradoxes inherent in the approach and use them to make some new wealth of leadership treasure.

Downsides

In his book *The Empowered Manager* Peter Block writes, "If I pursue politics in a positive way, will I be successful?"[2] He concludes that there is no way of knowing the answer because "every act of creation is an act of faith . . . and . . . the essence of faith is to proceed without any real evidence that our effort will be rewarded."[3] The same question can be asked of servant-leadership.

Will you be successful if you practice servant-leadership? There is no way of knowing. However, we do know and have experienced some downsides of practicing servant-leadership that you might prepare to experience along your journey.

Meeting your shadow side recognizes that as you journey toward becoming a servant-leader you will likely uncover some things about yourself that you might not like, might not want to encounter, and would rather not know. For example, are you really ready to share control, can you be humble, are you capable of uplifting others with the knowledge that they may surpass you on the organizational chart? Servant-leadership is the virtual antithesis of the things that most of us know and take for granted about leadership. Thus, the process of becoming a servant-leader may likely force you to question some of your most cherished assumptions about yourself, others, and the nature of organizations. You might not like the answers you find.

All talk and no action stems from the fear that we may not get it right. The literature on servant-leadership is rich and compelling. Numerous books, articles, and tapes are available to help us live more spiritual, connected, meaningful, and servant-based lives. The books are fun, insightful, and easy to read. Unfortunately, many people become entangled in the books and forget to take action. Hence, we know of people who claim to be on the journey toward servant-leadership but have yet to leave the safe port of their local bookstore.

My way or the highway mentality frequently besets those who seek to live more-balanced lives and practice servant-leadership. Remember, there are as many ways to be a servant-leader as there are servant-leaders. Find and use an approach that works for you. Do not, however, demand that others follow the same path.

Anger, frustration, vulnerability, and despondence are some of the most common feelings associated with the journey toward servant-leadership. This is not to say that there will not be good feelings, gains along the way, and more than ample joys. However, this journey will require you to accept the good with the bad. To begin this journey unwilling or unprepared to meet and feel a variety of challenges and emotions is both unwise and unrealistic.

Not everyone wants to be empowered will likely be the reason that you may experience some of the feelings described in the last point. As you journey toward servant-leadership it is paramount that you remember that not all of your peers, superiors, and subordinates will jump for joy when you start to lead in this new way. Some will be downright hostile. Therefore, don't expect a party, celebration, or promotion because you are leading in a new way. Then again, if you are expecting all those things, maybe you are not being a servant-leader!

Neglecting the other aspects of your life can occur on your journey. Servant-leaders cultivate a wonderful balance of mind, body, and spirit. To work on one area to the exclusion of others frequently leads to states of "dis-ease." Therefore, try to resist the temptation to become out of balance while traveling on the path toward servant-leadership.

In the past few years people/organizations have increasingly turned toward servant-leadership to help overcome the many difficulties of organizational life. Servant-leadership, however, is not a panacea, and it is all too easy to forget that the path upon which you are embarking is loaded with all the frustration, hostility, and periods of inaction that characterize all approaches to leadership. The previous section outlined some of the headaches and heartaches you are likely to encounter. You can enhance the likelihood of a safe and successful journey if you prepare for them now.

Finally, *actions speak louder than words* is a simple reminder that a lot of talk about serving will do you no good if all that others see are the same old attitudes and behaviors. Talking servant-leadership is easy. Practicing servant-leadership requires significant effort. The following section outlines some methods you might use to facilitate your servant-leadership efforts.

Practicing Servant Leadership

Though loaded with potential traps and pitfalls, the journey toward servant-leadership can be successfully negotiated by engaging in a variety of activities. In Table 5.1 we specified some of the techniques associated with the different paths toward servant leadership. Those actions will definitely assist in the process. Some other general activities in which you might participate include the following:

- Engage in dialogue, discussion, education, and training. Many of the barriers to practicing servant-leadership stem from misconceptions and myths about its meaning and practice. Thus, simply spending time exposing yourself and others to its core values and principles can go a long way toward understanding the essence, purpose, and practice of servant-leadership.
- Join or create a servant-leadership study group. We know a few managers who have selected servant-leadership-related books or articles and then held breakfast, lunch, or evening meetings for discussion with peers, associates, superiors, and subordinates. These meetings were most successful when they focused on exploring both the merits of the writings' content as well as how to apply the principles espoused in those readings in day-to-day situations.

- Attend the Servant-Leadership Conference. Each year The Greenleaf Center for Servant-Leadership in Indianapolis hosts a national conference that attracts speakers of national acclaim (e.g., Block, Covey, Wheatley, etc.) and people who have done both consulting and research on the topic. The conference is a wonderful place to meet fellow travelers and participate in lively discourse about the nature and practice of servant-leadership. The Greenleaf Center for Servant-Leadership also has memberships, books, tapes, and produces a newsletter that may be of interest.
- Other activities that might help in your journey could include: decorating your office to include a host of servant-leadership reminders (e.g., poster, calendar, pictures, etc.), engaging in daily prayer/meditation/reflection, keeping a servant-leadership journal, developing a hobby that promotes connection to your spiritual side and right brain, and exercising on a regular basis.

Engaging the flow of servant-leadership is a necessary part of your journey. Fortunately, there are many ways to facilitate the process. At the heart or core of all the approaches, however, is developing a mind-set that propels you to serve rather than be served.

Conclusion

Despite the relatively recent acclaim given to servant-leadership by the media and popular press, the concept really is not that new. There have long been leaders who lead from below; leaders who sought to enable, ennoble, and empower those with whom they work; leaders who through compassion, humility, and great personal/professional sacrifice inspired others to achieve great outcomes. In many ways, servant-leadership is the conscious practice of the Golden Rule.

The reason that concern for spirit in the workplace now resonates with so many people is because many of our leaders and organizations simply do not practice the Golden Rule. We are increasingly paying the price for such leadership and organizational practices.

Though simple in concept, servant-leadership is decidely difficult in practice. There are numerous ways to get started. There are pitfalls, landmines, and traps to encounter. This essay was written in the sincere hope of encouraging you to embark on the journey and to provide a guide for moving through the many obstacles you will encounter.

6

Trust: The Invaluable Asset

Jack Lowe Jr.

Jack Lowe Jr. is CEO of TDIndustries, an employee-owned company headquartered in Dallas, Texas. TDIndustries is a national mechanical construction and service company that has received numerous awards for quality, including the Contractor of the Year Award from the Associated Builders and Contractors of America. TDIndustries has been profiled in several books published in the 1990s—most notably Robert Levering and Milton Moskowitz's book, The 100 Best Companies to Work for in America. *Jack Lowe is a longtime trustee of The Greenleaf Center's board and currently serves as its chair.*

In this essay, Jack Lowe addresses the important role that trust plays within TDIndustries and discusses how servant-leadership has contributed to the strong trust that exists within their corporate system. He provides a practical perspective on how servant-leadership is implemented within TDIndustries.

What Is Trust?

Stephen Covey says that, "Trust is the glue of life. It's the most essential ingredient in effective communication. It's the foundational principle that holds all relationships—marriages, families, and organizations of every kind—together."[1] He further explains that trustworthiness requires character, the desire to act in a trustworthy way, and competence, the ability to perform the entrusted task. For example, unless your closest friend had the competence for brain surgery, he or she wouldn't be entrusted with performing brain surgery on your child. To that end, to be successful, you and your organization must be trustworthy. To be trustworthy, you—both individually and organizationally—must have the ability to perform the tasks entrusted to you.

Why Is Trust Important?

It is impossible to attain and maintain global competitiveness in serving customers without continuously, aggressively improving the processes we use to serve those customers, and this improvement is impossible without the eager participation of everyone from the front line through middle management to the executive office in our organizations. We cannot get this eager support unless we have a high-trust environment. Robert Levering, the coauthor of *The 100 Best Companies to Work for in America,* says that a great place to work is one where you trust the people you work for, have pride in what you do, and enjoy the people you work with.[2] At a May 1996, 100 Best Symposium, he showed a study that indicated that high-trust companies significantly outperform industry norms (see Figure 6.1). More specifically, in TDIndustries' own industry, the construction industry, the Construction Industry Institute conducted an extensive study of 262 construction projects and found that projects that had a high trust level among participants had a very favorable impact on cost (see Figure 6.2). Our relationship with our customers and our suppliers and our internal relationships cannot adapt quickly enough to the demands for continuous change and continuous improvement unless we have a high-trust culture.

TDIndustries

TDIndustries is a national mechanical construction and service company headquartered in Dallas. We install, maintain, service, and modernize air conditioning, plumbing, and piping systems in commercial, industrial, and

Figure 6.1
"100 best" (1993) vs. the rest.

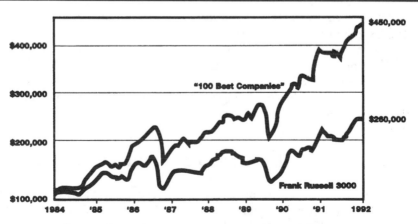

Total Return (equally weighted portfolios)

Source: BARRA

Figure 6.2
Cost-trust curve for 262 projects.

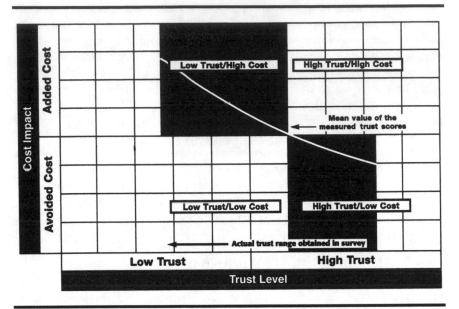

residential facilities. It is owned by its approximately 900 employees, who refer to each other as *partners*. With offices in Houston, San Antonio, Austin, Tyler, Longview, and Laredo, the company operates primarily in Texas under the trade names: TDMechanical, TDService, Tempo Mechanical, CDC Service, and TDI Air Conditioning and Appliances. Our customers include building/facility owners and operators, general contractors, and home owners and home builders. They buy from us because of our partners' reputation for performing on time, in budget, and with integrity. TDIndustries' mission statement is: "We are Committed to Providing Outstanding Career Opportunities by Exceeding Our Customers' Expectations through Continuous Aggressive Improvement."

Scrvant-Leadership at TDIndustries

The founder of our company, my father, Jack Lowe Sr., was a natural servant-leader even though he was unfamiliar with the term until he discovered Robert Greenleaf's pamphlet in 1971. At about the same time, we realized that many of our supervisors had little or no training in effective leadership. For the last 25 years servant-leadership has been the core principle that has directed the leadership development of all our supervisors from the front line to our senior managers. To make this philosophy pervade, each part of our organization has required a total commitment of management and company assets to build a community where employees trust management to listen to and hear their thoughts and ideas, and where management has learned to trust the judgment of employees. This philosophy has underpinned a broad array of community-building activities that pervade our organization. Some examples follow:

- **Employee Ownership.** Since 1952 when our first Employee Stock Ownership Plan (ESOP) was initiated, TD has become more and more widely owned by its partners (employees). Today, senior management owns about 25 percent of outstanding shares, and the balance is owned by other partners who could, if they wished, nominate and elect an alternate slate of directors and replace existing management. (I hope they don't.)
- **Open Book Management.** Revenues, orders booked, backlogs, profitability, customer satisfaction, and partner satisfaction are regularly shared widely throughout the organization.
  1. *Partner Roundtables.* Approximately 20 times a year I meet from 7:00 A.M. until 10:00 A.M. with different groups of 15 to 20 partners for breakfast and open discussion.
  2. *Friday Forums.* Two Fridays a month about 60 of us spend an hour together. One of these meetings is a sharing of business results, and the other is usually a presentation with an outside speaker. At these get-togethers we recognize partners who have celebrated a 5-, 10-, 15-year, and so on anniversary. They are presented with gifts ranging from Cross pen-and-pencil sets at their 5-year anniversary to a $3,000 gift of their choice at their 30-year mark.
  3. *Quarterly Conferences.* Each quarter about 125 of us spend several hours together. Each of our 10 business unit managers report their last quarter's results, their year-end projections, recent orders booked, customer satisfaction, and business outlook. At this gathering we also review our safety records, our accounts receivable, our cash flows, and our experience with our health care team.
- **Training.** In addition to a great deal of job-specific skill training, we provide a fairly comprehensive array of other development programs:
  1. *New Partner Orientation.* Orientation (some might call it indoctrination) continues in a structured process for about one year. After three months, a new partner is invited to attend a business report Friday Forum and introduced to the regular participants. I spend about 15 minutes with them after the meeting, they are given a tour of our shops and offices, and they receive two hours of additional safety training. After 6 to 12 months they become

eligible to enter our long-term benefit plans (401k, ESOP, Long Term Disability, Group Term Life Insurance). They all attend a two-hour explanation of these benefits, which are part of their beginning to think more about a career and less about a job. I lead most of these meetings.

Once or twice a year we conduct "TDOpportunities" for new partners who have been with us for more than one year. This is an all-day workshop where I explain some of the history of TD, how the total company is organized and what the various business units do, and encourage them to think widely about their career opportunities at TD. This is also their first structured introduction to servant-leadership. The morning also includes other managers talking about various career opportunities. The afternoon is the highlight of the day. Joe Charbonneau, an internationally recognized management trainer and motivational speaker, delivers a message of opportunity and optimism that significantly changes the self-image of many who hear it.

2. *Leadership Development.* All supervisors are expected to continuously develop their leadership abilities. Since the mid-1970s, Ann McGee-Cooper, a well-known author, lecturer, business consultant, creativity expert, and widely recognized leader in the emerging field of brain engineering, has led a workshop for newly appointed supervisors that we (cleverly) call TDLeadership Development I (TDLD I). This is a one-day workshop centered around servant-leadership. It includes sections entitled Life-long Learning as a Leadership Skill; The TD Philosophy: A History of Shared Leadership; "Theory X" and "Theory Y" Management; Productivity and the Self-fulfilling Prophecy: The Pygmalion Effect; Emotional Bank Accounts: Building Team Trust; Chain-dumping: Dealing with Negative Team Members; Effective Listening and Communication; Valuing Diversity; and Quality, Customer Service, and Servant Leadership. During the past year, 60 partners attended TDLD I, In addition, 60 others attended a one-day diversity workshop. This workshop helps participants to understand how diversity and empowerment are inseparable business necessities for profitable workforce utilization, to view and utilize diversity as a competitive business advantage, and to develop beginning group and personal strategies for implementing diversity. And 150 others attended a two-day in-house workshop on Stephen Covey's "Seven Habits of Highly Effective People."

3. *TDPartners in Quality.* We have been pursuing an aggressive quality initiative since 1990. In support of this, all second-year partners participate in a two-day workshop to introduce them to the principles, tools, and advantages of teamwork that underpin a successful total quality management effort. This workshop in-

cludes Joel Barker's "Discovering the Future: The Business of Paradigms"; The Cost of Quality; Quality and Servant Leadership; DISC Profiles of each participant and their implications for successful teamwork; and Deming's classic "Red Bead Game," which demonstrates that most problems are "system" problems, not "people" problems. Throughout the workshop, participants, working in teams, use the tools they are learning to work on real company problems. At the conclusion, they report their results to a group of our senior managers. We developed this workshop in-house and each session is facilitated by Bob Ferguson, an executive vice president, another manager (typically a superintendent), and me. This year we will conduct four of these workshops.

Does TD Have a Trusting Culture?

While building trust is a journey, not a destination, there is considerable evidence to indicate progress on that journey:

- In 1993 TDIndustries was included in the national best-seller *The 100 Best Companies to Work for in America* by Robert Levering and Milton Moskowitz.
- Since 1978 we have conducted an annual anonymous Partner Opinion Survey consisting of approximately 30 questions about various aspects of working for TD. The survey conducted at year end 1996 resulted in a 93 percent overall favorable response. Some results are indicated in Figure 6.3, which includes some national benchmark data.
- Satisfied employees are a prerequisite for satisfied customers. The services our partners have furnished our customers have resulted in a current overall customer satisfaction rating of 8.9 on a scale of 10. (Our goal is to be solidly over nine in each business unit and customer group. When we get there, we'll raise the goal.)
- In 1989 we very nearly lost our company. It was our first loss year in more than 30 years, but it was a dandy. We started the year with a net worth of about $10,000,000. We had a pretax loss of about $5,000,000. Our bank, whom we owed $15,000,000, went under; so we then owed the FDIC, and they wanted their money. (We eventually paid them in full!) Much was required for us to survive this situation, but the essential ingredient was the trust and the spirit of our partners. Even though we had to make quite a few painful layoffs, very few partners "jumped ship."

But that's just the beginning. As we had done before when major issues faced our company, we invited everyone with more than five years service to a meeting one night to discuss our situation and talk

Figure 6.3
National studies vs. TDPartner opinion survey.

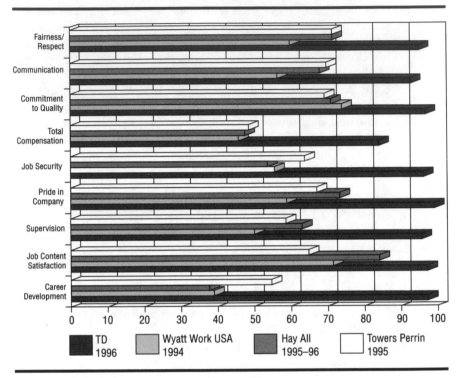

through what we would do together. About 150 attended. Most were pretty familiar with our situation because it was openly discussed and they regularly saw our financial statements. I told them I had been trying to borrow money or raise capital but had been unsuccessful. I told them that I felt we needed to terminate our Defined Benefit Retirement Plan, which was overfunded by $1,000,000. Further, I told them I felt we needed another $1,000,000 to have any chance of surviving. The only source for that extra $1,000,000 that I could imagine was from the retirement funds we would be distributing from the terminated plan. This was not a pleasant option, but it was the only one I could see.

After much discussion, a plan was agreed upon. I spent the next 60 days going from office to office and job site to job site explaining our situation, outlining our plan, and asking for their support. (Obviously, no one could be required to invest their retirement funds into such a precarious situation.) If everyone had invested according to the plan, we would have raised $1,500,000. We raised $1,250,000. And the rest is history.

What Have Been the Results of This Trusting Culture?

TD has experienced some gratifying results from the trusting relationships we enjoy coupled with the tools and techniques of TQM. Some examples include:

1. In 1990 we turned our medical plan over to a team of partners. Since then they have increased coverage and reduced costs. The total savings to the plan exceeds $6,000,000. The last two years they have waived partner premiums in December because of the outstanding results achieved during the year.

2. Employing the tools of quality and empowering (an overused word) teams to address our risk management, we have experienced dramatic reductions in workers' compensation, general liability, and vehicle liability losses (see Figure 6.4). This has resulted in millions of dollars in savings.

3. Partners can choose to invest in our ESOP and/or 401k. TD invests 30 percent of its pretax profits in our ESOP and 401k. In 1996 our

Figure 6.4
Workers' compensation/vehicle/general liability: total claims.

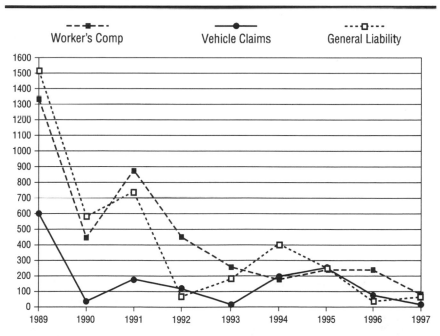

partners invested $1,851,000 in these plans and TD invested more than $2,274,000.

4. In 1993 we were included in the best-selling book *The 100 Best Companies to Work for in America*. In 1996 the Associated Builders and Contractors of America, a national trade association with almost 20,000 members, named TDIndustries as Contractor of the Year.

5. Each year Forbes publishes a list of the 200 most profitable small, publicly traded companies in the United States. Since we are not publicly traded, we are not eligible to be included. But our Return on Investment (Forbes's profitability measurement) would put us in this exclusive group.

Summary

Trustworthiness, which requires character and competence, can only flourish with leadership that trusts, supports, and encourages. At TD we call that servant-leadership. These trusting relationships allowed us to celebrate our 50th anniversary this year. They got us through our crisis in 1989. They also provided the culture that allowed the tools and techniques of total quality management to take root and lead to the strongest customer satisfaction, partner satisfaction, and profitability in our history.

7

Accountability as Covenant: The Taproot of Servant-Leadership

Ann McGee-Cooper

Dr. Ann McGee-Cooper is internationally recognized for her pacesetting work as a brain engineer. Her Dallas-based consulting firm, Ann McGee-Cooper and Associates, Inc., has worked with a wide range of clients. Ann is the author of the book Building Brain Power *and coauthor of* Time Management for Unmanageable People *and* You Don't Have to Go Home from Work Exhausted! *She is a former trustee of The Greenleaf Center and was a keynote speaker at The Greenleaf Center's 1995 conference.*

In this thought-provoking essay, McGee-Cooper suggests a new paradigm is emerging through which accountability within an organization, is based on a shared vision—a vision created through the process of establishing servant-leadership.

Why do we monitor rather than mentor people? Why does accountability end up last rather than first in our priorities? Why do we spend less time with those who we expect might "miss the mark" while giving those we expect to succeed our full attention? Is accountability as concerned with a person's development as with what they produce? As a leader in a research team working with many corporate clients, we have been both curious and suffered anguish in pursuit of meaningful solutions to these questions.

In today's climate of accelerating change, we are surrounded by shifting paradigms. One of these is accountability. The current reality of boss controlling and judging defines *accountability* as an obligation to account for and give an explanation of one's actions and to bear the consequences for those actions.

However, a new paradigm is emerging, which begins with covenant. By creating a shared vision and agreeing on core values and mission, we can design the shared map of where we want to go as a team. Accountability then becomes the rudder to keep us on course. If it is mutually created up front through the process of establishing servant-leadership, a whole new paradigm emerges of what accountability means. *Our deepest sense of self defines this new relationship. We lay out the role of each of us . . . how each can best support the other in achieving this shared vision. Both will be leaders AND followers, both will answer to the other on promises made. Failures will be explored as opportunities to learn and grow. Each will expect to unlearn and change.*

Exploring This New Paradigm—A New Way Unfolds

We all know well the old paradigm of not being personally responsible or accountable. Our American culture is saturated with a victim consciousness, entitlement mentality, and codependence. Simply turn on the television and see the plethora of talk shows dedicated to giving those who have been dumped on a voice and a million-viewer audience, feeding this belief system. Examine the leaflets and billboards encouraging you to file a lawsuit. Listen for bashing of polarized groups, which is presented as negative humor, or "politically correct" issues discounted as a social tool to avoid consequences rather than acknowledgment of the need to correct past unfairness. Note the strategy of dirty politics, labeling, and blaming with sound bite slurs and innuendos . . . short-term thinking, finger-pointing, and projecting blame on others rather than looking inward for solutions. "They are doing it, so we will too" is seen as the way to get ahead, and those who stick to the high road are labeled naive.

Yet, when all is said and done, there is still ultimately accountability. Talk-show hosts become accountable as witnesses in murder trials for the outcome of public surprises that explode into violence; voters become accountable to vote yes or no on tort reform; consumers become accountable for the kinds of businesses we support with our dollars. We may not see our participation in the bigger picture and thus think of accountability in a much smaller context of one person answering to another. Yet stepping back to consider the connections, how one's behavior influences another, opens profound new possibilities and awareness.

In the old paradigm, "bosses" periodically judge the performance of each employee, controlling when, how, and even if performance reviews happen. Calling someone on the carpet, checking to see that each person is performing, and measuring and monitoring progress was seen as the job of the manager.

We have begun to learn that one *manages* things, but not people. It takes *leadership* to inspire the best and most effective performances within people. And this comes from the new paradigm, which is two-way, open-ended, and ongoing. The servant-leader asks to be coached and given honest feedback as well as offering the same to those served. Making it safe for teammates to be honest and being accountable to change, grow, communi-

---

Accountability Paradigm

Hierarchy, Boss as Judge over Employee	**Servant-Leader/Coach/Mentor**
Top-down, one person judging Boss controls "when," "how," and even "if" accountability happens	Two-way, open-ended *INTER*dependent, teamwork Open flow created proactively
Reactive Punishment/reward Accountability a "have to"	*Proactive* Celebration/fail forward Accountability a "want to," "get to"
Seen as judging failure rate Win/lose Based on distrust	Seen as discovery process Win/win/win Based on trust
Legalistic Monitor Expectations fixed	Holistic Mentor Expectations in constant flux (growth and change anticipated)
Accountability as excuse/justification	Accountability as dialogue to raise level of "collective intelligence"
Extrinsically driven	Intrinsically driven

---

cate, and resolve differences in a spirit of mutual respect is the foundation of this new paradigm. Either party can initiate accountability, seen as skillful discussion or dialogue. "Help me understand . . ." or "Could we get curious together about why or how . . ." is the spirit of this new mutual dialogue.

Coaches ask:

What am I doing that helps you succeed?

What am I *not* doing that you need to succeed?

Where and how am I micromanaging?

What am I doing that you would like to do?

When and how do I shoot the messenger?

By becoming accountable to our team members in all directions, we signal a new level of shared trust and *INTER*dependence. Strength through difference begins to take root. And a collective intelligence begins to replace a competition or hierarchy of singular intelligence (putting the "smartest" person in charge or competing on each issue for who has the "right answer"). In either case, much is lost because building on collective intelligence will always go significantly beyond what the single brightest individual might propose.

Reactive versus Proactive

In a punishment/reward mind-set, accountability is a "have to." It can be seen as unnecessary with good performers and something distasteful to have to do with lesser performers. But still, it is seen as one-way and done reactively, looking back on the performance of one person by another.

In the new paradigm, this process flows daily, as partners create shared goals, celebrate shared accomplishments, and harvest lessons learned. Each so-called failure is seen as an opportunity to learn and is used to "fail forward." What does this teach us? How can we each benefit and leverage our collective resources to become more successful? In place of a hierarchy, each person's role is defined. Though the servant-leader may initiate this process, if it is truly successful, soon any teammate will call for an accounting *because it is rewarding and safe to measure progress, celebrate, recalibrate, and learn from mistakes.* Identifying problems early brings valuable lead time for all. Problems can quickly be turned into opportunities because the focus is on solving rather than blaming. And because the coach is seen as a resource rather than a judge, she or he is invited in early and often or as needed.

Win/Lose versus Win/Win/Win

If accountability is seen as searching out failure or level of success, a person's self-esteem is directly proportional to how much success is recognized. However, if accountability is seen as a mutual discovery process, then each person is recognized as highly important to the process before it begins. In the new paradigm, high self-esteem is continually nurtured. Within this context, the servant-leader and team work together to create a win/win/win situation. Rather than competing for who gets a raise, bonus, or other rewards, why not work collaboratively so that all persons get what they identify as important to them personally? If this happens, not only do these primary partners win, but the customers, families, teammates, and community will most likely also benefit. This is the true definition of synergy, where the whole is worth more than the sum of the parts. In win/lose situations, there is always distrust because the assumption is that only one party can win. If I win, you lose. However, in the new paradigm, we commit to stay engaged until we find a way for all to win. This calls for "thinking outside the box," for discovering paradigm shifts, for making creative leaps. "Grow the pie instead of merely dividing an existing pie."

Legalistic versus Holistic

An adversarial relationship exists in the old paradigm. "I am the boss and it is my job to make you honor your commitments." A contract implies that each of us will only honor the specifics as spelled out. Loopholes are painstakingly sought out. Distrust underlies this paradigm.

In contrast, holistic thinking tells us that the whole can be no stronger than the weakest link. If we invest major energy trying to cover our backside or litigating differences rather than searching out more imaginative solutions, we all lose. In the first situation, expectations are fixed, and we assume that we are only accountable to the letter of the law. However, in this new time of fast change and in this new paradigm, we know that we need to operate at the level of covenant, by developing a high level of mutual trust. We establish a broad definition of shared goals and individual roles and responsibilities. Knowing that the situation will be in constant flux, we expect to renegotiate our needs and solutions as the situation changes. In this paradigm, the level of shared trust is key. No person or party can be seen as more important. Each person is a potential leader of that about which they know the most. Yet simultaneously, each must equally be a follower of all others, synergizing and supporting the areas where others lead and know most. This is precisely why Robert Greenleaf's concept of servant-leadership is so powerful!

He challenges us with the following:

> *Anybody could lead perfect people—if there were any. But there aren't any perfect people. And the parents who try to raise perfect children are certain to raise neurotics.*
>
> *It is part of the enigma of human nature that the "typical" person—immature, stumbling, inept, lazy—is capable of great dedication and heroism if s/he is wisely led. Many otherwise able people are disqualified to lead because they cannot work with and through the half-people who are all there are. The secret of institution building is to be able to weld a team of such people by lifting them up to grow taller than they would otherwise be.*
>
> *Individuals grow taller when those who lead them empathize and when they are accepted for what they are, even though their performance may be judged critically in terms of what they are capable of doing. Leaders who empathize and who fully accept those who go with them on this basis are more likely to be trusted.[1]*

Extrinsic versus Intrinsic

In the old paradigm, accountability contributes to an extrinsic definition of self-worth: "I am valuable if my boss and my company or others in authority (teacher, parents, critics, etc.) think I am." In the new paradigm, account-ability encourages each person to begin with unconditional love and accep-tance of self and others. An intrinsic definition of self-worth causes each person to be guided by personal values, then personal and shared vision. Be-cause each is free to speak openly and honestly, accountability is about ask-ing, "Are we on course?" If anyone has information that the ship is headed in the wrong direction, a storm is coming up, or the sails need mending, early discovery is celebrated and acted upon by all. The goal is a successful journey and great joy and satisfaction comes from shared progress. Consequences impact all and are shared.

This is dramatically different from the old paradigm, which leaves all internal partners essentially competing with each other for power, position, rewards, and recognition. In this new time of fast change, collaboration is re-placing competition. We may compete for clients and markets but still, our behavior must be collaborative. Our competitor for Job A may become our partner as we team to perform in high-risk markets on Job B, where neither can afford the level of risk alone. Our resources of air, water, earth, and bio-diversity are shared no matter what. Awakening to this implication demands a new and more complex awareness of shared accountability.

In the old paradigm, accountability involves laying blame and offering excuses. In the new paradigm, accountability is more often centered on dia-logue to raise the level of collective intelligence and therefore to create more fruitful options. It is more about learning together and changing synergisti-cally. Rewards are more about collectively achieving something of tremen-dous intrinsic value than they are about money, profit, or bonuses. Dollars, profit, and bonuses are the result of intrinsic accountability but not the mo-tivator.

The Cornerstones of This Challenging New Paradigm: Shared Leadership, Shared Vision, and Proactively Anticipating Change

Everyone must become both leader and follower, taking full responsibility for what they know best and the unique talents and perspective belonging only to them, while respecting that those balancing talents and perspectives of all others must be considered and integrated. It is fascinating to discover that within teams who know how to dialogue, creating much richer shared mean-ing, collective intelligence rises to become much higher than the brightest member of the team. However, in teams where individuals compete to be right and have the last say, the collective intelligence falls below the level of the least bright team member because the brighter members begin to cancel each other out with power plays and intimidation. Others duck and choose not to surface their insights because it is not safe to do so. Negative humor is often used as a power tool to coerce and control. Teams who use or allow negative humor will stay stuck in the old paradigms and may not realize why.

Creating a shared vision is primary and central to all else. As noted by Peter Senge in *The Fifth Discipline,* creating a personal vision must precede the creation of shared vision.[2] If not, the power of a compelling shared vision will co-opt those who have not defined themselves with a personal vision. They will eventually feel coerced by the group because of the void of self-identity and personal meaning. However, once each has clearly created and aligned personal vision with a shared vision and purpose, this alignment becomes a powerful motivator and energizer. Now great energy comes from being accountable to this passionate shared vision. But with something magnificent to achieve, even people's immune systems become engaged and stronger, based on internal biochemical changes triggered by the commitment to something inspiring. This fascinating connection first emerged in *Man's Search for Meaning,* a true story written by Dr. Viktor Frankl, a prisoner in a World War II Nazi concentration camp.[3] Dr. Frankl observed that those who carried a burning purpose in their lives were far more likely to survive than those who may have been younger, stronger, or in better health but lacked this strong personal vision.

What Results Can Be Expected?
What Are the Outcomes from the New Paradigm?
Does It Work?

Most of us thrive on and relish meaningful challenge as we grow stronger, more capable of managing risk and stretching personal performance when being supported by committed partners. It is not only much harder for most to perform alone during times of rapid change, but we pay the price for our blind spots by learning of them too late. When we each proactively and intentionally partner with opposites and balance weaknesses with strengths, we each have enormous opportunities to change and grow positively. In today's world, if you *don't* change, you get left behind and that's far more painful and damaging. As leaders, if we don't give the people we serve every opportunity to grow and change, we are hurting them more. We are also betraying our sacred trust as leaders, not only to those we lead but also to those we collectively serve.

When people are empowered to achieve shared goals, accountability takes on a new meaning of purpose and commitment. At the conclusion of a recent meeting, one of our close colleagues asked the group in a servant-leader style, "What kind of accountability do you want to create?" The leader did not impose her ideas or give a hard date when results were due. Rather, she deferred this decision to them. The surprise was that they wanted accountability and imposed an ambitious time frame on themselves even though all were at a very busy time with other work. "If we don't put this up front, it won't get done. It's too important to let slide. Let's commit to completing this by the end of December (six weeks hence)." Because the vision was shared, because this team created and owned the plan, because the purpose and outcome were believed to be pivotal, this team chose to hold themselves and each other accountable for results. The servant-leader was asked by the group to circulate the results on the agreed-upon date. Roles were defined and consequences spelled out.

We begin in life confronted by the challenge of learning to be accountable to oneself. Until that is mastered it is far more challenging to participate with others. Think of accountability as the taproot that reaches deep into soil and rocks, drawing precious nutrients and life-quenching water while anchoring the plant against wind and storms. Is this not the role of accountability in our lives? Without this process, dreams, goals, and promises go unfulfilled, which may discourage further dreaming. But by closing the loop and choosing to learn from all that happens, whether pleasing or disappointing, we send a taproot deep into the soil of shared experience. With each accounting we learn and grow stronger.

> The best test, and difficult to administer, is: do those served grow as persons; do they, while being served, become healthier, wiser, freer, more autonomous, more likely themselves to become servants? And, what is the effect on the least privileged in society; will he benefit, or, at least, will he not be further deprived?[4]

PART TWO

Stewardship

I have noted people such as Abraham Lincoln and Pope John XXIII who held great power and did not seem to suffer the common corruptions of power. I believe that this was because their own deep spiritual resources were strong. If some of the serious corruptions of holding and using power are arrogance, impairment of one's imagination, or personality distortion, then perhaps the first step in protecting oneself from those impairments is to sustain a sharp awareness of the danger. The reference to Abraham Lincoln and Pope John XXIII suggests that part of the defense against these losses as a result of holding and using power may be the cultivation of a deep inner spiritual life.

Robert K. Greenleaf
Reflections on Leadership

In his groundbreaking book *Stewardship: Choosing Service Over Self-Interest,* Peter Block has defined stewardship as "the willingness to be accountable for the well-being of the larger organization by operating in service, rather than in control, of those around us. Stated simply, it is accountability without control or compliance."

Robert Greenleaf's view of all institutions was one in which CEOs, staffs, directors, and trustees all played significant roles in holding their institutions in trust for the greater good of society. Stewardship, like servant-leadership, assumes first and foremost a commitment to serving the needs of others. It also emphasizes the use of openness and persuasion, rather than control. Stewardship and servant-leadership are closely aligned ideas that reflect the growing trend within many institutions.

8

From Leadership to Citizenship

Peter Block

Peter Block *is the author of three best-selling books:* Stewardship, The Empowered Manager, *and* Flawless Consulting. *He is cofounder of the new School for Managing and has been at the center of changing organizations for 25 years, consulting to businesses, schools, and governments around the world. Peter was a keynote speaker at The Greenleaf Center's 1994 conference.*

In this essay, Peter Block urges a shift in our focus from "leadership" to "citizenship." He suggests that one of the benefits of this shift is to create the capacity for many more people to achieve what we have traditionally expected our leaders to accomplish. Block offers a persuasive view that suggests servant-leadership may provide a gateway for this transition from leadership to citizenship.

In a radio interview in 1991, the Nobel Prize–winning author Laurens Van der Post stated that the era of leaders is over. He said that what we had created in Nelson Mandela is an example of how we had gone too far in our search and glorification of leaders. We had made a god of Mandela, when in fact he was just a man. When we create a god, we at the same time create the possibility and conditions for the devil. He also believed that the way we glamorize leaders is a way of escaping from owning our own responsibility for the world we have created.

The people of South Africa, not Nelson Mandela, have brought some freedom to that country. Neighborhoods, cities, and civic and political associations are engaged in the process of deciding what that country will become. The leaders of that country are more products of the culture and its people than creators of it. Leadership in this era is more effect than it is cause. To keep focusing on the selection, training, and definition of leaders is to keep us frozen in the world of monarch, autocrat, and entitlement. It postpones the day when we will experience a world of community and accountability. The question of citizenship stays in the background, in the shadow of our attraction to leadership.

This is not an argument against leadership, rather a concern about the energy we have for the subject. Our attraction to leadership, our very interest in it, becomes the obstacle to authentic change or transformation. If we believe that leadership is the essential ingredient to high performance, then it has serious consequences about how we think about our institutions and what will improve or change them.

At a minimum we need to question the power of the leadership industry we have created. Once an idea becomes an industry, it loses it meaning. Everyone claims it as their own and it becomes commercialized. The question of leadership that began as a search for spirit and vision has now been commodified. We operate as if leadership can be packaged, and thereby be sold and then purchased.

What is stunning in this industry is not the suppliers, it is the willingness of customers to pay for the solutions. And to do it over and over again. The most frequently asked question at conferences on leadership is, "What is the next fad?" Our expectations of real results are so low that:

1. We accept that what we are now doing is a fad or fashion.
2. We are still willing to show interest and purchase the next solution.

Suppose Van der Post was right about the end of the era of leaders. What would it mean to stop our pursuit of leaders and leadership and, in effect, to lose interest in them?

Our loss of interest would not eliminate leaders. We would still have teachers, managers, doctors, mayors, senators, and presidents. Sergeants, coaches, professors, conference speakers, authors, and senior engineers. So what would change?

First, we would ask all of them to sit down. There is no need for them to stand up since we will not be watching them so closely. We might ask them to sit with us, to join us. We need their experience, their wisdom, even their direction. It is just not necessary to look up at them.

Second, we could have a garage sale for lavaliere microphones, laser pointers, overhead projectors, and podiums. Perhaps we could export them to cultures at an earlier stage in the industrial food chain. Call it economic development or foreign aid. We will not need loud speaker technology for a few. We will need new amplification methods so that everyone's voice can be heard. Learning replaces instruction, participation replaces presentation, questions become more important than answers.

Third, we can wind down the managed efforts to change organizational culture. We can stop acting as if management needs to articulate and drive a culture they have defined. We have been acting as if culture is created by the words and model of the leaders. Vision statements advocating customer service, economic success, employee trust, and teamwork continue to be sold and distributed. This is patriarchy at its most concealed. The mindset that there is a population waiting to be told what norms and values they are to live by expresses a loss of faith in human capacity.

Culture is the emergence of shared meanings, not as a product of top-level intentions. Culture is created by the stories, tradition, and behavioral consent of the community. The attempt to sell culture to your own people makes a commodity out of the search for community and meaning.

The Fiction of Change

Part of the reason for seeking leaders is the belief that we are living in an era of great social change. If we can be realistic about change, we might relax a little about leaders. There is a tendency to confuse speed with transformation. Just because I can exchange more information faster and faster does not mean that the content of our dialogue or the nature of the way we organize human effort has shifted. If we can take our eyes off of technology for a moment and see the tenacity of the beliefs that guide our culture, including our workplaces, we are most likely entrenched in a period of surprising stability. We do not need great leaders if tomorrow will be much like today.

The fundamental aspects of our organizations are remarkably resistant to a change in thinking and practice. The workplace may be flatter, leaner, focused more on customers and cycle time and mission. But when you get beneath the language, the way we distribute power, purpose, and resources and the way we view labor and the core worker has changed little in the last 20 years. We are still organized for consistency, control, and predictability. We still have financial and human resource practices that reek of a parent-child relationship. Too many of us are still seeking the approval of our bosses and fear anarchy from our subordinates.

The longing for change does not create it. The electronic revolution does not define our lives despite what the electronic industry and the media would have us believe. Think of a top spinning on a table; it rotates faster and faster, and still does not move from its spot. Speed, yes; change, no. For about 85 percent of the people at work, the core beliefs about organizing human effort remain untouched by the technological and marketplace changes that swirl around us.

Focusing on Citizenship

Draining the energy out of leadership takes us to an exploration of citizenship. *Citizenship* is our capacity to create for ourselves what we had sought from our leaders. Is it possible for each of us to:

- Create and articulate a vision?
- Be accountable for the well-being of the whole?
- Set and pursue goals that sustain the institution?
- Establish boundaries and set limits?

- Create structure and order that suits our purpose?
- Become a role model?

We have vested maturity and accountability for the whole in those with power. In doing this we have created the conditions where citizenship is not required and often discouraged. The fear we have of abandoning leadership is that lawlessness and chaos will result. We fear entitlement and individual self-interest will prevail. Through the way we have organized human effort, we have lost faith that people are capable of using freedom in a responsible way.

For some people and some groups, these pessimistic expectations often seem to be grounded in fact. We open the door and no one walks through. The paradox is that we have created a world so dependent on the centrality of leadership that citizens and employees have developed a learned dependency. If you ask citizens and employees what they want, they most often affirm the need for a kinder monarch. People seek the safety and comfort of someone at the top keeping the vision alive, promising a safe and prosperous tomorrow. They keep asking management to define their roles, develop a better pay system, judge their performance more objectively.

The trap we fall into in the face of passivity is to believe the solution is better leadership. Avoiding responsibility, compliance, and caution on the part of employees and citizens is a bigger problem than control and self-centeredness on the part of "leaders." The solution is not to keep trying to create better leaders, it is to explore how to become accountable citizens.

The reluctance for citizens and employees to be accountable for the well-being of the whole is exactly the reason for de-emphasizing leadership. If we keep focusing on the centrality of those in charge, we sentence ourselves to the continuing decay of citizenship and accountability.

Elements of Citizenship

Without getting lost in definition, citizenship is our agreement to receive rights and privileges from the community and, in so doing, to pay for them through our willingness to live within certain boundaries and act in the interest of the whole. At the core of citizenship is the desire to care for the well-being of the larger institution, be it an organization, a neighborhood, or a country. This requires accountability. This is the purchase price of our freedom.

One reason we seek leadership and lose faith in the principle of self-governing systems is that we live in a culture of entitlement. Entitlement is claiming rights without payment, the wish to be granted what is requested and to do our own thing. Entitlement destroys institutions and community. It is the wish to go to heaven and not have to die.

Citizenship is accountability that is chosen. This is most likely to happen when we have been able to overcome our isolation. High-control systems thrive on our isolation; they breed it, reward it. One hundred years ago self-management was called mutiny. One of the first thing totalitarian states do is establish a curfew and deny the right of assembly. Rediscovering citizenship depends on overcoming our isolation and paying attention to the way we come together.

The Power of Assembly

A very direct way of experiencing the presence of community and the existence of a larger whole is when we assemble in one place at one time. Community is felt in concert. In convention. We feel this when we go to concerts, to conventions. It is limited, though, by the way we design our communal events. We turn conventions into passive listening experiences. We have stages, all eyes aimed at the front, at the leader/speaker.

The microphone, the screen, the show is in the front. The community sits in judgment and reception. Applause, sleep, and questions are the options for citizens.

Even in a town meeting, the structure illuminates the leaders—town council on a platform, soft chairs, one microphone per person. Citizens sit on ground level, folding chairs, one microphone per mob.

The architecture, the structure of assembly, the intent of convening are currently born of the leadership mind. This steals accountability from us all. It reinforces isolation and passivity. We need to redesign concert and convention to be as a communal undertaking.

We now possess the large-group methodology and the technology to assemble people as citizens and make their voice, ideas, and accountability the center of attention. We regularly take groups in the hundreds and engage them with each other. Mixed in diverse groups, strangers can get more connected to each other in two hours than they are connected to the people in their regular workplace. We can poll their ideas and summarize them instantaneously. We can have 20 subgroups meeting on common subjects and display their output on a video screen visible to all.

These methods can be used to collectively define vision, assess current conditions, set strategy and goals, and make commitments. We do not have to live out our intentions through a leader, we can do it directly with each other. If citizenship and community were our prime intent, we would redesign the way people convene each and every time they come together.

Means of Engagement

Citizenship is a much broader question than simply the ways in which we meet. In an article entitled "Bowling Alone," Robert Putnam describes how people no longer bowl in leagues, they bowl as singles and pairs.[1] This symbolizes our isolation, the decline of social investment in each other, and the

waning of civic engagement. The organizations that once brought us together—church, union hall, social club—are in decline. His research suggests
that the economic and political viability of a community are highly dependent on our connection with each other.

This gives special importance to the institutions where people do con-
gregate, the workplace. The workplace has the potential to be the place
where community is revived and common purpose is reawakened. If we turn
our attention from leadership to citizenship, we would begin to understand:

- *The power of changing the conversation.* The culture shifts when the
  conversation shifts. Focus on the questions more than the answers.
  Structure time so that dialogue becomes possible. Appreciate that
  the struggle with difficult issues is what builds commitment and understanding. Minimize the manipulation and wordsmithing in our
  conversations and fill them with learning. Try to bring the way we
  talk to each other in line with our espoused beliefs. Have a conversation and then be willing to reflect on the quality and meaning of the
  conversation. And make this reflection the norm.

- *Connection precedes content.* Each shift in technology, work process,
  curriculum design, role, or responsibility needs the existence of trust,
  dialogue, and relationship if it is to be successful. This requires an investment in time and patience. Feelings need to be valued. Relationships need to be discussed. The struggle and the questions are often
  the solution. We need to structure our way of being together in a
  way that recognizes this—very different thinking from expecting the
  leader to define, answer questions, sell the changes.

- *Confront people with their freedom.* Each of us has to define meaning
  and purpose for ourselves. Take this off of the leader's back. Put it
  where it belongs. Each person has a vision, has a worldview. Our task
  is to help each person uncover and express their vision for the organization they are a part of. Common vision will emerge from this dialogue. Leaders do not need to be the ones to express the vision and
  enroll others. Enrollment is a choice to sign up, not a strategy of persuasion. Each person needs to confront whether they are living their
  values. Each of us needs to be a role model, walk our talk, articulate
  longings, offer hope and inspiration. This is the nature of citizenship.
  When we leave these tasks to leaders, we let people off of the hook
  and conspire to create a culture of entitlement instead of a culture of
  accountability.

Conditions for Self-Governance

We have the ideology and experience for self-managing institutions, we only
need to broaden the practice. Self-governance hinges on employees' willing-

ness to provide to each other what the leader previously provided. Peer accountability is the glue that preserves chaos from anarchy and lawlessness. Employees and citizens making promises to each other and holding each other to account is what sustains community. This is what civic engagement entails. Neighbors deciding to come together, making demands on each other to create a safe place to work and live.

In practical terms, we will always need bosses, some hierarchy, clear structure, measures, and rules to live by. The workplace stops spinning so fast and really begins to change when we redefine the role of the boss and reassign who is responsible for creating the structure, measures, and rules. Clinging to our attraction to leadership keeps change in the hands of the few. We want to transfer it to the many. This is the power of citizenship.

So what do bosses do? The task of the boss is to convene people and engage them in the everyday challenges of how to plan, organize, lay out the work, discipline, and make sure the right people are on the team and doing the job right. Bosses become convenors and a focusing lens, not visionaries, role models, and motivators. Citizenship is the willingness to struggle with the pain of making a human living system move toward a common goal.

The Will of Citizenship

Something more is required of each of us if we want a culture of accountability. Each of us has to confront our own beliefs about what is possible. What we think is possible for others, of course, is really a projection of what we think is possible for ourselves. We have all experienced moments of accountability, we just think they were the exception. Organizations based on connection and common purpose will emerge when we begin to:

1. Believe that employees and ourselves are capable of using freedom in service of the well-being of the institution. What you see is what you get. If eight employees act responsibly and two abuse their freedom, why do we stay so focused on the irresponsible two? We have designed practices and policies for the two; it is time to create organizations that fit the eight employees who are committed and care.

2. Value the act of convening as a primary part of our job. Defining the critical questions and deciding who needs to be in the room are the tasks for every moment. Meetings are not a distraction from work. Thinking is not lost production. People contracting with each other and deciding together is the work.

3. Learn how to design a gathering. Robert's rules are for order, not for building commitment or rethinking work. The ways we currently think about meetings are based on the industrial model of efficiency. Clear agenda, minutes, votes, time-controlled per item, leader in charge, tension postponed. Methods for living systems that

have been developed for training environments need to be brought into everyday working environments. Learn about the use of dialogue, open space methods, valuing tension and conflict, surfacing the diversity of purpose, encouraging face-to-face exchange of wants, fishbowls. Learn about conference models and how to use large-scale interactive designs. These are proven methods for both getting decisions made and evoking high levels of commitment. Sophisticated strategies for designing productive interaction currently reside in the hands of trainers and consultants. They belong in the hands of each of us.

4. Decentralize ourselves. Be a focusing lens, be willing to define the difficult issues, and then be a powerful equal. Create circles and become one voice among many. We don't need someone in the center. Get the boss out of the center, stop looking for a Sun King. Being boss is one role among many, and it is not the most critical role. Democracy is not defined by the actions of its elected officials, it is defined by the actions of citizens. Same with the workplace. Product is created and service is delivered by those who do the work. An organization is not the shadow of those who run them. Use the special powers of a boss no more than once a year and even then only when more collective efforts have been exhausted. Learn to listen, ask questions, express doubt, and live without answers. Be surprised. Learn to say no to those who want to be our leader.

5. Forge partnerships with others at your own level. Lateral relationships are the hardest to manage in the patriarchal world we live in. Stop expecting your own boss to build a team and bring distant territories together. Acknowledge the importance of your own acts of citizenship. If we are to truly be accountable for the well-being of the whole organization, then we need to be willing to give up territory. Turn over control to other departments, to neighbors. Transfer a portion of your budget to another unit that may be doing work that is more vital to the institution than your own. Accept the fact that people in your unit may not be the brightest and the best and deserve the highest pay. The consuming attention to leaders and followers distances you from the essential work of cocreating an organization with those at your level. Attending to your leadership turns your attention from your citizenship. If you insist on being a role model, set the example for how to cooperate with, yield, support, and affirm the actions of peers both within and outside without your department.

Citizenship, self-management, and engagement come together when we collectively learn to rethink and redesign the places where we assemble. Authentic change needs to be self-inflicted. Our institutions need fixing, and we need bosses willing to shoulder the responsibility of their position. What turns the corner, though, is when people come together to collectively re-design the structure of their own experience. It may be redesigning the work itself, the pay system, the offer to a customer, the strategy or the physical lay-out of an office. Unfortunately, we have lost faith in people's capacity to come together on their own and be productive. We have become contemp-tuous of democracy. Camels being designed by committee and the like. This need not be so.

Our bias toward monarchy and our belief in the centrality of the leader has us ignore collective and communal successes and celebrate the heroism of the individual. If we can just let leadership be, and choose to focus on cit-izenship, we have the knowledge and experience to create accountable insti-tutions, which is an important step toward an accountable culture, which is the essence of democracy.

9

Dharamshala Dreaming: A Traveler's Search for the Meaning of Work

Susana Barciela

Susana Barciela is an editorial writer for the Miami Herald. *Previously, she wrote* What Works, *a weekly column that covered everything from tyrant bosses to the end of lifetime employment. Born in Havana, Cuba, she grew up in Miami, Florida, where she resides. Before becoming a journalist, she spent 10 years in New England and the Midwest, and in various corporate management jobs.*

This essay describes a trip to the Himalayas that was both literal and philosophical, a search for both meaning and means. It explores why we work, our values, and our personal purpose and challenges us to find work that is fulfilling while building workplaces that serve more than the privileged few.

Some pilgrims go to the mountains seeking the meaning of life. I traveled to the mountains seeking the meaning of work—which qualifies as life for many of us Americans.

In my case, the mountains were the Himalayas. Actually, I went to the foothills. I landed in Dharamshala, India, the town known best as home of the Dalai Lama, for a business conference of all things. For me, a Cuban American from Miami, it was a long stretch in more ways than the 13,452 frequent flyer miles to get there.

An Unexpected Invitation

I almost didn't go. The fax had arrived in February inviting me to this oddball workshop on transformational leadership. Off the bat I didn't like the words.

Transformational leadership? I weary of faddish terms that roll off tongues as easily as employees fall from payrolls. Today firms tout the relationship leader. Team leader. Manager leader. Servant-leader. Fill-in-the-blank leader. Too many words, not enough practice.

But the invitation had come from Dinesh Chandra, a Plantation, Florida, consultant with a background in total quality management and an interest in spiritual topics that had led him to me. We had been talking off and on about values in business for about a year and he didn't appear to be a flake.

Dinesh was one of the facilitators of the workshop, along with Peter Block, author of *Stewardship: Choosing Service Over Self-Interest* and a couple of other hot management books. Both of them did work I respected. Cautiously, I checked my natural aversion toward management consultants, in particular those who write business best-sellers.

I began to think of this Himalayan conference as a serious possibility.

Of course, buried underneath a stack of publications and papers on my desk, I proceeded to forget about the invitation for a month. Then one Monday, I woke up and couldn't shake Dharamshala from my thoughts.

I wanted to go.

After a year reading the *The Tibetan Book of the Living and Dying*, Tibetan Buddhism both fascinated and impressed me. How could I pass up the chance to visit the town that was home to the Dalai Lama? For years I had been meditating, practicing yoga, and chanting in Sanskrit in my own search for peace. How could I ignore the chance to visit India, birthplace to these practices? I might never have another chance to see the Himalayas. How could I say no to the highest mountains in the world?

Yet reasoning does little to appease the gods of doubt. What if the conference were a joke? Other than Dinesh, an acquaintance, everyone else going would be a stranger. The cost, the time, the hassle were daunting.

"It's a crapshoot," Peter Block told me when I tracked him down to confirm the event was for real. "But I think it's worth enough for me to give up a week of my life for no pay" (personal communication, March 11, 1996).

To be honest, I knew of Block by reputation but hadn't read any of his books. I also knew he had been one of the founders of Designed Learning, the consulting firm that had come to my company, and not impressed me, the year before.

It's hard to practice what you preach.

"God is a four-letter word in business," I told Block.

Of course, he said, "How can you be objective about God? It's personal."

Secretly, I was fishing for a reason not to go. It would be easier to stay in my comfort zone. Much easier to not stretch, not push myself, not risk any crisis.

"So this is," I asked Block, "about change from the inside out?"

"And the reverse. Both," he said. "This is about human beings and the search for meaning in their lives."

Don't come if all you want to do is journalism, he challenged. "Come as a participant," Block said. "And if you go, you have to write about it."

The Journey Begins

Friday, March 16, 12:48 A.M. Miami

Today I paid for my flight. Tonight I can't sleep. In 12 days, less than two weeks, I'll be leaving.

I called Dinesh for reassurance before pulling out my plastic for the airfare, $1,665 and change. The itinerary gets me to Delhi a day early. I leave a day late. "You can stay on the farm where we'll be for as long as you like," Dinesh said.

"So, you are coming?" he quizzed.

"Yes, I think so," I said, surprising myself.

Now, at 1 A.M., my dog, Bud, twitches in his sleep on the floor next to me. And I'm scared. The mantras don't calm me. I don't know what I fear more: traveling by myself to a strange place, the strangers I'll have to trust, facing tough questions about my mission and my work.

I'm afraid of the spiritual part of the journey. I'm afraid of opening up. I'm afraid of revealing myself. But I am more afraid of not trying to.

This transformational stuff, I figured, had something to do with personal purpose and spirit, discovering what they were and aligning one's work with them. The subject was near to my heart, and my profession.

Work, you see, is my job. I'm a journalist paid to cover workplace issues for the *Miami Herald*. Since 1993 I've written a weekly column touching on issues ranging from bozo bosses to the end of lifetime employment.

Born of memories of my immigrant parents, honed by my own minimum-wage labor, polished to perfection after I graduated to the corporate managerial elite, my biases are obvious in the columns I write. Mostly, I chafe at the inhumane workplaces we create and tolerate.

The truth is, we lowly workers and big bosses alike treat each other poorly. Look at the people who say they believe in ethics and respect but treat colleagues, employees, and clients with none. Look at the status of those who do the work and those who manage it. Look at the employees who would rather complain about their treatment than work toward improving it.

I caught on to the ways of business early on. In high school, when I worked a part-time clerical job in a hospital, there was the administrator who didn't direct so much as *good day* to me. Until the day I quit, and he learned I was leaving to attend Harvard University. He saw fit then to meet me and wish me well. As if going to Harvard now made me a different person. As if as a minimum wage part-timer I hadn't existed, didn't think, couldn't learn or possibly do better.

Yes, people are our most valuable resources—as long as the firm doesn't have to pay them much and they keep their mouths shut.

Not surprisingly, I've seen many people grow bitter about their work. Settling into victimhood, some blame everyone but themselves for their job woes.

Others attracted me more. These folks, programmed by the same social pressures, chose to explore less traditional tracks. I began writing about businesspeople who brought their spiritual beliefs to work as a moral compass. I learned about managers who sought to serve both clients and employees. I sought out those for whom meaningful work outweighed the size of the paycheck. I found people who had traded high-pressure and high-paying jobs for simpler, more peaceful lives. More than hippie throwbacks, these people were seeking meaningful livelihoods and humane ways to do business.

Maybe I saw this only to validate myself.

My first 10 years in corporate America, I worked in managerial-type jobs for four Fortune 500 companies—Procter & Gamble, American Express, Harte-Hanks, and even my current parent company, Knight-Ridder. Each time I switched jobs, names and faces changed but not the phenomena. I would picture myself doing what my bosses and their bosses did and voilà, I knew I would hate it. I didn't want to treat employees like generic expenses. And I never have been good at keeping my mouth shut.

The truth is, it took all that time chasing MBA illusions of success to realize that the prize was booby-trapped. So five years ago, by chance, I found myself writing for a living. It's the only job I've managed to hold onto more than two years. I don't manage people and, I imagine, earn considerably less than classmates who graduated with me from Harvard Business School in 1983. I've never been happier.

Yet more than ever, I wondered what kept more folks from finding their calling when, somehow, some people were creating both meaningful work and livelihoods. I wanted to know how we could create humane workplaces. What I could do with my own behavior, my own writing, within my own work group? For no good reason, I thought I might find better answers in the Himalayas. What I found were 17 other businesspeople as perplexed as I was.

Friday, March 29, 12:40 A.M. Miami time.

By the streaks of red and gold outside my window, it's just after dawn. In three hours we touch down in Frankfort. A six-hour wait, then onto New Delhi. Ever since I decided to buy the plane ticket two weeks ago, I have been assailed by alternating bouts of dread and excitement.

This odd business conference could push me to a higher level, to a clearer direction. I'm tired of being tired.

It could also be a bust. The eight-page fax from the Centers for Disease Control listed every horrible disease I'll be exposed to in India:

malaria, rabies, dengue fever, typhus, polio, hepatitis, parasites, etc., etc., etc. The vaccines hurt, as the doctor promised, like a kick in the pants. The guidebook warns of theft, haggling with vendors, lost passports, and the legendary Indian bureaucracy that can turn any minor glitch into days of delay. Maybe I should have stayed home.

Maybe. But I will be sorry if I don't go. Crisis is a small price to pay for growth.

Even in the middle of the night New Delhi is hot, 78 degrees Fahrenheit, and muggy. It has taken 24 hours to get here. The air feels like Miami, enveloping me as I walk outdoors. Somewhere midair between Frankfort and Delhi, I realized I left at home all the phone numbers given me in case no one appeared at the airport to pick me up.

Not to worry. As I exit customs, a small dark man in a beige uniform holds a sign with my name. No problems, no snags. Not even with the Indian bureaucracy.

The man, Ravi Rao, chauffeurs me out of the airport crowds and we head south along rocklined streets that look under perpetual construction. At 3 A.M. Delhi appears deserted, haunted only by ramshackle buildings and ghostly cows. Shuttered storefronts and living quarters look all crammed together. Ravi points to worn boxlike apartment buildings. Government housing, he says. They look like the projects at home.

Turning down a dirt road, houses grown in size and luxury. Past a series of closed gates, we stop at one labeled Khurana Farm. A guard slides open metal doors and another world unfolds. Inside, statues beckon toward a circular driveway, and in the darkness I make out sweeping trees, lush greenery, and an ultramodern, split-level house.

"Excuse me," I ask Ravi, somewhat embarrassed. "Who is Mr. Khurana?"

Ravi hesitates. "A businessman," he says, sounding surprised.

"I take it he's successful."

"Mr. Khurana is the highest taxpayer in all of India," Ravi informs me. It is a description I will hear time and again, from different people in different cities during the length of my stay.

I learn much more about wealth, and its relative nature, in the next few days. Ravi is shocked that my Olympus camera cost $200. I am shocked when he tells me the farm, occupied only on weekends and by occasional guests, employs about 25 servants.

Having servants is not unusual, however, among the 200 million that make up India's middle class. With more than 700 million people living in miserable poverty, labor sells cheap. Imagine a country with close to 20 percent of the earth's population in the midst of an industrial revolution. Imagine the country opening its enormous markets to outsiders, and eager multinationals jumping in.

This is India today. An economic free-for-all fuels opportunities for the country's entrepreneurs and educated professionals, even as foreign influences disrupt cultural traditions. Meanwhile, pervasive social problems—overpopulation, poor public health, corruption, income disparity—persist.

When I meet the owner of the farmhouse, Ashwani Khurana is much younger than I imagined. Richer, too. Having made millions running a private lottery company, he is indeed one of the nation's highest taxpayers, though not its wealthiest citizen. In a country where corruption is as pervasive as poverty, paying that much in taxes means he reports more income than others who are much richer and more corrupt. Everything is relative.

These days, Ashwani is preoccupied with the environment. He has donated 30,000 trees to the City of Delhi in the last six years and is on track to give 70,000 more. He's already been to a previous transformational workshop in Dharamshala. He's going again this time to meet Peter Block.

> Sunday, March 31, 7:05 A.M., New Delhi
> I'm surprised at how comfortable I feel here. Of course, you can get used to servants offering tea every time you turn around. I seem not to be shocked by poverty, crowds, or the seedy-decayed looks of things outside the farmhouse. Perhaps you get used to being light-years richer than folks around you, too.

Altogether, 18 of us are headed to Dharamshala. By the time the charter plane takes off, I've met Anil Sachdev, managing director of Eicher Consultancy Service in New Delhi and the facilitator who has organized the conference in India.

I've also met Peter and Barbara Block. Both of them have backgrounds in organizational development and training, though Barbara has retired from the field. Peter still consults, now on his own since detaching from two consulting firms last year. I connected with them from the start, despite having all met while under the influence of jet lag.

As a group, we meet for the first time at the airport Monday morning. Executives have flown in from all over the country—Calcutta, Madras, Mumbai, Bombay, Pune. We clamber into an 18-seat Archana Airways plane, shoehorn luggage into storage compartments, and surprisingly take off about on time.

To the Mountains

If beauty has anything to do with transformation, the process begins on the plane. Below us, terraced farms cut into the mountains like waves molded to the curving slopes. Ant-sized trucks chug along roads that roller coaster around the tops of hills. Unassuming rivers trickle at the bottom of deep valleys they have carved for centuries out of the earth.

Three hours later, we land on a speck of an airstrip. We are surrounded by mountain giants all green at the base, topped by white, set against a backdrop of impossibly blue, blue sky.

A 40-minute drive to Upper Dharamshala gives a first taste of Himalayan life. The taxi takes hairpin turns over rutted pavement. On the right, the roadside is a sheer drop. The road feels too narrow, but oncoming cars pass. Just barely. Rhesus monkeys run, climb, stare.

We drive past the Tibetan hospital where long-robed monks roam the sidewalks. Ahead, a shiny, maroon Jeep Cherokee bounces toward us. I expect tourists. I see instead four Buddhist monks inside the jeep, a sticker affixed to their windshield: *Free Tibet.*

Those of us here for the transformation workshop fill Glenmoor Cottages, the guest house where we are meeting these four days. For our discussions, the furniture has been cleared out of the living room in the main house, a beautiful British-style summer residence, stone and white topped by a red tin roof.

We begin after lunch, sitting on mattresses on the floor around the perimeter of the room. Someone lights a candle and Anil kicks off, innocently enough, asking folks to tell why they have come. When he says, "You can make money, and be successful, and still have values," I feel choked. The room is too small.

It only gets harder for me when Anu Aga speaks. A month ago, she was in London visiting a new grandson. But everything has changed since. Her husband died of a heart attack on the way to the airport to welcome her home.

Anu had been the human resource director for Thermax, the family firm in Pune south of Bombay. She's taken over as chairperson, now one of only a handful women chief executives in all of India. She's been besieged by work, business, and family demands since.

Anu reveals all this to strangers without wavering, a small smile visiting her face. She doesn't sound self-pitying or bitter. Only deep circles under her eyes hint at her sorrow.

The organizers figured she wouldn't make it to the conference. She figured coming would give her needed time to think. And grieve in her own way, I suspect.

I, who was devastated a year ago after the death of a beloved aunt, am awed by Anu's presence. It dawns on me. Today, April 1, 1996, would have been the 67th birthday of this aunt, Tia Ñica—my Tarot teacher, confessor, and muse.

"All of us have work to do while we are here," Barbara tells the group. "We just have to get on with it."

Maybe it's the setting, or the tone set by Anil, Dinesh, and Anu. I am surprised, and impressed, by the raw honesty. In settings like this, high-powered business executives often play mine-is-bigger. *Mine is the best company. Our customers love us. Workers think we're great.* I see little of that posturing here.

Well, just a little.

"I have 600 people working under me and I am managing with the power of love," says M. K. Jalan, an entrepreneur from Calcutta who began importing steel and ended up building a lucrative trading business.

Despite the bravado, his questions hit the mark for many in the room. Now 48 and set for material needs, M. K. is wondering what to do in his next 25 years. He also broaches the subject of honesty.

M. K. questions: Does he really need to reveal *everything* to his workers, his vendors, his family? Should he be transparent, that is, not hide those inconvenient details so easily left unsaid? What if revealing production costs to a customer is bad for business?

"When I have been transparent, I lose," M. K. says. "If I tell the cost I'm honest. Then they want me to lower the price and won't pay so much."

And what if his workers were to ask M. K., the man who manages with love, how much top management makes? M. K. admits, he wouldn't tell.

"How can you manage with love and hold back?" retorts K. V. Mathew, chief executive of L&T-McNeil Ltd., an equipment manufacturing company in Bombay.

K. V. has been stirring under the blanket he has wrapped around him. I'm not sure if he's agitated by a worsening flu or the discussion. He speaks faster and faster:

> *People are very liberal with love. But do we really mean what we say? Are we prepared to be transparent? To love unconditionally?*
>
> *We say to workers we want you to take ownership, to participate. Behave as owners. But when it comes to profits, we say no, the shareholders are the owners. Is this practicing what we preach?*
>
> *I am reluctant to speak of love, because I feel it's a big hypocrisy. I go to the orphanage and volunteer there, but I can't love those children unconditionally. I can't love them like I love my children. And I want to be able to love unconditionally.*

I really like K. V. His rootedness will bring us back to earth over and over again. And M. K., who surprises me by speaking little in the following sessions, will be among those who visibly shift most.

By now a number of folks have mentioned they, like Ashwani, have come to hear Peter Block. Last to introduce himself, Sundar Iyer takes an altogether different tack.

"I am here because my boss called me up and told me I was going to Dharamshala and I said okay. I don't know what transformation leadership is. I never read any of the materials sent," says Sundar, one of two national sales managers for Silicon Graphics at the conference. Then, with apologies and a mischievous smile, Sundar adds he has never heard of Peter Block.

The ice is definitively broken.

The Himalayan cold seeps into the summer house. Thankfully, we are brought blankets and pots of hot chai, the ever present milky-sweet Indian tea that reminds me of my own cafe con leche.

Uncomfortable Questioning

The respite is short, though. When Dinesh asks what are our "transformation" questions, out tumble those things that run around in the head when work lets up and sleep hasn't kicked in.

Can anything good come without commitment and attachment? Should you do what you enjoy, or learn to enjoy what you do? What is my role in the divine play? What is the force that keeps partners together? Can we forget and forgive? Am I the image I project?

What happens when you start managing perception? Isn't that manipulation?

"In the United States," I say, "It's called management."

Is it right to insist on your values and to change the organization? Is it possible? Or do you just do whatever the company says, accept it, put your own values aside?

Peter tells us he is questioning his role as the expert. How much does commanding the center of attention have to do with service to others? How much is about arrogance and control?

Me, I want a more humane work world, not that I know what that really looks like.

We all want definitive answers to questions that don't have them.

How do you use your personal transformation to transform the organization?

"Your transformation is enough," Peter suggests. "Maybe that is the purpose of the business—a place where the transformation can take place. Money is just the economics that allows it to happen."

Tuesday (I think) April 2, 7:10 A.M., Glenmoor Cottages

I am sitting here on the terrace, overlooking a breathtaking valley. The new sun bathes everything in gold. Below, houses cut into the sides of the hills like jeweled steps in a staircase. Above, taller hills, covered in lush green. The air smells, well, clean. I do not recognize the odor.

At 6,300 feet, we are below the snow line. Yet the room was ridiculously cold last night, until I crept under the fat quilt and tucked its sides around me as if I were a mummy. Drifting off exhausted, I could hear a few diehards singing traditional Hindu songs.

The colors, the coolness, the quiet here invite meditation. I smile recalling the secret of upper management once confided to me by an executive: the higher the rank, the closer the attention span approaches that of a gerbil. Some call that efficient. I'm not convinced.

You need quiet to hear your heart above the din of your ego. The static that bombards us in our daily work life too easily separates us from our own humanity. Standing still, somehow, helps us reclaim it. Standing still in the shadow of the world's tallest mountains couldn't have been a better reminder.

The questions don't end by day two of the conference. But we begin to debate answers. Organizational structure, for example, reveals underlying assumptions about people and business.

"We organize like a triangle, for dominion," Peter says. The chief executive occupies the top point, employees arranged underneath to carry the burden. "I long for communion, like a circle," he says. "To be in a circle means redistribution of power."

But how to get there. To go from patriarchy to community. To bridge the chasm between the managers and the managed. I argue that we should. Because long term, the only way to maximize the value produced by a group is to cultivate the productive power of each individual. And you can't goad individuals into performing at peak through control, nickle-and-diming, or micromanagement.

Such a transformation, like any change profound and irreversible, rarely happens overnight. Anil tells of his father, a civil planning officer in the Indian army whose career had topped out. Life after work consisted of eating, drinking, and playing cards. Until one day a card buddy interrupted their game to go see a guru and Anil's father followed.

The next day, Anil's father stopped drinking and smoking and turned vegetarian. He and the family became devotees of the guru, embarking on a spiritual path that included meditation and retreats at the Chinmaya Ashram, a short drive from Dharamshala.

"Change happens with respect to the changeless," Anil says. "Like a fault line, cracks develop undetected. Then one day, something happens. You realize there is something deeper. You are in touch with what really lies inside."

Anil believes the only way to change the world is to change yourself. Good people make good leaders. Good leaders articulate what people really need, but only when they understand what that need is. Then the power comes from the people, not because the leader tells them what to do, but because you are describing what they want and filling a void. This describes servant-leadership.

The Power of Serving Others

Again, I am reminded of my late aunt. Anil has described a process Tia Ñica fell into naturally, though she would never have called it leadership, much less servant or transformational. Her concern was to find livelihoods, and hope, for people she cared about. She ended up transforming her dilapidated Havana community by teaching art to her neighbors.

We, her family and longtime friends, called her Ñica. Professionally she was Antonia Eiriz, a Cuban painter who gathered international awards and critical praise during the 1960s. She is still recognized today. One of her works was selected for the art exhibition accompanying the 1996 Olympics in Atlanta.

But in the 1970s, she stopped painting. She stopped cold at the height of her professional success. As if nothing had changed, she retired to a quiet life in a wood house built by my grandfather in Juanelo, the working class barrio where she was born and where everyone knew her. Concerned about helping others develop skills and confidence, Ñica began teaching neighbors how to work papier-mâché.

The project evolved into an after-school activities program. When kids began bringing home polychrome paper roosters, parents wanted in as well. Soon, people all over Juanelo were collecting discarded newspapers, learning to draw with dots and lines, painting with Mercurochrome and sculpting with flour paste.

The kids created their own theater, with their own words and masks, all captured in an award-winning documentary *Art of the People.* Juanelo later mounted its own papier-mâché exhibition. And Ñica traveled the island training other teachers.

What started out as a small idea took root and bears fruit still. In Cuba today, tourists buy tie-dyed cloth and papier-mâché crafts descendant from the modest techniques taught by Ñica in Juanelo.

To this day, from seeds Ñica planted, uncounted folks earn their livelihoods from creative work. One of the first neighbors she taught works as a restorer for Cuba's National Museum of Fine Arts. Another has traveled to international crafts shows exhibiting papier-mâché pieces. And the man who grew up across the street from Ñica is one of the most talented craft artists in the country, though he is schizophrenic and couldn't keep himself clean much less earn anything before learning papier-mâché.

All this because of Ñica, who would be embarrassed by too many accolades. Because her actions came from the heart, not the ego. And they were based on an unshakable belief in the power of people to create. Everyone can draw, paint, and create, she said. When we create from our core, we are like God. Even if the end result is a purple paper chicken, the creative process itself can transform your being.

Ñica saw it happen in people who never imagined they could create art. I think it was the taste of their own limitlessness.

I think that's how it could be in business, too.

People desire to grow, to create, to learn and improve, I believe. We want compassion and joy. It's exhilarating to shine.

What is it that stops us? What darkness drives us to build and tolerate inhuman institutions? And what keeps us from creating human ones?

The Geshe's Visit

Geshe Sonam Rinchen, a Buddhist monk, arrives after lunch smiling, smiling. The Geshe, a title bestowed on learned monks, bows and sits with us on the floor along with Ruth Sonam, his Oxford-educated translator.

We are staring. There is something spellbinding about the Geshe's face, his beautiful smile. He radiates.

He is a teacher at the Library of Tibetan Works and Archives, an international center for scholarly studies in Dharamsala (as spelled by the Tibetans without the second *h*).

An hour ago, he tells us, the Library's director asked if he would meet with us at Glenmoor Cottages. He asked, "What do they wish me to speak about?" The director replied, "They'll tell you."

Learning we are businesspeople, Geshe Rinchen professes little knowledge of our field. Then he launches into a 40-minute extemporaneous talk:

> *The thing about desire and attachment emotions is that when they begin, they feel like friends. But they bring trouble in the long term. They are possessive. They make us reluctant to let go.*
> *Those emotions may be very attractive for a businessperson.*

He flashes a sly smile. "But if you gather in and can't let go," he squeezes his hands as if churning, until he opens them in the shape of a bowl, "you can't gather in more."

I get the feeling the Geshe knows more than he owns up to.

We need to weigh the impact of our actions, he suggests, both in the short and the long run. We should consider the impact not only on ourselves and our spiritual growth, but on our company, our country, even our planet. We have to control our mind, so that the mind—its anger, greed, and other disturbing emotions—doesn't control us.

Without having heard M. K.'s questions about transparency, the Geshe answers them. When you feel you have to hide something, he says, ask yourself whether you should be doing that something:

> *We all need things and money. We all need personal livelihood. But it should be earned in an honest way, within the noblest values of society. This doesn't really go against the ways of business. If what you do in the long term is exploitive and destructive, then one has to restrain one's greed, that is, the desire for a quick profit.*

If we just talk and not change our attitudes, nothing will happen. If we change, then it has a snowball effect. More and more people start to change. We have to change by changing our minds, the way we think. That changes the physical and verbal actions and radiates to others.

When we can hold disturbing emotions at bay, we can remain calm and clearheaded in the face of any obstacle. "If the thought in our heart is good, then whatever we display is okay, even anger," he says.

The idea is to be like a delicious mango: ripe on the inside and ripe outside. If you can't be that mango, better to be ripe on the inside and appear tough outside. The worst mangos are those that appear ripe outside, but inside are hard as stone. The Geshe says:

There is nothing wrong with going to work. If you work sincerely, with a certain amount of affection for those that have given you the opportunity, then work becomes a spiritual practice. If you are doing it with a good heart, then everything comes. If the employer has affection for the workforce, all the better. If all they think of is profit, not so good.

Translator Ruth Sonam tells us that the Geshe is touched by us, that we've come together from different cultures and are meeting here with openness and desire to learn from each other. He hasn't seen many business folks on such pilgrimages.

Geshe Rinchen, from the Trehor region of Kham in Eastern Tibet, ran away from home at age 12 to join a neighboring monastery. After an uprising against the Chinese in 1959, like the Dalai Lama and other persecuted monks, he fled into exile.

The Geshe doesn't mention that more than 1 million Tibetans, from a nation of 6 million, have died at the hands of the Chinese since their invasion of Tibet in 1950. He doesn't talk about the 6,000 Tibetan monasteries and temples gutted, about the uncounted monks and nuns tortured, the forests stripped of trees, or the systematic attempts by the Chinese to obliterate Tibetan culture.

When he is asked how he feels toward the Chinese, he answers simply:

I don't think their behavior is honest. Never mind their behavior with respect to Tibet, but with their own people. The craving for control is very strong.

But I can truthfully say I don't feel angry. There are too many of them to get angry with.

Geshe Rinchen laughs and we join him in his gentle humor.

After questioning, poking and wondering for 15 hours, after listening and drinking chai with the Geshe, what more was left to say?

My fears were unfounded, I decide. There was no crisis. There's nothing to getting out of the comfort zone. I would coast the rest of the conference.

Right.

Gathered after dinner, still basking in the Geshe's glow, it doesn't take long to figure out my relaxation had been premature.

Facing What We Fear

This session is about personal limitations. We are to confront our dark sides. Face the anger that torpedoes loving intentions. The arrogance that turns charity into condescension. The disturbing desires that sabotage honesty.

Dinesh starts by telling of his wife. Not that he lied to her necessarily, only held back on the whole truth. By the time he realized she knew the truth all along, she was dying of cancer. By then, little time was left for real authenticity in their relationship.

Now, he says, he only wants honest relationships. And he knows fear of intimacy gets in the way. It's a personal limitation he pushes against. For him, confronting the memories in a supportive community is a way of healing.

For us in the room, the tension has grown hotter than the fire in which we are to burn whatever limitation holds us back. Like my thoughts, the hot wood sizzles and cracks—the only sounds in a silence so oppressive breathing feels difficult.

I don't want to stir. I don't want to look at their faces. I don't want to know their pain. I don't want to know my own.

Too late. Those that follow Dinesh speak in voices as hushed as in confessional. They expose deep hurts.

I must end this affair that has paralyzed my life.

I'm going to try, again, to mend my ragged marriage.

I can't stand the war in my home between my mother and my wife.

Others reveal studied introspection. Barbara wants to let go of her inner critic. Peter wants to let go of arrogance and the need to control. Me, I own up to craving approval.

Any way you slice it, vulnerability isn't easy. Those who say nothing appear most shell-shocked. Pinned by the silence that hangs between each revelation, each one of us is thinking, thinking. Who will go next?

What I don't say, I obsess over in the silence. How much does fear censor my behavior? Do I, even subconsciously, tone down my writing? Why can't I curb anger and frustration? How much energy have I wasted pretending I am someone else at work?

I flash on Harvard Business School and past corporate jobs, where the game demanded dress for success *and* think for success. You could look forward to the ultimate career, one that began with a six-digit salary, followed by more money, fame, and five-star vacations. You fired people, moved for promotions, jumped ship for a better offer. You didn't blink at marketing cancer or useless, overpriced services, or playing fast and loose with truth or the law. Business was business.

I don't want that game anymore—though old programing dies hard, and I know I get sucked in every now and again. There are advantages to being older. Earning enough to cover the basics, being clearer about values, I don't need promotions for show. When you don't need what the corporation offers, you have little to lose.

After all, at the end of the tiring day, we suffer our demons alone.

Wednesday, April 2, Glenmoor Cottages, Dharamshala

You think the world will shake and change. Yet the sun rises behind the foothills, clearing the mist from the valley below as every other morning. The wooded hills still ooze peace.

The demons may not be gone, but few wish to mention them the morning after. It's too soon, too raw. We comment on the power of silence. We move on.

Creating Community

What is it that creates a community anyway? Is it shared pain, like last night's? Is it noble purpose? Do we need enemies—like Hurricane Andrew, the Soviet Union, or a vicious competitor—to unite us?

"How can I, or anyone else who chooses to call himself a leader know everyone's dreams? And then articulate them year after year?" Anu asks.

"What if," Peter responds, "executives had term limits?"

The ultimate goal really does make a difference.

In the aftermath of Hurricane Andrew, employees at my newspaper put forth more than their best efforts. Hundreds of us, even some who had lost their own homes, worked 14-hour days to get information out to those who needed it. Volunteers woke before dawn to deliver newspapers to ravaged neighborhoods. Strangers became concerned coworkers. We served each other and our community. There was no time, and no reason, for half-truths.

Staring at devastation beyond imagination, 2,000 employees fused in single-minded purpose: to resurrect South Florida. We acted as one. But it didn't last. It rarely does.

After crisis passes, purpose dissipates. Colleagues who once collaborated bicker over petty territorialities. We point fingers, trying to blame anyone and everyone *else* for mistakes we all contribute to. Our egos hurt. Our arrogance divides us from each other, and the communities we claim to serve.

Increasing shareholder value doesn't cut it as a purpose to die for.

"Profit is a requirement," K. V. reminds us.

Profit is necessary, of course. But not sufficient. "Profit as a purpose leads to despair. If it's the prime purpose, sooner or later, customers get exploited," Peter argues. "Growing richer or bigger may sustain you at age 30. After that, how many Mercedes can you drive? Why does bigger mean better."

Even a big, noble goal like reducing poverty isn't enough. Peter insists:

> *How is important also. Because the end is always used by corporations as justification to do inhuman things.*
>
> *I see you as organizing agents. You are here because you are at a crisis of success. What will I do with this prison of success? How can I renew myself, so I can renew my company? There are many great answers. It starts with you deciding you have to relate to your company in a different way.*
>
> *Community is not the point. It's the container.*

Everyone wants to know the *how*. How does anyone create an organizational container that nurtures honest communication and a higher purpose?

Dinesh describes a South Florida bank where tellers give marbles to each other to show appreciation. M. K. says his employees have coffee together every morning. Shree Sridhar, a Silicon Graphics sales manager, recalls an office where the intercom was banished so that people would actually talk in person. In a town south of Delhi where there has been no ethnic violence, Anil tells us, Hindus and Muslims smoke around the fire together.

K. V., once again, brings us back to the earth.

> *I'm not against idealism, but we should also look at our feet. Rituals can become an opium, too. That is not enough. We have to take tougher subjects: the systems, the processes, the structure. Otherwise, we end up with all this drinking coffee and hugging and end up with another religion.*

People find many ways to say *ah ha*.

M. K. now believes he can live with transparency. "The introspection really helps," he says. Others realize *they* have to change. That if introspection is hard, communicating honestly with others is harder. That, deep at the heart, your problem is often the same as my problem.

Even K. V. feels renewed faith that many, many people around the globe are interested in building better communities.

Regardless of the hours we talk, we find no prefabricated answers. Peter offers us his truth:

> *Just because there are no answers doesn't mean there is nothing I can do about it. The struggle is the solution. Values and organization: we want them to come together. The ultimate test is how to take these ideas to improve the quality of lives for workers at lower levels.*
>
> *If you can't do that at your level, how can you ask others to do it? You have no right to demand.*

Demand that those who better understand their experience, at every level, find their voice and speak up. The point is not to replicate this experience. But to spread, to a large number of people, the idea that we are creating our lives.

The reason blaming others is appealing is because it feels good. God gave us choice. With freedom comes wrongdoing. If there was no evil, what would happen to good? The fact that we're going to die gives meaning to what we do. If you want cultures of caring, community, and compassion, it only comes with choice and freedom.

The problem is that we've created institutions designed to take away choice. Most of you are in places designed for predictability and control. If you don't have a sense of choice and freedom in your life, how can you offer it to anyone else? If I want accountability, I need choice. Anything else is business as usual, perhaps with a humane touch.

Peter seems to speak without effort, in language that flows clear and convincing. He articulates in cohesive thoughts with conviction. It is his gift. Aided I'm sure by 30 years of practice. When Peter speaks, you want to believe. Is it the power of the ideas? Or that of the speaker?

Procedures without purpose are just going to fail. You need the purpose to sustain you and you need your feet on the ground.

Ultimately, what you do has to survive the Tibetan plain of the marketplace. New age stuff that is like cotton candy dies in the marketplace. Yet if you get to the practical too soon, forget about the purpose.

Most of my industry is willing to get to the practical without doing the grounding. As Bharat would say, we have 84 million lifetimes to go through before we get to Nirvana, and that's if there are no stops or setbacks.

Peter says he's questioning his knack for drawing attention, his disposition to control. Funny how we battle hardest those things we don't like in ourselves.

This is why it pays to search for your calling. To find the things we love and care about, and inspire us to create value for all of us. That's what we try to pin down on day three when we each write personal mission statements. They run the gamut:

To be like a mango.

To spread the word that one can be successful and lead a virtuous life.

To be more introspective, experience the power of silence, and be less manipulative.

To follow a path as loving as possible.

The statements are heartfelt. Like Barbara's:

To move from the outer life to the inner; from the manmade to the natural; from the complicated to the simpler lifestyle; to serve, not self-serving service, but compassionate service. To regain innocence.

My calling is to write. And as I articulate my personal statement, I feel the power of intention: to use the gifts I have been given, particularly writing and life experience, to urge people to discover what is human in all of us.

Feeling the Spirit

We are ready for a break and it comes in a most welcome field trip to Norbulingka Institute, an arts center dedicated to preserving Tibetan culture in exile. It's been three days since I've ridden in a car and now the mountain roads seem less narrow, the drops not as threateningly steep. I have the funny sense that the pine-cloaked mountains, strong and protecting, are watching over us. Their beauty, or maybe the thin air, makes me lightheaded.

Going there I really don't know what to expect. In any case, I am not prepared for this. A blue, decorated archway, superimposed on a wall of solid stone blocks, frames the entrance. Inside, the sound of running water wipes away the noise of passing traffic. Prayer flags flap in the wind. Buildings are painted in soothing blues, reds, and yellows, decorated with delicate flowers and birds and an abundance of carved columns.

We cross an arched wood bridge and an interior patio and head for the temple, the first floor of a red building. Lifting the red and blue flag hung over its doorway, we enter barefoot. I bring with me a white gauze, a prayer scarf given to me by a Buddhist friend for blessing.

Save for a couple of elderly women, the temple is empty. And silent. Not the agonized silence of self-reproach, but an absence that sounds like surrender. Undoubtedly this is a holy place. I sit on the stone floor cross-legged, close my eyes, and disappear. When I return, the others are gone. I have no idea how much time has passed.

When I join my subdued friends outside, we climb three flights to a terrace on top of the temple building for yet another breathtaking view of the Himalayan foothills. I wonder if we can see Tibet.

Only after returning to Miami do I discover that we visited a place that serves as a house for the Dalai Lama, as an alternative to his main residence near the big temple by McLeod Ganj.

Thursday, April 4, 6:05 A.M., Glenmoor Cottages

Last night, our last in Dharamshala, called for celebration. Ajai Singh, Glenmoor's owner, built us a big bonfire to ward off the cold.

"One must thank God to live in a place such as this," Mr. Singh told me.

Glenmoor has belonged to his family 50 or so years. As a child, he came every summer and just loved the place. A few years back, he built cottages and began renting rooms. He and his family now live amid the beloved mountains year round.

"I hear you only like nice guests," I told Mr. Singh.

"God has been good," he replied, "to provide us only with the very best."

On this, our last morning, I am running late. I've lost my way back to Glenmoor after an early hike to the Church of St. John in the Wilderness, an idyllic spot where Lord Elgin, as in the Parthenon marbles and Viceroy of India, was buried in 1863. My heart is racing from rushing and climbing. So much for peace.

I'm glad to squeak into the living room on time, breathless. We have only a couple of hours left together for final thoughts and well wishing.

Sundar, who's been uncharacteristically quiet, tells us he's been bothered since the night we fed limitations to the fire. He didn't speak out then. But after much thought and little sleep, he doesn't like how he manipulates people. He calls himself dishonest. This is not easy for Sundar to get out. His voice is raspy, halting, his eyes teary. He tells how he awoke Shree, his coworker, in the middle of the night to detail how he, Sundar, had manipulated him over the years. He tells us how he vowed to Shree that he will stop.

Sitting quietly nearby, Shree shows no sign of anger or mistrust.

Paying the price of owning up to his demons, Sundar is being harsh with himself. It's not as if he can't be honest. Indeed, the first time he spoke to this group he was quite frank: He was at this conference because the boss ordered him here. Sundar thought he was along for the ride. As it turns out, the ride took him farther than he expected.

I am not sure this will be a turning point for Sundar, or for any of us. Though I can't imagine any of us ignoring this experience entirely. Each step, no matter how small or tenuous, counts. Maybe one day, like Anil's father, one of us will wake up and change an entire life. Meanwhile we slog along, taking our hits, getting lost and sidetracked, finding our path again, learning the hard way, learning to make it easier.

The vans have arrived to take us to the airport. I have one last question, one I have been afraid to pose to the group: I ask for permission to write their stories.

Almost in unison they nod their heads and encourage me. They tell me to use their real names. They want me to write.

"Susana," K. V. turns to me. "I don't want your being a part of our group to cloud your journalistic judgment."

I am so amused. Here is the man who criticizes himself for not loving unconditionally and he is offering me unconditional trust. Like the tin man in *The Wizard of Oz*, K. V. only thinks he doesn't have a heart.

The Journey That Doesn't End

My fears were right, after all. So were my hopes for this trip.

The wheel of fortune spins. We perceive the fates to bless some more than others. But in our jobs and outside of them, each of us chooses to make the best or worst of whatever befalls us. We solve one crisis. Another is sure to follow. As Peter observed, "This is the 22nd year of my midlife crisis."

I traveled to Dharamshala afraid of finding my crisis, and found those of 17 others. We all wanted transformation to be over already. The truth is, transformation never ends.

We can comfort ourselves living on the surface. But that's not enough for those who long for work that is deeper and more satisfying. Even in business and even in America. It's up to us to create it.

The point isn't to go to the Himalayas. Learn to climb.

10

Quiet Presence:
The Holy Ground
of Leadership

John J. Gardiner

John J. Gardiner is a professor of educational leadership at Seattle University. He serves as a founding member of the National Leadership Group of the American Council on Education and as chair of the board of the Pacific Northwest Postdoctoral Institute.

In this essay, Gardiner offers a series of thoughtful meditations that link together the ideas of Robert Greenleaf with those of others—from David Bohm to Vaclav Havel—around the theme of "quiet presence" as the place where leadership and the Spirit meet.

> *Leo . . . is a person of extraordinary presence.*[1]
>
> —Robert K. Greenleaf

> *The English "holy" is based on the same root as "whole."*[2]
>
> —David Bohm

Our state of being is the real source of our ability to influence the world. Yet our collective state of being, human consciousness, is not adequately developed to cope with the growing number and intensity of global crises that seem to threaten the viability of our home planet. In the words of Vaclav Havel, "Without a global revolution in the sphere of human consciousness, nothing will change for the better in the sphere of our being as humans, and the catastrophe toward which the world is heading, be it ecological, social, demographic or a general breakdown of civilization will be unavoidable."[3] A worldwide revolution in the sphere of human consciousness, in our personal and collective states of being, is needed to avert global disintegration. A revolution is needed in how we relate to each other as people and how we relate to the whole of creation.

Wholeness is our natural state; unrelated separateness is an illusion. As Charlene Spretnak observed, "We do not need to invent a ground of connectedness, but only to realize it."[4] We are all one, but we do not live in that knowledge. Human beings need to become more aware of the interrelatedness of their existence. As David Bohm emphasized, "You cannot think of existence as local."[5] Or as Thich Nhat Hanh said, "You cannot just be by yourself alone. You have to *inter-be* with every other thing."[6] The separate self is an illusion that now threatens the survival of our species. We are all part of a universal consciousness that defines the essence of our being. Mahatma Gandhi observed, "A drop in the ocean partakes of the greatness of its parent although it is unconscious of it; but it dries up as soon as it enters upon an existence independent of the ocean."[7] Consciousness is a deep internal awareness of the whole. As individuals, we are places of potential consciousness, loci where the universal consciousness can manifest.

The global revolution that is needed is one of wholeness and integrity, of being true to our inner being and, thus, to the greater Being of which we are all a part. The road to global renewal begins within our selves. In the words of Hermann Hesse's *Siddhartha,* "To change the world, change yourself."[8] It is the task of each one of us to awaken to the knowledge that we are part of a great, interconnected whole, part of a universal consciousness. Transforming the sense of separation to one of unity is the key to the most important human transformations: personal, corporate, and global.

Reconnecting to our peaceful core involves rediscovering what we are and what we have always been. Ralph Waldo Emerson said, "The highest revelation is that God is in every man."[9] This deep knowledge transforms into an all-encompassing awareness of our nonseparateness and unity, the new consciousness of which Vaclav Havel spoke. With this new way of being, great focused energy will be released personally, corporately, and ultimately, globally. Human connection will transcend to new levels of alignment and synergy, ones envisioned by history's great religious and spiritual leaders.

Seeing with Eyes of Wholeness

Gandhi noted that "faith is nothing but a living, wide-awake consciousness of God within."[10] We fear discovering the godlike in ourselves, for that discovery implies great responsibility for our circumstances as they are. Yet, in the words of Teilhard de Chardin, "We are not human beings having a spiritual experience. We are spiritual beings having a human experience."[11] And the time is now "to build the Earth." In that great awakening to our oneness in Spirit is the great hope and enthusiasm of our species and of the Earth. As Emerson reminded us, "In the awareness that God is acting through us, we find determination, courage, and strength."[12]

The leaders of this global revolution will be people of quiet presence, the calm ones at the center of great corporate and global enterprise, the eyes

of the storms. Robert Waterman noted that "most of the renewing companies had a calm at the center."[13] The leader in this new world will be such a
quiet presence.

Kevin W. Kelley, in his wonderful book *The Home Planet,* said, "Space
offers us a chance to see our world with new eyes, a perspective that may
have great significance for the planet for all of the future."[14] Seeing with eyes
of wholeness, the astronauts have become our generation's prophets and
mystics. As astronaut Edgar Mitchell observed, "The peaks were the recognition that it is a harmonious, purposeful, creating universe; the valleys
came in recognizing that humanity wasn't behaving in accordance with that
knowledge."[15] Yet the vision of Earth from space was inspiring and wonderfully hopeful. As Muhammed Ahmad Faris of Syria noted, "From space I saw
Earth—indescribably beautiful with the scars of national boundaries gone."[16]
And there was cause for even greater hope: "My mental boundaries expanded when I viewed Earth against a black and uninviting vacuum, yet my
country's rich traditions had conditioned me to look beyond manmade
boundaries and prejudices. One does not have to undertake a space flight to
come by this feeling."[17] Rakesh Sharma, astronaut from India, offered comfort regarding the possibility of transformation in global consciousness, of
seeing with eyes of wholeness, for those of us who have not yet circumnavi-
gated our home planet.

Authentic Living Relationships

*Interrelatedness has been experientially grasped in myriad cultural contexts
and variously expressed as the core perception of the wisdom traditions. Yet
the forces of modernity continually deny and degrade it. Human society
needs grounding in the unitive dimension of our existence.[18]*

—Charlene Spretnak

The future of our planet and its life forms depends on increasing the level of
authentic relationship among human beings. The concept of relationship offers great promise in restructuring our consciousness regarding interconnectedness. In redefining relationship as a *living* reality, instead of a coming together of two selves, a new paradigm is created that serves our emerging
collective consciousness. The Stone Center model of human relationships,
developed by faculty at the Harvard Medical School and the Stone Center,
Wellesley College, is proving to be a powerful tool for breaking down the old
models of male-female relationships. The context of relationship offers new
hope for responding to "the primary motivation for all humans . . . a desire
for connection."[19]

People need each other to live more abundant lives. Integrity comes from sublimating our egos and giving ourselves entirely to life. Physicist Fritjof Capra noted in his recent book, *The Web of Life:*

> Our self, or ego, does not have any independent existence but is a result of our internal structural coupling. . . . To overcome our Cartesian anxiety, we need to think systemically, shifting our conceptual focus from objects to relationships. Only then can we realize that identity, individuality, and autonomy do not imply separateness and independence. . . . To regain our full humanity, we have to regain our experience of connectedness with the entire web of life.[20]

The Particle-Wave Metaphor

One of the great metaphors of our time is the particle-wave of quantum physics. The basic building blocks of the physical world, it was discovered, behave in some situations like waves and in other situations like particles. As Robert Gilman questioned, "Might we humans also, in some mysterious way, have both particle-like individuality and wave-like shared beingness and interconnectedness?" Noting that we are interconnected in profound ways, Gilman explained the nature of the human crisis:

> Philosophically, interconnectedness stands in opposition to separateness—the idea that we are each isolated, sovereign, and self-contained. Since most of the distinctive institutions of western civilization—materialistic science, market economics, our legal system, the Bill of Rights—are based on the assumption that the world is composed of discrete units, the idea of interconnectedness rattles the foundations of our whole society.[21]

The essential nature of matter, we are taught by the particle-wave metaphor, lies in its interconnections; a web of relationships is the essence of all living things. This web of life is fundamentally interdependent and spiritual in character. As Fritjof Capra emphasized:

> Ultimately, deep ecological awareness is spiritual or religious awareness. When the concept of the human spirit is understood as the mode of consciousness in which the individual feels a sense of belonging, of connectedness, to the cosmos as a whole, it becomes clear that ecological awareness is spiritual in its deepest sense.[22]

Consciousness of the unity of all life lies at the heart of being. Yet we live in a reality that is fragmented and thus lose the energy of the whole. Our language forms a prison that limits our thinking to a segmented reality—not one that is infinite and whole.

Beyond Interdependence to Wholeness

The issue is integrity. We are disjointed from our spiritual roots. When the love of the whole, the love of God, replaces our idolatry of self, we live in integrity. The change must begin within each of us. We must be the change we wish to see in the world. The global revolution must begin within the hearts and minds of each of us; and the global shift of consciousness is at hand. As David Bohm revealed:

> *If you reach deeply into yourself, you are reaching into the very essence of mankind. When you do this, you will be led into the generating depth of consciousness that is common to the whole of mankind and that has the whole of mankind enfolded in it. The individual's ability to be sensitive to that becomes the key to the change of mankind. We are all connected. If this could be taught, and if people could understand it, we would have a different consciousness.*[23]

The revolution needed is one of integrity, being true to one's inner being, to the Being of which we are all part. We are the doors through which the creative force, the universal consciousness, is manifested on the planet. As William Blake proclaimed, "If the doors of perception were cleansed, everything would appear to man as it is, infinite."[24]

In *The Seven Habits of Highly Effective People,* Stephen Covey described the growth in people from dependence to independence, and finally, to interdependence.[25] David Bohm suggested that the step highly effective people must now make takes them from interdependence to wholeness.[26] The questions that bring us to this transcendence are basic: What are we? Individuals or people united on a common or holy ground? What is the difference implied in component and wave? Is our essence, that which we have been resisting, the wave?

David Bohm noted: "In the West, society has mainly emphasized the development of science and technology (dependent on measure) while in the East, the main emphasis has gone to religion and philosophy (which are directed ultimately toward the immeasurable). If one considers the question carefully, one can see that in a certain sense the East was right to see the immeasurable as the primary reality."[27]

To move beyond interdependence to wholeness, people must be brought to understand that they create the world they see. We are not victims of circumstances, but the predominant creative forces in our own lives. The journey to wholeness begins with a profound knowledge of being whole oneself. The metanoia from being a reactionary individual to an all-powerful person changes "the path of least resistance,"[28] by changing the structure of human perception.

In *The Path of Least Resistance,* Robert Fritz identified three insights that lead to change in human affairs: "You go through life taking the path of least resistance. . . . The underlying structure of your life determines the path of least resistance. . . . You can change the fundamental underlying structures of your life."[29] Changing the underlying structure of our perceptions to seeing with eyes of wholeness our fundamental interconnections with each other and with all of life is at the heart of the global transformation. Liberation from the ego illusion, at the heart of the world's major religions and the modern sciences of biology and physics, is also at the heart of the transformation. The new leadership must move from the transformational emphasis of James MacGregor Burns[30] to the transcendent emphasis of Robert K. Greenleaf.[31]

According to Robert Greenleaf, "Spirit is the driving force behind the motive to serve."[32] In fact, service to others may be the driving mechanism to bring on the global transformation on a personal level. The day of the servant-leader may be upon us. Connection with one's core and with that of others is the key. Our self is not separate, in fact, but rather a field within larger fields.

Service to others offers the mechanism to move our attention outside of ourselves. And with the servant-leader come the new principles that leave a leader of an organization humble and servant first.

Quiet Presence

I was born on February 6, 1946, in the British mandate of Palestine. My grandfather on my father's side, a logger and judge and a man I never met, was killed in the death camp of Auschwitz. My grandfather on my mother's side was a great servant-leader—a man who refused elective office but served his community in many ways with joy and spirit. Like Robert K. Greenleaf, he was a quiet presence, a calm in the eye of great social, political, economic storms; like Greenleaf, he practiced meditation and prayer, connecting to the Spirit from which he received great nurture and guidance, and a deep sense of inner peace; like Leo in Hesse's *Journey to the East,* he modeled leadership by being a joyful servant of all.

When I was six years old, my father decided to move his family to the United States. I was angry and bitter about being taken away from my homeland and my grandfather, whom I loved above all people. Outside of a house that he had loaned to my parents on the Mediterranean coast, I had an enlightening experience in which I deeply felt that I was part of the whole and in which my anger and bitterness dissipated, enabling me to say farewell to my grandfather in a loving way. I had touched the timeless awareness, the "implicate order" of which David Bohm spoke, a place of peace and power, harmony and joy, a place of unconditional love. I had also touched my dharma or truth directly, knowing then that my life mission was to bring people together to help heal themselves and, thereby, the planet.

Now, as an adult and professor of leadership at Seattle University, I long to do all that I can to help manifest that dream of a world reborn. The human heart yearns for peace: inner peace, communal peace, and world peace. I believe that our world needs global dialogues, symposia on issues that require international cooperation, and conferences and/or workshops that promote the psychotechnologies that will encourage movement toward a world reborn. I have joined with several colleagues to create a Pacific Northwest Postdoctoral Institute for global dialogue, leadership development, and professional renewal to address these needs. Working together, we *can* renew the earth.

Service Above Self

When my son, James, was in kindergarten, I was asked to coach his soccer team. Not knowing much about the game, I invited Mike Xu, a doctoral advisee from mainland China and a friend, to co-coach the team with me. Mike agreed to serve if he were given the role of senior coach, a condition to which I readily agreed. After Adam Arterbury scored our team's first goal with a kick of over 20 yards, Mike pulled Adam out of the game and asked him to name the two members of his team who were closer to the goal than he was. Adam was benched for much of the game until he was able to remember the names of those players. It was in that first game that the principle of assist became embedded in the minds and hearts of these young children. Over the next several years, the teams coached by the mantra of "an assist is as good as a goal" could not be stopped; they were unbeatable!

During the past decade, I have often wondered how our world would be different if the principle of assisting or serving others was viewed equally with that of scoring or gaining for one's own. Service above self could lead to the changes that would bring about global renewal. And the changes would begin with quiet presence, a quality of being found within each of us. Speaking of renewal, Kate Steichen noted:

> Renewal most naturally occurs in late fall and winter when the leaves are off the trees and life appears still. Renewal is the time to remember our true nature. How do we do that? We remember who we are by becoming silent witnesses, by being instead of acting. Renewal is the time to be a human be-ing. . . . The very act of renewal is a surrender of doing.[33]

Quiet presence is an act of renewal.

God-Centered Leadership and Meditation

John Ruysbroeck, the great medieval mystic of Flanders, said, "You are as holy as you will to be."[34] We are each one part of the other, each one part of the whole, to the degree that we will to be . . . and as we strive to Be, whether invoked or not, God is present.

In his recent book, *Leading Minds: An Anatomy of Leadership,* Howard Gardner celebrated the lives of Mahatma Gandhi and Jean Monnet as leaders whose lives would serve as models for a new world leadership, one extending beyond the boundaries of nation-states. In the words of Howard Gardner, "for both Monnet and Gandhi, in the deepest sense, their methods were their message."[35] They become conscious of deep, universal truths regarding global cooperation and the nature of being, and they repeated these truths quietly and persistently to all who would listen until these truths were widely accepted. They led by example, by the example of their quiet presence.

> The secret of meditation is stillness, to allow the focusing of mental and spiritual energy. . . . Through meditation, the ego which creates the illusion of separation is subdued, the meditator becomes one with the object of his meditation—sometimes just for an instant, ultimately for eternity.[36]

Robert K. Greenleaf was a lifelong meditator:

> I prefer to meditate, I have come to view my meditating as serving. Somehow the quiet and peace of anyone's meditation communicates and enriches the culture. I feel the fruits of other people's meditation.[37]

"Listening for signals as I was, all the time—and still am," led Robert Greenleaf to hear the Spirit's call for him throughout his life. "Meditation will serve, at all stages of life," he emphasized. Regarding this quiet presence, he observed, "There are many signals all of the time that will cue one to the ideas that will make life more rewarding at all stages. But one is likely to hear those signals only if one is alert to signals, all the time."[38]

In old age, Robert Greenleaf came to accept that he could "best serve by being." That leadership of being, that quiet presence, that living in the present moment is greatly needed in our rapidly changing world. The quiet presence, a God-centered being, balanced and true, centered in values of integrity and compassion, will be the model for the next millennium.

Robert Greenleaf proposed the creation of circles of friends, which he called Seekers Anonymous, people who would participate in "healing, in the sense of being made whole." Seekers Anonymous, he said, in a prophetic passage, would seek to serve.

> Those who see themselves as part of Seekers Anonymous will learn to listen attentively and respond to that faint flutter of wings, that gentle

stirring of life and hope. By their gentle and sustained listening, they will make the new prophet who will help them find that wholeness that is only achieved by serving. And out of that wholeness will come the singleness of aim and the capacity to bear suffering that a confrontation with the basic malaise of our time, the failure of our many institutions to serve, may demand.[39]

Deepak Chopra, who studied timeless awareness, suggested that "human awareness is capable of touching dharma directly, of latching onto it and thus guiding its own evolution."[40] Francisco Varela, as cited in Joseph Jaworski's book, *Synchronicity, the Inner Path of Leadership*, stated:

> *When we are in touch with our "open nature," our emptiness, we exert an enormous attraction to other human beings. There is great magnetism in that state of being which has been called by Tungpa "authentic presence." . . . And if others are in that same space or entering it, they resonate with us and immediately doors are open to us. It is not strange or mystical, it is part of the natural order. . . . All we have to do is to see the oneness that we are.[41]*

Joe Jaworski's life story models the generative leadership he teaches. His book on synchronicity is essential reading for those wishing to live the new way of being, for those wishing to understand "the journey toward wholeness—thinking whole and being whole."[42] The remarkable work of Sperry Andrews and the Human Connection Project in developing the psychotechnologies to move people into collective and global consciousness is worthy of wide recognition and attention.[43] So is the work of Paul Hawken at Findhorn studying "the actual palpable experience of one's own consciousness merging with a group consciousness" among a community of people experiencing "the consciousness of God."[44] So too are the amazing results of Joe Jaworski's efforts with extending Peter Senge's work on dialogue and David Bohm's understandings of the implicate order to global leadership development and decision scenarios.[45]

The Holy Ground of Leadership

By being fully present, being open in mind and body and heart, listening unconditionally, one can model the new leadership that places service above self. As Robert Greenleaf noted, "A qualification for leadership is that one can tolerate a sustained wide span of awareness so that he better 'sees it as it is.' "[46] Authentic listening, focused attention, is at the heart of the essential transformation.

Diana L. Eck observed:

> Attention is key to the disciplines of the spirit. Attention can turn any activity to prayer. . . . It is intention, paying attention, that transforms the ordinary moment.[47]

Duane Elgin declared that "the quality of our shared attention is the most precious resource that we possess as a human family and is basic to our evolution as a species."[48] Collective attention, as it is being studied and implemented by people like Sperry Andrews, Paul Hawken, and Joe Jaworski, holds the key to seeing with eyes of wholeness as a global people. Their work, and the work of many others like them, will propel our species to the place of peace envisioned by our great prophets and spiritual teachers. The holy ground of leadership is our own quiet presence.

> When you can *actually* see "what is," without trying to change it, suppress it, go beyond it or escape from it, then you will see that "what is" undergoes a tremendous change. That is, when the mind is completely silent in observation, then there is radical change.[49]

Change, whether for us individually or for us collectively, does not have to be slow. Authentic acceptance can lead to rapid change. And we can be a quiet presence for one another in profound ways, speeding our interconnected transformation. Perhaps, W. B. Yeats said it best:

> We can make our minds
> so like still water
> that beings gather about us
> that they may see, it may be,
> their own images,
> and so live for a moment
> with a clearer,
> perhaps even with a fiercer, life
> because of our quiet.[50]

The holy ground of leadership is our own quiet presence.[51]

11

Quaker Foundations for Greenleaf's Servant-Leadership and "Friendly Disentangling" Method

Richard P. Nielsen

Richard P. Nielsen is a professor in the Department of Organization Studies, Wallace E. Carroll School of Management, Boston College. He works in the areas of ethics, leadership, learning, and change methodologies. He has worked and traveled widely in Europe, Asia, and Latin America.

This is a groundbreaking essay on two little-known aspects of Robert Greenleaf's work—the Quaker roots of servant-leadership and Robert Greenleaf's successful efforts at increasing by tenfold the number of African-American managers at AT&T in the 1950s and 1960s. Nielsen demonstrates that servant-leadership has numerous roots, including the "Friendly" roots of Quakerism.

> *Walk cheerfully over the earth answering that of Go(o)d in everyone.*
> —Old Quaker Motto

> *To be gentle and humble is not the same thing as being weak and easygoing.*
> —Angelo Giuseppe Roncalli

Robert Greenleaf was a member of the Religious Society of Friends (Quakers). His religion and corresponding spiritual philosophy for acting and learning with others greatly influenced his servant-leadership approach and, in particular, his method of "friendly disentangling." This essay illustrates and explains how the method is both widely applicable and built upon Quaker foundations for acting and learning with others.[1]

This article proceeds as follows. First, Greenleaf's method of friendly disentangling is illustrated in two case examples of his practice at AT&T. Second, two case examples of how the Quaker leader John Woolman (eighteenth century), who used the method and who Greenleaf explicitly credits as the model for much of his own work, are illustrated and explained. Third, the method is linked to Quaker principles of acting and learning with others. The four key Quaker principles discussed in relation to the cases are (1) "that of Go(o)d in everyone," in our "prior we" relationship, (2) tradition system entanglements as causes of problems rather than solely individual responsibility, (3) friendly and cheerful affect, and (4) continuing experimental action-learning. Finally, strengths and limitations of the method are discussed.

Robert Greenleaf defined his concept of servant-leadership as follows:

> The servant-leader is servant first. . . . It begins with the natural feeling that one wants to serve, to serve first. Then conscious choice brings one to aspire to lead. . . . The difference manifests itself in the care taken by the servant—first to make sure that other people's highest priority needs are being served. The best test, and difficult to administer, is: do those served grow as persons; do they, while being served, become healthier, wiser, freer, more autonomous, more likely themselves to become servants? And, what is the effect on the least privileged in society; will they benefit, or at least not be further deprived?[2]

How does one do this? One method Greenleaf used was friendly disentangling, which was based on the life and work of the Quaker servant-leader, John Woolman.[3] John Woolman was a Philadelphia area cloth merchant and ethics activist in the colonial era.[4] He developed and used friendly, disentangling dialogue with merchants and farmers to address the issues of slavery, peacemaking with Indians and the British, farmer-banker relations, trading practices with Indians, and child labor.

Woolman's method was explicitly used and taught by Robert Greenleaf while he was a manager, management training director, and corporate vice president at AT&T. The method has four key parts:

1. Frame to oneself a "we" fellowship relationship with others and look for the source of current problematic behavior within the biases of an embedded tradition rather than solely in the behaviors and governing values of individuals.
2. Approach those involved in a friendly manner.
3. Ask for help in disentangling a problematic behavior from potential biases within "our" embedded tradition system.
4. Work with those who are agreeable to experiment with alternative behaviors and/or governing values that do not rest on the troublesome biases of the tradition system.

The Woolman method can also be considered a type of "triple-loop action-learning" that holds open for question (1) the appropriateness of behaviors, (2) the governing values that drive behaviors, and (3) the embedded tradition systems where the governing values are nested.[5] That is, in triple-loop action-learning (friendly disentangling is a type of triple-loop action-learning) the social tradition is both criticized and treated as a partner in action-learnig. The tradition system is respected but also considered to have potential negative biases that can be reformed and transformed, just as individuals and their governing values and behaviors can be reformed and transformed.

The first two case examples in this essay describe how Robert Greenleaf explicitly used the Woolman method to help AT&T greatly increase its employment of women and black managers. The third and fourth examples show how John Woolman, the Quaker servant-leader, developed and used the method to end slavery in colonial Pennsylvania and resolve dysfunctional lose-lose disputes between farmers and lenders.

Robert Greenleaf and Equal Employment Opportunity for Women at AT&T

Robert Greenleaf, a graduate of Carleton College, began work at AT&T as a laborer's assistant in a line crew in 1929. In 1964 he retired, after having served as corporate human resources vice president and director of management development and research. Among the management issues he was concerned with was equal opportunity for women employees. He explicitly used Woolman's method and taught this method within AT&T. At the time, most operations managers did not hire women. He used the method of friendly disentangling in his approach to the issue of blue-collar hiring discrimination against women.[6]

1. *Frame to oneself a "we" fellowship relationship with others and look for the source of current problematic behavior within the biases of an embedded tradition system rather than solely in the behaviors and governing values of individuals.* When dealing with sensitive and controversial issues it is not uncommon to become dysfunctionally emotional, overly defensive, and unnecessarily adversarial. Uncomfortable and anxious situations can elicit overly aggressive behaviors, which Greenleaf prepared himself against. In preparation for his meeting with the operations managers, he reminded himself that he had worked with most of the operations managers for many years and they were for the most part basically good people. He reminded himself that they were on the same team, the same side, and had overcome difficulties together in the past. In addition, Greenleaf framed the issue such that the source of the problem concerning

blue-collar employment discrimination against women might lie in the embedded tradition system of AT&T and not solely in prejudicial values and behaviors of individual operations managers. Some system level biases might be entangled with the individual behaviors.

This framing to oneself is not as strange as it may appear. For example, in a perhaps reverse type of preparative framing to oneself, coaches and athletes before competitive games frequently "psych" themselves up by focusing on the "opposition," the "enemy," and the intense, competitive engagement to come. Some coaches even quote negative things that "they," the opposition coaches and players, are reputed to have said about "us."

2. *Approach those involved in a friendly manner.* Greenleaf's first motion toward each of the operations mangers was friendly and respectful, not adversarial or critical. He reviewed with the managers their common experiences at AT&T, people they knew and liked in common, times when they had worked well together in the past, and their common concerns.

3. *Ask for help in disentangling a problematic behavior from potential biases within "our" embedded tradition system.* He asked the operations managers for help in understanding potential system level entanglements. In his conversations with some of these operations managers it was revealed that a reason why some of them did not hire women was because they did not think women were strong enough to do the heavy lifting that the job required. Greenleaf further inquired about what it was that had to be lifted and carried. He found that the heaviest objects that had to be lifted regularly were 50-pound rolls of telephone wires. It also appeared true that regular lifting of these 50-pound rolls of wire would be too much for most women.

4. *Work with those who are agreeable to experiment with alternative behaviors and/or governing values that do not rest on the troublesome biases of the tradition system.* In the conversations, Greenleaf inquired about ideas for potential experiments that might address the women, heavy lifting, nonhiring entanglement. One of the operations managers suggested an experimental packaging of the wires in 25-pound rolls instead of 50. The experiment was tried. It was found that women could regularly lift 25-pound rolls. It was also found that most of the men also preferred the 25-pound rolls instead of the 50-pound rolls. Greenleaf did not press. He explained his perception of entanglements and the disentangled experimental solution. The packaging was changed. More women were hired. Few women were not hired because of the heavy lifting–physical differences issue. Generally, the women hired performed very well and helped lead to the hiring of many more women.

Robert Greenleaf and Black Management Development at AT&T

In addition to the discrimination-against-women issue at AT&T, there was also the issue of equal opportunity for black people. Robert Greenleaf was concerned with the development of black managers and used the method of friendly disentangling to address this concern.[7] When Greenleaf began work at AT&T there were very few black managers, with the exception of a few telephone operator supervisors. In significant part through his efforts, between 1955 and 1964, before the 1968 Civil Rights Act, AT&T increased the total of black managers from about .5 to about 4.5 percent of total managerial employment.

1. *Frame to oneself a "we" fellowship relationship with others, and look for the source of the current problematic behavior within "our" shared tradition system rather than solely in the characters or idiosyncratic views of individuals.* Greenleaf reminded himself that he had worked well, for his entire adult working life, with many of the managers who were not hiring blacks for managerial positions. He reminded himself that "we" have shared and overcome many difficulties, and most of us very much like being "phonemen" and being part of the AT&T system and tradition. In the potential heat of dealing with this sensitive issue, he did not want to forget that most of the managers he knew at AT&T were basically good people and that he was much like them. An important part of why blacks were not being hired for managerial positions was that there was an "institutional bias" within the AT&T tradition system that silently and perhaps subconsciously kept people from considering blacks for managerial positions. Many of the managers he knew had entered AT&T when its tradition was already established. While they might be maintaining a biased tradition, they did not create it. He reminded himself that such tradition-system biases might be at least as important as individual and group prejudices against hiring blacks for managerial positions. The issue was too important to ignore or avoid. He wanted to prepare himself simultaneously to confront an important issue critically and realistically at the tradition-system level in all its complexity, and to approach people he cared about in a cooperative rather than adversarial manner.

2. *Approach those involved in a friendly manner and suggest that there may be some problems in our shared tradition system.* Greenleaf personally visited many managers, and he believes that he personally spoke to most managers at one time or another in his management development programs. Before raising the issue of black management development, he would explicitly express a friendly attitude, respect, and appreciation toward the managers. Whenever he could,

he would review past successful relationships with them. He would explicitly mention the many years he and they had worked well together at AT&T. He would then frame the subject he would like to discuss as consideration of potential biases in "our" system with respect to the issue of black management development. He suggested that such biases might be at least as relevant and important as potential individual or group differences with respect to the issue.

3. *Request help in disentangling a specific behavior from a troublesome assumption within the tradition system.* Greenleaf asked managers individually and in groups for their help in understanding how the issue of black management development might be entangled with potential biases in "our" tradition system. Many of the managers had been framing the issue in terms of the "unsuitability" of blacks for management roles; Greenleaf challenged this framing. Several observations emerged from the discussions. Some managers observed that since they didn't see any black managers at AT&T, they just didn't think of blacks as candidates for managerial positions. That is, the informal tradition of not having black managers led them to not consider the possibility. Other managers observed that it appeared that not many blacks had the training or experience required for managerial consideration and thought part of the reason for this was that since blacks were not expected to become managers, they were not encouraged to complete such training or gain such experience. Several other managers observed that most blacks did not apply for managerial training or positions and thought this might be related to a fatalistic expectation. That is, there was little point in applying for managerial training or positions because the implicit tradition was not to hire many black managers.

4. *Work with those who are agreeable to experiment with alternative behaviors that do not rest on the troublesome biases of the tradition system.* Greenleaf repeatedly asked managers individually and in groups for consensus-building help in developing and interpreting experiments in disentangling reform. One experiment involved recruiting blacks for management training programs. Another experiment involved offering black technical specialists a broader range of experiences that would better prepare them for managerial positions. For the most part, blacks did well in the management training classes and exercises, and in the rotating work assignments that led to managerial positions. There were no top management orders to increase black hiring for managerial positions, no quotas, goals, or timetables, and no management performance reviews tied to black management development. Nonetheless, over a 10-year period black employment in management grew from about .5 to about 4.5 percent. Apparently Greenleaf's use of the Woolman method was at least somewhat effective.

Perhaps ironically and unnecessarily, after Greenleaf retired, in the period between 1973 and 1979, AT&T was pressured through the rate-setting powers of the FCC to accept a consent decree with the EEOC whereby affirmative action quotas were agreed upon. At the end of a very acrimonious internal and external seven-year struggle, in 1979 AT&T had increased its employment of black managers to about 9 percent.[8] Although several other factors influenced black managerial employment, in both the dialogic Greenleaf period and in the adversarial consent decree period, the increase in black managerial employment levels was approximately 4.5 percentage points.

John Woolman, Slave Freedom, and Productivity in Colonial Pennsylvania

John Woolman developed and used his four-step method to address several ethics concerns in a 30-year period during the mid–eighteenth century.[9] He used the method in conversations with individuals and small groups. Woolman was a member of the Society of Friends (Quakers), which was at the time the dominant economic and political group in Pennsylvania. Within the Society of Friends he is considered the primary leader in eliminating slavery from the Society and, derivatively, from Pennsylvania.[10] Slavery was peacefully, gradually, and voluntarily eliminated from the Society of Friends in the late eighteenth century; shortly thereafter it became illegal in Pennsylvania. By 1800, of the states south of New England, only Pennsylvania had outlawed slavery. According to Nash and Soderland's *Freedom by Degrees: Emancipation in Pennsylvania and Its Aftermath*, Quaker influence was primarily responsible for this action.[11]

According to Greenleaf, "Some assume great institutional burdens, others quietly deal with one person at a time. Such a man was John Woolman, an American Quaker, who lived through the middle years of the eighteenth century. He is known to the world of scholarship for his journal, a literary classic. But in the area of our interest, leadership, he is the man who almost singlehandedly rid the Society of Friends (Quakers) of slaves."[12] Woolman devoted 30 years to this issue. Many Quakers were wealthy, conservative merchants and farmers who owned slaves; by 1770 no Quakers owned slaves. The Society of Friends was the first religious group in the United States to formally denounce and forbid slavery among its members. Woolman addressed the slavery issue with farmers and lenders as follows:

1. Before meeting with the slaveowner farmers and merchants, he framed to himself a "we" fellowship relationship with them and reminded himself that there might be important tradition system biases causing problems and conflicts, and that these biases could be at least as important as individual differences. He recorded his

preparatory thoughts and feelings in his journal: "From small beginnings in errors, great buildings, by degrees, are raised; and from
one age to another, are more and more strengthened by the general
concurrence of the people: and as men obtain reputation . . . their
virtues are mentioned as arguments in favour of general error: and
those of less note, to justify themselves, say, such and such good
men did the like."[13]

Woolman believed that good people could contribute to unethical behavior in part because they were entangled in what he
called "biases" and "oppressive customs." He observed, "The
prospect of a road lying open to the same degeneracy, in some parts
of this new settled land of America, in respect to our conduct toward the negroes, hath deeply bowed my mind in this journey. . . .
Deep-rooted customs, though wrong, are not easily altered."[14] He
was as concerned about the people doing the problematic behavior
as about the direct victims. He explained, "We feel a Tenderness in
our Hearts toward our Fellow Creatures [the slave owners and
traders] entangled in oppressive Customs."[15]

2. In a friendly and not a coolly analytic, positional, or adversarial manner, Woolman approached the farmers and directed the conversation in terms of potential negative bias entanglements in "our" tradition system. In addressing the slavery issue with a group of
farmers who were opening up new farmland, Woolman spoke with
them as follows: "Dear friends . . . as you are improving a wilderness, and may be numbered amongst the first planters in one part of
a province, I beseech you . . . to wisely consider the force of your
examples, and think how much your successors may be thereby affected: it is a help in a country, yea, and a great favour and a blessing, when customs first settled are agreeable to sound wisdom: so
when they are otherwise, the effect of them is grievous; and children
feel themselves encompassed with difficulties prepared for them by
their predecessors."[16]

3. Woolman asked slave owners for their help in disentangling the
slavery-related problems from negative biases in "our" tradition system. The slave owners, from their positions of authority and perceived
economic self-interest, had been framing the ethics issue in terms of
a laziness problem among the slaves. They spoke of "the untoward
slothful disposition of the negroes," and said, "one of our [free
white labourers] would do as much in a day as two of their slaves."
Woolman challenged this framing through a criticism of the tradition system within which this ethical framing was nested. Emerging
from the discussions were the observations that "free men, whose
minds were properly on their business, found a satisfaction in improving, cultivating, and providing for their families; but negroes,
labouring to support others who claim them as their property, and

expecting nothing but slavery during life, had not the like induce-
ment to be industrious."[17]

4. Woolman asked for consensus-building help in developing and interpreting an experiment in disentangling reform. A decision
   emerged from the discussions to try an experiment where a few
   slaves would be freed and offered sharecropping opportunities. The
   productivity of these freed farmers was higher than that of the
   slaves. Within 20 years of this experiment (1790), many farmers
   adopted this ethical and political-economic reform. There followed
   formal Society of Friends Minutes, and later state laws, against the
   practice of holding and trading slaves, and by 1800 slavery was eliminated in Pennsylvania.[18]

Most of the farmers and merchants Woolman approached were wealth-
ier and more powerful than he. However, since they were all members of the
Society of Friends, it would have been considered inappropriate for them to
refuse to talk with him. As Greenleaf's position as a human resources manager gave him access to line managers to discuss black management development, Woolman's position as a member of the Society of Friends and, in his
later years, a "weighty" and well-known member, gave him access to the
wealthy and powerful Quaker farmers and merchants. Although most of the
farmers and merchants responded favorably and gradually to Woolman's efforts, not all of them did. Some even refused to discuss the issue with him.
This problem is discussed later in the section on the strengths and limitations
of the Woolman method.

Woolman and Dysfunctional Farmer-Lender Relations in Colonial Pennsylvania

As a small cloth and clothes retailer, John Woolman and other merchants
came in contact with many small farmers. Many of these small farmers had to
borrow money to carry them through the harvest season. The interest rates
were often higher than the profits from farming. This resulted in several
bankruptcies. Woolman did not approach the issue in a "Merchant of
Venice" adversarial manner.

1. Before meeting with the merchant lenders, he framed to himself a
   "we" fellowship relationship with them and reminded himself that
   there might be important tradition system biases causing problems
   and conflicts, and that these biases could be at least as important as
   individual differences.
2. In a friendly and not a coolly analytic, positional, or adversarial manner. Woolman reviewed with the lenders their commonalities of experience and concern for sound business practices.

3. Woolman asked the merchant lenders for their help in disentangling the high interest–farm bankruptcy problem from negative biases in "our" tradition system. He asked the lenders for help in understanding entanglements. Out of the conversations it became clear that part of the reason for the high interest rates was the bankruptcies. Lenders had to charge high interest because some farmers would not be able to pay back loans. Part of the reason for the farmers not being able to pay back their loans was the high interest rates. High individual lender risks were entangled with high interest rates.

4. Woolman asked for consensus-building help in developing and interpreting an experiment in disentangling reform. Woolman addressed one lender as follows: "I am now thinking of that . . . exhortation, Love as Brethren and propose to thee my Neighbor whether a way may not be opened for thee and thy family to live comfortably on a lower interest, which if once right attained, would I believe work in favor of us. . . ."[19] Emerging from the dialogues came an idea for experimenting with a system where if more people shared the risks with lenders, then interest rates could be lower. As an experiment, a lender greatly reduced interest charges and a Monthly Meeting (a community similar to a parish, at that time normally between 50 to 200 families) informally guaranteed repayment of loans made by Meeting members. The experiment worked. Woolman did not press but clearly and gently explained his perception of the success of the experiment and his perception of the entanglements and potential disentangled solution. The experiment became a common practice in New Jersey and Pennsylvania. Monthly Meetings and the substantially larger Quarterly and Yearly Meetings (thousands of families, similar to a diocese) would informally guarantee repayment of loans. With such risk sharing, loans could more easily be obtained and interest rates could be substantially less. Many such experiments were tried. For the most part, they succeeded and became something of an informal norm among many eighteenth-century Pennsylvania and New Jersey farmers, merchants, and lenders.

Quaker Principles for Acting and Learning with Others

1. Go(o)d in Everyone in Our "Prior We"

Perhaps the most important principle of Quakerism was simply stated by one of its founders, George Fox, "Walk cheerfully over the earth answering that of Go(o)d in everyone." Woolman assumed that there was some good in all of us, in the slave owners, the slaves, the slavetraders, the small farmers who were not repaying their loans, and the merchant lenders. Similarly, Greenleaf assumed that there was some good in the managers who were not hiring and promoting women and minorities as well as good in the women and minorities.

This Go(o)d in everyone serves as the foundation for action and learning. Greenleaf and Woolman were able to address and work with the good in a very wide variety of people. In terms of action, there is an assumption of a commonality of the good to address. That is, the cup is part full rather than part empty. Woolman and Greenleaf directed their actions to join with and build on what was good in everyone. They would look for and inquire about the good motivations and behaviors of people. This is not to suggest that the not so good does not also exist. It is more an issue of where we start from. Do we start from what we have in common that is good, or do we start from what is not so good and from how we differ?

2. Tradition System Entanglements as Causes of Problems

Another foundational belief of Quakerism, which has some commonality with postmodern perspective, is that individuals are in very important ways social constructions of the tradition systems within which they are born and socialized. That is, individual behaviors and values are greatly influenced by the tradition systems within which they are born and socialized. Further, there can be contradictions and dysfunctionalities among entangled system tradition components and that of Go(o)d in everyone.

As mentioned earlier, Woolman found and explained that "we feel a Tenderness in our Hearts toward our Fellow Creatures (the slave owners and traders) entangled in oppressive Customs."[20] Woolman explained in his journal that what he experienced and learned in conversations with slave owners and their children was that as children and neighbors of other slaveholders, they accepted slavery in significant part because their love and respect for their parents and community had become "entangled" with "oppressive customs," and implicit and explicit "teachings" that accepted slavery. Their entanglement with oppressive customs and their love for parents and community left "less room for that which is good to work upon them." Their minds and spirits did not easily lend themselves to the "general Movings of uncreated Purity." Protest, verbal attack, and criticism of them, their parents, and their community further hardened and closed the mind and spirit.

Similarly, Greenleaf found that the AT&T managers he dealt with were basically good people. When they came to work for AT&T, the implicit policies had already been established of not hiring women and minorities in certain areas. These implicit tradition system biases were entangled with basically good managers and managerial values concerning loyalty to the organization. They liked their identity as "phonemen." They wanted to cooperate and work hard for the good of their organizational community. Greenleaf helped them disentangle their, for the most part, good loyalties and productive behaviors from the biases in the tradition system of the organization and larger society.

This is a common problem in what might be called corrupt sectors. Individuals know that the public life in these sectors is corrupt. To survive and prosper, individuals join together on the basis of family, friends, ethnic group, and so on to help each other. "Ethnos" is much more important than "polis" and citizenship behavior. Out of entanglements between corrupt sectors and loyalty and cooperation with one's own group, there is systematic discrimination against and corrupt behavior against people not in one's own group.

3. Friendly and Cheerful

For both ethical and effectiveness reasons, Greenleaf and Woolman acted in a friendly and cheerful manner with those they were in actual and potential conflict with. For ethical reasons they were friendly because they believed it was important to respect and care for not just those one agreed with but also "those who were entangled in oppressive customs." It was important to respect and care for those one disagreed with and in opposition to because there was "that of Go(o)d in everyone."

This is not to deny that terrible sufferings and injustices exist. For example, Woolman felt deeply with respect to the terrible consequences of slavery that "Many Cries are uttered by Widows and Fatherless Children . . . Many Cheeks are wet with Tears, and Faces sad with unutterable Grief . . . Cruel Tyranny is encouraged . . . The hands of Robbers are strengthened, and Thousands reduced to the most abject Slavery . . . What pious Man could be a Witness to these Things, and see a Trade carried on in this Manner, without being deeply affected with Sorrow." Nonetheless, he also wrote that "we feel a Tenderness in our Hearts toward our Fellow Creatures [the slave owners and traders] entangled in oppressive Customs."[21]

Friendly and cheerful can also be an effective strength of the method. There is the old saying that when you laugh, the whole world laughs with you, but when you cry or are angry, you are more alone. There is also some support for this notion within the leadership effectiveness literature. For example, James Kouzes and Barry Posner have observed that positive affect and not solely intelligent and cognitively sound plans and policies can be very important for effective leadership.[22] Friendly and optimistic affect can make leaders more effective by helping in "inspiring a shared vision" and "encouraging the heart." Similarly, Howard Gardner has observed in his study of leaders and leadership behavior that friendly inclusiveness with increasingly wider circles of inclusiveness can be a very important characteristic of leadership development.[23]

4. Continuing, Experimental Action-Learning

George Fox, one of the founders of Quakerism, begins his journal with the assertion that "This I knew experimentally."[24] Action and learning are not alternatives, nor are they totally sequential. There are nuances of epistimological emphasis. There are nuances and emphases between whether action precedes learning or learning precedes action. For Fox, Woolman, and Greenleaf, the nuance is toward experimental learning, toward action preceding learning, toward learning through experimental action. Experimental action-learning is a key component of the method. Greenleaf with other managers developed experiments with 25-pound bales of wire instead of 50-pound bales, experiments with women doing traditionally male blue-collar work, experiments with blacks in management training programs and management positions. Woolman with other merchants and farmers developed experiments in tenant farming by former slaves and Meetings guaranteeing to lenders the loans of farmers in exchange for lower interest rates.

A key component of Quaker method is that experimentation needs to be continuing. There will always be mixtures of the good and less good, entanglements of the good with oppressive biases and customs. As one set of biases and entanglements appear and are more or less solved, other biases and entanglements emerge. Quakerism shares something of the postmodern perspective that as one group replaces another group in power, new biases and entanglements emerge and need to be addressed. There is a continuing opportunity and need for cocreation, leadership, and problem solving with "that of Go(o)d in everyone."

Strengths and Limitations

The strengths of the friendly disentangling method within servant-leadership include the following: (1) It facilitates peaceful change; (2) it reforms organization tradition biases; (3) it can sometimes as a by-product produce integrative, win-win results; and (4) it can facilitate belief conversion toward the ethical and not solely win-win behavior change.

Situations in which the method is less effective include: (1) when the people involved perceive no "we" fellowship relationship or when a conflicting "we" relationship is more important; (2) when there really is not much of a negative bias in the tradition system and the reason for the unethical behavior is primarily or fully individual; (3) when powerful people in authority frame ethics issues in a self-interested manner and ignore alternative frames; and (4) when the method is misinterpreted and stimulates negative us-versus-them cognitions and behaviors.

Strengths

1. *The method can facilitate peaceful change.* Peaceful change is one of the key strengths of the method. For example, Woolman used it to address one of the most difficult and violent issues of his time, slavery, yet his method facilitated first the peaceful, voluntary elimination of slavery in Pennsylvania and then the passing of Minutes and laws against it.

While Greenleaf was using the Woolman method, employment of black managers at AT&T increased from about .5 to about 4.5 percent. This change occurred without any enforcements such as top management orders, performance reviews tied to hiring and promotion of black managers, and external court orders or consent decrees. The peaceful changes during Greenleaf's time are in marked contrast to the later intense, external conflicts between AT&T and the EEOC and FCC, internal conflicts among top management under the consent decree quotas, and employee resistance to the preferential hiring and promotion of black managers.

The peaceful Woolman method and politically generated and legally enforced change are not necessarily mutually exclusive. Paul Ricoeur has observed, "The state of law is . . . the actualization of ethical intention in the political sphere."[25] Politics can provide the space for ethics to act; law can be the result of ethics-driven politics. The Woolman method can serve as peaceful preparation for changes that may later be encoded as rules or laws.

What is it about the Woolman method that facilitates peaceful change? Several parts contribute: friendly affect, consciousness of a "we" relationship, consciousness that sources of conflict may be caused as much by tradition system-level biases as individual or group differences, consensus-building experimentation, and the user's sincere interest in transcendent and not solely individual welfare.

2. *The method can help reform organization traditions.* The focus on potential biases in "our" tradition system is one of the method's key strengths. It is designed to address and improve ethical organization traditions by identifying and correcting such negative biases. This focus is particularly important compared with more individually focused methods. In the slavery example, the focus was on considering and reforming the slave economy. After identifying the biases—the inhumanity of slavery, the low productivity of slavery, and the perceived "untoward slothful disposition of the negroes"—and trying the experiment of paid workers and sharecropping, many farmers and merchants voluntarily discontinued the practice of slavery. Later they voluntarily voted to outlaw it. The terrible slavery-supporting bias in the economic tradition system of the Pennsylvania Society of Friends and later the state of Pennsylvania was reformed and transformed.

In the AT&T example, the apparently largely systemic and institutional bias within AT&T with respect to the training, hiring, and promotion of black managers was significantly improved. Although black managers remained in the minority, the culture changed from one where black managers were practically nonexistent to one where it was not uncommon to find them in all areas of the company. This is not to suggest that the problem was solved, but that a significant improvement appears to have been made with respect to the managerial and leadership role of blacks in the AT&T society.

3. *As a by-product the method can generate effective, but not perfect, integrative win-win solutions.* The focus of the Woolman method in the cases considered was more on transcendent tradition system-level concerns than on individual criteria: In all these cases, though there were not perfect solutions without any negative effects, integrative, win-win solutions mostly resulted. That is, what emerged appeared to be not so much win-lose outcomes or compromises but solutions that were large enough to encompass and reconcile many, if not necessarily all, diverse extremes.

    For example, in Pennsylvania the slave owners increased their productivity with paid workers and sharecroppers, the slaves gained freedom and employment, and the conscience of society benefited by eliminating slavery. One group that may not have benefited economically were the slave traders, who were generally different from the farmer and merchant slave owners.

4. *The method can facilitate belief conversion toward the ethical and not solely win-win behavior change.* Belief conversion toward the ethical is a strength of the Woolman method relative to win-win negotiating and enforced regulatory approaches. The Woolman method neither explicitly compels nor rewards. The decision to experiment with a solution to an ethical problem is made after some voluntary agreement has been reached that a negative bias in the tradition system needs to be addressed. That is, some belief conversion toward the ethical occurs before behavior change. People may reject what they think is an unworkable or inconvenient solution to the negative bias in the tradition system, but, nonetheless, some belief conversion occurs. While this is a strength relative to win-win negotiating and forcing methods, other methods such as Socratic dialogue can stimulate belief conversion.

Limitations

1. *The method can be ineffective when the people involved perceive no "we" fellowship relationships or when a conflicting "we" relationship is more important.* Insiders may regard the person trying to use Woolman method as an outsider or relative outsider and can choose not to consider seriously or even to resist the changes suggested. For example, Rufus Jones, George Walton, and Robert Yarnall, representing the American Friends Service Committee, tried to use the Woolman method in helping Jews emigrate from Nazi Germany.[26] They visited Gestapo headquarters in 1939, in part in response to the

"Day of Broken Glass," November 9, 1938. They addressed Reinhard Heydrich, who was Heinrich Himmler's immediate subordinate, head of the SS, and in charge of the Dachau concentration camp, through two of his deputies in a foyer outside his office where he could hear the conversation.

Their written and spoken words to him and his two deputies were as follows. They first reminded them that there was a history of friendly relations between the German people and the British and American Friends Service Committees. "We have had close and friendly relations with the German people throughout the entire post-war period."[27] In addition, they indicated that there were some shared points of view. "We have always been concerned over the conditions of the Peace Treaty and in spirit opposed to these conditions."[28] They tried to remind the Nazis that the Quaker relief efforts were built on a foundation of previous service to the German people. "We came to Germany in the time of the blockade; organized and directed the feeding of German children, reaching at the peak no less than a million two hundred thousand children per day. . . . And at the time of 'Anschluss' we were distributing food to a number of Nazi families."[29] They reminded the Nazis that during this period of service no propaganda or conversion efforts had been made. "We have not used any propaganda or aimed to make converts to our views. . . . We have come now in the same spirit as in the past and we believe that all Germans who remember the past and who are familiar with our ways and methods and spirit will know that we do not come to judge or criticize or to push ourselves in, but to inquire in the most friendly manner whether there is anything we can do to promote life and human welfare and to relieve suffering."[30]

Matters of relief, quicker emigration, and transient camps were discussed. Heydrich announced through his deputies that everything the Quakers asked for would be granted. For a few weeks Jews from Germany were able to emigrate through the American and British Friends Service Committees. According to Clarence Pickett, then executive director of the American Friends Service Committee, as a result of this visit to the Gestapo, "Workers in our Berlin Center found they had a new freedom in making emigration arrangements for Jewish families and in bringing relief. This short reprieve meant the difference between life and death to some families, at least."[31] However, in the light of subsequent history, Jones, Walton, and Yarnall had relatively little positive influence in changing Nazi policy or helping German-Jews escape.

Clearly, in some circumstances, the effectiveness of the Woolman method is limited. While Jones, Walton, and Yarnall were able to communicate something of a positive "we" relationship, based on the Service Committees' record of feeding German children after World War I, that resulted in some relief and saved some lives, it did not last very long. It was relatively weak compared with the contradictory, distorted, destructive, and even depraved internal sense of "we" within the Nazi society.

2. *The method may be ineffective when there really is not much of a negative bias in the tradition system and the reason for the problematical behavior is primarily or fully individual.* The Woolman method may be less appropriate in situations where the ethical problem is primarily individual and personal. Traditions and systems are not always the primary or even an important source of the problematic behavior. As Chris Argyris has observed, some people blame the organization or the system simply as an excuse for avoidance of individual responsibility.[32] Although this is often true, the Woolman method sometimes can still help people to understand that no tradition system-level bias exists and that the ethical problem is primarily individual. Exploration of the tradition system can make it clear that the source of the problem is one's own behavior and thus can encourage the individual to change voluntarily. Exploration of a tradition system can also reveal that it supports ethical behavior, which can increase pressure on an individual to "get in step" with it.

3. *Powerful people in authority sometimes frame ethics issues in a self-interested manner and ignore alternative frames.* Many of the powerful farmers and merchants whom Woolman approached chose, at least initially, to frame the issue in terms of the "untoward slothful disposition of the negroes." This outlook conveniently shifted the burden to the victim. Woolman was able to overcome this framing with most of those people, but some chose to ignore alternative framing and did not change their behavior until they were required to either by the Society of Friends' Minutes or Pennsylvania law.

   Similarly, in the AT&T case, several powerful managers chose to frame the problem in terms of the "unsuitability of blacks" for management roles rather than the embedded and systematic channeling of blacks into nonmanagerial training, experiences, roles, and expectations. Although Greenleaf was able to overcome this framing with many managers, some only changed their behavior when they were required to by company policies and federal law.

   Powerful people can sometimes choose not to pay attention to or talk about an alternative framing that is not in their perceived self-interest. If the user of the method is considered an insider or peer, such people may feel some pressure to at least listen to him. The Woolman method sometimes can also trigger a positive response among people who articulate a biased, self-interested framing but simultaneously understand that the behavior in question is unethical. Many of the slave owners Woolman talked with already understood that slavery was unethical, but on the surface they accepted the biased framing and were inactive about the issue because they were benefiting from owning slaves. Some became willing to risk losing those benefits when Woolman spoke with them and they realized they were not alone in their reservations about slavery. Similarly, some of the managers Greenleaf spoke with already understood that it was unethical to discriminate against blacks. On the surface, they accepted the "unsuitability of blacks" framing and were inactive about their belief because they feared that other white managers and workers might disapprove of contrary actions. Some became willing to risk such disapproval when Greenleaf spoke with them and they realized they were not alone in their reservations.

However, there are circumstances where no conversational method is effective, including the Woolman method. Powerful people may understand what is unethical but choose to continue it because of their perceived self-interest. Correspondingly, less powerful people may choose to respond negatively because of fear of a powerful person who is supporting the problematic behavior.

4. *The method can be misinterpreted and stimulate negative us-versus-them cognitions and behaviors.* Raising the salience of a "we" fellowship relationship can have some negative consequences. A person considering the "we" fellowship relationship might respond positively to people within the "we" as insiders but might view people not part of the "we" as outsiders to be defended against or attacked. For example, during the Pennsylvania abolitionist movement, and the post-consent decree period at AT&T, some intense adversarial behavior occurred on all sides. There were heightened emotions about "their" evil compared with "our" righteousness. Sometimes the followers of Woolman and Greenleaf exhibited behavior as insensitive and nasty as the behaviors they were criticizing. Peacefully intentioned methods do not always result in peaceful outcomes. Sometimes peaceful methods can even stimulate, at least for a while, more violent and hostile reciprocal interactions. "I am we" can slip into "us versus them."

Conclusion

Robert Greenleaf's membership in the Religious Society of Friends (Quakers) and corresponding spiritual philosophy for acting and learning with others greatly influenced his servant-leadership approach and, in particular, his method of friendly disentangling. As the Greenleaf and Woolman cases illustrate, there are important parallels between the friendly disentangling methods Greenleaf and Woolman used. The method is linked to four Quaker principles of acting and learning with others: (1) "that of Go(o)d in everyone," in our "prior we" relationship; (2) tradition system entanglements as causes of problems rather than solely individual responsibility; (3) friendly and cheerful affect; and (4) continuing experimental action-learning.

The friendly disentangling method has important strengths and limitations. Strengths include the following: (1) It facilitates peaceful change; (2) it reforms organization tradition biases; (3) it can sometimes as a by-product produce integrative, win-win results; and (4) it can facilitate belief conversion toward the ethical and not solely win-win behavior change.

Situations in which the method is less effective include: (1) when the people involved perceive no "we" fellowship relationship or when a conflicting "we" relationship is more important; (2) when there really is not much of a negative bias in the tradition system and the reason for the unethical behavior is primarily or fully individual; (3) when powerful people in authority frame ethics issues in a self-interested manner and ignore alternative frames; and (4) when the method is misinterpreted and stimulates negative us-versus-them cognitions and behaviors. Nonetheless, as the preceding cases illustrate and especially in situations where the causes of problems and conflicts lie at least partially with biases within tradition systems and not solely with individual responsibility, the method has great potential. Walking cheerfully over the earth answering that of Go(o)d in everyone and disentangling individual behaviors and values from tradition system biases can be an ethical and effective method. And as John Woolman observed, this approach "in different Places and Ages hath had different Names. . . . It is deep, and inward, confined to no Forms of Religion, nor excluded from any."[33]

12

Servant-Leadership
and Enterprise Strategy

Jill W. Graham

Dr. Jill W. Graham is an associate professor of management at Loyola University Chicago. She has Ph.D. and M.M. degrees from Northwestern University and a B.A. from Wellesley College. Her research concerns various forms of virtue in organizational life, including principled dissent, organizational citizenship behavior, activist loyalty, servant-leadership, and value-driven strategic management. Her community service is focused on her local church, spirituality, healing racism, and economic development in disadvantaged inner-city neighborhoods.

In this essay, Graham examines the role that leader values play in relation to defining and implementing organizational purpose. She suggests that servant-leadership helps people and organizations to operate in a more mature and moral manner.

Servant-leadership is by no means limited to top-down hierarchical relationships. It can occur in any setting, between occupants of any organizational position or level, and in any interpersonal relationship. Wherever or whenever servant-leadership occurs, the leader's example and nurture of others results in the healthy growth of those who are led. Servant-leaders who hold executive-level positions, however, may have an even broader impact, one concerning strategic decisions for the direction and functioning of an organization as a whole. For it is typically at the most senior levels of organizational responsibility that major organizationwide strategic decisions are made and policies are put into effect.

The highest level of strategy specifies the very purpose of an enterprise. Little systematic attention has so far been directed to how the choice of enterprise purpose might be influenced by the value preferences and priorities, business philosophy, and ethical beliefs of servant-leaders. (The whole field of strategic analysis from an ethical perspective is quite young.[1]) Strategic decisions, moreover, must not only be made but implemented as

well, and servant-leadership may be even more important at the implementation stage of the strategy process than at its formulation.

In the first part of this essay, a variety of enterprise strategy options will
be positioned relative to one another in terms of what stakeholder interests
are given greater weight. An enterprise strategy option that is consistent
with the values of servant-leadership will then be identified. The special challenges of implementing that enterprise strategy will be outlined, but servant-
leadership will be seen as uniquely able to lead a way through those challenges. The essay's concluding section summarizes the distinctive strengths
of servant-leadership with regard to implementing a morally appealing but
extremely challenging organizational strategy.

Varieties of Organizational Enterprise Strategy

Strategy in the most comprehensive sense refers to a pattern of decisions that
concern the full range of intentions of an organization with regard to what it
will do, how it will do it, and why.[2] Various levels of strategy deal with issues that
apply to particular parts or phases of an organization's activities. The highest
level of strategy, which in turn affects decisions made at all subordinate parts and
phases of an organization's activities, has been termed "enterprise strategy."[3]
Enterprise strategy concerns "what a firm stands for"[4] and answers the questions, "For whom does an organization exist?" and "How does it add value to
its stakeholders in order to legitimize its existence and ensure its future?,"[5] as
shown by "a commitment to a set of purposes, values, and ethical principles."[6]

Some organizational stakeholders (i.e., owners) primarily seek economic returns to capital, and others (e.g., customers, employees, vendors,
and the community) seek noneconomic (or "social") as well as economic
benefits in return for other forms of contribution or trade. Based on these assumptions about stakeholder values and interests, a variety of enterprise
strategies that provide value to stakeholders can be arrayed along a main continuum where value is composed of various combinations of economic and
social costs and benefits (see Figure 12.1). Three additional dimensions that
intersect the main continuum (to serve customer, employee, and vendor welfare, respectively) are also conceivable.

Each strategy shown in Figure 12.1 is defined and/or illustrated as follows:

- *Profiteering enterprise strategy* is maximization of profits *without constraint* in order to increase owners' wealth. This is based on the
  philosophical principle of the primacy of property rights.[7] Examples
  include sales of illegal drugs and the operation of textile sweatshops
  employing indentured foreign workers.
- *Classical economic enterprise strategy* is profit maximization *within
  the law*, but otherwise without regard to the cost or benefit to

Figure 12.1
Varieties of enterprise strategy.

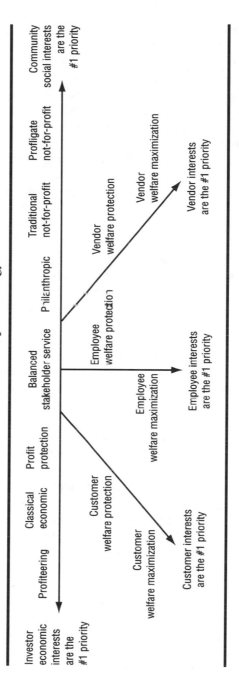

stakeholders other than owners. This strategy defines the assumed rationality of the firm within modern microeconomics and describes the avowed philosophy underlying many firms in a market economy.

- *Profit protection enterprise strategy* is profit maximization within the law to benefit owners, modified to restrain costs inflicted on other stakeholders whose displeasure could threaten future profitability. This strategy, although clearly instrumental in its evaluation of the importance of interests other than those of owners, does pay them some attention. Nevertheless, property rights of owners are still the highest priority interest. Examples include Levi Strauss and Reebok, which led the name-brand clothing industry in forcing their foreign subcontractors to improve working conditions, in order to appease their domestic workers and customers whose concerns about the issue threatened production and sales at home.

- *Balanced stakeholder service enterprise strategy* is production over time of positive net value for all stakeholders (even at the expense of maximizing shareholder wealth, or the welfare of *only* customers, employees, vendors or the community), so that no stakeholder group is used purely instrumentally to serve others. Ben & Jerry's Homemade Ice Cream is an example of a firm that explicitly attempts to balance the needs and interests of all its stakeholders.

- *Philanthropic enterprise strategy* is a profit protection or balanced stakeholder service strategy, modified to include regular and substantial contributions to benefit common community interests. Here community social welfare has a higher priority than other stakeholder claims, so that those others are used instrumentally to generate support for community interests. An example is Greyston Bakery in New York, which sells gourmet pastries at a high profit to finance a variety of housing and social service programs in its inner-city neighborhood.

- *Traditional not-for-profit enterprise strategy* is maximization of some community social benefit at the lowest possible economic cost. Most 501(3)(c) organizations serving educational, cultural, religious, medical, social service, or environmental purposes exemplify this enterprise strategy.

- *Profligate not-for-profit enterprise strategy* ostensibly is maximization of some community social benefit *without* regard to economic cost, sometimes (actually) to line the pockets of unnamed beneficiaries. Scandals revealing the corrupt mismanagement of a nonprofit organization (e.g., the Foundation for New Era Philanthropy) are revealed from time to time.

Additional dimensions along which enterprise strategies may vary concern other primary stakeholders such as customers, employees, and vendors, all of whom are presumed to desire a combination of economic and social benefits that evidence courtesy and concern for their short-term needs and long-term welfare. The extreme in each case aims to give the named stakeholder group everything it wants, regardless of the cost to other groups. An intermediate position is modeled after the profit protection enterprise strategy, in that the interests of other stakeholders are responded to instrumentally, that is, greasing the squeaky wheel so that progress toward the primary goal is not threatened.

Servant-Leaders' Likely Preference for Enterprise Strategy

Strategic decisions are influenced by many factors, both from within an organization and from its external environment. The value preferences of those with responsibility for making strategic decisions, while not by themselves determinative, are among the factors that influence those decisions. When high-level strategic decision makers are also servant-leaders, the values underlying servant-leadership will influence the choice of enterprise strategy.

Since one of the defining characteristics of servant-leaders is that they use their resources (including their power) to serve *others'* interests, not just their own, it is unlikely that their choice of enterprise strategy will be driven by pure ethical egoism. That means that servant-leaders' preferred enterprise strategy is unlikely to be what Freeman and Gilbert term "managerial prerogative enterprise strategy,"[8] where an organization's purpose is to maximize the personal interests of management. (See Table 12.1)

More generally (with one possible exception), it is unlikely that servant-leaders will prefer any enterprise strategy favoring one stakeholder group's welfare above all others, especially when the favored group is already well off. This rules out both profiteering and classical economic enterprise strategies that favor the property-based interests of owners above all others. It also rules out customer, employee, or vendor welfare maximization enterprise strategies, since all of those ignore the interests of all but the single favored group.

It is possible, however, that servant-leaders might favor a single stakeholder group that represents those "least privileged" in society. Freeman and Gilbert define a "Rawlsian enterprise strategy" as one where an organization promotes inequalities among stakeholders "only if these inequalities raise the level of the least well-off" stakeholder.[9] Servant-leaders might be inclined to do this directly, by working for a traditional not-for-profit organization that focuses on social justice, or indirectly, by choosing a kind of philanthropic enterprise strategy where money is made in one activity to help finance the efforts of others working for Rawlsian justice.

Except for the type of philanthropic organization just described, servant-leaders are unlikely to prefer any instrumental enterprise strategy that attends to multiple stakeholder interests only insofar as addressing the interests of

Table 12.1
Freeman and Gilbert's Philosophically Grounded Varieties
of Enterprise Strategy

Name	Description of Corporate Purpose	Primary Underlying Value or Philosophy
Stockholder enterprise strategy	The corporation should maximize the interests of stockholders.	Property rights
Managerial prerogative enterprise strategy	The corporation should maximize the interests of management.	Ethical egoism
Restricted stakeholder enterprise strategy	The corporation should maximize the interests of a narrow set of stakeholders, such as customers, employees, and stockholders.	Priority to those who have the most to gain or lose
Unrestricted stakeholder enterprise strategy	The corporation should maximize the interests of all stakeholders.	Utilitarianism
Social harmony enterprise strategy	The corporation should maximize social harmony.	Pro: consensus Anti: conflict
Rawlsian enterprise strategy	The corporation should promote inequality among stakeholders only if inequality results in raising the level of the worst-off stakeholder.	Justice
Personal projects enterprise strategy	The corporation should maximize its ability to enable corporate members to carry out their personal projects.	Respect for individual autonomy

Source: R. Edward Freeman and Daniel R. Gilbert, *Corporate Strategy and the Search for Ethics* (Englewood Cliffs, N.J.: Prentice-Hall, 1988), pp. 72–82.

most groups ensures the uninterrupted ability to serve the "highest good" of maximizing benefits to the most favored (and already well-off) stakeholder group. This rules out profit protection (to benefit owners), and even customer, employee, or vendor welfare protection (where those stakeholders are already well off).

What remains? Servant-leaders in strategy-making positions in business organizations are most likely to prefer a balanced stakeholder service enterprise strategy, where no group is used merely as an instrument to serve others, and all stakeholders' welfare is recognized as legitimate and important, where the organization's purpose is, over the long term, to benefit all interested individuals and groups. This definition of organizational purpose is in closest accord with the service-oriented values of servant-leaders who recoil at viewing some people merely as means to serve others as ends.

Implementing a Balanced Stakeholder Service Enterprise Strategy

The process of strategic management includes both the formulation and implementation of strategy. There are two reasons why putting a balanced stakeholder service enterprise strategy into practice is arguably more challenging than other strategic options. First, this strategic choice encourages all stakeholder groups, over the long term, to have a reasonable expectation of being well served by the enterprise; yet the timing of those benefits is rarely made explicit by the strategy itself. As a result, in the short term, groups are likely to have conflicting preferences about whose interests should be served first. Second, given the long-term time horizon inherent in this strategy, it is vital that the organization prosper over an extended period of time, so that it is able to distribute benefits to all stakeholder groups.

What these conditions combine to mean is that an organization with a balanced stakeholder service enterprise strategy must have distinctive abilities both at managing conflict and at adapting successfully to change over time so that it prospers indefinitely in its environment. Although those challenges are important to all organizations, they are especially relevant for balanced stakeholder service organizations. When that enterprise strategy has been chosen in part because of the value preferences of servant-leaders in the organization, however, the continued presence and influence of those servant-leaders is likely to help make the strategy successful.

Servant-Leading through Conflict and Toward Adaptive Change

Building on the observations of Robert Greenleaf[10] and James MacGregor Burns[11] that leaders have the potential of enhancing the moral development of followers, I have outlined a set of theoretical linkages between leadership style and level of moral reasoning among subordinates.[12] This line of inquiry is relevant to implementing a balanced stakeholder service enterprise strategy because of the threats posed to that strategy by stakeholders whose level of moral reasoning ties them to an exclusive concern for self-interest (regardless of the costs borne by other stakeholders), and to familiar (but dated) patterns of behavior and ways of understanding the environment. Servant-leadership helps both leader and led to advance toward postconventional moral reasoning, which has two effects that are relevant here: Each person's welfare function is broadened so that it includes more than self or own-group interests; and people are freed and encouraged to think creatively, which is an essential component of adaptive change for an organization.[13]

This argument is based on the models of cognitive moral development identified by Lawrence Kohlberg[14] and refined by Carol Gilligan.[15] Each stage and level of moral reasoning has its own distinctive logic, which is used to identify, motivate, and justify behavior that is plausibly "moral." A summary of the logics used at each level is shown in Table 12.2, and a suggestion of what leadership styles encourage each level of moral reasoning is shown in Table 12.3.

Preconventional moral reasoning: At the earliest level of cognitive moral development, morality is defined solely by what an unquestioned authority figure (e.g., parent, teacher, soldier, boss) declares to be right and wrong. Right action is that which buys favor from an authority figure, thereby protecting or enhancing self-interest. This makes preconventional morality essentially instrumental in character. As such, it contains no restraint on unbridled egoism, on the one hand; and, on the other, no basis for independently assessing the suitability of authoritative pronouncements, or otherwise challenging the status quo. For a preconventional moral reasoner, "I was just following orders" is an adequate moral defense for any behavior, no matter how outrageous or outdated.

Table 12.2
Stages of Moral Development

Level 1: Preconventional

Stage 1: Uncritical obedience to rules set by an external authority who controls rewards and punishments.

Stage 2: Instrumental performance of explicit exchange agreements if nonperformance would adversely affect self-interest.

Level 2: Conventional

Stage 3: Fulfilling role obligations arising from specific interpersonal relationships.

Stage 4: Fulfilling fixed social duties arising from membership in a specific group, institution, or society.

Level 3: Postconventional

Stage 5: Utilitarian calculus taking all stakeholders' interests into account.

Stage 6: Utilization of self-chosen, universal ethical principles to seek creative solutions to ethical dilemmas that serve the common good while respecting the individual rights of all interested parties (including self).

Sources: Adapted from Carol Gilligan, *In a Different Voice: Psychological Theory and Women's Development* (Cambridge, Mass.: Harvard University Press, 1982); and Lawrence Kohlberg, "Moral Stages and Moralization: The Cognitive-Developmental Approach," in *Moral Development and Behavior,* ed. Thomas Lickona (New York: Holt, Rinehart & Winston, 1976).

Table 12.3
**Leadership Styles Encouraging Various Levels of Moral Development
among Organizational Stakeholders**

Leadership Style	Level of Moral Development	Moral Referent(s)
Preconventional		
Autocratic or coercive leadership	Uncritical obedience to external authority	Authoritative rules and instructions
Path-goal or trans-actional leadership	Instrumental compliance with exchange agreements	Enforcible contracts and job descriptions
Conventional		
Leader-member exchange and consideration	Meet interpersonal role obligations	Personal relationship with supervisor
Institutional leadership	Fulfill social duties from group membership	Cultural expectations
Postconventional		
Transforming	Utilitarian calculus	Cost and benefits for all stakeholders
and Servant-Leadership	Discern and apply universal principles	Principles of justice

Source: Adapted from Jill W. Graham, "Leadership, Moral Development, and Citizenship Behavior," *Business Ethics Quarterly* 5, no. 1 (1995): 43–54.

A variety of leadership styles reinforce preconventional moral reasoning among subordinates by relying exclusively on rewards and punishments to influence their behavior. If the emphasis is on positive outcomes of subordinate action, such leadership can be described as clarifying path-goal relationships. If the emphasis is on negative outcomes of subordinate (in)action, such leadership can be described as autocratic or coercive. Neutral terms include initiating structure and transactional leadership. Because these command and control leadership styles all depend on the preconventional moral logic of individual self-interest, however, they tend to work against the generosity of spirit and capacity for empathy that are needed to find integrative solutions to stakeholder group conflict.

Command and control leadership is likely to be most effective for subordinate behaviors that are concrete and specifiable in advance, such as regular on-time attendance, reliable effort expended on quantity and quality of output, and compliance with work rules. Although convenient for management in the short run, such ready obedience provides no check on the possibility of unethical rules or instructions; authority is obeyed without question. It also contains no encouragement or support either for alertness to environmental change, or for innovative ideas for responding to it. In short, command and control leadership encourages dependency and short-run expediency rather than independent thought and action that can help meet the challenges of the future.

Conventional morality: The second level of moral reasoning moves away from individual authority figures to social systems of rules and responsibilities. The focus of moral concern broadens from protection of self-interest to performance of social duties. While these obligations may be articulated by individual spokespeople, they have authoritative force because the hearer takes seriously his or her identity as a member of a social group with behavioral customs and normative expectations; the member is loyal to the group. Leader-member exchange that favors in-group members and leadership that is high in consideration of all followers help create strong interpersonal and/or social relationships that broaden self-interest to include service to a dyad or group, thereby giving rise to social norms that favor in-group loyalty.

The dedication to duty and within-group generosity engendered by conventional moral reasoning is less self-serving than the instrumental ethnic of preconventional morality, yet it too has its limits. In general, conventional moral reasoning is oriented toward the status quo and encourages resistance to change. This hinders the development and communication of innovative ideas that are so critical to an organization's ability to adapt in the face of environmental change. Group or personal loyalty, moreover, can lead to *group-think,* the uncritical acceptance of majority opinion.[16] The combination of inertial forces and groupthink reduce an organization's ability to ensure the long-term success of the enterprise, so that all stakeholder interests can be served.

Gilligan's critique of moral development theories identifies another danger of conventional morality: the potential for imbalance caused by an abdication of self-interest by those who devote themselves entirely to the needs and interests of others.[17] While her analysis of conventional morality focuses on women and family relationships, an analogous imbalance is conceivable within organizations: the "organization man's" [sic] workaholism, for example, may entail sacrificing self-interest to organizational goals to an extent that is not only generous but potentially self-destructive.

Finally, the within-group generosity of spirit supported by conventional morality ignores the needs and interests of stakeholder groups other than one's own. Group loyalty implies a boundary that defines not only who is *in* but also who is *out*. This insensitivity to other stakeholder groups poses still another threat to implementing a balanced stakeholder service enterprise strategy.

Postconventional morality: Both the first and second levels of moral reasoning have the advantage of simplifying moral decisions by relying on external authorities to distinguish right from wrong. The third level moves from external definitions of morality (be they determined by individual authority figures or social convention) to independently arrived at principled beliefs that are used creatively in the analysis and resolution of moral dilemmas. When an individual moves from the relative passivity of levels one and two to become an active subject at level three, the limitations of the other levels of moral reasoning are overcome: respect for and careful balancing of all interests avoids both excessive attention to or abdication of self-interests; and independent analysis and moral courage counteract the threats posed by uncritical dependence on a single authority and/or groupthink.

Servant-leadership has what Burns describes as an "elevating power"[18] that may both provide a model for and help to nurture the personal development of followers that is necessary to advance toward postconventional morality. In servant-led organizations with a balanced stakeholder service enterprise strategy, serving the needs and interests of all stakeholders is part of the purpose and normal functioning of the enterprise, and opportunities for wide participation in discussions about policies and practices provide the means for that end. The consequence of such organizational ends and means is an ethically elevating climate that frees participants from the need to guard self-interest without regard for the cost to others (in the manner of preconventional morality), or to subordinate self-interest and/or out-group interests entirely to in-group interests or organizational goals (as is possible with conventional morality). Instead, participating stakeholders, encouraged by the servant-leaders, are responsible both for informing others of their own needs and interests, *and* for inquiring about those of others—the object being to serve in a balanced way all those needs and interests that do not violate moral injunctions such as not harming others. Integrative solutions are devised to resolve conflicts—for example, by applying universal moral principles behind a Rawlsian veil of ignorance (of which interests are one's won)[19]—so that some interests are not systematically favored over others. The role of the servant-leader is to envision, espouse, facilitate, and model this "adaptive work."[20]

Conclusion

One of the functions of strategy is to point the direction ahead, to signal the path to be taken, and also to designate which paths have not been chosen. If the chosen path is an especially challenging one including a plausible means of traveling it in the strategy is all the more important. In this essay, we have seen that the special challenges of the morally appealing balanced stakeholder service strategy are addressed by the empowering and ennobling influence of servant-leadership because it helps people to grow toward postconventional morality. Selfishness, in-group myopia, naive gullibility, and complacent confidence in the perpetual adequacy of the status quo all are lessened when people are challenged, motivated, and empowered to assess and balance interests of all stakeholders in terms of universal moral principles; and to think creatively about innovative adaptations to enhance their organization's ability to serve all its stakeholder interests over the long term.

Burns describes servant-leadership when he defines as "transforming" leaders who model and encourage postconventional moral reasoning by "rais[ing] the level of human conduct and ethical, aspiration of both leader and led"[21] in terms of "near-universal ethical principles of justice such as equality of human rights and respect for individual dignity."[22] Heifetz calls for servant-leadership when he notes that making progress on complex issues where there are no simple solutions "demands not just someone who provides answers from on high but changes in our attitudes, behavior, and values. To meet challenges such as these, we need a different idea of leadership and a new social contract that promote our adaptive capacities."[23]

In other words, we need leaders who inspire and empower us to grow. Such servant-leadership is likely to mean more common selection by organizations of a balanced stakeholder service enterprise strategy. And by increasing the adaptive capacities of subordinates through encouraging postconventional moral reasoning, servant-leadership also makes it more likely that organizations will succeed in achieving balanced stakeholder service.

13

Within Our Reach: Servant-Leadership for the Twenty-first Century

Bill Bottum with Dorothy Lenz

Bill Bottum, chairman of Townsend & Bottum Family of companies, has spent more than 40 years in the construction industry. Townsend & Bottum has specialized in constructing power plants around the world. Bill Bottum is a long-time board trustee of The Greenleaf Center whose interests include writing and lecturing on the application of spiritual principles in the business world. Dorothy Lenz has degrees in journalism and English. She is currently minister emeritus at the First Congregational Church in Ann Arbor, Michigan. Over the past 30 years she and Bill's wife, Olivia (a nurse and aviatrix), have translated Bill's engineering mode of expression into language meaningful to others.

In this essay, Bottum and Lenz provide a personal look back at the evolution of management and leadership theories that have led to a growing emphasis on servant-leadership in many institutions. Bottum, who was a friend of Robert Greenleaf during the 1980s, offers good insights into Greenleaf's influence on his own company and the promise that servant-leadership holds for the twenty-first century.

High moral values and excellence must dominate the twenty-first century if progress is to have positive meaning. Through ideas like those of Robert Greenleaf's servant-leadership, such a way of life is now well within our reach.

Outside of my family, the highest priority in my life work since 1949 has been a continuing study of Jesus' Sermon on the Mount and how it applies to all aspects of life, particularly the world of business.

Until about 10 years ago there was outright hostility to such an idea, as well as to practices consistent with it, such as team building, collaborative effort, and caring and compassion in the workplace. Psychologists tended to scoff at the Sermon as impractical, especially in its emphasis on control of anger. Team building was called "love and kisses" and was disdainfully rejected by our client when we were building the Detroit Resource Recovery Power Plant. In our industry, conflicts were more typically resolved by spud wrenches to the head.

For the past 47 years I have been continually monitoring management theories and psychological research, seeking correlation between them and the guiding principles of the Sermon. To facilitate study, I translated the eight Beatitudes, which summarize the Sermon, into nonreligious language, which could be applicable as guiding principles in the world of business.

Guiding Principles for Business Based on the Beatitudes

1. Self-transcendence
2. Service-sensitivity to needs of others
3. Commitment to values
4. Achievement, productivity
5. Nurturing the positive in people
6. Integrity
7. Team building, peacemaking
8. Growth through adversity, endurance

I have watched with amazement as these ideas that were scoffed at 30 and 40 years ago are now beginning to be accepted as the most practical way to do business. Today they are called team building, partnering, strategic alliances, and total quality management.

Scientifically validated surveys are reporting that not only are the Guiding Principles most effective in family and work situations, but they have a dramatic positive impact on stress reduction and the immune system. Some say that they even retard the aging process. All of our amazing automatic bodily and mental control systems respond to these principles with healing and enhancing impulses.

In the world of business, Deming's 14 Points for total quality management and Peters and Waterman's eight attributes of successful companies (from their book *In Search of Excellence*) echo the Guiding Principles (see Figure 13.1). Stephen Covey's work abounds in compatible concepts.[1]

The first breakthrough for me in my study came from the work of Dr. Ernest Ligon and his Character Research Project in the 1940s, 1950s, and 1960s. Ligon was a research psychologist as well as a Methodist minister. He developed a church school program for preschool children to mature adults, based on the teachings of Jesus and built around the Beatitudes, and he did extensive psychological research, statistically validated, on the application of

Figure 13.1
Guiding principles and attributes.

1. Self-transcendence	2. Service-Sensitivity to needs of others	3. Commitment to values	4. Achievement, productivity	5. Nurture the positive in people	6. Integrity	7. Team building/ peacemaking	8. Growth through adversity, endurance
Open, teachable, flexible, adaptable, able to change, so able to grow (Bias for action—try it—change it)	Service to customers (Close to the customer)	Commitment to ideals beyond self— toward making the world better	Achievement orientation	Overcome prejudice and antipathy	Genuine, sincere, open authentic, trusting and trustworthy (Simultaneous loose-tight properties)	Individual: Equanimity, overcome anxiety Calm, sure, serene, yet enthusiastic	Growth through adversity Learning, teaching, training
Humility Unselfishness Self-actualization Self-transcendence Servant-leader (Simple form, lean staff)	Compassionate Understanding of coworkers Empathic listening	The business entity must stand for something—have a corporate culture that gives meaning and purpose to its endeavors	Productivity Enthusiasm Goals, objectives Focused will (Autonomy and entrepreneurship) (Stick to the knitting) Creativity	Nonvengeful Nonjudgmental Control anger Forgiveness, no grudges See positive in people Recognize talents and capacities of people (Productivity through people)	Quality of products and services Total integrity	Organizational: Conflict resolution Team building Inclusiveness	Courage Steadfastness Dedication Perseverance Endure to the end (Hands-on, value driven) Difficulties and problems necessary to growth

( )=Attributes described *In Search of Excellence* by Peters and Waterman

Points for Total Quality Management—Deming

1.	2.	3.	4.	5.	6.	7.	8.
• Lead people and help employees to learn.	• Create constancy of purpose for better product and service.	• Adopt the new philosophy, new religion, in which careless mistakes and negativism are unacceptable	• Continual improvement of production methods. • Take action to accomplish the transformation.	• Eliminate numerical quotas. • Remove barriers to pride of workmanship. • Drive out fear.	• Improve quality by improving the process. • Don't award business on price tag alone.	• Break down barriers between staff areas. • Work as a team.	• Institute teaching and training. • Institute a vigorous program of education and retraining.

159

these principles in daily life. Included was a great deal of research on anger, its causes and consequences, and control, which contradicted conventional psychological beliefs of the time. Ligon's dream was to raise a generation of Christians. Our family participated in Ligon's program, finding it interesting and helpful and Ligon himself inspirational.

Chester Barnard of AT&T generated the first major breakthrough in management theory. In 1938 Barnard, inspired by the Western Electric experiments in the late 1920s on the influence of human factors in productivity, wrote *The Functions of the Executive*.[2] In the face of the then contemporary theories of scientific management and mechanistic behavioral ideas, he believed that the survival of an organization depends on willingness to cooperate, ability to communicate, and integrity of purpose. (Robert Greenleaf was a ghostwriter of speeches and articles for Barnard in later years.)

Another turning point came in 1960 when I read Douglas McGregor's book *The Human Side of Enterprises,* a major, if unknowing, support for the Guiding Principles. In his book, McGregor describes what he calls management "Theory X" and "Theory Y."[3]

McGregor says that how workers are supervised depends on what managers believe about people: Theory X describes the management style of managers who believe that people are basically lazy and have to be coerced or manipulated into working; Theory Y describes the style of managers who believe that people want to work and be productive, needing only to have obstacles cleared out of their way.

I gained new insight into McGregor's theories from Abraham Maslow who had been studying motivation and had come up with his hierarchy of needs. From 1965 until his death in 1970, Maslow went around the country studying people who had made the greatest contributions to the world. He found them to be self-transcenders (the first Guiding Principle) and inspired by spiritual "Being Values." His last three books were all on this subject—*Toward a Psychology of Being: Religions, Values, and Peak Experiences;* and *The Farther Reaches of Human Nature.*

In 1974 Ron Lippitt, a clinical psychologist, and Ken Cowing, a Methodist minister, came to me to say that they would like to help in the quest to apply Sermon on the Mount values to business. Ron has started The University of Michigan's Institute for Social Research and had helped set up the National Training Lab in Bethel, Maine. Ken had joined the business world as an organizational development consultant. They demonstrated and taught Townsend and Bottum some techniques and tools that they had developed in the areas of team building, communication skills, and conflict resolution—all aspects of the Guiding Principles.

The next pivotal point for me was discovering an assessment tool called the Life Styles Inventory, developed by Dr. Clayton Lafferty, clinical psychologist, through an organization called Human Synergistics. Life Style information has been gathered on about a million people and the resulting data processed and validated by the University of Michigan's Institute for Social Research. In 5 percent of the people a pattern was found that characterizes those people most effective in all life situations such as marriage, family, work, and play. People having such a Life Style pattern are able to cope with stress without physical or psychological damage. This pattern is called the Ideal Profile.

When giving a Beatitude talk in 1981 at the First Baptist Church in Ann Arbor, Michigan, I met Dr. Joe Fisher, who had done a lot of work on this research while he was president of Human Synergistics. He and I decided to plot the personality traits found in the Sermon on the Mount (which we called the Beatitude Profile) on the same chart as the Ideal Profile to see how they compared. We found that the Beatitude Profile is the Ideal Profile extrapolated out almost to the limits of the four positive life styles the Ideal Profile describes, and a dramatic shrinking back of the self-defeating Life Styles.

We were excited to find this evidence that the message Jesus taught 2,000 years ago represents the most effective way to live in our world today, and we believe, in all times and places.

From this Beatitude-Profile project came a most exciting by-product. I had included Bob Greenleaf among a number of theological experts I had asked to fill out a Beatitude Profile using the Life Styles Inventory. He misunderstood and filled out the Life Styles Inventory on himself rather than on the Beatitudes. So I have in my archives a priceless treasure in the form of the original profile of Bob Greenleaf in a self-appraisal. And to top it off, it turns out to be a modest and unassuming version of the Ideal Profile.

It was not until 1979 that I read Robert Greenleaf's 1970 treatise "The Servant as Leader," and realized that the servant-leadership he described fit perfectly the value scheme of the Guiding Principles. Servant-leadership looks at what is motivating the leader, rather than the workers, and concludes that the most effective leaders are those motivated not by power and greed, but by a desire to serve. This desire to serve almost always comes from deep transcendent spiritual impulses, which see servant-leadership as the appropriate means toward the achievement of objectives and goals that benefit all of humanity.

Bob Greenleaf said the test of servant-leadership is the effect it has on its followers. If it truly is servant-leadership, Bob said, it will cause the followers to "grow as persons, (and) while being served, become healthier, wiser, freer, more autonomous, more likely themselves to become servants." He adds, "What is the effect on the least privileged in society; will (they) benefit, or, at least . . . not be further deprived?"[4]

Not only was servant-leadership correlated with the values of the Guiding Principles, but Greenleaf had also come up with a name for his idea that did not have religious overtones that might exclude some people. Bob was a

Quaker and told me at our first meeting in 1980 that he got a lot of inspiration from the story of Jesus' washing the feet of his disciples. Still, you will look in vain in his message to find reference to this. Bob believed his message applied inclusively to all religions and cultures, and he did not want anyone to feel excluded.

When he created servant-leadership in 1970, Bob Greenleaf merged the essence of his 40 years of being management idea man for AT&T's top management with ideas from Hermann Hesse's novel, *Journey to the East*. The man who was the servant in the mystical pilgrimage described in Hesse's novel turned out to be the man who had been the spiritual leader all along.

The immediate situation that provided the catalyst for the merging of these ideas into servant-leadership was Bob's serving on the Massachusetts Institute of Technology (MIT) Commission that was to deal with a student uprising. Bob took time out from those tense meetings at MIT to go down to the bookstore to see what the students were reading. He hoped that this would help him understand where the students were coming from. When he found that the most popular books were by Hermann Hesse, he read them. Bob then recommended that police rather than the National Guard be used at MIT to maintain order, because he said that the police were trained to react by saving lives rather than taking them. Bob's wisdom was borne out shortly thereafter by the events at Kent State, Ohio, where the National Guard was used and students were killed.

Most of us who have come to be part of Bob Greenleaf's servant–leadership movement remember clearly and can swap stories about the first time we read that original essay. When I read it, I told my secretary that all of my great heroes like Gandhi had died before I got to meet them and talk with them. I asked her please to track down Bob Greenleaf wherever he was so I could meet him before it was too late. It was not easy, but she finally found him in a Quaker retirement center at Kennett Square, Pennsylvania, not too far from Philadelphia.

I called Bob immediately and he agreed to see me if I would come there to visit him. We talked for five hours straight that first visit and kept up frequent communication for the last 10 years of his life.

Although Bob Greenleaf coined the term *servant-leadership* in 1970, the basic idea has popped up in unlikely places throughout human history. For example, out of the injustice and brutality of the feudal age came noblesse oblige—the obligation of nobility—reminding chivalrous young knights that the more gifts, resources, and abilities that they had been given, the more responsibility they had to serve and to share with those less fortunate.

The ancient Greeks raised the cry of "Arete" (ah-re-tay) to lift the human spirit to the heights of valor and virtue. Their athletic games were administered with the "arete" of fairness and excellence.

In the sixth century B.C., the prophet now called Second Isaiah foretold the "Suffering Servant" of Israel. About the same time Lao Tzu and Buddha were saying similar things; and Bob Greenleaf always added Confucius as a servant-leadership supporter, as well as John Woolman, who persuaded people against slavery one by one, and Pope John XXIII.

In our company we had started to work with team building, an application of the Guiding Principles, in 1974 and have used it on almost all of our major projects since then. One of the most helpful programs for implementing servant-leadership was putting 145 of our people through a week of communication skill training.

We also benefited from somewhat superficial aspects of servant-leadership—like eliminating status symbols such as reserved parking spaces, and by using round tables at which there is no head of the table and communication is enhanced because everybody is able to see everyone else eyeball to eyeball.

The real benefits, though, came during the times of tough downsizing and layoffs made necessary by the dramatic drop in the demand for energy when the energy conservation program in the United States became so successful. From the turn of the century until the Arab oil embargo of 1974, use of electricity had steadily increased by 7 percent per year, doubling every 10 years. Since 1974 it has increased barely 1 or 2 percent per year. The downsizing trend continues today.

Trust and goodwill, which had been built up during past operations, and concerned outplacement programs were what ensured survival rather than organizational meltdown for us. There was very little trouble or legal action during our downsizing. I believe this was true because of the attempts we had been making to follow Bob Greenleaf's principles.

One time, due to a combination of circumstances, we had a cash flow crisis and could not meet payroll without help from the bank and bonding company. Normally this would throw a company into bankruptcy. We proposed as an alternative to this scenario the ultimate team-building form: a three-way agreement among the bank, the bonding company, and ourselves. It was far riskier for the bank and the bonding company, but if it worked, it would not only save our company and pay our creditors all we owed them but also would save the bank and bonding company $2 to $3 million each. They ran background checks on each of our employees to see if there were any potential integrity leaks. Then, based on our past reputation and the high trust level they had in our people, they went along with our proposal. With a great deal of struggle and determination from our people, it worked and we survived.

During those difficult times, the services of an outplacement specialist proved most helpful. We established the ground rule that each supervisor was responsible to try to find a job for each of his or her people who was being laid off. It makes a lot of difference when a manager intercedes for a person with another manager. We also established a ground rule that if there was a choice, the one who found it the most painful to break the bad news was the one who should do it.

When our company was doing operating and maintenance work on power plants and refineries in Saudi Arabia, our people there, led by our manager Bill Gay, provided a good example of servant-leadership. We in the home office didn't even know about the problem until we noticed that our profits took a temporary sudden dip. We had up to 1,000 employees in Saudi Arabia from 20 different countries. Most of them were third country nationals, there on single status. We ran a camp to house them and provided meals. When our people took over the running of the camp, they found terrible conditions. The previous contractor had been shutting off the air conditioning at night to save on electric bills. It gets to be 110 to 120 degrees Fahrenheit there. They had also been skimping on meat to save money. There were not enough toilets and the workers had to stand in long lines to get to them. Our people did what they knew was right and corrected these conditions. You can imagine what happened to morale and productivity.

We found that a particular set of skills needs to be learned to enhance the environment for servant-leadership. These include communication skills and empathetic listening, conflict-resolution, problem solving, consensus decision making, and community building. We found these to be especially vital to the creation of servant-leadership and the key element in team building. We discovered that tremendous savings can be gained in cost and schedule by team building rather than the traditional adversarial relationship among owner, designer, and constructor.

One of our team-building methods was to get the top 20 or so project people from each of the key organizations, that is, owner, designer, constructor, and so on, together with facilitators. Each group was asked to list on newsprint the "prouds" and the "sorries" about the project and the other participants' behaviors in it. The "prouds" were usually hard to come by, but the "sorries" were voluminous. As each group reported to the others, a lot of "ah-has" usually came forth as each group recognized that the others had real problems, too, were just as interested in a successful project as they, and that the others' "dastardly deeds" were not just attempts to undermine them.

The next step was to sort out the newsprint by common problems and then get everyone from all groups to gather around each problem on which they wanted to work. Each group now was a composite of people from all original groups. By the end of the first workshop, there was common commitment to the success of the project and to working through any additional problems as they came up. Weekly problem-solving meetings were held thereafter with representation from all original groups of project participants. The common pledge was, "Whenever anyone has a problem, *we* have a problem. We're going to make it, and we'll make it together!"

Our team-building experience was key in getting us selected by the Department of Energy (DOE) to construct out on the desert in Barstow, California, Solar One, the first solar power plant in this country. Solar One utilized 1,800 sixteen-foot-square mirrors, each individually programmed to track the sun with its own computer. We had been selected on the basis of team-building experience as well as power plant experience. The DOE selection team had had substantial team-building training and watched carefully how we interrelated during our presentations to them. Usually being too much ahead of one's time gets one a bloody nose, but this time we benefited because not many of the 52 other companies bidding were into team building yet.

Bob Greenleaf had a diverse international spectrum of friends like Aldous Huxley and Gerald Heard, but the servant-leader aspect of his work started slowly and unobtrusively. For many years the movement had existed pretty much in the hearts and minds of Bob and a heterogeneous handful of us who were his friends and kindred spirits. Among them was Sister Joel Read who started and ran Alverno College in Milwaukee. There were the Jack Lowes, father and son, in the construction business in Dallas. Their company, incidentally, is listed as one of the top 100 best companies for which to work. They got Bob Greenleaf's attention because they ordered so many copies of *The Servant as Leader*—one for each of their employees. (They're still giving out copies to each employee.) They also used Bible principles in their business. There was Jim Tatum from Missouri who got community colleges going and nurtured them. There was Bob Lynn from the Lilly Foundation, and a theologian, Dick Broholm, of Andover-Newton Seminary, and Jitsuo Morikawa, head of the American Baptist Convention and minister at Riverside Church in New York, worked between the seminaries and urban renewal projects like one in Philadelphia, Fred Myers and Diane Cory rediscovered Bob for AT&T, publishing and distributing books and videos pertaining to Bob's work not previously available.

The servant-leader movement has really taken off since Bob's death in 1990. I believe that this new interest in servant-leadership is the result of a world evolved to greater receptivity to the ideas inherent in servant-leadership and of the outstanding job of promoting servant-leadership that is being done by Larry Spears, executive director of The Greenleaf Center for Servant-Leadership, and by Richard Smith and the other excellent members of the Center's staff.

Many books have been written about servant-leadership, and The National Society for Experiential Education has been linking with servant-leadership for the past 15 years. Experiential learning is an integral part of college programs. An important part of the educational process, it is also an excellent means of encouraging people to be volunteers or make careers in such programs.

The W. K. Kellogg Foundation has funded servant-leadership workshops and is now funding research on servant-leadership as it relates to the leaders of educational institutions. The Lilly Endowment has funded a great deal of research on servant-leadership aspects of the work of trustees in nonprofit organizations. Because of funding like this, many more institutions are now experimenting with servant-leadership.

The Michigan-based Sisters of St. Joseph Health System with 18,000 employees has servant-leadership as one of its guiding values and has institutionalized it. Everyone in the organization is to hold everyone else accountable for living out servant-leadership principles. In the office of John Lore, the CEO of this health system, is a statue of Jesus with a towel and a basin.

In 1996, 450 people came to the annual conference on servant-leadership held in Indianapolis. Speakers at the annual conferences have included Peter Block, Max DePree, Ann McGee-Cooper, Scott Peck, and Peter Senge.

In the second chapter of his book *Servant Leadership,* entitled "The Institution as Servant," Bob Greenleaf describes an organizational form appropriate to servant-leadership. It is the council of equals, that is, primus inter pares, first among equals. This council-of-equals framework was extremely important to Bob but was the riskiest, most unexplored territory. We began to experiment with it in the mid-1980's. When I called Bob for a list of those who had tried it so we could compare notes, he said that at that time there weren't any others experimenting with his complete idea. Bob himself helped us with lots of free telephone advice during that period.

When Bob wrote about the first-among-equals concept, he did have in mind some examples of companies that had used some aspects of the idea. He told me that the only models he knew for using primus inter pares were the big European companies in international competition, Unilever, Royal Dutch Shell, and Phillips, all of which have inside boards, each having a managing director who is a creature of the board. Such a manager is really a primus inter pares. In any case, Bob said he saw all three of those in action before he wrote his piece "The Institution as Servant." He said, "In other words, I knew about the governing board of inside directors who are working directors, which these companies do very successfully. . . . The only company in this country that I know about which did this was Exxon, when it was Jersey Standard. They had an inside board and later they abandoned that. I don't know why. They were very successful when they operated that way, with a chief who was really responsible to his peers."[5]

Today several organizations in the United States are experimenting with this primus inter pares/council of equals framework, and a growing body of case histories is available. Two engineering firms in Indiana, for example, have used it. One of them, Schneider Engineering of Indianapolis, has been operating with the council of equals and primus inter pares for seven years, and their business has more than doubled in that time.

Richard Smith, Greenleaf Center staff member and organization development facilitator, has been the consultant helping these two organizations to implement the concept. Smith is also working with a group of forensic engineers doing expert testimony on disaster situations, and with a group of cardiovascular surgeons. He says that the fact that these professional groups start out with a need to examine a feeling of equality among colleagues is a help to begin with. Richard is at the forefront of developing this application of servant-leadership as it expands from Bob's theory into the real world.

At the University of Michigan, the 250-person Housing Facilities Group is implementing the council of equals, complete with council handbooks and documentation on what happens in difficult instances in which trust has been broken among members. George San Facon, the primus inter pares for that council, says their growing edge is the need for each member of their council to have an inner journey and quest, perhaps even a contemplative practice, leading toward authenticity and mutual understanding.[6]

Over the years, I have watched four categories of leadership tools evolve from conceptualization through implementation. In the first, which includes team building, conflict resolution, strategic alliances, collaboration, and communication skills, conceptualization was complete about 1970, but it was not in popular general practice until 1985. Servant-leadership, the second category, was conceptualized by Bob Greenleaf in 1970, but implementation did not begin to take off until his death in 1990. It is now generally popular. Greenleaf's organizational form, council of equals, first among equals, and consensus, conceptualized in 1970, began to be used in 1984 and is only now being implemented in a number of organizations. The fourth category, new economic forms, especially ownership alternatives, has been conceptualized since the middle of the nineteenth century but is still in the experimental phases of implementation. See Figure 13.2, "Evolution of Leadership Tools." (Our company has experimented with a new ownership form consistent with the Guiding Principles, wherein the company owned itself for the benefit of employees.)

The old model for business was an organization that looked like a pyramid and was run in a top-down, coercive manner. The new organization, characterized by servant-leadership, looks more like an interlocking group of circles and stresses empowerment and seeing things as a whole. Decisions are more likely to be made by consensus in the new model and include intuition, compassion, and understanding, rather than just rational, linear thinking.

The new model is characterized by accountability without total control. An example of how this principle is being used effectively in our industry is seen in more forward-thinking utilities. These use strategic alliances with engineers, vendors, suppliers, and contractors in which all share in the rewards and risks of the utility's success or failure, as measured by certain critical operating ratios. No one firm has total control over all the factors, but each participant influences and impacts on the results. This method of lining up everyone's motivations and keeping everyone on the same team is the way

Figure 13.2
Evolution of leadership tools.

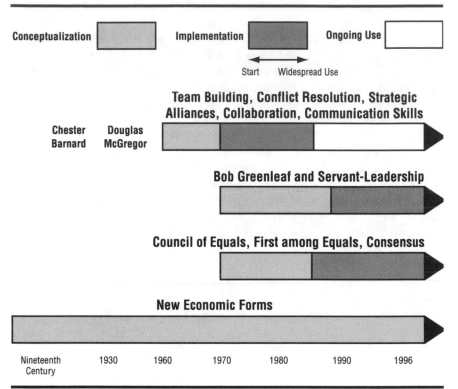

of the future. In the old conventional system there were always a number of conflicting incentives and motivations resulting in adversarial relationships. (See Figure 13.3, "Two Territories and Many Pathways.")

Although 25 years ago such concern for people would be considered a handicap in the business world, today there is evidence that the times are ripe for a dramatic change in leadership, one for which many of us have been struggling for decades. A recent study done by Paul Ray for the Fetzer Institute and Institute of Noetic Sciences, entitled "The Integral Culture Survey," indicates that a new cultural group has emerged in the United States.[7] Twenty-five percent of the adult population now in their middle years, or about 45 million people Ray calls "cultural creatives," are generating new ideas that are on the leading edge of cultural change. These people are more idealistic and spiritual and are concerned about relationships and personal development. They are more open to an alternative future. Sixty percent of them are women. Most of them have a high concern for ecology and a compassion for people. They epitomize the soul of servant-leadership. A generation ago such a large group with such an approach to life did not exist. The

Figure 13.3
Two territories and many pathways.

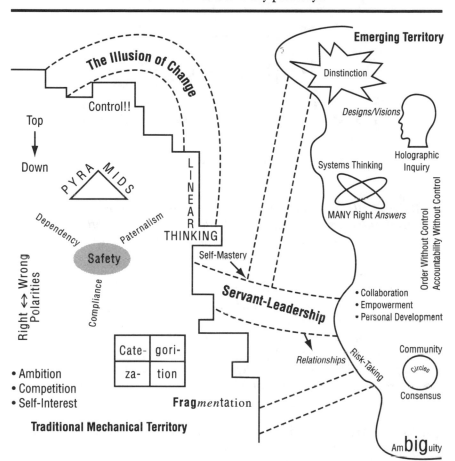

fact that people of this potential are now in their most productive years gives great promise for rapid progress toward more effective leadership in the twenty-first century.

This, along with the growing body of evidence that shows servant-leadership/Beatitudes most effective in both work and family-life situations, bodes well for the future. Human potential takes on new creativity as we get rid of the old restraints and find the productive power of self-directed work teams, councils of equals, and alliances in which everyone is serving and accountable to the others. Such a way of life is no longer just a dream but is well within our reach.

14

Followership in a Leadership World

Robert E. Kelley

Dr. Robert Kelley is an adjunct professor of business at the Graduate School of Industrial Management at Carnegie Mellon University in Pittsburgh. He is the author of The Power of Followership *and* The Gold Collar Worker. *Kelley was a keynote speaker at The Greenleaf Center's 1995 conference.*

In this essay, Robert Kelley addresses the flip side of leadership—followership— which is too often overlooked in traditional leadership theory. Kelley offers great insights into what makes for exemplary followership by his skillful answering of the question: "What is exemplary followership and why should anyone choose to take that role when most societal perks go to leaders?" His answer to that question offers a powerful rationale for the adoption of servant-followership by people and institutions. As Kelley say, "The best followers know how to lead themselves."

In *Journey to the East,* Hermann Hesse portrays a group on a mythical journey. The main character, Leo, is a servant and is viewed as such by the group. He does the cooking, the cleaning, and other menial chores. The journey is buoyed by Leo's good spirits and it proceeds well until Leo vanishes. The group, it turns out, cannot continue on its own without their servant and supposed follower, Leo. The journey is abandoned.

Some people interpret Hesse to mean that Leo, although a servant, was in reality the journey's leader. The conclusion is that without leadership—or what Robert Greenleaf calls servant-leadership—success is unlikely.

I interpret Hesse's story differently.[1] To me, Leo is the quintessential exemplary follower, the kind of person that no leader or group can succeed without. Leo knew what it took for the journey to proceed. He willingly did the tough work without any glory. He did not demand the limelight or constant praise. Leo was content with his role as servant. His departure provides a startling contrast to the lack of followership skills in the other group members. Without the servant-*followership* that Leo displayed, organizations and leaders fail.

The notion of being an Exemplary Follower is one of the most challenging in organizational life, not only because it is so difficult to master but because it is so hard to accept. In our leader-centric world, reasonable people might ask: What is exemplary followership and why would anyone choose to take that role when most societal perks go to leaders?

Followership is the organizational role where you spend the majority of your time. It focuses on all the hierarchical relationships you have with people who have organizational power and authority over you, especially leaders. Followership differs from teamwork, which is most often about worker-to-worker relationships—the horizontal—not the top-down relationships, or the vertical of leadership.

The negative image of followership in American work and social structure is every bit as powerful as the glittery popular notions of leadership. And I argue here as I have in my other writings that it is every bit as inaccurate.

The now-famous picture of a 16-year-old Bill Clinton shaking hands with President John F. Kennedy during an American Legion–sponsored civics program in Washington was a powerful campaign image because it supposedly captured the watershed moment when Clinton decided he could someday be president. It would hardly have had such resonance with voters if Clinton had described it as the moment he decided he wanted to be an administrative assistant in the White House. But in reality, much of the concrete successes in an administration can be credited to creative, capable assistants who get only broad policy directives from a president.

The dogma pounded into us from kindergarten on into retirement is that being a leader is something special to aspire to. Being a follower is something mundane to settle for. This is why readers of Hesse's story declare that Leo is really the leader in disguise; to call Leo, the hero of the story, a follower is too incongruent with our deeply held stereotypes.

Consider the unusual experience of Dave, who set himself on a successful career track and made an important contribution to his company when he stepped forward and shattered the traditional image of followership.

Now a vice president in one of the country's top pharmaceutical firms, Dave began his career with the company fresh out of college, thrown into a highly competitive management training program with 28 other employees. After two years, the 25 who remained were graduated from the program and pitted against one another in a horse race to determine who would win coveted top management jobs. In the end, only Dave and nine others remained on the company's fast track.

Dave recognized the brutal nature of the leadership race early on. He decided to continue with the program but with a radical change in course. Dave was moving to the follower track and leaving the leadership contest to others. At a company ceremony marking graduation from the training program, many in the group talked about their plans for reaching the highest ranks of management—how their ideas and skills would see the company through the next 20 years.

Dave's talk caught the group by surprise. Yes, many of his fellow trainees did have great ideas and brilliant minds, he said. But for any of them to reach the highest leadership positions in the company, they were going to need sharp, dynamic, independent-thinking followers working along with them. Dave was putting them all on notice that he was aspiring to be that kind of follower, rather than racing against them for the leadership slots.

The pitch had such an impact that Dave heard from every one of his fellow graduates by the next day, all asking for his assistance. And the strategy has paid off in his long-term career. His vice president's job carries leadership responsibilities and he fulfills them well. "But I have never coveted a leadership role," he says. "My career goals were to contribute to, rather than compete with, my colleagues—to earn their respect and trust. My promotions have resulted from good followership."

The added benefit of taking the followership route is that Dave has avoided the dark side of the glitzy leadership track. Among the 10 management trainees still with the company, Dave is the only one who is on good terms with each of the others. Some are higher in leadership positions than Dave, some are lower. There are even people younger who have passed him up, and he has gone out of his way to help them in their climb. "My strategy paid off for me," says Dave. "I avoided the struggle for leadership, kept my friends, and did a good job without constantly guarding against power and politics."

My research shows that many star workers, like Dave, have figured out how much they play the followership role in their day-to-day work. They have waved off the negative popular notions and concentrated on developing a definition that elevates it to its proper status:

> Exemplary followership means being actively engaged in helping the organization succeed while exercising independent, critical judgment of goals, tasks, potential problems, and methods. Exemplary Followers have the ability to work cooperatively with a leader to accomplish the organization's goals even when there are personality or workplace differences. They are key players in both planning courses of action and implementing them in the field.

This definition contrasts with what the average person thinks followership is: a work behavior that shows managers and coworkers that "I know how to toe the line and not threaten the leader, take orders without question, and stick to the boundaries of my job description."

The stars have figured out that day-to-day realities of the workplace put the lie to societal snubbing of followership. Although this is a relatively new field of research, my work shows that 90 percent of most workers spend as much as 90 percent of their time as followers. And followers actually contribute about 90 percent to the success of any organizational outcomes, while leaders account for 10 percent. It is the way the business world is set up, but the glamour bias pushes workers to devalue what they spend most of their time doing. For every committee where a worker holds court as chairperson, there are dozens more, over the span of a career, where she or he is merely a member.

When I pointed out the followership-leadership ratio in a consulting session with some General Motors executives, the reaction was predictably hostile, so I had them crunch some numbers, which many business leaders love to do.

"Of the 400,000 employees at General Motors, how many would fall into the leaders category—the people who you think make things happen?" I asked. The group agreed the number was about 2,000. So I told them to do the math. One-half of 1 percent are leaders, and if you follow models of effectiveness already established out there, this group has an impact equal to 10 percent of the workforce, which is a lot of power in proportion to their numbers. Yet, it is still not enough to account for or guarantee success.

That calmed them somewhat, but I think these seasoned executives wanted to believe their leadership accounted for as much as 50 percent of the productivity in the organization. They had to confront the fact that 90 percent of the success is coming from people who implement their directives. Leadership skills are important, but follower skills are probably more important when it comes to adding bottom-line value to the corporation.

In the course of researching my book *The Power of Followership,* many well-known leaders and followers reacted in extremes to my ideas on cultivating bright, creative followers in the business world. Many of them were wildly enthusiastic, but a few were surprisingly hostile to the concept.

One of these was Red Auerbach, coaching titan and past president of the Boston Celtics basketball team. After reading my article "In Praise of Followers" in the *Harvard Business Review,* he responded: "Can you imagine a team in which players picked other players and decided on the substitutions? It is absolutely ludicrous. Or can you imagine a business run by people without authority or by people who are not in a position to assume the responsibility of failure? It would undoubtedly flounder."[2]

Now, Auerbach may very well be correct that in a few limited situations—military operations, for instance—the only call is for one leader to bark out orders, with followers carrying them out precisely as directed. And although there are many in the Auerbach mold who would prefer all of life's endeavors be run that way, very few do.

Even on Auerbach's most successful squads, the creativity, innovation, and spontaneity on the court seem to belie his words. Perhaps he issues the overall commands, but team members carry them out with independence and distinctive style. When they lose, they seem as downcast and responsible as Auerbach.

Very few situations depend on robotlike conformists to achieve a goal. In fact, a lot of evidence suggests the opposite. The domineering, ego-centered style of leadership—what I have labeled the "Big L" leadership attitude—brings far more failures than successes. Most societal disasters, ranging from the Iran-Contra fiasco to the space shuttle *Challenger,* result from conformist following.

If you were to jot down the name of every supervisor you've had in your career and rate each according to his or her ability to lead, it's likely only a few would get high marks. My surveys show that workers admire less than 20 percent of the bosses they've had. The same would be true of the number of coworkers you've known who make dynamic, effective followers. A lot of people you work with every day go through the motions of completing assignments but don't add anything to the process.

At different points in their careers, even at different times of the working day, most workers have to play both roles, though seldom do they perform equally well. Part of that has to do with awareness and training.

There is a clamoring for business leadership seminars and specialized courses in graduate schools, but when was the last time someone in your workplace came up to you and said "Hey, I just finished this great training course on how to be a star follower. You really should get in on this; it's hot stuff"?

So followership dominates our work lives and the organizations that coordinate them, but it is rarely discussed. Star performers are keenly aware of both the importance of followership as a developed skill and the lack of information about it. As a result, many of the best performers have developed their own systems for sharpening followership ability but my research has uncovered some common themes that account for much of the increased effectiveness.

The Follower Style Chart

Two primary factors distinguish an Exemplary Follower from an average one: independent critical thinking and active participation in the destiny of the enterprise. (See Figure 14.1.) The best followers we studied bring enthusiasm, intelligence, and self-reliance into implementing an organizational goal. They are actively engaged in making the organization a success, whereas average coworkers are more passive, withholding their best thinking and efforts.

Many of these stars choose followership as their primary role at work because it is more closely tied to the actual work than the leadership role. Yet the jobs held by most workers also have a leadership component that demands workers fill the role temporarily, often on a moment's notice. Like Leo in Hesse's novel who plays a leadership role later in the story, the stars become adept at moving back and forth. They know when to turn their respective followership and leadership switches on and off as appropriate.

Some Exemplary Followers enjoy the challenge of dual roles and have a talent for switching hats as situations demand. Others treat followership as a temporary proving ground where they log experience that will qualify them

Figure 14.1
Followership styles.

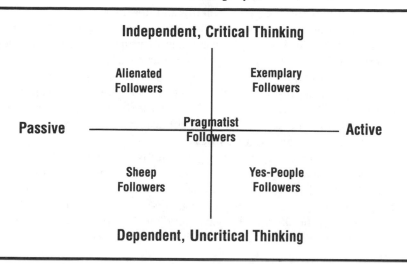

for upper management. Whatever the motivation, followership is seen as a critical skill.

Just as there are different leadership styles, people have separate styles of followership. As seen in Figure 14.1, my studies show that followership style is determined by how well the worker performs on two behavioral dimensions: a measurement of independent, critical thinking and a ranking on an active/passive scale. These factors then yield five separate styles of followership.

When your mother warned you, the child, about blindly following your friends, she probably recognized better than most the reality of this world—that most of our lives are spent following others' directives. The worry in her mind was "What kind of follower were you going to be?" Her point was to dissuade you from the most negative type, what I refer to as the Sheep Follower.

One reason that ranchers prefer sheep over other animal stocks is because they're passive and completely dependent—usually not an upstart, critical thinker in the flock. Because of their herd instincts, they can be trained to perform necessary simple tasks and then wander around while awaiting further direction.

Yes Followers are also in the negative section of the critical thinking chart. They are more enthusiastic and involved than their sheep coworkers but they are aggressively dependent on leaders for direction. They will do whatever the leader says but they need the leader to say it. Yes Followers can be more dangerous than sheep, either because they do exactly what they are told and no more or because they tell leaders what they want to hear, not what they need to know. Insecure executives tend to surround themselves with Yes Followers, producing a management structure that operates in a dangerous vacuum without critical thinking and new ideas.

Alienated Followers are critical thinkers and very independent in relations with management, but they're passive in carrying out their role. They have a personal dislike for leaders in the organization or they are unhappy with their work situation. Most started out as exemplary followers, but someone or something turned them off. Alienated Followers are often cynical and skeptical. They tear down what the leader is trying to build up. Their energy is channeled into fighting against the leader or organization rather than toward their work or a mutually desired future.

In the center of the Follower Style chart is the Pragmatic Follower group. These are capable workers who eschew their independence for political expediency. Or they are system bureaucrats who carry out directives to the letter, even though they might have valuable ideas for improving them. They are constantly monitoring the wind direction and their motto is "better safe than sorry." They manage to survive even the most sweeping changes in the workplace.

The last section of the chart is the most valuable filled—the Exemplary Followers group. Workers in this category never stop thinking for themselves. They do not follow blindly; but when they disagree with the leader, they do so constructively with the organization's best interest at heart. Plus, they carry out their assignments with great energy, paying attention to policy implications down the road as well as the details of implementation. Exemplary Followers are self-starters and creative problem solvers, applying their talents for the benefit of the organization even when confronted with bureaucratic inanities or nonproducing colleagues. And because they have these qualities they get consistently high ratings from peers as well as supervisors.

Exemplary Followers are those who can take on a project with minimal preparation. As a supervisor, you can trust them enough to turn your back on it and know that it will get done in the best way possible (even if it's not the way you originally had in mind). A leader who has an Exemplary Follower on staff doesn't need to worry about hands-on supervision, time-consuming explanation of assignments, or being visited with problems along the way to implementation. Exemplary Followers are independent and responsible members of the team and they believe they add as much value to the organization as anyone in upper management.

Exemplary Follower Strategies

The late Frank Wells played the follower role to Michael Eisner when they were enlisted by the Walt Disney Co. Board of Directors to help rebuild the moribund company in the 1980s. Disney had originally recruited Wells for the CEO slot, but he turned it down. Instead, he suggested that Eisner was a better choice and offered to be Eisner's number two. "(Frank) is a great devil's advocate. I mean, he will ask questions that nobody's ever thought of, and he will take the opposite side of everything," Eisner said in describing Wells's followership style. "But he's a deal maker, not a deal breaker and that's very unique."[3] Wells's value was that he thought for himself, but his thinking was directed at producing successful outcomes for the organization. Wells's untimely death in a helicopter crash left a void in the company that has yet to be filled two years later—even by Hollywood power broker Michael Ovitz.

Like Wells, the Exemplary Followers I observed in my research fall under the broad behaviors just outlined, but they also exhibit some common specific behaviors that have propelled them to a followership skill level well beyond their average coworkers:

1. They know how to lead themselves well.
2. They have focus, commitment, and incentives beyond personal gain.
3. They build competence and credibility to have maximum influence in the workplace.
4. They exercise an honest courageous conscience when carrying out assignments and implementing policies.
5. They control their own ego to work cooperatively with leaders.

Leading Yourself

The best followers know how to lead themselves, and they've demonstrated personal reliance that makes managers comfortable in delegating. Exemplary Followers take their responsibilities seriously, initiating and following through with minimal supervision. They do not see themselves as underlings of the manager doing the delegating. More often than not, they see their work as different but equal to the manager's in any given work situation because they know how critical the implementation role is to the overall success of the assignment.

"The decision as to whether an order has authority or not lies with the person to whom it is addressed . . ." not with the boss issuing the assignment, Chester I. Barnard wrote half a century ago in his seminal business management study "The Functions of the Executive."[4] Leadership authority is only on loan from the followers, who can demand its return at any moment. That assessment is even more true in today's stripped-down organizational flowchart where the worker in the benefits section of a major corporation is likely to report directly to a senior vice president. No longer are there the layers and buffers of management that once regulated the flow of assignments and criticism. Followers have more direct involvement in receiving assignments and reacting to them.

Commit and Focus

Exemplary Followers are often purposefully committed to something—a cause, a product, an organization, an idea, a person—in addition to their own lives and careers. For some, this commitment is a passion that engages their hearts as well as focuses their minds, emotionally fueling their everyday work activities.

Jessye, a star medical researcher in a Chicago hospital, told me during a training seminar that her career goal was to help eradicate diabetes. She had a personal connection, she said, watching her mother struggle with the disease for 20 years and then die from it. She was willing to work with any leader who could help find the cure to diabetes faster than she could alone.

Some leaders mistake a follower's commitment to their goals for personal loyalty. Although in some cases that may be true and end up benefiting the organization, Exemplary Followers like Jessye are almost always devoted to something beyond individual personalities or personal gain. They may be committed to a principle, developing a new product that will change lives, or focusing on the bottom line—increasing profit and publicity for the organization.

In fact, most Exemplary Followers see their managers more often as equals in the process of reaching a goal. The work is considered important enough that titles and protocol are not necessary to achieve results. Exemplary Followers consider their leaders part of the team, but if they detect too much ego in the leader that conflicts with their mutual goal attainment, or if the leader starts to swerve away from the goal, they will strive to get the leader back on track. If they cannot, then they will end the working relationship with that leader, even if it means subverting the leader or personally leaving the organization.

For secure, intelligent managers, the advantages of having Exemplary Followers on staff are enormous. On the plus side, the high enthusiasm generated on projects that include these workers is infectious. The work is generally more creative and of higher quality; morale is higher and schedules stay on track.

Develop Competence and Credibility

Exemplary Followers are keenly aware of a harsh but important reality of the workplace: Some of the most enthusiastic, committed, nicest workers can also be the most incompetent, the most lacking in useful work skills. As I repeat to all my clients and students: "Highly committed and motivated incompetence is still incompetence."

Exemplary Followers almost always have higher competency standards for themselves than those of the leader or the general work environment. They also are sharp observers of new technology and societal trends, working to keep their skills up to date. They are the first among their peers to take advantage of continuing education programs and performance improvement seminars, even suggesting programs that managers don't know about.

Average followers are not nearly as proactive. They may sign up for a course if it's pushed by management, and they're likely to be competent only in those skills that bear directly on their day-to-day work. They require frequent hand-holding sessions in the boss's office when problems arise. They are reluctant to take on extra assignments that improve their expertise, often pointing to the clock or the boundaries of their job description as excuses.

Meanwhile, the most competent followers know their weaknesses well. They also are aware of their strengths, of course, but knowing in what areas they may fall short prompts them to take action to correct them. If they're asked to produce in an area where they don't feel qualified, they look for assistance on their own. If they can't find help on their own, they don't waste the company's time going in circles. They speak up and work with the leader on a solution.

Exemplary Followers are also invaluable as members of project teams. Unlike the prima donnas in the workplace who must stand out in front of other team members, the best followers treat their coworkers as colleagues, not as competitors.

Use Your Courageous Conscience

In my experience, Exemplary Followers spend considerable time and effort worrying about the ethics of their actions on the job, often more so than leaders. There are some exceptions to this, but I've discovered that in the vast majority of cases where a Exemplary Follower is directed to implement a new policy or take on a controversial assignment, the dictates of personal conscience come in to play. In the traditional leader-follower dynamic, the leader makes the decisions and sets the ethical framework for the group, while the follower is expected to do as told. But that is not how it works with the best followers.

In some cases, leaders are forced to choose from among a series of bad options or make their decisions within sharply defined boundaries and under enormous pressures that followers don't have. In these cases, ethics is seen as just one of many factors that must be considered in the final decision; it can get lost in the pack. But that is precisely why conscience is included in the range of skills that make up exemplary followership. Even though there are times when it can be very inconvenient, leaders need their Exemplary Followers to fulfill an ethical watchdog role. More important than the leader's image, the organization's future can depend on how effectively a follower follows her or his conscience. A lot of evidence suggests that this aspect of exemplary followership needs more attention.

A study by University of Pittsburgh business management professor William Frederick found that 70 percent of middle managers reported organizational pressures to conform and often compromised personal principles.[5]

These ethical compromises occurred even though managers rated honesty, responsibility, and independence as the most important personal attributes, while relegating obedience last on their lists.

In a survey I conducted involving 250 brainpowered workers and managers, 30 percent responded that they "often" or "always" accept what authority leader figures tell them without any questions. And 30 percent also reported that when the leader asked them to do something that was not right for them, they usually did it anyway. After analyzing 10 studies of ethical problems in business, Rick Wartzman of the *Wall Street Journal* concluded: "Even the most upright people are apt to become dishonest and unmindful of their civic responsibilities when placed in a typical corporate environment."[6]

When the courageous conscience skill comes up for discussion in training sessions, most participants bring up the obvious first-level responsibility of avoiding or correcting existing wrongs. Stopping there would provide organizational benefit, but there is more to it. A corresponding duty exists—to use the courageous conscience to make positive contributions. The stars champion a worthy idea even in the face of strong organizational resistance, or they deal with a problem before it grows into a crisis.

Disagree Agreeably: Controlling your Ego to Work Cooperatively with the Leader

Exemplary Followers fulfill their obligations by first trying to work cooperatively with the leader. They try to make the leader's job easier rather than be a constant thorn in the side, like alienated followers. They proactively try to support the leader and to fill in gaps that the leader might have.

But in any work situation, conflicts will inevitably arise. At this point, Exemplary Followers try to curb their own ego so that it doesn't get in the way of progress. They distinguish between their own preferences and an honest assessment of the ideas under discussion. Drawing on their multiple perspectives, they try to understand the leader's view while being sensitive to the leader's public image.

After all this, they may find they are still in disagreement and do not feel that it is in the organization's or the goal's best interest to acquiesce to the leader. The issue might be over a positive contribution, such as new product strategy, or an ethical concern, such as targeting problems that could compromise company values. Whatever the conflict, they do their homework and argue persuasively without being threatening or self-righteous.

When "push comes to shove" though, they openly and unapologetically disagree with leadership if it becomes necessary, and they are less likely to be intimidated by titles since they view it as more of a face-to-face interactive partnership. At the same time, they are careful not to develop a reputation for challenging every issue that comes down the pike. Exemplary Followers choose their battles carefully, weighing the necessity of panning the entire idea, or working to modify parts of it. With organizational perspective, they realize that the people delegating an assignment to them may have likely been directed to do so by someone above them.

Not even the best followers win every battle, but by following the seven steps developed from my observations of Exemplary Followers, you can substantially increase the chance that your view will carry the day and limit any negative fallout to your career:

1. *Be proactive.* Exemplary Followers presume that the leader wants the best outcome and operates from that assumption until it is proven false. In addition, they believe that leaders would rather have input before the fact when there is still time to act on it.

    Exemplary Followers are experienced enough to know that leaders often make decisions without complete information (or different information). They appreciate that leaders cannot see some problems brewing because they are further removed from the front line. Or leaders might miss some downside ramifications of their decisions that followers can catch. Also, being more closely attuned to other followers, they can sense how their colleagues are reacting to the leader's decision or situation. Given access to this information, leaders can often self-correct before going off a cliff.

2. *Gather the facts.* Only a foolish follower champions a cause with incomplete information or, worse, with allegations based on rumor and innuendo. Exemplary Followers take time to get the facts of a situation before making a case to leaders. Columbia University business professor Harvey Hornstein's study of 200 brainpowered workers found that 9 out of 10 who had to summon the courage to challenge managers—on everything from pursuing radically innovative product ideas to revamping nepotism-riddled hiring procedures—said they felt comfortable doing so because they had the facts on their side.[7]

    Once the Exemplary Followers we studied had convinced themselves that their arguments were grounded in strong evidence, they proceeded on the assumption that management did not have access to the same material. They began their conscientious response with an informational talk or memo to a supervisor.

3. *Seek wise counsel.* Exemplary Followers trust themselves to gather facts, but, in controversial areas, they know better than to try to interpret them without benefit of a second opinion. Instead, they seek wise counsel. Followers who want to be sure of their findings rely on the perspective skills of those they respect to get a fresh outlook. When Exemplary Followers seek assistance, they are looking for someone—a respected business executive or a recognized expert colleague in another department—who can view the situation from both the follower's position and that of the organization's leadership and make an informed judgment. A follower's adviser should

have a track record for keeping confidences, be knowledgeable about the responsibilities of leaders, be experienced in the ways of office politics and protocol, and be willing to play devil's advocate to test the strength of the follower's position. If they know the particular department, problem, and players, all the better.

4. *Play by the rules.* Most organizations have norms and protocol for airing disagreements. Exemplary Followers realize that company leaders take the procedures they've put in place to deal with these issues very seriously. So they find out what these are before taking any action. Then, they go the system route first, usually trying to work the issue out privately with the leader who is directly involved. When that fails, each step in the system is followed until there is a resolution to the problem. The key point here is that the Exemplary Follower always wants to be perceived as part of the community working within the framework, not an outsider trying to tear it down. Only after the internal steps have been exhausted or found to be untrustworthy do they go outside the system.

5. *Persuade by speaking the language of the organization.* Exemplary Followers always orient their position according to the values and vision dear to the organization and its leaders. They make their arguments based on what they'll do for the organization, and more rarely, what the organization stands to lose by not accepting the argument.

Proactive followers at the health care products giant Johnson & Johnson were alarmed when one faction of corporate leadership made plans to market the company's baby oil to adults as a suntan product. The followers grounded themselves well in research linking sun exposure to cancer and also referred to the company credo, which corporate officers take seriously: "Our first responsibility is to the doctors, nurses and patients, to mothers and all others who use our products and services." The followers also came up with other marketing ideas for adult use of the baby oil. Putting the whole package together in the language and methodology of company leaders' decision-making process eventually won them over. Viewed in the light of current medical research, the decision to end the suntan marketing campaign saved the company a confrontation with health care professionals and possible lawsuits from consumers.

The key to Exemplary Follower behavior here is to change bad leadership decision through conversion, not intimidation. Leaders are more favorably moved to accept an argument framed in terms consistent with the values and vision of the organization and backed up by solid, objective information.

6. *Prepare your courage to go over heads when absolutely necessary.* No Exemplary Follower operating in the bottom-line fixated business environment of the 1990s, no follower who will likely work for sev-

eral organizations over the span of a career, can expect to breeze through the years without facing at least one crisis of conscience over a disagreement with the leader.

Corporate leaders do not always take well to workers who challenge policies and directions forged in top officers' suites. Hal Sperlich, who moved from Ford to Chrysler when top executives blasted him for repeatedly pushing his idea for a new vehicle—the minivan—says corporate life is much easier in the short term "if you go with the flow . . . the corporate environment just doesn't reward people for challenging the status quo."[8]

But the long-term effects of going along and getting along can be very hazardous to career health, especially in situations that involve serious ethical and legal issues.

Exemplary Followers work on their confrontation and courage-building skills on a daily basis, practicing insightful, positive challenges to small directives in order to establish both a reputation and experience level that prepares them for the heavy crises that will eventually present themselves.

7. *Take collective action or plan well to stand alone.* It is easier to find courage to take a conscience stand when others are with you. Exemplary Followers know their voices are stronger when blended into a chorus of colleagues all singing from the same page. While the group approach can be threatening to some leaders, Exemplary Followers have been successful at making changes when the go-it-alone approach fails.

In those cases where Exemplary Followers have been forced to stand alone, wise planning has helped cushion the blow. Some have lined up other job options in the event there is retaliation against them. Others have established special savings accounts as a financial cushion should they be forced to find another job or as a hedge against having to hire an attorney.

Followers may agree to suspend their decision-making power and vest it in a leader. But Exemplary Followers make sure leaders understand that their control has only been suspended, not surrendered.

By following the seven steps of Exemplary Followers who have learned to disagree agreeably, you will greatly increase your chances of success in the leadership confrontations all exemplary workers are bound to face.

Conclusion

"The brave carve out their own fortune," Cervantes wrote in *Don Quixote.* Exemplary followership in a leader-centric world is not easy. First you must overcome the negative stereotypes. Then, you have to deal with the power and authority issues. Finally, you need to learn the skills of the Exemplary Follower. This is a tall order for anyone.

But considering that you spend up to 90 percent of your time in the follower role, the personal payoff can be great. Plus, when you consider the meager return that society has gotten from its huge investment in leadership training and leader worship, perhaps it is time to give followership a chance. A good leader with 10 (or 100 or 1,000) less-than-competent followers can achieve little. On the other hand, 10 Exemplary Followers don't even require a leader; if they get stuck with a less-than-competent one, they can still accomplish their goals. With widespread great followership, leadership perhaps becomes a nonissue.

15

Healing Leadership

Judith A. Sturnick

Dr. Judith A. Sturnick is president of The Sturnick Group for Executive Coaching and Consulting to Corporations, Higher Education and Healthcare, located in the San Francisco Bay area. She is also a senior associate with The Education Consulting Institute in Washington, D.C. Dr. Sturnick served as a campus president for 11 years (the University of Maine at Farmington and Keene State College). Author of numerous articles, chapters in books, and two books of her own, Dr. Sturnick is working on a book dealing with women and prosperity. She is a member of The Greenleaf Center's board of trustees.

In this essay, Judith Sturnick addresses the need for the healing of our many wounded leaders and organizations. Drawing on her own personal experience, and that of others, Sturnick suggests that depression, fatigue, and overwork have become commonplace in the 1990s and that it is imperative that we concentrate on the development of healing kinds of leadership—servant-leadership—in the decades to come.

We live in "interesting" times; the ancient Chinese curse has come true and is now embedded in our lives and work. As the times we live in are interesting, so are the opportunities and challenges for leadership within and at every level of our organizations.

Interesting is one of those blanket words that camouflage numerous meanings, both pungent and subtle. In contemporary leadership situations, *interesting* may in actuality be a code word for *mangled, wounded, disempowered, disenchanted, confused, disheartened.* Our public vocabularies are carefully detached and objective, the better to obscure that which is uncomfortable and painful. In not many corporate, business, or educational settings, after all, may we speak of agony and spiritual evisceration—to say nothing of the accompanying bleak depression.

Many of the leaders and administrators with whom I work are profoundly depressed. Depression is indeed a sign of these times. Many of these bright, dedicated leaders believe (or behave as if they believe) that depression can be willed away. Many of them also believe that they are not allowed to show fear or uncertainty; they dare not fail in any endeavor; it is normal to lose control of one's life; the sacrifice of personal life for the efficacy of work is legitimate; pain is merely temporary (best to ignore it!); relentless fatigue is a necessary accompaniment of leading contemporary institutions; time is inherently unmanageable; self-care is therefore impossible (or irrelevant); and joyful life lies somewhere in the misty future.

These are some of the symptoms of deeply wounded leaders, individuals who are in need of healing at the most profound levels of their being, whether or not they can risk consciously acknowledging this. The title of this essay, "Healing Leadership," has meaning on at least two levels: restoring our leaders by bringing them back to emotional, spiritual, intellectual, and physical health; and from the wisdom and insight gained through that healing process to provide, in turn, leadership that heals and transforms the quality of life and work within our organizations.

Earlier I used the term *disheartened*. Here are some living examples of disheartened leaders. A senior executive from an international, megacorporation confides, as he passes his 50th birthday, that he is weary of his highly salaried job and detached from his 30-year marriage. His eyes fill with tears as he talks about his unhappiness.

At a stress management seminar for presidential leadership, one man tells the group that his physician has warned he will die in his job if he does not make significant life changes immediately. This man, still in his forties, tearfully informs us that the demands of his position make it impossible to undertake those changes; he is reconciled to death by stroke or heart attack on the job.

The president of a private college has only three years to complete before retirement; she finds herself weeping several times a day, without obvious cause. Sadly, dealing with the reasons for the tears is not her issue; instead, her issue is how she can keep from breaking down in public. In her stress and fatigue, she does not have the energy to worry about why. She asks me for "maintenance help" to "get through" the time until she can retire.

Each of these individuals had lost heart for their lives and work. These are not simply stories related from a cool distance. I too have wandered in the wilderness of exhaustion and suffering, unable to see the pathway out. A few years ago, in my 11th year as a campus president, I brought in an outside consultant to conduct a retreat on stress reduction with my leadership team and me. In her debriefing alone with me at the close of the retreat, she told me, "Judith, consider this conversation an intervention. If you do not change your life now, you will not be alive a year from now." (Is it any wonder that years later I resonated to similar words spoken by another president in my workshop?)

The consultant's words were incomprehensible to me at first. Finally I stuttered, "You don't understand. If I do not continue in this job, what will I do?"

Very quietly and firmly, she gave me a response that is permanently imprinted on my mind and heart. "The question," she said, "is not what you will do. The question is: If you continue in this job, *what will you be?*" Four months later, following probing introspection, I resigned from my position to seek healing and a different way of life.

Let me state truthfully what a long, hurtful, arduous, sometimes confusing, zigzag journey I traveled after my resignation. That healing process, which was filled with self-doubt and depression, was not easy on any level, and many times I thought of abandoning it in order to slide back into the oblivion of denial. For the first time, I understood on a gut level the meaning of "dis-ease." Remembering now how hard it was to stay with my own healing work, I truly acknowledge its dark complexity. Yet I also acknowledge how vital was that dark complexity to re-creating and deepening connection with my inner spirit.

The voice that speaks within each of us guides us to the centered balance: that place of health from which our dearest impulses spring. This balance becomes the standard by which we can weigh our life choices. Through our deepest listening in that centered stillness, we define our personal equations of life and work, mind and feeling, striving and rest, body and spirit.

During my own 10-month struggle to reshape my life, I determined that in the present and future my livelihood must provide daily soul-grounding. Spirit and sacred life; spirit and sacred work; spirit and sacred health. As Matthew Fox has said: "There is no Eucharist without our labor. In fact, Eucharist is our labor, our thank-you for being here."[1] There is sweetness in speaking of work and Eucharist in the same breath. How, I wondered as I pondered his words, could organizational life be yoked with the purposes of the human heart? Consequently, issues of healing leadership are now central to my work.

So many questions lie at the heart of this process. Many individuals are "called" to lead (although they may not use that language). Is it possible to create healing patterns for work without losing the passion of the call? Is it possible to play a highly public leadership role and still live a healthy life? Even if a leader comes to terms with self-healing, is organizational healing possible—or worth the enormous effort it requires? Can the healed leader throw herself or himself into the task of healing the organization without once again taking on unhealthy patterns? When must an individual choose to leave the institution to preserve hard-won health? These are tough questions without analgesic answers.

Six Stages of Healing Leadership

From the journeys I have witnessed, as well as from my own healing, I can make the following observations about healing leadership and the six stages— (1) consciousness of health; (2) willingness to change; (3) a teachable moment; (4) healthy support systems; (5) immersion in the duality of our inner lives; and (6) the return to service in leadership—that an individual passes through.

First things first, as the adage goes. Change is not possible without a "health consciousness." There must exist a frame of reference, a consciousness about personal and institutional health. By what measure, and in what ways, are we and our organizations ill—or healthy? Although we may not have answers, we are conscious that health could be a possibility for ourselves and our organizations—and that we are not now healthy. This is a sorrowful realization.

Such personal consciousness may require a triggering event, perhaps something as forceful as an intervention, as it did in my case. Although we ordinarily do not think in these terms, formal and informal interventions can help jar us loose from unhealthy life patterns. As is true of addiction interventions, a leadership intervention is for the purpose of confronting and defining the problems at hand, cracking open the shell of denial to expose (but not destroy) the vulnerable self, and providing both support and wisdom for creating—or re-creating—the healthy self.

Out of this individual consciousness, then, emerges the second stage: a desire to change one's life and one's self. Often the very act of bringing in a coach or an outside consultant indicates the leader's willingness (albeit unconscious) to explore new possibilities individually and within the organization. During the ensuing conversations around matters of organizational behavior, team development, or leadership strengthening, an individual leader may ask for advice and begin to pose new questions. Thus appears stage three: the teachable moment, which is also the vulnerable moment.

Timing is of immense consequence here. Epiphany emerging from the teachable moment is a remarkable experience. But in itself, this is not enough. Because the resulting steps are harder, we may try to evade the covenants of healing that lie beyond the moment of revelation. Since insight without changed behavior is meaningless, however, epiphany must be followed by altered actions.

No matter how determined a person may be, however, behavior change cannot occur in a vacuum; a support system (stage four) is needed, whether initially that be only one person, several people or a group, or a community. Part of the unhealthy past pattern is the isolation that often accompanies leadership positions. Frozen in that isolation, we lose our ability to reality test and to belong fully to the human race; we disconnect our circuits of intimacy. Nevertheless, while isolation compels us to unhealthy behavior, connectedness holds at least the possibility of health.

But connectedness to what? Often our organizations (loosely, a type of community) are torn between setting apart their leaders as icons or demonizing them—often simultaneously. (In his writing, Walter Wink speaks wonderfully of the angelic/demonic dualisms within our institutions.[2]) There is irony in the fact that personal and organizational dysfunctions result in the loss of the powers of discernment at the very time we must make sensible judgments about the communities we seek and where to find them. It is wise to remember that unhealthy organizations cannot provide a healing space for their leaders; indeed, they are often antagonistic to that struggle to heal. At the same time, not all "intentional communities" are safe, so various are the human motivations within them. All the more difficult is this quandary to find healing space and supportive humanity.

Additionally, our own ambivalence about community, within institutions at least, comes into play. The ego strength that motivates and energizes us in our leadership roles also keeps us skeptical in our detachment. Yet effective leadership, acting out of health consciousness, is nourished by relationships with peers and colleagues, self, family and friends, mentors and teachers.

Effective healing processes require, then, at some point (and perhaps at most points), a human support system. We simply need the help of others to determine the causes and extent of our woundedness, as well as to witness our return to health. Since we cannot heal what we cannot acknowledge or understand, we need safety to explore and discuss what is happening to us. For that exploration, community can be an abundant wellspring.

Exploration is really a tao kind of a word, for, both initially and intermittently throughout the cycle, we are plunged into the cruelest darkness. A black cloak of fear, self-doubt, and uncertainty muffles our senses. This is the time during which we must allow another human being to be present to the sorrow of our private sagas: When we cannot tell our stories, freely and with absolute truth (as best we understand it), we remain stuck in our woundedness.

A decade ago, we paid considerable attention to the condition of the wounded healer and, as a corollary, the wounded leader. It is easy to become caught in our stories, retelling our personal myths without ever breaking the circles of pain and dysfunction. Nevertheless, healing means moving beyond seductive cycles of grief into patterns of renewal. A system of human support that critiques our realities with love and encouragement helps us move on; we are then no longer wounded leaders but healthy healers of ourselves and our organizations. In the terminology of Chris Argyis, we come to understand the "defensive routines" by which we have protected and rationalized the illness of our own, and our institutions', behaviors.

Refuge in safe communities liberates us to experience stage five: absolute immersion in our inner life, a kind of baptism of the self. The state of being we seek through the healing process is, at its core, within us. Although our inner shadows are real and must be confronted, they are rarely as virulent as we fear them to be. That fact is essential knowledge, not only for the conscious act of rekindling our own light, but to keep us from applying demonic myths, not just to our organizations, but to ourselves.

It is said that when the nineteenth-century transcendentalists Emerson and Thoreau walked together in the forest near Concord, Thoreau saw the shadows and Emerson saw the sunlight. Both elements are reality. In order to confront, like Joseph Conrad's Kurtz, the heart of organizational darkness, we must believe in the potential of light, too. We need to know this for, ultimately, as we enter the sixth stage, most of us feel the urgency to bring our healthy selves back into the still unhealthy systems—even though we know the integrity of our healing will be ferociously tested.

Why return to unhealthy organizations? Because many—perhaps the majority—of leaders seek to serve. Although that particular language may not be universally accepted by individual leaders, most of us are motivated by dedication to a greater set of principles or vision. A healthy perspective on servant-leadership (by any other name) reflects an equally healthy insight, gained from our authentic odysseys through pain and blackness, into our own egos and motives. Whatever wise perspective we have learned allows us to recognize that, despite our best hopes, not all organizations can, or wish to, heal. It is not a unique experience to attempt healthy leadership and find no followers.

Studies of organizational development show a consistent reality about states of health and disease. An intriguing fact is that when a healthy individual enters a dysfunctional organization, she or he must become dysfunctional, too, to survive in that culture. Sick organizations really do contaminate.

The Components of Healing Wisdom

Near the beginning of this chapter, I raised the issue of how the healed (and still healing) leader knows when it is necessary to leave the institution. The answer is logically simple and emotionally tangled; in such circumstances, though, reason must carry the decision. When a leader who has reached a state of health perceives that she or he is being drawn back into sick behavior and thinking, and it is clear that the organization cannot or will not deal with its dysfunctional issues, it is time to go. As each of us is responsible for our own health, we are responsible, too, for making the sane distinctions between healthy and unhealthy environments, as well as about leaving or staying.

But let us return to the leader's reentry into the organization, a process that is itself a significant, unpredictable undertaking. In returning initially to our institutions, we bring with us the transformative energy of new knowledge, along with a revitalizing of some old truths and a discarding of others. Whether or not we are welcomed back, we now carry *possibility* within us. The potential exists to teach our organizations, according to our best understanding, these components of healing wisdom: (1) comprehending and honoring boundaries; (2) releasing obsessive and destructive perfectionism; (3) seeking creative responses to ambiguity; (4) acknowledging, however tentatively, a spiritual reality within our institutions; (5) fostering personal and organizational experimentation; and (6) maximizing the elements of discovery and surprise.

The attention to boundaries is compelling. Although we do not always establish them, healthy boundaries are as crucial to our organizations as they are to individuals. Effective leadership service requires boundaries that remind us how to keep service redemptive rather than sacrificial.

Healing insight helps us also to confront issues—exacerbated by personal and institutional transitions—of obsessive perfectionism and abhorrence of failure. (What an anomaly it is that we fear both success and failure, roughly in equal measure). We live in a time of tangled and inchoate change without clearly illuminated choices. At times it is incomprehensible that we no longer have time to catch our breath in the midst of change. As Peter Vaill (who has written so eloquently of modern change as "permanent whitewater") and I have recently discussed, we no longer have the luxury of spaces in which to pause, reflect, and restabilize before we are hit by the next wave of upheaval. Change occurs and, before we can process and fully adapt to its ramifications, new changes supersede and dislocate our lives and our institutions once again. How hard it is to hold our center!

Healing leadership recognizes this reality and at the same time understands the logic of the illogical chaotic. The precise decision, the perfect action are not possible in this world of tumbling and colliding forces. The best judgments may not hold true a moment later. Accepting the fallibility of structures and the unpredictability of sequences, then, means also accepting our own inevitable failures. Unhealed leaders who invest too much in impossible flawlessness can neither learn nor lead their organizations through transformative learning.

When we depersonalize ourselves by denying the omnipresence of ambiguity (as unhealed leaders do), we have no resources for dealing with it or for creating organizational environments in which ambiguity can be addressed. No wonder so many leadership theories and reengineerings throw us into the gaps and crevices of our institutions. Releasing our expectations of flawlessness is therefore an act of pure health. As an aside, an organization moving toward health no longer expects the impossible of its leaders. The healed organization (in those systems in which healing is possible) comes to grips with ambiguity and fallibility, just as do its leaders.

Another component of healing leadership is to acknowledge, however tentatively, the nature of spiritual reality within our institutions. We can differentiate between calling our institutions (which are often almost demonically destructive) "spiritual" and recognizing the possibility of a spirituality within them. I am struck by a comment in one of Parker Palmer's essays: "The link between leadership and spirituality calls us to reexamine our denial of the inner life."[3] An institution may not have an inner life (surely a debatable point, since the Fetzer Institute recently underwrote a small conference to explore whether or not institutions have vocations), but its human leadership does. The health of our organizations requires, and healthy leaders allow, space for questions about that inner life to be posed and legitimized by the people within those structures. Our purpose is not to seek a monolithic answer but, rather, to create the possibility of many dialogues around what is human, what is the higher purpose of leadership ethics and institutional values, and why acknowledgment of the inner life matters, individually and organizationally.

Healing leadership that encourages organizational healing does focus on dialogues and questions—rich, complex, complicated, and contradictory voices and perspectives. "Why are we here?" is as much a query for the organization as for the individual.

The process of both public and internal dialogue, however, simultaneously demands the capacity to listen. Sometimes we behave as if dialogue is actually an unfolding of parallel and competing monologues, rather than interconnected questions or statements with responses. As healed leaders strive to listen with care and thoughtfulness, they nurture their organizations to do likewise. When this process comes alive, there is the flicker of health.

Since the tried and true solutions of the past no longer fit (and perhaps never really did), a healing organization is eager for the freedom to experiment with ideas, options, challenges, new ways of relating, new definitions of one's identity in work. Dialogues foster verbal experimentation: Will this work? Is this possible? What happens if we do this? Verbal experimentation leads to experimental actions, which give rise, in turn, to discovery and surprise. Organizations are as capable of this sequence as are individuals.

Too seldom in our analysis and discussion of healing do we dwell on the power of surprise. Earlier I talked about ambiguity; one powerful outcome of ambiguity is surprise. Without stable and secure answers, we are constantly in a process of discovering the unexpected. Surprise brings us to a halt, then to reflection and, to the unveiling of unanticipated outcomes. The healthiest leadership is, at one and the same time, a product of unfolding surprise and a catalyst of such discovery within the organization.

Discovery has another healing advantage: the recovery of truth. Our institutions provide cover and denial behind which we can hide from pain and self. Yet as dialogue raises questions that eventually route us to discovery, we begin to discern the authentic in ourselves and our organizations. What possibilities may result from institutional discovery and recovery? How many conjunctions of personal and organizational discovery does it take to transform our institutions, to heal the wounds that institutions inflict on individual lives and to create healthy, new infrastructures for those institutions?

More than one leader is needed to seek answers to these questions and to foster constructive change within our organizations. In our culture, we are enamored of heroes: Daniel Boone, Clayton Powell, Christa Macauliff. The problem with the Leader-as-Hero is that when the Hero leaves, the decapitated institution bleeds to death. Or when the Hero is turned into the Scapegoat, the institution cannibalizes itself. In any case, healing leadership means restructuring organizations so that more leaders are simultaneously servants to the institution's highest purpose—and leaders responsible for accountable directions.

Sharing power and service is healing in itself, acknowledging as it does the presence of numerous valued leaders. Opening the organization to many leadership roles at all levels invites an infusion of varied perspectives, a multitude of options and solutions from which the best actions (as these are understood in the moment) can be determined.

Healing leaders, confident in the efficacy of questioning, can both stimulate and participate in the institutional healing process. Truly, by our healing we are known. As the comedian Lily Tomlin reminds us, "metaphysical fitness" is also necessary for health.

Yes, we do indeed live in interesting times. Toxic institutions, toxic work, and toxic leadership define many aspects of our lives. But so too are our realities defined by organizational health, spirited work, and heartened leadership. We discover a healing path and then offer our leadership to heal our institutions. In our journeys, many of us are learning new ways of wellbeing and wellspringing. As we do so, we are raising a counterpoint of intriguing riddles and questions to arouse the energy of these most interesting times.

PART THREE

Spirit

I do not want to define or explain spirit. There is, in my theology, a mystery before which I simply stand in awe. At the threshold of the mystery, I ask no questions and seek no explanations. I simply bow before the mystery, and what it wants to say to me comes as gently as doves as I achieve the quiet. Spirit is behind the threshold of the mystery. I don't know what it is, even though occasionally I get intimations about it, but I do have a belief about what it does. When a leader has spirit, it builds trust; it builds trust not only between leader and follower but also between followers.

Robert K. Greenleaf
On Becoming a Servant-Leader

Robert Greenleaf said that spirit represents the drive behind the urge to serve—the force that takes one into an active role as servant. "As the driving force behind the urge to serve," wrote Greenleaf, "spirit may be a profound manifestation of the deep good and strength in a person, and a primary ingredient that makes a civilized society possible."

There are many understandings of the word *spirit* as it relates to servant-leadership. The essays contained in this section share their own insights on the natures of spirit and servant-leadership.

16

Leading from Within

Parker J. Palmer

Parker J. Palmer is a writer, teacher, and activist who works independently on issues in education, spirituality, community, and leadership. Among his widely acclaimed books are The Company of Strangers, To Know as We Are Known, *and* The Active Life. *His latest book is* The Courage to Teach: Exploring the Inner Landscape of a Teacher's Life. *Palmer travels widely, offering workshops and retreats. He serves as a senior associate with the American Association of Higher Education and as senior adviser to the Fetzer Institute.*

This essay has been updated and expanded considerably from its initial publication in 1990. Parker Palmer addresses the need for all leaders, from the president to classroom teachers, to look inward and to understand their motivations in providing leadership. Palmer examines the "shadow side" of leadership and suggests that we should all strive to uncover our own spiritual nature, which may open our capacity for compassionate, moral leadership.

Introduction

In the last decade or two, we have done a lot of moaning about the lack of moral, humane, and visionary leadership in the public arena.[1] But today, if we have eyes to see, we can look around the world and find those moral, visionary, humane leaders. We can find them in South Africa, we can find them in Latin America, and we can find them in eastern Europe.

I want to begin these reflections with the words of one of those people, someone whose credentials for leadership are far more authentic than mine. In 1990 Vaclav Havel (playwright, dissident, prisoner, and then president of Czechoslovakia) addressed the U.S. Congress. It was surely one of the most remarkable speeches ever delivered on the floor of our national legislative body:

> As long as people are people, democracy, in the full sense of the word, will always be no more than an ideal. In this sense, you too are merely approaching democracy uninterruptedly for more than 200 years, and

your journey toward the horizon has never been disrupted by a totalitarian system.

The communist type of totalitarian system has left both our nations, Czechs and Slovaks, as it has all the nations of the Soviet Union and the other countries the Soviet Union subjugated in its time, a legacy of countless dead, an infinite spectrum of human suffering, profound economic decline, and, above all, enormous human humiliation. It has brought us horrors that fortunately you have not known. [I think we Americans should confess that some in our country *have* known such horrors.—P.J.P.]

It has also given us something positive, a special capacity to look from time to time somewhat further than someone who has not undergone this bitter experience. A person who cannot move and lead a somewhat normal life because he is pinned under a boulder has more time to think about his hopes than someone who is not trapped that way.

What I'm trying to say is this: we must all learn many things from you, from how to educate our offspring, how to elect our representatives, all the way to how to organize our economic life so that it will lead to prosperity and not to poverty. But it doesn't have to be merely assistance from the well-educated, powerful and wealthy to someone who has nothing and therefore has nothing to offer in return.

We too can offer something to you: our experience and the knowledge that has come from it. The specific experience I'm talking about has given me one certainty: consciousness precedes being, and not the other way around, as the Marxists claim. For this reason, the salvation of this human world lies nowhere else than in the human heart, in the human power to reflect, in human meekness and in human responsibility. Without a global revolution in the sphere of human consciousness, nothing will change for the better in the sphere of our being as humans, and the catastrophe toward which this world is headed—be it ecological, social, demographic or a general breakdown of civilization—will be unavoidable.[2]

I doubt there has ever been, from a more remarkable source, a stronger affirmation of the role of spirituality in the world of human affairs than Havel's words "consciousness precedes being" and "the salvation of the world lies in the human heart." He points us toward the heart of the matter—the formation of the human heart, the reformation of the human heart, and the rescuing of the human heart from all its deformations.

Material realities, he tells us, are not the fundamental factor in the movement of history. Consciousness is. Human awareness is. Thought is. Spirit is. Those are the deep sources of freedom and power with which oppressed people historically have been able to move immense boulders and create remarkable change.

But let me say something that Vaclav Havel was too polite to say: It is not only the Marxists who have believed that matter is more powerful than consciousness. It is not only the Marxists who have believed that economics is more fundamental than spirit. It is not only the Marxists who have believed that the flow of cash creates more reality than does the flow of ideas. We capitalists have believed these things, too, and Havel was simply too nice to say it. But we can say it to ourselves. We can remind ourselves that in our own system of thought we have a long and crippling legacy of believing in the power of the external world much more deeply than we believe in the power of the internal world.

How many times have you heard or said, "Those are good ideas, inspiring notions, but the *reality* is . . ."? How many times have you heard people trying to limit our creativity by treating institutional realities as absolute constraints on what we are able to do? How many times have you worked in systems based on the belief that the only changes that really matter are the ones that you can count or measure or tally up externally? This is not just a Marxist problem. This is a human problem, at least in our twentieth-century, technological society.

We are not victims of that society, we are its co-creators. The great insight of our spiritual traditions is that external reality does not impinge upon us as a prison or as an ultimate constraint. Instead we *co-create* that reality. We live in and through a complex interaction of spirit and matter, a complex interaction of what is inside of us and what is "out there." The wisdom of our spiritual traditions is not to deny the reality of the outer world, but to help us understand that we create the world, in part, by projecting our spirit on it—for better or worse.

Vaclav Havel has said some hard things to his own people about how they conspired in the domination of a tyrannical communist system through their own passivity. We too are responsible for the existence of tyrannical conditions, of external constraints that crush our spirits, because we too co-create reality through the projection of our internal limitations. Our complicity in world-making is a source of awesome and sometimes painful responsibility and at the same time a source of profound hope for change.

The great spiritual traditions are not primarily about values and ethics, not primarily about doing right or living well. The spiritual traditions are primarily about *reality*. The spiritual traditions all strive to penetrate the illusions of the external world and to name its underlying truth—what it is, how it emerges, and how we relate to it.

In my own tradition, I have been rereading some of Jesus' sayings that I was taught to regard as ethical exhortations, as guides to what we *ought* to do. For example, "The person who seeks life will lose it, but the person who is willing to lose life will find it." That, I now understand, is not an ethical exhortation. It is not an "ought" statement. It is simply a description of what *is!* Time and again, things Jesus said that we take as ethical pronouncements are simply his statements of what is real. That is the nature of great spiritual teaching.

The insight that I want to draw from the spiritual traditions, and from Havel, may be best summarized in a word from depth psychology: *projection*.

We share responsibility for creating the external world by projecting either a spirit of light or a spirit of shadow on that which is other than us. We project either a spirit of hope or a spirit of despair, either an inner confidence in wholeness and integration or an inner terror about life being diseased and ultimately terminal. We have a choice about what we are going to project, and in that choice we help create the world that is. Consciousness precedes being, and consciousness can help deform or reform our world.

The Shadow Side of Leadership

What does all of this have to do with leadership and with the relation of leadership to spirituality? Here is a quick definition of a leader: A leader is a person who has an unusual degree of power to project onto other people his or her shadow, or his or her light. A leader is a person who has an unusual degree of power to create the conditions under which other people must live and move and have their being, conditions that can either be as illuminating as heaven or as shadowy as hell. A leader must take special responsibility for what's going on inside his or her own self, inside his or her consciousness, lest the act of leadership create more harm than good.

I want to look here at the shadow side of leadership. Many books on leadership seem to be about the power of positive thinking. I fear they feed a common delusion among leaders that their efforts are always well intended, their power always benign. I suggest that the challenge is to examine our consciousness for those ways in which leaders may project more shadow than light.

By *leaders*, I do not mean simply the heads of nation-states. I am talking, for example, about classroom teachers who have the power to create the conditions under which young people must spend half of their waking hours, five days a week, week in and week out. We know that there are classrooms where the leader projects a welcoming light under which new growth flourishes. But we also know of classrooms where the leader casts an ominous shadow under which nothing can grow.

I am talking also about parents who can generate the same bipolar effects in a family, or about clergy who can create congregations that lurk in the leader's shadow or thrive in his or her light. I am talking about the CEOs of corporations who face the choice between shadow and light every day, but who often do not even know that they are making a choice, let alone know how to reflect on the process of choosing.

The problem is that people rise to leadership in our society by a tendency toward extroversion, which too often means ignoring what is going on inside themselves. Leaders rise to power by operating very competently and effectively in the external world, sometimes at the cost of internal awareness. Leaders, in the very way they become leaders, tend to screen out the inner consciousness that Vaclav Havel is calling us to attend to. I have met too many leaders whose confidence in the external world is so high that they regard the inner life as illusory, a waste of time, a magical fantasy trip into a region that does not even exist. But the link Havel makes between consciousness and reality, between leadership and spirituality, calls us to reexamine that common denial of the inner life.

I think leaders often feed themselves on the power of positive thinking because their jobs are hard. They face many external discouragements and they get little affirmation. Thus they feel a need to psych themselves up even if it means ignoring the inner shadow. Of course, leaders are supported in this by an American culture that wants to externalize everything, that wants (just as much as Marx ever did) to see the good life more as a matter of outer arrangements than of inner well-being.

I have looked at some training programs for leaders, and I am discouraged by how often they focus on the development of skills to manipulate the external world rather than the skills necessary to go within and make the spiritual journey. I find that discouraging because it feeds a dangerous syndrome among leaders who already tend to deny their inner world.

The Nature of Spirituality

Spirituality, like leadership, is a very hard concept to pin down. *Leadership* and *spirituality* are probably two of the vaguest words you can find in our language, and when you put them together you get something even more vague.

So let me share a remarkably concrete quote from Annie Dillard's wonderfully titled book *Teaching a Stone to Talk*. Never have I read a more evocative description of the inner journey:

> In the deeps are the violence and terror of which psychology has warned us. But if you ride these monsters down, if you drop with them farther over the world's rim, you find what our sciences can not locate or name, the substrate, the ocean or matrix or ether which buoys the rest, which gives goodness its power for good, and evil its power for evil, the unified field: our complex and inexplicable caring for each other, and for our life together here. This is given. It is not learned.[3]

Annie Dillard is saying several things that are very important for a spirituality of leadership. She is saying first, that the spiritual journey moves inward and downward, not outward and upward toward abstraction. It moves downward toward the hardest concrete realities of our lives—a reversal of what we traditionally have understood spirituality to be.

Why must we go in and down? Because as we do so, we will meet the violence and terror that we carry within ourselves. If we do not confront these things inwardly, we will project them outward onto other people.

When we have not understood that the enemy is within ourselves, we will find a thousand ways of making someone "out there" into the enemy—people of a different race, a different gender, a different sexual orientation. We will deal with our fears by killing the enemy, when what we really fear is the shadow within ourselves.

Annie Dillard is saying we have to go down and in, and on the way we will meet our own monsters. But if we ride those monsters all the way down, we find the most precious thing of all: "the unified field, our complex and inexplicable caring for each other," the community we have underneath our brokenness—which, Dillard says, is given, not learned. Great leadership comes from people who have made that downward journey through violence and terror, who have touched the deep place where we are in community with each other, and who can help take the rest of us to that place. *That* is what great leadership is all about.

That is also what Vaclav Havel is talking about, because the downward journey is what you take when you are under a stone for 40 years. That is what you have a chance to do when you are a victim of oppression. Is it not remarkable that Nelson Mandela used decades in prison to prepare himself for leadership rather than for despair? Under the most destructive circumstances, he went down, he went in, he dealt with the violence and terror, and he emerged as a leader able to take people toward "our complex and inexplicable caring for each other." It seems to me that this is a powerful image for the spiritual journey, the journey that leaders must take if Havel and Dillard are right.

Now the question is, why would anybody want to take such a difficult and dangerous journey? Everything in us cries out against it. That is why we externalize everything—it is far easier to deal with the external world. It is easier to spend your life manipulating an institution than dealing with your own soul. We make institutions sound complicated and hard and rigorous, but they are simplicity itself compared with our inner labyrinths!

Let me tell you a little parable about why one might want to take the inner journey, a parable from my own life. About 10 years ago, when I was in my early forties, I decided to go on that amazing program called Outward Bound. I was in the midst of a midlife crisis—one that began at age 17 and persists to this day!—and I thought Outward Bound might be a way to stretch my soul.

I elected to spend 10 days at a place called Hurricane Island. I should have known from the name what was in store for me. Next time I will choose the program at Pleasant Valley or Happy Gardens! It was a week of sheer terror. It was also a week of amazing growth and great teaching and a deep sense of community, the likes of which I have seldom experienced.

In the middle of that Outward Bound course I faced the challenge that I had most feared. The leaders backed me up to the edge of a cliff 110 feet above solid ground. They tied a frayed and very thin rope to my waist and told me to back down that cliff.

So I said, "Well, what do I do?"

The instructor, in typical Outward Bound fashion, said, "Just go!"

So I went and slammed down onto a small ledge, with considerable force.

The instructor looked down at me. "I don't think you quite have it yet."

"Right. *Now* what do I do?"

"The only way to do this is to lean back as far as you can. You have to get your body at right angles to the rock face so you'll have your full weight on your feet."

Of course I *knew* that he was wrong. I knew that the trick was to hug the mountain, to stay as close to the rock face as I could. So I tried it again, and BOOM! I hit the next ledge, hard.

"You still don't have it," the instructor said.

And I said, "Well, what do I do?"

And he said, "Lean way back and take the next step."

The next step was a very big one, but I took it. Wonder of wonders, I began to get the knack. I leaned back, and sure enough, I was moving down the rock face, eyes on the heavens, making tiny, tiny, tiny movements with my feet but gaining confidence with every step.

When I got about halfway down, a second instructor called up from below. "Parker," she said, "I think you better stop and look at what's happening beneath your feet."

Very slowly I lowered my eyes, and there beneath my feet was a large hole opening up in the rock.

To get around the hole, I was going to have to change directions. I froze, completely paralyzed in sheer terror.

The second instructor let me hang there for what seemed like a very long time, and finally she shouted up, "Parker, is anything wrong?"

To this day, I do not know where these words came from, though I have 12 witnesses that I spoke them. But in a high, squeaky voice I said, "I don't want to talk about it."

"Then I think it's time you learned the motto of the Outward Bound School."

"Oh, great," I thought. "I'm about to die, and she's giving me a motto!"

But then she yelled up to me words that I will never forget, words that have been genuinely empowering for me ever since. "The motto of the Outward Bound Hurricane Island School is, 'If you can't get out of it, get into it!' "

I have believed in the idea of "the word become flesh" for a long time, but I had never had a real experience of it. But my instructor's words seemed so profoundly true to me in this existential moment that they entered my body, bypassed my mind, and animated my legs and feet. It was just so clear that there was no way out of that situation except to get into it. No helicopter was going to come; they were not going to haul me up on the rope; I was not going to float down. I had to get into it, and my feet started to move.

Why would anyone ever want to take the inner journey about which Annie Dillard and Vaclav Havel write? The answer is: There is no way out of my inner life so I'd better get into it. On the inward and downward spiritual journey, the only way out is in and through.

Out of the Shadow, into the Light

The shadow lives of leaders are inevitably projected onto institutions and society. If they are to create less shadow and more light, leaders need to ride certain monsters all the way down. Here is a bestiary of five of those monsters, and a few thoughts on how the inner journey might transform our leadership at each of these points.

One of the biggest shadows inside a lot of leaders is deep insecurity about their own identity, their own worth. That insecurity is hard to see in extroverted people. But the extroversion is often there precisely because they are insecure about who they are; they are trying to prove themselves in the external world rather than wrestling with their inner identity.

This insecurity takes a specific form that I have seen many times, especially in men, and I see it in myself: We have an identity that is so hooked up with external, institutional functions that we may literally die when those functions are taken away from us. We live in terror of what will happen to us if our institutional identity were ever to disappear.

When leaders operate with a deep, unexamined insecurity about their own identity, they create institutional settings that deprive *other* people of *their* identity as a way of dealing with the unexamined fears in the leaders themselves.

Here is a simple example. I am astonished at the number of times I call an office and hear "Dr. Jones's office—this is Nancy speaking." The leader has a title and a last name; the person who answers the phone has neither; and the boss has decreed that it be done that way. This is a small but powerful example of depriving someone else of an identity to enhance your own.

Everywhere I look I see institutions depriving large numbers of people of their identity so that a few people can enhance theirs. I look at schools and I see hundreds of thousands of students passively memorizing information delivered by experts. These students have been deprived of an identity by the educational system so that teachers can have more identity for themselves, as if this were a zero-sum game, a win-lose situation.

As I go around the country talking to people in higher education, I always ask students, "When was the last time that you were asked to relate your life story to the things you are studying?" They say, "What? Our life story doesn't count here." The whole idea in higher education is to replace their "little" life stories with the "big" story of the disciplines. The whole idea in an expert-dominated, technocratic form of education is to devalue those little parochial stories on behalf of the "true" one. And think of what we do to patients in a hospital. Talk about depriving people of identity so that leaders can have more for themselves!

It is not always this way. There are organizations led by people who know who they are "all the way down," whose identity does not depend on a specific role that might be taken away at any moment. If you are in that kind of organization, you are with people and in settings that *give* you identity, that empower you to be someone. I believe this is a core issue in the spirituality of leadership.

The great spiritual gift that comes as one takes the inward journey is to know for certain that who I am does not depend on what I do. Identity does not depend on titles, or degrees, or function. It depends only on the simple fact that I am a child of God, valued and treasured for what I am. When a leader knows that, then the classroom is different, the hospital is different, and the office is different.

The second shadow of leadership that is inside a lot of us (and please understand that I am talking about myself and my struggles here as much as anybody else's) is the perception that the universe is essentially hostile to human interests and that life is fundamentally a battleground.

Have you ever noticed how often people use "battle" images as they go about the work of leadership? We talk about "do or die" tactics and strategy, about using our big guns, about allies and enemies, about wins and losses. The imagery suggests that if we fail to be fiercely competitive, we will lose, because the basic structure of the universe is a vast combat zone. The tragedy of that inner shadow, that unexamined inner fear of failing, is that it helps create situations where people actually have to live that way.

Our commitment to competition is a self-fulfilling prophecy. Yes, the world is competitive, but only because we make it that way. Some of the best operations in our world, some of our best corporations, some of our best schools are learning that there is another way of going about things, a way that is consensual, cooperative, communal. They are fulfilling a different prophecy and creating a different reality.

The spiritual gift we receive as we take the inward journey is the knowledge that the universe is working together for good. The universe is not out to get anybody; the structure of reality is not the structure of a battle. Yes, there is death, but it is part of the cycle of life, and when people learn to move with that cycle there is coherence and great harmony in our lives. That is the spiritual insight that can transform this particular dimension of leadership and thus transform our institutions.

The third shadow in leaders I call "functional atheism"—the belief that ultimate responsibility for everything rests with *me*. It is the unconscious, unexamined conviction within us that if anything decent is going to happen here, I am the one who needs to make it happen.

Functional atheism leads to dysfunctional behavior on every level of our lives: workaholism, burnout, stressed and strained and broken relationships, unhealthy priorities. It is the reason the average group can tolerate only 15 seconds of silence; people believe that if they are not making noise, nothing is happening!

The great gift we receive on the inner journey is the certain knowledge that ours is not the only act in town. Not only are there other acts in town, but some of them, from time to time, are even better than ours. On this inner journey we learn that we do not have to carry the whole load, that we can be empowered by sharing the load with others, and that sometimes we are even free to lay our part of the load down. We learn that co-creation leaves us free to do only what we are called and able to do, and to trust the rest to other hands.

The fourth shadow among leaders is fear. There are many kinds of fear, but I am thinking especially of our fear of the natural chaos of life. Many leaders have a deep devotion to eliminating all remnants of chaos from the world. They want to order and organize things so thoroughly that the nasty stuff will never bubble up around us—such nasty stuff as dissent, innovation, challenge, change. In an organization, this particular shadow gets projected outward as rigidity of rules and procedures. It creates corporate cultures that are imprisoning rather than empowering.

The insight we forget from our spiritual traditions is that chaos is the precondition to creativity. Any organization (or any individual) that does not have a safe arena for creative chaos is already half dead. When a leader is so fearful of chaos as not to be able to protect and nurture that arena for other people, there is deep trouble. The spiritual gift of the inner journey is to know that creation comes out of chaos, and that even what has been created needs to be turned to chaos every now and then so that it can be re-created in a more vital form. The spiritual gift on this inner journey is the knowledge that people and organizations not only survive but thrive in chaos, that there is vitality in the play of chaotic energy.

The final example of the shadows that leaders can project on others involves the denial of death. We live in a culture that simply does not want to talk about things dying. Leaders everywhere demand that they themselves, and the people who work for them, artificially maintain things that are no longer alive, maybe never have been. Projects and programs that should have been laid down 10 years ago are still on the life-support system.

Fear pops up again in this denial of death—fear of negative evaluation, fear of public failure. Surprisingly, the people in our culture who are least afraid of death, in this sense, are the scientists. The scientific community really honors the failure of a hypothesis because the death of an idea produces new learning. But in many organizations, if you fail at what you are doing, you will find a pink slip in your box. Again, the best organizations and leaders are asking people to take risks that may sometimes lead to failure, because they understand that from failure we can learn.

The spiritual gift on the inner journey is the knowledge that death is natural and that death is not the final word. The spiritual gift is to know that allowing something to die is also allowing new life to emerge.

Inner Work in Community

Can we, should we, help each other deal with the spiritual issues inherent in leadership? We *must* help each other, because these are critical issues. The failure of leaders to deal with their own inner lives is creating conditions of real misery for lots and lots of folks and unfulfilled missions for lots and lots of institutions. Too many organizations in our society are in deep trouble because of the leadership shadows I have tried to name. One way out of trouble is for us to start helping each other recover the power of the inner journey. How might that happen?

To begin, we could strive to elevate the value of inner work. It would be wonderful if the phrase "inner work" could become a central term in our schools, in our businesses, and in our churches—if we could help people understand that the phrase really means something. The activities that constitute inner work are as real and as important as any outer project or task—activities like journaling, reflective reading, spiritual friendship, and meditation. We must come to understand that if we skimp on our inner work, our outer work will be diminished as well.

A second thing we can do is to remind each other that although inner work is a deeply personal matter, it is not necessarily a *private* matter. There are ways to come together in community to help each other with that inner work. I have been very touched by the Quaker tradition, where they know how to come together in support of people engaged in deep inner work. They come together in a way that is supportive but not invasive, that asks a lot of probing questions but never renders judgment or gives advice. They come together in a way that respects the mystery of the human heart but still allows people to challenge and stretch one another in that mystery.

In a beautiful little book called *Letters to a Young Poet,* the German poet Rainer Maria Rilke has a definition of love that still astounds me. "Love is this—that two solitudes border, protect, and salute one another."[4] This is the essence of being together in inner work. It avoids the invasive and violent notion that are have in our culture of getting in there and fixing each other up. It affirms the possibility of being present to a person's solitude, a person's mystery, while that deep inner work goes on.

I wish I had time to tell you, as a person who has struggled through two bouts of that deep inner work called depression, about the healing that came as a few people found ways to stand at the border of my solitude in that experience. Because they were not driven by their own fears to either "fix" or abandon me, they provided lifelines to the human community. It *is* possible for people to be together that way—if we have education for leadership that is not simply about the skills to manipulate the external world but also the personal and corporate disciplines of the inner world.

Finally, we need to remember that all of the great spiritual traditions at their core say one simple thing: Be not afraid. They do not say you cannot *have* fears; we all have fears, and leaders have fears in abundance. But the spiritual traditions say you do not have to *be* your fears; you do not have to lead from fear and thus engender a world in which fear dominates the lives of far too many people. We can lead, instead, from an inner place of trust and hope, creating a world that is more hopeful and more trustworthy.

New leadership is needed for new times, but it will not come from finding new and more wily ways to manipulate the external world. It will come as we who lead find the courage to take an inner journey toward both our shadows and our light, a journey that, faithfully pursued, will take us beyond ourselves to become healers of a wounded world.

17

The Killing Fields:
Institutions and the Death
of Our Spirits

Diane Cory

Diane Cory, author of the AT&T Teaching Tales *and the* AT&T Teaching Verses, *is an independent consultant who works primarily with The Learning Circle, an organization devoted to bringing the best people, resources, and materials to businesses and groups interested in becoming learning organizations. Diane's focus is on individual and collective leadership skills and concepts and practices that hamper or empower organizations. Her areas of expertise include the learning organization, whole brain thinking, team building, servant-leadership, creativity, and the wellness of the individual and the organization. She is a member of The Greenleaf Center's board of trustees.*

In this essay, Diane Cory reflects on the idea that institutions are killing our spirits and that we need to confront the fear that exists inside ourselves before we can move forward as servant-leaders. Cory, who knew Bob Greenleaf during the last decade of his life, calls forth his vision and challenges each of us to first look inward in order to effect meaningful change in the outer world.

There is a lie that must be named and a truth that must be told. *Our institutions are killing our spirits.* We are allowing it to happen. In exchange for an illusion of power and control, safety and security, we have betrayed our souls because *we are afraid.*

We are afraid of losing our jobs. We are afraid to think for ourselves inside organizations. We are afraid of our bosses and our bosses' bosses. We are afraid of our colleagues and what they might say and how they might betray us in meetings or behind our backs. We are afraid we won't meet our deadlines. We are afraid of foreign competitors. We are afraid to "dream great dreams." We are afraid to be kind.

Whatever nobility and greatness we might once upon a time have claimed as our own by founding and sustaining the institutions of our country, we have squandered with a pettiness and cowardice repeated every minute of every working day in meetings and conversations that should disturb our sleep and haunt and torment us in the small hours of the night.

There is no excuse. There is nowhere to hide from the depth and breadth of what we have done to ourselves and to the legacy of love that has always been our heritage by allowing the institutions that we have created to destroy our spirits through fear.

At the end of a workshop with a group of about 75 employees and managers from a Fortune 50 organization, we concluded our work together with a check-out session. We were coming together one last time to share our perspectives about what had been accomplished and learned.

As participants expressed their thoughts and feelings, one woman finally gave voice to what had been hinted at in rumblings and murmurings from members of this team but that was never stated with straight-out clarity during the two days.

Because we had some cardboard, life-sized characters from the book *The Wizard of Oz* in the room, the woman used them to illustrate her concerns. "I see the Scarecrow," she said, "and I am reminded that we have the brains we need to accomplish our vision. I see the Tin Man and I am reminded that we have the heart to accomplish our vision. But when I look at the Cowardly Lion, I stop because I do not believe that we have the courage to accomplish our vision."

Where is the courage then? The courage we will need to break the icy lies that have frosted and clouded our perception and frozen the beatings that should have been our hearts. Where is the courage?

In *The Book of Qualities,* author J. Ruth Gendler writes about 77 human qualities as if each one were an individual person. With her poet's eye she helps us see ourselves anew by taking individual qualities and writing about them as if they were individuals. When she speaks about courage she says,

> **Courage**
> Courage has roots. She sleeps on a futon on the
> floor and lives close to the ground. Courage looks
> you straight in the eye. She is not afraid of
> powertrippers, and she knows first aid. Courage is
> not afraid to weep, and she is not afraid to pray,
> even when she is not sure who she is praying to.
> When courage walks, it is clear that she has made
> the journey from loneliness to solitude. The people
> who told me she is stern were not lying, they just
> forgot to mention that she is kind.[1]

After listening to thousands of managers and employees from corporations churches, schools, government agencies, and nonprofit organizations, what has become clearer to me is that unlike Courage, we are, for the most part, deeply afraid of people we perceive as powertrippers in our places of work. We are afraid of power, of our bosses, of people who are above us in the hierarchy. We are afraid of what they might do to us in these rapidly changing and uncertain times.

But what does Gendler say about Courage? "She is not afraid of powertrippers, *and she knows first aid.*" What does that mean? And why does she follow her comment about powertrippers with her comment about first aid?

Perhaps it is because so many of us have confused managing and leading with powertripping. And like bulls in china shops we wreak havoc and inflict pain on others without being conscious of it or responsible for it. So, in our meetings we wound each other and call it *efficiency* or *practicality* or *teasing* or *getting to the bottom line.*

What passes for effective, efficient meetings these days is mostly superficial conversations that, with exquisite care and capacity, avoid clarity and honesty and substitute verbal extroversion and battle for productivity.

When we engage in intellectual battles and power struggles and unconsciously believe that this is a survival-of-the-fittest scenario that serves us well in meetings, we naturally leave in our wake wounded ideas, sickened hearts and spirits, devastated and cynical minds. No wonder we might need first aid.

In his book *The Tao of Leadership,* John Heider collects his beliefs on leadership into short meditations that can startle and alarm us with their different perspectives. In meditation number 28, "A Warrior, a Healer, and Tao," he writes,

> The leader can act as a warrior or as a healer.
> As a warrior, the leader acts with power and
> decision. That is the Yang or masculine
> aspect of leadership.
> Most of the time, however, the leader acts as
> a healer and is an open, receptive and
> nourishing state. That is the feminine or Yin
> aspect of leadership.[2]

What does it mean to be in "an open, receptive and nourishing state" as a leader? When I have asked people if they experience their organizations, or their leaders as open, receptive, and nourishing, they routinely laugh, look incredulous or ask me if I am kidding. Why is that, I want to know? Why have we allowed our leadership and our institutions to behave in ways that I believe are destroying our spirits?

I think about the Quaker John Woolman who Robert Greenleaf speaks of in *The Servant as Leader.* Woolman pursued his goal of ridding the Society of Friends of slavery by asking landowners two questions: "What does the owning of slaves do to you as a moral person? What kind of an institution are you binding over to your children?"

For our use, we might rephrase these questions slightly: "What does living in fear do to you as a moral person? What kind of an institution are you binding over to your children when you allow yourself to live in fear?"

I believe that by living in fear and accepting it as the norm in our institutions we have confused positions of authority with leaders and abuses of power with leadership.

That's one reason I believe Robert Greenleaf began reflecting on and taking a deeper look at leadership. He went beyond the accepted models of hero, king, priest, or president to look for an archetype that was ultimately more whole. My assumption is that Bob wanted to help us look again at our deeply held beliefs and, like John Woolman, influence and persuade us with his ideas and questions toward a more sustainable and healing concept of leadership at the individual and institutional level.

In a book entitled *The Tao of Pooh,* the author explores what *courage* is by looking at the root of the word—where it meets the earth of our language—and finds that it comes from the French word *coeur,* which means heart. He speaks through Winnie the Pooh who is talking with his companion, Piglet.[3]

Pooh states that although his friend and neighbor Kanga is not necessarily brave, she would do a brave thing for her child, Roo, because she cares about him—hence, Pooh's logic and the author's conclusion that courage comes from caring. We will be brave and find the courage we need to do the things we need to do when we care enough about someone or something.

In 1986, when I visited MIT and sat in a reflective conversation with Peter Senge, author of *The Fifth Discipline,* asking him a series of questions about leadership, he expressed ideas that echo Pooh's thinking.

At the end of our two hours together, Peter summarized his reflections by saying that for him leadership ultimately comes down to two things—truth and love. Peter said he believes that when we care deeply enough about our visions of the future—the things that we truly want to create and bring into being—when we love them enough, we are willing to tell the truth about current reality—where we are now.

So where are we now? How would we describe our current reality? Robert Greenleaf's writings on servant-leadership reflect his deep concerns about the reality of the 1960s and 1970s. One of his greatest concerns seems to have been how our leaders and our institutions could care most deeply for the human spirit while they went about the work they were created to do.

By making explicit his intuitive insight about serving and leadership, Bob articulated a paradox that acts as a mirror reflecting back to us the limits of our previously held concepts. His thinking and writing help explain why the structure of leadership with a foundation of servanthood provides us with fundamentally different results than other leadership structures.

I am deeply concerned by what we have done and what we have left undone in our institutional designs, our workplaces, and our beliefs about leadership. I am deeply concerned that there are not enough among us who might answer what has become the faintest call to truth pulsing in our veins.

Who will come? Who will look at what must be seen and named? And who will find enough compassion to hold what we have done and are doing even now? Who will heal the death we run from even as we deal it out unconsciously and with what feels like a hideous lack of caring?

Before I met Robert Greenleaf I watched a commencement speech that he videotaped for graduates of Alverno College. In that speech Bob said something that struck me as profound and funny at the same time. He said that when he had retired from AT&T, he had hung up his sword.

Now that's an interesting image for a Quaker to have, I thought. So the first time I met Bob and his wife, Esther, I recalled those words to him and told him that I had come to get his sword. He looked surprised for a moment, then he chuckled quietly, looked at me, and said, "I said that?" He hadn't remembered that he had used that image.

One day when I was remembering our visits with Bob and Esther, my friend Fred Myers reminded me that Bob reflected for a moment about the image of the sword and speculated that perhaps he had incorporated it into his writing because he had been deeply moved when he and Esther had visited the place in Spain where Ignatius of Loyola, the founder of the Society of Jesus, had hung up his sword.

These days, however, the image of that sword burns within my mind. Every time I hear comments by managers and employees that reflect their pain, humiliation, loss, confusion, and, ultimately, their fear, that sword burns brighter behind my eyes.

"What is going on here," I ask myself, "that there could exist this level of stress, anguish, and paralyzed action in our organizations? How is it that leaders speak in the kind of abstracted numbers about downsizing and reengineering that remind me of body count totals from the Vietnam War?"

There are days when I think that I cannot stand what I see any more. I feel myself consumed by the image of that sword Robert Greenleaf hung up when he retired. I feel myself become that sword of flame and brightest anger at the betrayals I sense that we are all committing by our continuing to run away from our fears instead of stopping, slowly turning to face them, and then acknowledging that what we see in the mirror of truth is ourselves.

A great deal of the talk and writing about leadership and organizations is bright with academic displays of intellectual giftedness and occasional anecdotes or stories with an entertaining, sentimental, or touching moment. This is talk and writing that speakers and authors intend with a sad lack of awareness to serve as an awakening for us all.

But it is not enough. For most of what has been said and written has only served our complacency. It has focused on what we might be without the grounded honesty of looking in the mirror of self-reflection at what we have created and become.

Visions are born daily. Yearned for, spoken forth, dreamed of, cradled in committees and communities around the globe. But these visions will only be illusions. Illusions of love for something not yet created until they are served by truth. Not just one truth but all our truths. All of them. Held in the hands of paradox so that they might all be different, unique, and even completely opposite and yet still at the end—at the same time—be true.

The saints and mystics tell us that the opposite of love is not hate or apathy but power. Power comes with a price. Stop for a moment, sit quietly, and gently search within yourself. What did you have to give up of yourself in school? In church? In colleges and universities? In your places of work?

How about your native common sense and your unique giftedness and intelligence? How about your creativity and imagination? How about your joy and enthusiasm? How about your capacity for love and compassion? How about your spirit and soul?

In the movie *Excalibur*, Merlin, mentor to King Arthur and court wizard, is asked at a celebration what is the most important quality that a knight must have and he answers, "Truth. That's it. For when a person lies, they murder some part of the world."

What is the lie we have not named and the truth that must be told? *Our institutions are killing our spirits,* and we are allowing it to happen. In exchange for an illusion of power and control, safety and security, we have betrayed our souls *because we are afraid*.

That sword I told Robert Greenleaf I wanted now burns brightly within me. Where is yours?

Feed Me
The temple of reason
wavered in its own image.
Particles of logic
changed to wave.
Hairline cracks of love
webbed the foundation
of dualism.

"Feed me,"
the masses cried.

There were no loaves.

There were no fishes
handed out from hands
that worked with wood
and water.

The temple of reason
stood still and empty.
Waiting.

Thinking its thoughts.
Coupling with itself.

"Feed me,"
the child whimpered.

There was no breast
to suckle.

"Feed me,"
the woman
whispered.

There were no arms
to circle and hold her.

"Feed me,"
the man
demanded.

"I have only arguments,"
stated the thinking,
alone at last.

"Feed me,"
cried the temple.

18

Lives in the Balance: The Challenge of Servant-Leaders in a Workaholic Society

Diane Fassel

Dr. Diane Fassel *is the author of* Working Ourselves to Death *and* Growing Up Divorced *and coauthor of* The Addictive Organization. *She is a management consultant and mediator. Fassel was a keynote speaker at The Greenleaf Center's 1996 conference.*

In this essay, Diane addresses the need for servant-leaders to reject the deeply embedded acceptance of workaholism that is particularly present in modern America. She persuasively details the ways in which workaholism is detrimental to both workaholics and to the organizations with which they are associated, and she offers specific suggestions for overcoming workaholic behaviors.

The test of a vision is whether it stands the ravages of time, whether it holds up under circumstances unknown and unanticipated when the vision was first articulated. Knowing that Robert Greenleaf spent his entire work life of 40 years at AT&T, that he immediately changed out of his corporate suit and tie and put on "grunge" clothes the minute he arrived home, that he puttered in his garden in summer and his workshop in winter, that when asked if he would type a document or do a drafting job, he refused, saying he had no inclination for such jobs—knowing just these few things about Greenleaf's approach to work, I wonder how he would have fared in our workaholic society? Would he find contemporary corporations places where the listening, healing, and commitment to the growth of people, which is so core to the servant-leader, all but lost in a flood of hype about being lean, mean, and highly productive? How would Greenleaf react to mechanistic euphemisms of "right sizing" and "reengineering"—modern metaphors for sacrificing people in order to squeeze the last cent out of production?

Perhaps the man whose most oft-quoted statement concerns whether "those served grow as persons . . . become healthier, wiser, freer, more autonomous, more likely themselves to become servants" would find this a dangerous and exciting time. Dangerous because our very souls are at stake given the type of organizations we have created, the pace we expect ourselves to go, and the values that are sacrificed by our busyness. Exciting because never before has so much seemed possible, not just in the building of material empires, which will surely fail, but in the possibilities for the human spirit. I want to discuss the danger of one aspect of our corporate and individual culture—workaholism—but first I want to present some images that carry layers of meaning and that I refer to when I need to make sense of the changes that compel us today.

Three Images

The world is a much more frantic place to live and work than when Greenleaf first articulated his vision of the servant-leader. Yet never before have the values he espoused been more needed. I don't know how you make meaning of the upheaval that is going on in our lives, especially our lives in institutions today. I have found myself carrying around three images that speak to me of our current situation.

The first image is of a lily pond that is half full of lilies. You know the pond I'm speaking of—Monet painted it beautifully—those round, green pads with white flowers. According to gardeners and pond tenders, lilies in the pond double every day. I think of the pond as half full of lilies. In my mind's eye I observe the pond and think. "There's nothing to get excited about. The pond is only half full. I have lots of time to decide what I'll do." But because of the doubling effect, the next day the pond is full. This is my image for the rapidity of change. We're lounging around thinking we have all the time in the world and overnight the pond is choked. The pace of change is increasing exponentially and our psyches, indeed our entire beings, feel unprepared and often bewildered by the speed.

The second image is a nexus with nodes and it is an image for what organizations have become. Think of what we used to call a jungle gym in a playground—that rounded structure of steel bars connecting to other bars that you could climb all over. Instead of the traditional organizational diagram with boards and CEOs and reporting relationships going up and down and sideways with broken and unbroken lines, think instead of the jungle gym or a nexus with nodes. Charles Handy says in his book, *The Age of Paradox:* "The challenge of tomorrow's leaders is to manage an organization that is not there in any sense in which we are used to. A corporation is nothing more than a nexus of contracts."[1] Perhaps some of the disequilibrium we are feeling in organizations is that the old organizational diagram is hardwired in our brains, while the actual process we experience is one of relationships, contracts with ever-changing parties, and no real place to land physically. Hence, not only are things faster but all the relationships are different—all of which adds to our stress.

The third image is the S-shape or sigmoid curve. This is a classic depiction, which has been used for many years, to show the learning process as well as the predictable growth and decline of organizations. Envision a line that starts in a valley and rises up to an arc then curves back down. The curve or wave is back in vogue these days. John O'Neil uses the curve in his book, *The Paradox of Success,* to describe leaders who attain mastery (the peak of the curve) and then begin to descend; their energy dissipates and stagnation sets in. The same is true for organizations.[2]

Ian Morrison, author of *The Second Curve,* counsels leaders to become vigilant about those faint blips on the radar screen that eventually could become the core business replacing the first curve (your current business) with a powerful second curve (your new business).[3] Knowing when and how to leap from the first curve to the second curve is essential to the survival of any business.

It is difficult to remember that at the very peak of the curve when we are feeling exultant, celebrating our victories, and basking in our mastery, we are also at the point where the descent begins. It is hard to move to the new and the unknown in the sweetness of success, but it is necessary. O'Neil says of this precarious time on the peak: ". . . external voices of warning and internal voices of need may go unheard amid the din of congratulations or the cocoon of a leader's isolation. Paradoxically, the summit of success is fertile ground for the shadow to grow in. It is where we are most vulnerable to hubris, and thus a dangerous place to linger too long."[4]

These three mental images are not meant to simplify a world that is admittedly complex but to remind me that change (the lily pond) is not difficult; it is the most natural process there is. Resistance is difficult. The nexus with nodes reminds me that nothing is as it appears in institutions and that as soon as we write something down or codify it, that is the sign it has served its usefulness. What endures are values and relationships, and those are rarely static. Finally, I think of the S-curve as a warning that as soon as something succeeds, it is time to go on to the next thing, lest we turn our successes into idols to be worshiped rather than markers along the way to a goal.

The images of the lily pond, the nexus with nodes, and the curve are organic reminders that we are in a natural process. They are also about change, speed, and the necessity to keep up. They evoke fear that we will fall behind the big engine that is driving business processes in America. The downside or the shadow of these images is that we feel compelled to go faster and faster, often against our better instincts. Busyness, overwork, and work stress are hallmarks of this decade. Out-of-control workaholism has led Peter

J. Gomes, the minister of Harvard's Memorial Church, to ask: "How ought men and women in search of the virtuous life and a culture that celebrates the classical trinity of the true, the good, and the beautiful to proceed in a culture that knows how to make a living, but not a life worth living?"[5] Compulsive busyness is a serious impediment to servant-leadership and ultimately results in the downfall of individuals and organizations.

Working Ourselves to Death

First, a definition of workaholism: *Workaholism* is an addiction to incessant internal and/or external activity with the belief that if I were not active, I would have no right to be or exist. I arrived at this definition because I often have heard workaholics complain about how many hours they actually worked. Thus, you could assume that a workaholic was a person who was addicted to a job. But workaholism does not relegate itself to being practiced only at work nor do you have to be employed to be a workaholic.

The essence of workaholism is compulsive activity. The workaholic measures self-worth in terms of accomplishment of tasks and suffers from the sense that there is never enough time to do all that needs doing and so one always comes up short. Life in the United States appears to have been ratcheted up to warp speed of late. In fact, it is interesting to note that during the 1990s, when many major corporations gained awareness of drug and alcohol problems among the workforce and acted to address them, workaholism was becoming the new drug of choice in corporate America.

Workaholism masquerades as a positive trait in the cultural lore of our nation. We are rewarded for overwork by being featured in the pages of the company newsletter. We routinely read magazine articles about high-achieving, stressed-out men and women who describe themselves as "happy workaholics." And it is not unusual to read in a daily newspaper a headline like one I saw in my local paper recently, "Workaholic Vice President of University To Retire" shouted the headline. Funny, I mused, I've never seen a headline that said "Drunk University V.P. Says He Quits" or "Sex-Addicted Provost To Hang It Up." These and many other social approbations for workaholism convince me that a progressive and potentially fatal disease now receives a great deal of support in our society. The pervasiveness of workaholism means that any person who attempts to recover from it is a personal, private revolutionary in the very fabric of the nation.

A disturbing trend in corporations is the tendency to judge those employees who work at a human pace—say 40 hours a week—as the deviants, while those whose loyalty knows no bounds, who work without regard to limits are considered "normal." This was exactly the problem I faced with a client. My task was to resolve a conflict in a human services agency. The conflict devolved into a virtual war between staff members who met their obligations in 40 hours per week, and insisted on time at home and with family, and staff who put no boundaries on their service. The second group, the all-out workers, felt that the 40-hour-a-week people were not loyal or committed to the agency.

A distorted culture, which took hold in the agency, pitted self-care against organizational commitment. In the organizational culture, those who pushed themselves to the limits of their physical and emotional well-being, and sacrificed their families and loved ones as well, were the heros. The other group became fierce in their attempts to maintain a balanced life. They struggled with feeling apologetic for having to leave to attend to family emergencies. They resented a workplace that they experienced as guilt inducing. Ironically, this agency served oppressed people, but lacking a systems perspective, it never occurred to them that the oppression they were trying to solve with their clients was flourishing in the workforce.

The preceding example, in one form or another, is all too common in our institutions. Juliet Schorr, author of *The Overworked American,* points to economics as the culprit.[6] It takes two adults earning income to support a family in the way that one person was able to provide support prior to 1970. The work week has lengthened to 43.5 hours on average for the first time in this century. People in Fortune 500 and Service 500 companies typically work 56 hours a week. Vacation time is down to 14 days from 16 days a year and that is because people voluntarily are not taking all the vacation days they have coming to them. Permanent work-related disabilities are up 16 percent in the past year, and 93 percent of these injuries are due to more overtime and employee turnover.

The physical boundary between work and home is fading. Not only are more people taking work home, but no matter where your work location, you are never far from a pager, cell phone, voice mail, E-mail, and fax. These technologies are both time compressors—everything is more immediate because of them—and boundary erasers—you can never get away from work, it follows you everywhere.

Many myths underlie our fascination with workaholism, but three in particular are of interest to our concern about becoming servant-leaders who are responsive in this milieu.

The first myth is that workaholics are more productive and therefore profitable to organizations. Repeatedly, this myth has proven to be wrong. We have confused activity with productivity. Workaholics are addicted to activity and all the things that go along with activity: speed, peaks-and-valleys performance, crisis, and obsessiveness around projects. In addition, workaholics operate on less restful sleep than others and consequently they are tired and prone to more mistakes.

Productivity has nothing to do with incessant activity. Productivity is the result of visionary planning coupled with efficient action. The most productive workplaces are economical in the use of all resources, human and material. All of us have the experience of struggling to the point of exhaustion with something, only to get a good night's rest and discover an obvious solution the next day. Productivity seeks the most elegant, simple solution, the one with no waste. Activity, for the workaholic, is its own reward. In the workaholic organization, constant activity gives the illusion of productivity and frequently results in one crisis after another. Crisis takes so much attention that leaders rarely have time to plan.

The second myth states that no one ever died of hard work. Many people are dying of overwork and work stress. The most blatant example is Japanese men between the ages of 40 and 52 who have been dying from a disease dubbed *karoshi* (death from overwork). Karoshi victims were working 13 hours a day (78 hours per six-day week) over a two-year time period. They usually collapsed with a brain hemorrhage or a heart attack. Karoshi is the second-largest killer of men in this age group.

Why does workaholism kill? It kills because most workaholics produce enormous amounts of adrenaline. Adrenaline, also known as epinephrine, is an adrenal hormone that constricts blood vessels and raises blood pressure. In other words, it rouses the body to respond to danger. The adrenaline high is the physical form of the addictiveness of work. In fact, many workaholics claim they are addicted to the production of their own adrenaline and without that "high," activity would not provide the same fix.

Adrenaline is a marvelous substance in that it temporarily masks the body's pain and gives us a sense of power and self-transcendence. Rightfully used, adrenaline is the substance that surges when we are in danger and enables us to perform physical feats that would not be possible in the normal course of events. Here is where the literalness of the body is so instructive. Many of us run on adrenaline daily from the moment we walk into the still dark morning until we wend our way home. Why? Because the body determines that daily life presents dangers to the organism and produces adrenaline to fight (face it) or flee (get to safety). We are accommodating ourselves to higher and higher levels of stress and the body is reacting exactly the way it is supposed to react with doses of adrenaline on a continuing basis.

Adrenaline gives us the illusion that our bodies have no limits. When adrenaline is rushing we can go for hours without sleep, food, or attending to bodily needs. This masking property of adrenaline results in our not being attuned to small problems or signals that might be coming from our bodies. Stress may indeed be taking its toll and indicating that toll through backaches, headaches, heightened blood pressure, nervous stomachs, but we don't note those symptoms or we push through them, emboldened by the next hit of adrenaline. Thus, when most workaholics hit bottom, they do so through a catastrophic illness like a stroke or a heart attack. Many of these catastrophic illnesses could be prevented if we lived in a milieu that valued a balanced life. However, the pressure is on performance, and rewards go to high achievers, with the result that self-care and stopping are unpopular. Our concept of ourselves is that we are "do-ers."

The third myth is that workaholism can be managed with stress-reduction techniques. This myth is partly true. If you address your stress and engage in daily stress-reducing practices, your stress will decrease. Reducing stress does not necessarily stop the internal and external compulsion to activity. The compulsion continues unabated and sometimes becomes less worrisome because you feel better physically as a result of reducing stress. In this sense then, stress reduction actually serves to support your workaholism.

Leaders of institutions should confront the ethical aspects of offering stress-reduction programs to employees. Stress-reduction programs are straightforward and effective. Usually, employees fill out a questionnaire that enables them to identify their degree of stress. Then a program is designed that, if adhered to regularly, will bring down stress as measured by such physical factors as blood pressure, pulse, headaches, backaches, insomnia, ulcers, and self-referrals to the company medical department. The point is that these stress-reduction programs are effective. They get results; you feel better and are more able to cope. Yet these programs are only half the equation. The other half of the equation is served when the same inventory that employees use to measure their work stress is applied to the systems of the corporation. When we can identify non-value-added stress that is coming from the company itself, when we can remove non-value-added stress, then we are on the way to a workplace where true health is possible.

Examining the corporation as well as the individual for evidence of dysfunctional stress is both an ethical issue and a systems issue for the servant-leader. It is an ethical issue because it is immoral to reduce employees' stress so as to adjust them to last longer in dysfunctional work environments. The process of dealing with individual stress can give the impression that the individual is to blame for being unable to cope. Those of us in organizational consulting often find systems issues hiding underneath isolated individuals collapsing from stress. The dysfunctional patterns and structures of the organization usually manifest first in individuals who "can't cope." It is treacherous to blame individuals whose outcry offers a warning of more serious organizational breakdown.

Understandably, the servant-leader may be oriented to first serve individuals in becoming healthier, wiser, and freer. Before long, however, the leader must face the living organization and deal with the processes and structures that are in dynamic interaction with individuals. The astute leader will distinguish stress reduction as a Band-Aid, but definitely not the cure.

For years I have felt that stress reduction by itself is only a temporary measure in ensuring the overall health of organizations. I knew that we should be able to measure the organizational factors that were inducing stress, but I couldn't figure out how to perform such a measurement. Recently, I discovered and began working with a simple but elegant instrument that identifies non-value-added stress in organizations along six universal dimensions. Employees complete a 15-question survey, which is scanned electronically and produces a graph showing where the non-value-added stress is.

Observing a team of employees looking over the graph of their department's results, I witnessed the empowerment that comes when individuals have information that enables them to make effective systems change. Additionally, there is something wonderful about having the whole system in the room and around the table. The individuals were there with their commitment to take responsibility for their own stress by following the program the company had provided. The system was in the room, too, as each person committed him-or herself to take responsibility for addressing areas of corporate functioning that were sources of stress. As one man exclaimed, "It doesn't get much better than this!"

There is more that can be written about the myths supporting our love of excessive busyness but these three—"Workaholics are more productive," "None ever died of hard work," and "Workaholism can be managed with stress-reduction techniques,"—seem to me to be intimately tied to one another and deep in the heart of our cultural ethos. As such, the servant-leader will rarely confront one without having to address the other. Usually, when we decide to confront any one of these myths, like the proverbial thread that unravels the whole ball, we find ourselves dealing with all three.

Ultimately, it is not possible to resolve the problem of the workaholic organization without servant-leaders acknowledging the degree to which they are prone to workaholism themselves. The seduction of being on the cutting edge with a revolutionary approach to organizations can be an excuse for workaholism. It is easy to lose balance when the cause is so worthwhile. This is where the servant-leader leads by example. We first must become human to ourselves and before others. In so doing we can be part of a business whose primary purpose is not profit but the creation of a positive impact on employees and community.

Balancing for Our Lives

These days everywhere I turn people are calling for more balance. Frankly, most of the prescriptions leave me cold. They seem mechanistic and superficial, as if achieving balance, like getting the right exercise routine, will solve our problems. So many solutions to the balance question propose more things to *do*. Of course, workaholics love the idea that they can get well, they can recover from over work by another kind of work—get busy about recovery! When people describe balance, I envision the playground teeter-totter, which is a board on a fulcrum. As a child, I always hoped the person on the other end was equal to my weight or else I was dangling up in the air or crashing to the ground. Perfect balance was two equal weights going up and down. Somehow, I don't think this is really the balance we are seeking.

Nevertheless, the notion of balance does entail equilibrium among components. Erik Erikson wrote that finding balance in life consists in pursuing work, love, and play in equal measure.[7] He observed that those who attained inner balance and lived the richest and fullest lives were people who had all three elements. Those who concentrated on one area, say work, to the exclusion of others were most likely to feel unhappy as the years passed.

In *Divided Lives,* a study of women and balance, Elsa Walsh found that women were happiest when they devoted time and attention to work, love, family, friends, time for self, sense of place, and sense of self.[8] Conversely, women were sad and disappointed when they ignored one or several areas or failed to understand the importance of one of the areas in making an important decision about their life.

Helen and Scott Nearing, authors of the 1953 classic *Living the Good Life: How to Live Simply and Sanely in a Troubled World,* championed human rights, vegetarianism, and the joys of simple living.[9] They also insisted on balance and developed a daily schedule that incorporated their philosophy. The Nearings divided their waking hours into three equal parts. They spent four hours a day on "bread labor," that is, activities that provided for their basic needs and netted money. Four hours were devoted to their professional interests—for Helen her music and for Scott his economic studies. The last four hours went to social and citizen activities. Obviously, this lifestyle suited them. Scott lived to be 100 and Helen lived to be 91 years. They built their last stone house at the ages of 91 and 70, respectively. They lived simply, harmed no one, and believed they had the abundance of the wealthiest persons on earth. They went quietly about their daily activities and attracted many seekers who were burned out with the rat race of competition and success.

On the organizational front, studies of good stress and bad stress point out that balancing three factors at work is essential for health. The three factors are job demands, job supports, and job constraints. When one is in a demanding job but lacks support in the form of resources, skills, and emotional understanding, and when one also lacks the ability to control or put constraints on the job, then burnout is inevitable. Conversely, too much support and constraint without a challenging, demanding job results in boredom. Thus, balance, in all these instances, requires variety of activities equally distributed over the course of a day or week.

Putting Joy Back into Jobs

Robert Greenleaf thought that two things which needed balancing were a sense of purpose and an ability to laugh. He had the humility as well as the humor to write this inscription that appears on his gravestone: "Potentially a good plumber ruined by a sophisticated education." He also said, "If I had the chance to rub Aladdin's lamp, one rub, one wish, I would wish for a world in which people laugh more. One can cultivate purpose to the point of having a glimpse of the ultimate and still remain connected with people and events, *if* one has humor, if one can laugh with all people at all stages of their journeys."[10] Greenleaf saw purpose and laughter as "twins that must not separate. Each is empty without the other. Together they are the impregnable fortress of strength."[11]

Having fun and experiencing joy at work function like an immune system of the organization. You cannot plan to have fun, you cannot control being joyful. Fun and joy are the result of something, not the thing itself. They are a benchmark. When fun goes out of work, it is the sign that something is dysfunctional in the organization. When the immune system of the organization is down, then all sorts of disease take hold.

In interviews with employees of corporations I've inquired when they had the most fun at work. I've asked them to remember a time they emerged from a meeting or a day at work and said "That was fun!" Inevitably, they describe times when they have delighted in a project, felt lost in it with no sense of time or any limitation. They suspended judgment, criticism, and analysis of themselves and others and felt no judgment coming from others. Often they talk about activities that seem to have the same structure that we experience in games.

Games have a goal and rules and therefore provide a structure for letting go and having fun. Listening to my interviewees, I began to appreciate that employees have fun when there is a background of predictability (rules, structure, expectations, and goals) and a foreground of unpredictability (challenge, the unknown, problems). Receiving information and having the right skills helps them let go and enjoy a project. The presence of a person who functions as a coach and provides safety is important. And finally, setting appropriate limits of risk seems to enhance their ability to concentrate on the task.

These interviews taught me that servant-leaders can take specific actions to reduce stress and foster fun at work. One thing they can do is buffer the workforce against unnecessary change.

At a meeting of people who work in health care, several nurses said that their jobs were changing almost daily. They were expected to perform duties that they had not trained for and they felt they were being asked to stretch into new skills about 60 percent of the time. Others in the audience, no matter what their position in the system, declared they were experiencing the same demands. On further examination, it became clear that many people were operating at a dysfunctional level of stress due to the fear that they could not meet job requirements. The fear of not being able to keep up is common in other organizations as well.

Fear is the opposite of fun. Whereas fun consists in letting go and actually letting yourself flow with an activity, fear is awareness of potential for harm with a subsequent tightening of the body that often results in the thing you fear happening. It is almost impossible for people to learn when they are afraid. I remember trying to learn to downhill ski. The ski instructor told me to override my natural inclination to lean back because leaning back resulted in falling down. Instead, he urged me to lean forward, which only resulted in sheer terror as I saw myself careening down the slope at ever-increasing speed. Of course, my fear of falling kicked in, I leaned back, and fell! When I finally took myself down the bunny slope a million times and then gradually attempted hills commensurate with my skill, I could relax into my new skills and prove to myself that they worked even when my instinct was to do the wrong thing.

There is a great need these days for servant-leaders to become coaches, mentors, and facilitators. While encouraging people into the adventure of change, leaders should consider their needs for safety. It is hard to ski down the steepest slope of competition when you are not sure you have a secure job, much less the wherewithal to do it. Fostering joy in the job is actually an invitation to servant-leaders to be willing to share their own uncertainties about the business environment. I admire most those leaders who let me see their fears as well as their strengths. I distrust a leader who has it all together, because no one in their right mind has it all together in these times. The nature of the change we are going through lends itself to candor and compassion as well as high-powered problem solving.

Joyful leaders give hope because they restore perspective. In their presence we understand that joy is simply an essential "rightness." It is the experience of living with yourself, your successes and failures. It is letting go into the realization that the world wants to do you good and everything will be all right. In the end, joy at work results in balance and gets us laughing at ourselves, and in that laughter the perfectionism so characteristic of workaholism crashes to pieces.

Four Factors Servant-Leaders Can Affect

Besides striving for balance and joy in the workplace, servant-leaders can do other things to positively address the pervasiveness of workaholism in organizations. Here are four concrete actions that promote healthy work environments. They are actions that are in response to four typical problems in fast-paced organizations.

1. *Problem:* The current climate is one in which emphasis is put on doing everything in teams or with an attitude of teamwork. The downside of operating in open corporate cultures that value teamwork is that teams require more meetings, involve more people needing to be in on everything, and make more demands on time. In the service of including all voices, the process becomes laborious and tedious and adds to people's stress.
   Action: Move teamwork, which is a value, to another dimension. Accentuate the need for trust, accurate and complete communication, and especially the importance of delegating certain people to attend meetings on behalf of everyone. Be precise about what decisions require total participation. Be as careful about including others by communicating as by inviting physical participation at meet-

ings. Meg Wheatley, who applies the new physics to organizational issues, has observed that "life moves with what works, not necessarily with what is right."[12] Teams and participative management are surely "right" in a servant-leader organization, but so is creating solutions that work and make sense for the group.

2. *Problem:* Statements coming from management that say "We want you to take care of yourselves" but the unspoken expectation is that being at work all the time is true loyalty. The variation on this problem is that you, as the servant-leader, make the above statement and then you pick up the slack so that others can have the time they need.

   Action: Robert Greenleaf was adamant that nothing changes until we change. He said "The servant views any problem in the world as *in here,* inside oneself, not *out there.*"[13] The servant-leader is in the humbling position of knowing that anything advocated for coworkers had better have been directly experienced by the leader. Lacking that experience, the servant-leader must be prepared to learn along with coworkers and be willing to place oneself before the group. Moreover, many of us get enamored of glitzy programs that promise to turn around our companies and propel us into the next wave. But my experience is that the really profound changes happen unexpectedly when one person has the courage to speak his or her own truth. No communication program in the world can equal that moment in an organization. True servant-leaders desire to move into the place of truth-telling about themselves and the organization.

3. *Problem:* Many of us live too often on adrenaline highs, mistaking them for true sustained energy. Adrenaline is to true action like sentimentality is to emotion. Sentimentality tries to make more emotion than a situation warrants. Adrenaline tries to make more excitement than a situation warrants. In the end, you mistake sentimentality for real feelings and adrenaline for healthy action.

   Action: Create work that has focus, meaning, appropriate support, and parameters. Work is inherently satisfying but not when it is "make work" or busy work. The role of servant-leaders is not to micromanage the workforce but to deal with the larger questions of life as they apply to work. Involving everyone in crafting mission-vision-value statements is not just a fad but a serious process in creating and claiming work that has meaning beyond the satisfaction of our personal goals.

   Adrenaline highs are the result of spending too much time reacting to crisis and handling deadline-driven projects. When servant-leaders focus their attention on planning the big picture, attending to core values, and seeing that those values are concretized, then work actually gives energy rather than depletes.

4. *Problem:* The belief that the effects of stress and overwork can be resolved by a vacation or a few days off, not examining the job or organizational expectations.
   Action: Inventory the organization for systems stress as frequently as
   workers measure their individual stress. We seem to know far more
   about the sick individual and what contributes to his or her stress
   than we do about the sick organization and what would contribute
   to its health. We back off from doing an inventory of the organizational factors that are resulting in non-value-added stress because
   we are afraid that we would have to change the entire organization.
   The prospect seems overwhelming. But my experience with organizational assessments of this type is that non-value-added stress is
   often in one or two areas of work. Those areas can usually be handled easily and without huge upheavals. Changes of this sort are
   good examples of small changes that have a ripple effect in the organization. They do a great deal for morale and release energy for
   other, more important activities.

I do not believe that I have ever come across the word *workaholism* in
Robert Greenleaf's writing. This is understandable because the word first appeared in the English language in 1968, and Greenleaf's essay, *The Servant as
Leader,* was published in 1970. He probably wasn't aware of the word. However, he was aware of the effects of workaholism and in a few cogent para-
graphs in *The Servant as Leader* he discusses the importance of withdrawal.

Greenleaf says that the "ability to withdraw or reorient oneself, if only
for a moment, presumes that one has learned the art of systematic neglect, to
sort out the more important from the less important—and the important
from the urgent—and attend to the more important, even though there may
be penalties and censure for the neglect of something else."[14] Further on he
counsels leaders to learn to pace themselves by appropriate withdrawal as one
of the best approaches to making optimal use of one's resources. Greenleaf
obviously knew the value of stepping back, taking stock, retreating so as to
nurture the vision, and then engaging again. His always probing question is
"How can I use myself to serve best?"

I take Greenleaf's wisdom about withdrawal as his comment on the
dangers of workaholism for the contemporary servant-leader. He would be
the first one to say that you cannot use yourself to serve best when you are
stressed out and fatigued. So much of his concern that servant-leaders show
acceptance and empathy, in addition to foresight and taking action, indicates
that he would be critical of the exhaustion that characterizes so many contemporary workers.

I think Robert Greenleaf would have another, deeper concern about
our workaholic society, a concern that goes to the heart of what Greenleaf's

writings are about: turning the pyramid upside down. Becoming the servant first is such a profound change that it goes to the very essence of our identity as leaders. Such action equalizes people and flattens hierarchy. This was the core of Greenleaf's insight and he approaches it from every angle in his writing. The ordained Baptist minister and family physician Paulanne Balch, M.D., reflecting on Greenleaf's grasp of this important principle, puts it this way: "Once you assume that someone else's experience is less important than yours, you have taken the step necessary to making them an object, and you have taken the first step to oppress them. Thus, oppression doesn't begin with an action but with an attitude."[15]

When Robert Greenleaf advised servant-leaders to withdraw, it was not just to recoup strength but to realign with the core principle. When we put our work before ourselves, we lose ourselves to work. Ultimately we lose the meaning of work itself.

Greenleaf would understand that workaholism isn't a fad disease of our time. He would rightly see our enmeshment in workaholism as the tendency to become objects to be used and then to be used up in the service of activity. No matter how inspiring the activity, if its direction is away from self and other awareness, we end in false adrenaline highs and numbing busyness.

Adrienne Rich, commenting on the predicament we are in, observes that "suffering is diagnosed relentlessly as personal, individual, maybe familial, and at most to be 'shared' with a group specific to the suffering, in the hope of 'recovery.' We lack a vocabulary for thinking about pain as communal and public, or as deriving from 'skewed social relationships' "[16]

Robert Greenleaf had a prescription for resolving skewed social relationships. He aimed to achieve a new social balance by unbalancing the traditional notion of the hierarchial leader. Thus, I think in these times, he would direct us back to the rudder of all servant-leader actions: serving other people's highest priority needs. In so doing, his message resounds in our society with renewed power.

19

———

Servant-Leaders Making Human New Models of Work and Organization

Thomas A. Bausch

Dr. Thomas A. Bausch is a professor of management and former dean of the College of Business Administration at Marquette. Currently he also serves as president of the Middle East Business School in Amman, Jordan, and as the executive director of the International Association of Jesuit Business Schools. Dr. Bausch has had international experience in Venezuela, England, Brazil, Cameroon, Jordan, the Czech Republic, Russia, India, and Indonesia. His numerous publications include several previous articles on servant-leadership.

In this essay, Thomas Bausch suggests that what seems to be two mutually exclusive goals in our society—meaningful work for all and competitiveness in the world economy—are really two sides of the same problem. Bausch invokes servant-leadership as a unifying pathway to developing human dignity and fulfillment in the workplace. This, in turn, generates a type of self-motivation that leads to flexible, successful organizations.

Introduction

The primary purpose of work is the development of the full potential of the individual doing the work. Each of us as servant-leaders can only develop our fullness as a person as part of a community, both through serving others and working with others in communities as diverse as the family; a church; our local, state, national, and international communities; our voluntary affiliations; and, possibly more important than anything but family, our community of work. There is no such thing as an effective community without leadership.

Changes in technology, information, understanding of the organization as well as of the human person and communications are all changing the way work is organized. One result is the rapid emergence of the *virtual organization,* where definitions of place, assets, ownership, and stakeholder are changing and calling for something other than the traditional hierarchical model of leadership. This essay argues that the most appropriate paradigm of leadership for the virtual organization is servant-leadership. This form of leadership must begin with a deep understanding of the human person as the basis, and the only source of sustainable competitive advantage as we enter the new millennium.

The Virtual Organization: The Model of the Future

In the virtual learning organization of the future, and this will be the dominant form of organization, there will be no viable paradigm of leadership other than servant-leadership. For any organization, for-profit, not-for-profit, or governmental, the only source of sustainable competitive advantage will be the commitment to and trust in the mission and vision of the organization by highly competent employees. Technology, processes, location, or any other source of competitive advantage can be duplicated and surpassed with ever-shorter lead times. Although competence of individuals must be present, it also can be duplicated or surpassed. Therefore, the clear commitment by employees to organization mission and vision are necessary conditions for organization success. This commitment, in turn, depends on leadership that earns its legitimacy from within the organization, in part because of its commitment to the development of the full potential of each person. This will be present only if leadership has a deep understanding of the human person as a foundation for its commitment to the actualization of each person that makes the organization, as well as, in many ways, the other stakeholders.

Concepts and definitions of organizations are changing rapidly with ever more focus on the intangibles of mission and vision and the relationships among the persons striving for their implementation. We no longer identify organizations with physical assets. Many were aghast when Rockefeller Center was acquired by the Japanese, but this is symbolic of business firms no longer owning and managing real estate as they focus on core business. The leading bank in Milwaukee once owned and managed their home office, the largest and most outstanding office complex in the city. They sold it and now lease back the space.

I sit on the board of a major insurance company that is being driven by our core competencies, primarily based on the abilities of our executives and employees, into services we would not have conceived of, much less considered, 10 years ago. We have sold our headquarters building because, in the world of modern technology and the virtual organization, where we are driven by mission in a very competitive industry, location is determined in part by a strategic need for proximity to our customers. This calls for many local and regional offices focused on customer service. Our business also demands cost control in the processing of data, which can be done anywhere in the world, provided the communications technology is present. Our creative functions of product development and actuarial work can be located wherever we can attract the very best professionals.

As an insurance company, we manage a large portfolio. Our best-performing and most creative money management firm has no main office as this term has traditionally been used. It exists in space, the virtual organization, as its creative people live and work in a variety of locations to accommodate customer service and personal preferences. Money can be managed in Jackson Hole as well as New York.

I once left the headquarters of the Fidelity Mutual Funds in Boston in the middle of rush hour traffic. I asked a senior executive, "What demands that you be located in this mess?" The response was, "The front facade of this building is the logo on all of our printed material." So buy a Hollywood set and move your employees to Stowe! The real question the firm faces, as is true with any organization, although difficult to resolve in action, is very basic and straightforward. How does Fidelity in this new era of the virtual organization release the full potential of its employees? This is especially difficult to answer if community is necessary for the full development of people. Greenleaf tells us that developing this potential is the work of leadership. Is not this release and harnessing of potential what DePree, Drucker, Senge, and so many others write about?

As is so often the case, the poet, in this case Gerard Manley Hopkins, captures in a few words what it takes the rest of us volumes to say:

As kingfishers catch fire, dragonflies draw flame;
As tumbled over rim in roundy wells
Stones ring; like each tucked string tells, each hung bell's
Bow swung finds tongue to fling out broad its name;
Each mortal thing does one thing and the same:
Deals out that being indoors each one dwells;
Selves—goes itself; myself it speaks and spells;
Crying *What I do is me: for that I came.*[1]

What does it mean in today's world of rapid change as leaders seek to create organizations where the fullness of the person comes alive with the power expressed by Hopkins and mission and vision are achieved by the organization? How do we apply the concepts of Greenleaf?

Leadership in the Virtual Organization

One of the most articulate social philosophers, a writer, broadcaster, professor at the London Business School and a former executive, is Charles Handy, author of *The Age of Unreason*.[2] He wrote the concluding essay "Unimagined Futures" in the most recent publication of the Drucker Foundation, *The Organization of the Future*.[3] In this piece he pulls together many of the characteristics of the virtual organization. Implicitly it calls for the paradigm of servant-leadership. A few incisive quotes will make clear why servant-leadership is the model of today and the future.

> Organizations aren't the visible, tangible, obvious places which they used to be. No longer, for instance, do you have to have everyone in the same place at the same time in order to get things done.[4]

Observe how many office buildings in your town are being converted to condominiums, as professional workers are in the field, at home, and in their cars. The work of the leader is to coalesce and articulate mission and vision and develop commitment to them by people in these various diverse locations and circumstances. This is hard-nosed thinking in the existing world of productive business. In the insurance company I mentioned earlier, one of our major vendors is also a competitor, customer, and partner. The business context is no longer us versus them, it is one of creating a set of relationships around the accomplishment of our mission and vision that the employees must understand and be committed to to achieve in a wide variety of relationships.

Handy continues as he compares the new organization to the new physics where particles are "bundles of potentiality." He sees this term as a good description of people in the new organization. For the leader this means:

> Power, in the new organizations, comes from relationships, not from structures. Those who have established reputations acquire authority which was not handed down from above; those who are open to others create positive energy around themselves, energy which did not exist before. Love, or, to give it a more corporately respectable title, "unconditional positive regard," may not make the world go around, but it can certainly release unsuspected potential.[5]

This resonates with Robert Greenleaf when he writes:

> A new moral principle is emerging which holds that the only authority deserving one's allegiance is that which is freely and knowingly granted by the led to the leader in response to, and in proportion to, the clearly evident servant stature of the leader.[6]

Much of what is written in business ethics is of questionable analytical value for it is not grounded in first principles, to use a term so well developed by Covey.[7] The very first and most basic principle for ethical behavior in any organization is that a clear mission and vision and set of core principles must exist. Integrity (wholeness) as an organization and consistent ethical behavior depends on and begins with the integrity of commitment to mission and vision. As Handy notes, as he uses another metaphor from the new science, there must be trust in the "strange attractor":

> Francis Fukuyama, in *Trust: The Social Virtues and* the *Creation of Prosperity*,[8] argues that societies of high trust do better economically. I would extend his idea to organizations. Organizations which rely on trust as their principal means of control are more effective, more creative, more fun, and cheaper to operate.[9]

Handy continues:

> Chaotic and energetic but uncontrolled organizations can exhibit movement without meaning unless they have found their strange attractor, which gives them point and purpose. Some have called this the "soul" of the organization, another soft but pregnant word which fits the new language of organizations. It is, I now believe, the principal task of leadership to find the strange attractor which will give meaning to movement, and around which a field of trust can be built which will allow the organization to devote most of its energies to its product instead of to its own entrails.[10]

Again, does not this model of the future call for all the leadership qualities important to Greenleaf? Much of what Handy has to say is captured by the father of modern management, Peter Drucker, when he writes:

> . . . increasingly, command and control is being replaced by or intermixed with all kinds of relationships: alliances, joint ventures, minority participations, partnerships, know-how, and marketing agreements—all relationships in which no one controls and no one commands. These relationships have to be based on a common understanding of objectives, policies, and strategies; on teamwork; and on persuasion—or they do not work at all.[11]

The abilities of being able to persuade others, of developing understanding, of deeply caring about the growth of others, as developed by Greenleaf as he describes the work of John Woolman, Thomas Jefferson, and Nikolai Federik Severin Grundtvig, define the persons who will lead the organizations of the future.[12] It is fascinating that Greenleaf, the man drawn to the large bureaucratic organization of the mid–twentieth century, developed a paradigm of leadership that is so clearly the way to manage the virtual organizations of the future. But the explanation is simple. As Covey so clearly understands, the work of leadership is based in first principles, especially in an accurate and profound understanding of the human person and of the role of his or her work in the full realization or self-actualization of his or her personhood.

Work—What I Do Is Me: For That I Came

I was recently in a meeting of professional social workers and businesspersons. When the speaker noted her agreement with Drucker's prediction that most persons in the next century will extend their work lives to the age of 75 there was a very audible and spontaneous gasp of disbelief, certainly not one of buy in to the idea out of the fulfillment of work. One does not need to be very perceptive to note that something is missing as one observes commuters and the activities in our modern saloons in the late afternoon and early evening. There is no joy or sense of fulfillment of achievement for many on any particular day. Yet Drucker is correct. If we are serious about saving social security, Congress is dancing on the deck of the *Titanic* if our society does not deal with one consequence of living longer. It means working longer or going broke as a society. If people are to work longer in their lives, however, it is compelling to re-create work so it is meaningful.

One of my favorite stories is that of the three bricklayers who, when asked by a traveler to describe what they were doing, provided three different answers. The first said simply, "I am laying bricks." The second responded, "I am feeding my family by laying bricks." The third, with spirit, said, "Through my work of laying bricks I am constructing a cathedral, and thereby giving honor and praise to the Lord."

Fulfillment comes through service to a cause, an idea, a mission, or others external to ourselves; best a purpose with a transcendent character. Each of us has a right to the dignity that comes from a job with real purpose. The role of leader is to create this purpose for the unskilled worker as well as for the highly skilled technical workers or the executives in the organization. But this is not happening in our world of work today, and if my experience with many part-time MBA students is indicative of the wider world, there is less satisfaction than ever before. Often, if they do enjoy their work, it is for the wrong reason—money or power. The tragedy of Tom Wolfe's character Sherman in *Bonfire of the Vanities*[13] appears to be their future. They are part of a dehumanizing, eroding, community-destroying, and eventually self-destructive concept of professional work. This is the tragedy of careerism. There is little thought to value added, much less service.

In a conference held by the Notre Dame Center for Ethics and Religious Values in Business, Dennis P. McCann delivered a paper entitled " 'If Life Hands You a Lemmon . . .': Business Ethics from *The Apartment* to *Glengarry Glen Ross.*"[14] In it he traces the development, as it were, in the person of Jack Lemmon playing three characters, of a single individual through his career. In *The Apartment* he is a person without much sense of self or purpose, eager to please, who becomes part of a rotten culture, but who eventually has enough idealism to quit. But there is little sense of self. Mc-Cann traces the Lemmon character through *Save the Tiger* and concludes with *Glengarry Glen Ross* where the character is 20 years older and totally corrupt, as he purposefully sets out to commit fraud for the sake of the money. Mc-Cann's purpose is to develop what can be the slippery slope of unethical behavior for his students using film, and he does it well. In an even deeper way, however, as with *Bonfire of the Vanities,* the utterly corrupting nature of purposeless work, or work done only for money, comes through. As the dignity of the person is lost, it rots those around the person, the customers and all others in contact with the business, and eventually the business itself. All of this is in contrast to Greenleaf's definition of leadership and DePree's chapter on making vice presidents in *Leadership Is an Art.*[15] It is through giving work purpose and dignity that individuals grow and mature to serve as leaders.

The tragedy of the meaninglessness of work is captured by many of the persons interviewed by Studs Terkel in his book *Working.* The words of a professional, Nora Watson, call out for the servant-leader:

> *"Jobs are not big enough for people. It's not just the assembly line worker whose job is too small for putting his spirit into it, you know? A job like mine, if you really put your spirit into it, you would sabotage it immediately. You don't dare. So you absent your spirit from it. My mind has been so divorced from my job, except as a source of income, it's really absurd."*[16]

We must not underestimate the raw tragedy of unemployment and insecurity in our modern economies or the unethical nature of financial marketplaces that reward executives for firing people rather than making them productive and the companies profitable or the human costs of enforced mobility, even for those who may have highly marketable skills.[17] This is not to suggest that the realities of a global economy do not exist—they do, and the naive populism of a Pat Buchanan or Ross Perot are just as senseless as the idolatry of the rigid "financial theory of the firm" academic and professional advocates who bow five times daily to Wall Street. Yes, needed are institutional and societal changes such as work expected until 75, disconnection of health insurance and pensions from jobs, and entirely new models of education that focus on the needs of persons rather than the vested rights of the providers.

If the economic growth of our U.S. society has only been shared by a relatively small minority within our country, while at the same time many countries in the world are not sharing in growing prosperity, and many of those that are sharing in growth really have no development, only growing disparity,[18] then this is a growing force for violence and tragedy for our children. Greenleaf considers perspective and foresight as marks of the servant leaders. Obviously, these characteristics were missing in the steel, auto, computer, and other industries that have seen huge downsizings in the past few years. Or if consideration of "what is the impact on the poorest"[19] is a mark of leadership, then much of industry has not been headed by leaders. The problem is deeper for all involved with our organizations, however, if the only source of sustainable competitive advantage is the commitment of quality employees to the organization. Part of this commitment will be loyalty, not defined as the blind faith captured so well in the character Ditto in *The Last Hurrah*[20] or some sort of self-interest by the mediocre. Rather, loyalty is expressed in competent action and sacrifice for the sake of the ones served by the organization. John Haughey has given extensive thought to what he calls the dilemma of loyalty to the firm. He believes that the economic costs of the loss of long-term loyalty to be between $60 and $70 billion annually. But he also notes:

> Even more important than the economic loss, though much less measurable, is the human cost to both individual and society if loyalty goes the way of the dinosaur. In my former role as a pastor, I have observed first hand the cost to the spiritual and social condition of people who had been laid off by companies to which they were loyal. Not only did they suffer, but everyone around them suffered.[21]

The lack of servant-leadership that creates dysfunctional and nonproductive job environments and companies takes many forms. The most insidious may be the "it's a game to be played" phenomenon captured so tragically when Bill Clinton awarded Bob Dole the Medal of Freedom. I happen to believe that Dole deserves this award, but the process and timing, especially in the present political context, reminds me of two football coaches embracing after what was only a game to be won. Clinton, like so many of our CEOs, appears to have no sense of purpose or understanding of what it is to serve the common good or good society where deeply held ideas must be argued in the marketplace. Politics is only a game to be won. Likewise, many executives apparently see little of inherent value in their work, they must just prove that they are better than the next executive by a bigger salary or running a larger organization.[22] Covey captures the issue in his distinction between the ethic of character and the ethic of personality. How in these environments can the commitments to the purpose of the organization be fostered? The seriousness of the problem hits me each year as I teach approximately 100 part-time MBA students. I am regularly troubled by the many, maybe half, who do not admire and respect their CEO. Many just do not care about their CEO and dismiss him or her as useless while others subject their leaders to ridicule.

The most disturbing aspect of work today is not that its nature is dehumanizing as was true of the traditional assembly line and is still true in chicken processing plants and other places. It is not the type of work that results in a product that has no redeeming social value, such as the flood of rip-off diet books; nor is it designed to destroy people, like the gossip magazines; exploit, like the sex rags; or kill people, like creating cigarette commercials designed to appeal to teenagers. The most dehumanizing aspect of work today is primarily focused on relationships that corrode rather than build the human potential.

Serving as a waitress or waiter can be very satisfying and we have all known the person waiting on us who, through attitude and service made our day, made us more human. On the other hand, we have all experienced the restaurant where supervision destroys the job for the wait staff and often the enjoyment of the dining experience for the customer. The good jobs need not only be in the high-price upscale restaurants. Much of the success of the Starbucks Coffee House[23] chain is directly attributable to a set of human resource policies that builds people as persons as part of a team providing a valuable service. Several years ago while on a Boy Scout camping trip I had a long conversation with a very competent lineman for the local public utility company. For years he had loved his work and truly saw himself as building a cathedral. The utility began to focus on all of the nonessentials of paperwork and process and demoralized John and many of his colleagues.

These relationship problems also exist in the world of professional jobs. It is my observation that large accounting firms have restructured themselves in a manner that greatly reduces job satisfaction. A brilliant woman accountant, who was one of the few women to become partner in her firm left and started her own firm, which has been successful beyond her dreams, because the old firm did not allow her to service her clients. Many are the universities that do not reward good teaching and constantly denigrate that which drew many people into the intellectual life. And then the institutions complain about lack of institutional loyalty when the going gets tough or lack of student commitment to learning.

Ensuring the Meaningfulness of Work: The Job of the Modern Servant-Leader

Two high school educator friends of mine recently were intensely engaged in a conversation as I approached them so the three of us could begin our meeting. One was complaining about the laziness, sloppiness, lack of preparedness, and so on of his students. The second person, tiring of the tirade, finally responded, "Now that you have defined a high school student, what are you going to do about it?" The question sums up the task of the servant-leader in the modern organization. She must ask herself only three critical questions. What is the mission and vision of our organization? (For the high school it is to provide secondary education with the vision of helping each student achieve his or her fullest potential at that point in time.) What is the reality of the persons I must lead? (High school students do not fit any definition of mature; they are frustrating, challenging, and lovable; they often come from tough nonsupportive backgrounds; and they have open and creative minds and wills if properly led.) What am I going to do about it? (The high school teacher should meet each student where he or she is, use the finite resources available, and take each person to heights undreamed by utilizing the potential present.) And of course the most important servants are the school boards, superintendents, and principals who will serve the teachers by asking the same three questions.

Derek Abel, a leading strategy theorist, defines a business by asking three similar questions.[24] Who are our customers? (Mission and vision) What are their needs? (Reality) What are the competitive strengths and resources we have to serve the needs of these customers? (Resources) The leadership in any organization is not only asking these questions as it attempts to define the business, it is also asking them of each and every employee in the firm or organization. As the questions are answered, the executives should see the organization as a set of ever larger circles, rather than a bottom-to-top entity.

This image helps one to begin to understand the interdependence of the roles of the servant and the served. Those in the outer circle are the ones with the real feel for the customer and his or her needs, and the resources available, but each person in this circle is an expert in a small piece of the organization and does not see the big picture and the mission and vision in total. Developing, articulating, and conveying the mission and vision is the role of the servants in the center circle, the leadership of the organization. No matter how competent the people throughout the organization, Leo is needed to hold it together and give it purpose. No matter how good the Leos of the modern organization, they depend on the people in the outer rings of the organization for the information necessary to understand reality and to be the ones totally committed to serving the stakeholders of the organization.

The servant-leader is successful when each person in the organization is committed to serving the specific needs of the customer by stretching and growing as necessary. When I was a dean, one of the professors, after an out-of-town student called to convey the message that his computer had crashed, put his personal computer in his car and undertook the 120-mile round trip to deliver the computer to the student. This is servant leadership, for even if the student was poor and lazy, looking for a fail-safe excuse to extend the deadline for his paper, I am sure that this one action by the servant-professor resulted in immense growth of the student.

Tim Hoeksema, the CEO of Midwest Express Airlines, often rated as the airline with the best service in the United States, is a servant-leader. He tells the story of one of the station managers in a small airport who delivered one of his suits and shirts and a pair of his shoes to a customer of his size and build, after the airline misplaced the customer's luggage. The customer was thereby enabled to do a sales presentation to a very important client the next morning. The environment that Tim has created fosters this type of service by fostering the growth of employees and in that highly competitive industry has made Midwest the airline of choice in those markets it serves. Everything in the Midwest formula for success can be duplicated or surpassed, other than this intense commitment of the employees of Midwest to its mission and vision. The rest of the formula can change, as demonstrated by Southwest, today's most successful airline. But the same important ingredient for success is found in both companies—intense employee loyalty is present. Whenever I fly Southwest, my day is made by the take-charge, self-confident, and humorous attitude of all the employees. Southwest, under the servant-leadership of Herb Kelleher, develops the potential of its employees while serving customer and stockholder.

Servant-Leadership: Grounded in the Understanding of the Person

The real secret of servant-leadership, in my opinion, is that it is grounded in a deep and objective understanding of the human person. It creates an environment or culture that nurtures new meanings of work in large and small organizations. It does this by constantly striving to enhance the dignity of each and every person, most importantly the employees, impacted by the organization. This growing dignity, in turn, releases the creativity necessary if an organization is to have the dynamism necessary for sustainable success. Perspectives on creativity are many, for this concept lies at the very heart of the intersection of the three institutions of capitalism, democracy, and religious freedom that make our American society what it is. Each of our political leaders who has been judged great by history in some way was a servant-leader releasing the creativity of the American people. In other words, they found a way to cut to the heart of the person and release potential. Michael Novak sees this as part of capitalism:

> But capitalism, truly defined, does not come into existence until institutions are established that systemically support and nourish the creative capacities of human beings to invent, discover, and innovate and to practice the fundamental human right of personal economic initiative.[25]

Pope John Paul recognizes that dignity of person involves releasing creativity in service to others when he writes that the person's "principal resource is the person himself or herself. The human's intelligence enables the person to discover the earth's productive potential and the many different ways in which human needs can be satisfied."[26] John Paul continues, "The person discovers his or her capacity to transform and in a certain sense create the world through his or her own work . . . carrying out a role as cooperator with God in the work of creation."[27] He continues, "We as individuals fulfill ourselves by using our intelligence and freedom. In so doing we utilize the things of this world as objects and instruments and make them our own. The foundation of the right of private initiative and ownership is to be found in this activity."[28]

The real genius of the capitalist system is certainly not efficiency, for in a certain sense we are wasteful and given to all sorts of false starts and product introductions that fail or simply duplicate something else that is available. This type of inefficiency is a very low cost to pay for the tremendous release of human creativity, which is the greatest of all assets and also the most unpredictable. The servant-leader tolerates mistakes as creativity is released by persons developing potential and moving the organization toward its vision.

Too many of us work in an environment where the human person is not valued for creative potential. Often work is treated as a mere factor of production, expendable and fully interchangeable with capital or natural resources. This is manifested in the scientific management of work (Taylorism), which focuses only on scientific increase in productivity through the improvement of the efficiency of the worker. In reaction to Taylorism, the Humanist school emerged, centered on the intrinsic value of work, with the focus on the worker rather than on the object being produced. An understanding of the psychological nature of the person in the act of working is present, and that is good, but humanist thinking does not capture the full meaning of work that flows from a cultural and spiritual perspective. The results have been shallow at best and, in the hands of practitioners, manipulative at worst.

It is not enough to define work in just a cultural sense, although this must be understood. For example, how many of us ever ask some variant of the question, when we meet somebody for the first time, "Who are you?" Rather, we tend to ask, "What do you do?" I seldom call myself Dr. except when I call an M.D.'s office and desire instant access. I never call myself professor, except when traveling in other countries where Dr. or Dean means little, but Professor confers instant respect.

The true meaning of work is *spiritual,* a term that I believe can be used by persons with or without religious belief. As persons with dignity, each of us shares in a common spirit, called God's life in the Christian/Judaic tradition or similar concepts of unity in other religions, or something as basic as brotherhood. As such we are called to be cocreators with our God or with each other in service to each other. It is through this inherently valuable work that we develop our potential. The essential value of our work is in its impact on us as persons. This is not to deny that the product of our work will also have an impact on others. Nevertheless, we are the subject of our work. As a human person each of us has the right to develop our potential through our work in service to others as well as the obligations. We will contribute directly and indirectly to the mission and vision of our organization only insofar as the creativity in our potential is released. The job of the servant-leader is to translate this conceptual reality into the ongoing operating reality of our organizations.

I am grateful to Michael Naughton for providing us with a framework for moving from conceptual to practical ideas that can be implemented in today's virtual organizations by committed servant-leaders. He notes that the activity of work has four dimensions. There are two subjective dimensions called *function* and *remuneration* and two objective dimensions that we know as *process* and *product.* Naughton explains,

While each of the four dimensions interact and constantly overlap in the experience of work, each has unique characteristics. Function is the essential dimension of work which focuses on the changes work brings about in an individual's personality, character, and potentialities as a subject.[29]

Taylorism focused on the economic aspect of the process and Humanism on the psychological. To understand work fully, however, we must understand the more important spiritual characteristics of the human person, primarily the functional dimension. As Naughton emphasizes, the other three dimensions are rooted in the functional dimension of work. If the focus is only on a just remuneration, then the result will be the motivation of the bricklayer. Sustainable creativity focused on the mission of the organization will not be released. It also lends credibility to the stockholder model of the corporation rather than the stakeholder or, better yet, the common good model as developed by Michael Stebbins[30] at the Woodstock Center and based in part on the work of Bernard Lonergren. The later two models come to terms with the question Max DePree asks in *Leadership Is an Art,* "Who Owns This Place?"

The third dimension of work, process, focuses on one of the most important social issues of our era. If we believe in primacy of the person as a foundation for building an organization, the servant-leader is forced to ask two questions. How will this organization ensure that science and technology is a slave and not a master? What will be the workers' relationship to it? Or, in new forms of organization, how is an authentic community created in the virtual corporation? The fullness of person can only be developed in authentic community. If all are not in the same place and the persons involved are fluid and the organization is global, operating in all of the time zones, how is it held together as community? The organization must form community, if it is to release the full potential of its employees—and remember this is the only source of sustainable competitive advantage. It begins with fullness of commitment to mission and vision.

Developing this type of virtual community is possible to do in a vibrant manner if the technology of communication is harnessed in the context of commitment of mission and vision. My own experience indicates it can be done. Two of the most productive communities to which I belong and to which I commit myself are global. The mission and vision in both cases are crystal clear with buy in by most members. The servant-leader will be focused on the acculturation processes, annual meetings, reward systems and recognition, and other practical means of implementation and building the necessary community. If effective organizations with commitment to mission could be built by the English trading companies in the seventeenth and eighteenth centuries, organizations like the Hudson Bay Company or the East India Trading Company, it would appear that building purposeful communities can more easily be done today with modern technology. Of course this same technology can be misused to impose dysfunctional control systems.

The concept of product, the object made from the process employed, is also determined by one's model of the corporation as well as one's view of the person. If product is viewed as only a means to profit, then go for the pornography, useless diet books, and slander magazines. Destroy the environment. But if product is seen as the link through which the worker serves community, including the investor, then the servant-leader is concerned with community beyond the organization, the environment, and quality of product. Herman Miller is a wonderful example of a firm committed to manufacturing products that enhance the humanity of their customers. It is the excellent value provided to customers that makes the virtual organization of the money management firm mentioned in the beginning of this article so successful.

Servant-Leadership—The Answer

Servant-leadership as a concept may be more important today in our world of the virtual organization, knowledge worker, hunger for community, intense competition, and resource constraints than when Robert Greenleaf first conceptualized the ideas in the mid–twentieth century. But we have all long considered him to be a prophet. Just as the large organization, properly implemented, that Greenleaf loved allowed a specialization that grew people in community, so the technological and organizational developments of a new century can do the same—if harnessed by the true servant-leader committed to the growth of all involved with the organization. The spiritualization of work in no way calls for a soft approach to leadership. The servant-leader is in no way relieved of the ever harder options facing those in leadership. If nothing else, the characteristics of foresight and reflection will be demanded of the leaders of the virtual organization in greater quantity than ever before. The reality of the fluid global marketplace is upon us and not going away.

None of us like the massive layoffs that we have seen for the past two decades. But Greenleaf would argue that many of these are not unethical for there really is no choice, and for an action to be unethical, there must be choice. The unethical actions were those of building huge organizations that added no value, did not reflect changing technology, and probably only fed management egos. The servant-leader will also carefully hire employees and devote sufficient resources to training and acculturating them into the organization and make termination decisions early on if a poor fit exists. The servant-leader will also take ownership of the problem, if there is an employee who is not performing. These are the moral decisions and actions that will build both effectiveness and community in organizations and allow the virtual organization to become a facilitator of releasing human potential.

An example of taking ownership of the problem is the CEO of a family firm in one of the toughest of American industries who has a standing rule that must be accepted by anyone promoted to a management position. New managers cannot fire any one until 12 months have elapsed and then only if they have a documented record that nothing has worked. This creates an environment of trust and listening. And listening is a transferable skill needed by a servant-leader to build an organization.

Listening is the first phase in conveying purpose in building community. For workers to commit to building a cathedral, they must have a vision of a cathedral. The work of the leader is to articulate vision and purpose in a manner that resonates with the employees, which means listening first.

> The leader always knows what it (the direction) is and can articulate it for
> any who are unsure. By clearly stating and restating the goal, the leader
> gives certainty and purpose to others who may have difficulty in achiev-
> ing it for themselves.[31]

Greenleaf clearly saw the need for community. He saw that shared purpose is the first step in creating community. And he would say, do not tell me how the new technology destroys community, tell me how it can be used to create community. For instance, he draws on a quote from Paul Goodman, who is speaking through a character in *Making Do*, "If there is no community for you, young man, make it for yourself."[32]

He clearly saw in his leadership paradigm that the primary purpose of work is the growth of the person in service to others:

> Looking at the two major elements, the work and the person, the new
> ethic, simply but quite completely stated, will be: The work exists for the
> person as much as the person exists for the work. Put another way, the
> business exists as much to provide meaningful work to the person, as it
> exists to provide a product or service to the customer.[33]

Greenleaf hoped for a situation where "the significance of work will be more the joy of doing rather than the goods and services produced." He also understood that the greatest waste in modern business is the waste of human potential. He argued that not only does each person have a right to a job, but that

> The next step may be to acknowledge that every person is entitled to
> work that is meaningful in individual terms, and that it is the obligation
> of employers, in toto, to provide it.[34]

I conclude at the point I began. That is, in the virtual organization, more than ever before, the only source of sustainable competitive advantage for any organization is the commitment of quality employees to the mission and vision of the organization. What appears to be two mutually exclusive goals in our society—meaningful work for all and competitiveness in the world economy—are really two sides of the same problem. In an advanced industrial society like ours, we can only be successful and compete and maintain or improve our standard of living, and ensure that even greater numbers obtain it, if we build virtual organizations based on the dignity of the worker and the need for work to be meaningful. Dignity and fulfillment, in turn, generate a type of self-motivation that leads to not only a flexible organization but also a successful virtual organization. The "strange attractor" that will generate the work patterns and success of the future will be servant-leadership, as articulated by Robert Greenleaf and his disciples, and lived by persons like Max DePree in organizations like Herman Miller in our current world and in the virtual organizations of the future—when the servant-leadership fit is even better.

20

Seeking the Soul of Business

Christine Wicker

Christine Wicker is a senior religion reporter for The Dallas Morning News. *She is writing a book on individualistic spirituality, a trend that University of Chicago church historian Martin Marty calls one of the three greatest changes happening in American religion today.*

This essay originally appeared as a feature article in The Dallas Morning News. *In it, Wicker captures the essence of spirit and servant-leadership that is being advocated by a growing number of businesspeople.*

None dare call it religious.

But a management philosophy catching on at companies across America sounds so much like religion that adherents are sometimes at pains to make the difference clear.

This is spirituality. Ethics. Values. Common sense. And market imperative, they say.

The labels that identify it—stewardship and servant-leadership—might seem to have a religious ring. The original inspiration was the writing of Nobel Prize winner Hermann Hesse, whose work focused on man's spiritual loneliness.

In the 1970s a Quaker businessman named Robert Greenleaf began espousing "a new ethic" when he wrote an essay called "The Servant as Leader." It was based on an idea he borrowed from Hesse's novel *Journey to the East,* the notion that those who serve are best equipped to lead.

Today a number of business consultants and managers are elaborating on Greenleaf's philosophy, propagated at annual conferences put on by The Greenleaf Center for Servant-Leadership in Indianapolis.

Common threads include managers who see the search for life's meaning as a legitimate part of the workday and employees who seek to forgo personal ambition in favor of the common good. A goal of the philosophy is to judge employees and managers less on how much profit they generate than on how much help they give each other and the customers.

Seeing the workplace as the new community is part of the thinking.

"That's where people spend most of their time. That's where they're congregated," said Peter Block, who has done consulting work for Texas Instruments, Chrysler, Ford, and Levi Strauss on this form of management. "If you want to affirm or do something about citizenship and democracy and people reclaiming choice for themselves, then go to the workplace," he said. "I think that's where community gets lived out."

Echoes of the servant-leadership or stewardship business movement can be heard in books such as Stephen R. Covey's *The Seven Habits of Highly Effective People* and former Fortune 500 executive James Autry's book *Love and Profit: The Art of Caring Leadership*. Also among the proponents of this new orientation are Dallas business consultant Dr. Ann McGee-Cooper, author of *You Don't Have to Go Home from Work Exhausted!* and Max DePree, author of *Leadership Jazz* and chairman of Herman Miller, the office furniture manufacturer.

Advocates of the movement quote Jewish mystics, Buddhist masters, Hebrew prophets, Jesus, and Albert Einstein. They recite poetry and sometimes compose their own verses about work. They talk about reconciliation, surpassing self, and "being" rather than "doing."

"Work is about learning and transforming yourself," said business consultant and retired Southern Methodist University history professor Dr. Luis Martin, when quoting management guru Peter Senge to a group of Burlington-Northern Railroad employees.

"Love is more powerful than greed, but maybe not as prevalent," he noted.

"Are you personally and spiritually growing in your job? If not, something is wrong with your job or you, and you'd better do something about it because you are the only one who can," warns Dr. Martin, a former Jesuit priest.

Such ideas sound so spiritual that Dr. Martin repeatedly reminds his audiences, "This is not your Sunday school teacher talking."

"I don't know anything about religion," says Peter Block, a Jew who was once complimented after a speech by being told he sounded like a good Christian. "I'm just trying to figure life out. It's pure pragmatism for me."

Block, author of *Stewardship* and *The Empowered Manager*, departs radically from many traditional ideas about the marketplace. He believes, for instance, that businesses ought to downplay money as a motivation.

"People don't work for money," he asserts. "Sure they have to make a living, but after that . . . if you can't find some meaning, some way to be of service, then you'll say, 'Damn it. I want to get paid.' " He maintains that businesses ought to redistribute wealth from the top to the bottom: "You can't have a partnership if you don't share the profits. They ought to eliminate executive perks such as parking places and big offices."

In addition, Block believes managers and employees should think of themselves as holding power and wealth in trust for future generations.

He and others believe businesses will adopt servant-leadership ideas for practical reasons. They say shifting responsibility downward and adding life-affirming values to business is the best way to do more work with fewer people and create companies that can react to rapidly changing markets. Some executives back them up.

"We started down this road out of necessity," said Jim Walker, vice president in charge of AT&T's North American Global Business Communications System. In 1989 his division was losing a quarter of a billion dollars. He began replacing rules with values and dividing employees into small, virtually autonomous groups with far more power. Now, his division is making a quarter of a billion dollars a year, and he says the new management plan is a large part of the reason.

"The other ways won't get you there," he argues, referring to hierarchical management systems based solely on the profit motive. "We take our principles and religious values to work," he explains. "Another way to say it is we all know what's right." Sometimes such thinking leads the work community to reach out into the world at large.

At Perot Systems, chief executive officer Mort Meyerson began trying to establish a new sense of mission and open up communications in 1992. In late 1993, one of the things employees communicated was that they wanted to do more good works outside the office.

Now, Brenda Shaw, who heads the community relations program, goes through the office before Easter with empty baskets swinging from her arms. Anyone who wants to fill a basket for senior citizens takes one, makes it up, and helps deliver it to a retirement home. Perot Systems employees, some of whom had never seen a housing project, now get time off from the workday to volunteer at such places as a food bank, a women's shelter, or in public schools.

Meanwhile, the company has avoided what Ms. Shaw calls "checkbook charity." Why? "It doesn't do anything for your corporate soul," she said.

But self-sacrifice, humility, and power to the people haven't exactly swept the business community into a new age of economics. Most change has been cosmetic, notes Peter Block, who estimates that 60 percent of the companies that hire him want "a placebo" but no real reform. "Mostly, I get criticized not for being wrong but for being impractical," he said. "What they're really telling me about is their own despair."

Critics have said that business must be run on economic, rather than spiritual principles. Author Tom Peters is among those who have warned against linking spirituality and business too closely.

Mort Meyerson agrees and rarely uses the word *spirituality* to describe his management ideas. Nevertheless, his approach has angered some. After a speech outlining his ideas at the Massachusetts Institute of Technology, Meyerson was approached by a man who was so incensed that he was almost spitting as he talked.

"Don't you realize that business is about making profit?" he asked Meyerson.

Meyerson replied, "It's about that. But it's about a lot more, too."

Jack Lowe Jr., chief executive officer of TDIndustries, has practiced servant-leadership concepts all his business career, as his father did before him. "Our purpose is to be a great place for a lot of people to work for a long period of time," says Lowe, whose company has handled some of the biggest construction projects in the Dallas area. "To do that, we've got to amaze our customers."

As an example of the company's principles, he tells about a retired employee who reflected that workers had been allowed to make all sorts of mistakes as long as they didn't keep making the same ones, but "if you mistreated anyone, you knew you were out of here."

Lowe, whose office is a 10-by-15-foot space with only partition walls and no windows, acknowledges that putting servant-leadership principles into practice isn't easy. "We screw up all the time," he said. "Construction is a hard-nosed business. Sometimes we forget our principles."

But the method does have payoffs. The most recent edition of *The 100 Best Companies to Work for in America* included TDIndustries. Trust between management and employees was a big factor, says Lowe. For example, when a worker committee tackled the employee-owned company's health costs four years ago, they went down $4 million from projections and coverage increased.

The change in companies that adopt the stewardship or servant-leadership principles can be seen in their mission statements. An Atlanta hardware store, for instance, now has as its purpose not selling, but helping the customer make the best decisions.

The change can also be seen in the type of training offered. Dr. Martin, who consults all over the country with his Intellectual Fitness Center, includes history, sociology, and philosophy in his lectures.

The new thinking can also be seen in management. "My job is more like a consultant than a boss," comments AT&T's Jim Walker, who now briefs his employees as if they were a board of directors.

But no one pretends it is easy.

"It's scary," admits Richard Jacob, who as CEO and president of BriskHeat Corp. in Columbus, Ohio, says he is preaching revolution to the ruling class.

It has worked for him. When he took over in 1989, BriskHeat was not doing well. In 1994 he was named Entrepreneur of the Year for Ohio by *Inc.* magazine.

Many want to emulate his company's success, he said, but they don't want the change. "Lots of people want to go to heaven, but few people want to die," he said by way of analogy.

According to Peter Block, who has taught these ideas for years, implementation is enormously difficult. People try, fail, and try again.

"What's important is the effort they are making. Spirituality is in pursuit of something. We're not going to be God. That's arrogant. We're not going to make it. We aren't," he asserts.

"But community is about coming together in pursuit of some kind of purpose, some kind of goal that has meaning." And community is the only future, he says. "I think sooner or later all of us are going to get to the point that [we realize] 'I can't survive unless we choose 'we.' "

21

The Integration of Business Ethics and Spirituality in the Workplace

James Conley and Fraya Wagner-Marsh

James H. Conley and Fraya Wagner-Marsh are both professors of management in the College of Business at Eastern Michigan University. Both are members of the Academy of Management. Conley is a member of the Association for Business Communication and has recently begun to travel the country interviewing business leaders who espouse the servant-leader philosophy. Fraya Wagner-Marsh is a member of the Society for Human Resource Management and contributor to human resource management books and journals.

In this essay, Conley and Wagner-Marsh provide a useful survey of the influence that Robert Greenleaf's writings have had on current thinking in the areas of spirituality and business ethics. They close their essay with some suggested steps for organizations interested in exploring spirituality in the workplace.

Examples of ethical lapses by corporations are as close as the front page of the newspaper. Charges of corporate espionage and racketeering, minority bashing in the boardroom, alcohol advertising aimed at underage consumers, churning investment accounts, fraudulent billing practices, and other such unethical behaviors have created embarrassing news coverage that has been severely detrimental to the credibility of the business community. Many small organizations, as well as corporate giants such as Volkswagen, Texaco, Sears, Beech-Nut, Salomon Brothers, and General Electric have been directly touched by scandals. Even socially enlightened corporations such as The Body Shop can find their images severely tarnished overnight due to allegations of unethical conduct.[1]

Due to today's litigious environment, executives who choose to ignore unethical behavior are facing an increasing risk of both personal and corporate liability. The November 1991 U.S. Sentencing Commission guidelines

for corporate violators has intensified this personal aspect of the legal consequences of unethical business conduct. These guidelines have also increased
the rewards provided by adopting ethical compliance programs in the organization since they allow for leniency sentencing based on the presence of
such programs.[2] Penalties such as fines and probation for ethical misconduct
can vary dramatically depending on whether or not the company has implemented such a program. These traditional ethics programs tend to emphasize the prevention of unlawful conduct, primarily through the use of controls and imposing penalties for wrongdoers.[3]

There is also an argument that ethical commitment within a corporation may provide other types of rewards. Norman Bowie supports the notion
that, other things being equal, a moral firm will have a competitive advantage
that includes greater trust and determination among employees and perhaps
even higher-quality services and products.[4] Even though empirical attempts
to establish the relationship between corporate social responsibility and financial performance have provided mixed results,[5] some corporations such as
California-based Levi Strauss & Company are currently developing measurement tools to put an exact dollar figure on the income side of social responsibility.[6]

Traditional Approaches to Business Ethics

Most companies approach business ethics in a fairly straightforward manner.
Typically, some philosophical statement is presented by top management
that sets forth the corporate leadership's ethical positions on a variety of
business-related issues and includes a written code of ethics. Some studies
have found that approximately 93 percent of companies have written codes
of conduct.[7] Examples of companies known for exemplary codes of ethics are
Johnson & Johnson,[8] McDonnell Douglas,[9] and Security Pacific Corporation.[10] Many of these codes of ethics are frequently accompanied by a requirement that the employees sign some sort of declaration of intent to ad-
here to the principles and procedures of the corporation's code, perhaps with
some warning of the individual consequences of nonadherence.

More effective codes of ethics are often accompanied by some specific
procedures, appointed persons, or some type of ongoing communication
mechanisms that allow employees to report ethical concerns. Examples of
such mechanisms would be ethics ombudspersons, corporate ethics officers,
and ethics hot lines.[11] Once an ethics code and reporting mechanisms have
been established, companies typically engage in ethics training. The most
common approaches to ethics training are case studies, presenting and discussing rules or guidelines for decision making, frameworks to provide guidance in resolving ethical issues, and cognitive approaches focused on higher
levels of ethical thinking.[12] Companies that have strong ethics training programs would include Chemical Bank, Dow Corning,[13] Allied, Chase Man-

hattan, and General Electric. Recent studies have indicated that approximately 44 percent of companies provide some type of ethics training with 86 percent of the companies directing their ethics training to managers.[14]

The traditional programs described can be deemed a praiseworthy approach, so far as they go. And, depending on the length and perceived quality of the instructional effort, they would probably satisfy the courts that the organization in question had done its best to communicate its ethical requirements. However, little evidence is available on the actual impact of these traditional ethics programs. In fact, codes of ethics have been criticized because many of them only establish a minimal level of acceptable behavior, and critics say the codes are ineffective. This ineffectiveness is clearly demonstrated when a company with a strong code of ethics suffers a public scandal. One prime example of this is Dow Corning and their alleged cover-up of information about the toxic effects of silicone.[15] Therefore, while these traditional programs are indeed laudable, and similar ones should be offered within all business organizations, we contend that these ethical programs might be more effectively communicated within what could be called a spiritual environment.

Spirituality in the Workplace

A number of best-selling books have focused on the theme of spirituality in the workplace incorporating "a management model filled with heart—and soul."[16] Some of the better-known authors and publications would include: *Spirit at Work: Discovering the Spirituality in Leadership* by Jay Conger, *Leadership Jazz* by Max DePree, *The Soul of a Business* by Tom Chappell, *Stewardship: Choosing Service Over Self-Interest* by Peter Block, and *Making the Grass Greener on Your Side: A CEO's Journey to Leading by Serving* by Kendrick Melrose.[17] Also, several informative articles that include numerous examples of corporations that are incorporating spirituality in the workplace have appeared in various business publications.[18]

Specific examples of corporations and their leaders who have attempted to implement a kind of value-laden spirituality through their leadership and practice would include the following:

- Fred Huyghue, president of the SSiM Group Inc.[19]
- Truett Cathy, founder and president of Chick-fil-A
- John Teets, chairman of Greyhound
- Thomas Phillips, CEO of Raytheon
- Sanford McDonnell, chairman and chief executive of McDonnell Douglas
- Kenneth Olsen, founder and president of Digital Equipment[19]

- Bill Bottum, former president of Townsend & Bottum, Inc.[20]
- Tom Chappell, CEO of Tom's of Maine[21]
- Max DePree, former president of Herman Miller[22]
- Earle Hess, former CEO of Lancaster Laboratories[23]
- William Pollard, Chairman of ServiceMaster[24]

Other corporate examples would include Boeing Co., Lotus Development, and Medtronic.[25] The list continues to grow as more companies are trying to find a sense of meaning and purpose after the trauma of downsizing and reengineering.

Other evidence of this move toward spirituality in the workplace is revealed in a recent article describing "tomorrow's organizations," where one of the major emerging functions includes the "spiritual center."[26] Two of the essential duties of this center would be: (1) to infuse all organizational members with the vitality, enthusiasm, and spirit needed to acquire true excellence, and (2) to give every organizational member a true sense of meaning and purpose.

It has been suggested that the wellspring of this recent spirituality emphasis comes from the servant-leadership concept espoused by Robert K. Greenleaf, a devout Quaker and management researcher at AT&T.[27] According to the concept of servant-leadership, the leaders exist to serve their followers. In other words, a manager's main job is to serve his or her followers—to do what needs to be done to see that the followers can do their jobs effectively. Peter Block similarly defines *stewardship* as the willingness to be accountable for the well-being of the larger organization and being responsible for what's being created.[28]

This concept certainly fits with the contemporary management ideas of empowerment and participative management and goes well beyond Theory Y assumptions about workers. This new school of thought, according to Max DePree, incorporates "covenantal relationships" between leaders and employees where bonds are created that "fulfill deep needs and give work meaning."[29] DePree says that individuals need to weigh the pragmatic in the clarifying light of the moral and understand that reaching one's potential is more important than reaching one's goals.[30]

Another major contributor to the concept of spirituality in the workplace is Stephen Covey. In his national best-seller, *The Seven Habits of Highly Effective People* (1989), Covey talks about the importance of the "character ethic," a new level of thinking that is principle centered and character based.[31] Some of the main principles include fairness, integrity, human dignity, service, quality, potential, patience, nurturance, and encouragement. He emphasizes that "principles are guidelines for human conduct that are proven to have enduring, permanent value."[32]

Akin to spirituality, M. Scott Peck, author of *The Road Less Traveled* and *A World Waiting to Be Born*, talks about the importance of community:

"a place where there is authentic communication, a willingness to be vulnerable, a commitment not to walk away when the going gets tough."[33] Peck believes that we are at the beginning of an organizational revolution in group consciousness that deals more with emotions and communicating with each other.[34]

Spirituality and Business Ethics

We contend that spirituality and ethics complement each other and that the spirituality movement could produce a dynamic synergistic effect within the organization when combined with the organization's concern for ethical performance. Ethics deal specifically with morality and "the line between spirituality and morality has always been thin at best."[35] Peck alludes to this connection between "community" and ethics when he says that ethical integrity will be *guaranteed* when genuine community is introduced into a business.[36]

The new role of leadership in a spiritually based organization would be a key to developing greater individual commitment to ethical principles. One of the major problems with traditional ethics programs is that they are developed and administered top-down with top management developing a statement of ethical principles for the organization and then someone else indoctrinating employees with these principles. In a spiritually based organization, the leader's role is to be servant-led. Some of the characteristics of servant-leaders are that they listen, they empathize, they are aware, they have foresight, and they are committed to the growth of people.[37] Interestingly enough, these characteristics would also support the research by James Kouzes and Barry Posner that concluded that the most admired leaders are also the leaders "who make their followers feel valued, who raise their sense of self-worth and self-esteem."[38] This theme is also repeated by Dobbs when he identifies "compassionate leadership," characterized by honesty, caring, dignity, and respect for people, as the most crucial element for creating an ethical environment, one that supports integrity and initiative.[39]

Corporate Examples of Spirituality and Ethics

Some examples of spiritually based companies that have integrated spirituality with business ethics would include Lancaster Laboratories, Wetherill Associates (WAI), Medtronic, Toro Company, and TDIndustries in Dallas. This list is certainly not exhaustive but provides some diversity of industries and approaches. Lancaster Laboratories (a research-and-analysis lab employing more than 500 employees and reporting $25 million in sales) incorporates ethics into its mission statement. Earl Hess, former CEO of Lancaster, believes that it is significant that the company's mission statement was formulated to define not only *what* the company does but *how* it is committed to doing it. "The *how* part of the mission statement committed us to the provision of quality service with a client focus, to conduct ourselves ethically, in a spiritual way."[40] Earl Hess's commitment to mutual trust and honesty in dealing with others is also illustrated by the fact that he always wore a company name tag with a note that said "If I'm not living our values, challenge me."[41]

Wetherill Associates (WAI) is an automobile parts supplier that incorporates a basic operating philosophy known as the "principle of right action." This principle is summed up as follows: "Whenever an action is known or felt to be right, the action is to be taken. Whenever [an] action is known or suspected to be wrong, the action is not to be taken. We don't tell lies here, and everyone knows it. People trust us and this works well for us on both sides of the business, the sales side and the supplier side." Honesty is also a key element in dealing with WAI's employees. "We believe we have demonstrated beyond a doubt, that when people function in an atmosphere of absolute honesty, they feel safe, they are happier, they suffer no stress. And as a result, they are more productive and have a positive effect on everybody they deal with."[42] WAI also emphasizes that there is an *ethical* basis for *quality*. They believe that when there is an overall organizational commitment to a value system that is "ethics affirming," then quality of product and effectiveness of service will follow.

Medtronic is another company that strongly emphasizes the importance of honesty and integrity. However, such a strict policy of honesty, integrity, and mutual trust becomes even more complicated when a company operates globally and the tendency is to say that compromises are necessary to market successfully in some countries. Bill George, CEO of Medtronic, explains that Medtronic has developed a *worldwide* standard of ethics. In fact, George states that Medtronic decided to pull out of one country because the organization couldn't tolerate some of the unethical practices there.[43] Beyond honesty and integrity, the attitude of stewardship is woven throughout this organization starting with its mission: "to help people live fuller lives." Earl Bakken, the man who built Medtronic and is now over 70 years old, meets with every new Medtronic employee all over the world and tells the history and mission of the company and gives everyone a medallion incorporating a representation of the mission statement. He says, "Put it on your desk, and when you look at it . . . it will remind you that you are not here just to make money. But you're here to help people lead full lives." George believes that if a company makes profit, instead of providing service, the mission, the company eventually loses its soul.[44]

Toro Company and TDIndustries are both examples of spiritually based companies that have a strong commitment to employees that is often seen in their programs and value statements. One example would be Toro Company's "Pride in Excellence" program, which was developed by the entire management group. This program is a credo of employee empowerment and is aimed at creating a culture based on mutual respect and the worth of each employee, or "owner" (the term used by Ken Melrose, the CEO). The cornerstone of the "People Values" of the program include teamwork, win-win partnerships, giving power away, and respect for one another.[45] A similar example would be TDIndustries' Basic Values Statement that begins with "concern for and belief in individual human beings." TDI let their actions reflect their words in 1990 when it came time to lay off employees ("partners" in company parlance). One year after the layoffs, the company received the highest scores on its annual morale survey since it began surveying employees over a decade ago. These scores were evidence of the company's compassionate and caring approach to the downsizing.[46]

Conclusions and Proposed Actions

As the previous company examples illustrate, we contend that a more widespread organizational commitment to the spiritual underpinnings of the basic organization would enhance the effectiveness of development, dissemination, and acceptance of appropriate codes of ethics and guidelines for ethical behavior. The consequent value of combining spirituality and ethics would be hypothesized as threefold: (1) The ethical expectations of the organization would more likely be viewed by its constituents as emerging from the most credible moral plane, and hence be more willingly accepted; (2) the modeling of community and stewardship would provide a mutually reinforcing and socially supportive context for appropriate behavior; and (3) over time, conformance to the behavioral expectations and declared ethical norms of the group would lead to the *individual* internalization of those expectations and ethical norms, where the prescribed behavior is no longer that of mere conformity but "second nature."

To organizations that have not yet explored spirituality as a means to motivate employees and create a strong identity or "soul," the following practical, though admittedly challenging, steps are recommended:

1. Familiarize all levels of management with the literature that is developing on spirituality.
2. Familiarize management with some concrete examples of organizations that have been successfully infused with spiritual values.
3. Get management involved with one or more of the leading foundations or associations that are seeking to communicate these principles, such as The Greenleaf Center for Servant-Leadership or the Fetzer Institute.
4. Seek consultant assistance in implementing spirituality within the workplace.
5. Take, with advisement, personal steps toward strengthening one's own individual spiritual understandings.

22

Destiny and the Leader

Joseph Jaworski

Joseph Jaworski is the author of Synchronicity: The Inner Path of Leadership, *an exploration of the way leaders deepen their understanding of reality and gain the capacity to shape the future. Jaworski spent the first 20 years of his career as an attorney with the Houston-based firm of Bracewell & Patterson, specializing in domestic and international litigation. During this same period, he helped found three successful businesses in fields as diverse as life insurance, oil refining, and horse breeding. In 1980 he founded the American Leadership Forum to develop new leadership in the post-Watergate era. In the early 1990s he joined the Royal Dutch/Shell Group of Companies in London to lead a multinational team of experts in creating global scenarios. He has worked closely with the MIT Center for Organizational Learning (now The Society for Organizational Learning) to help build learning organizations. He is also a founder and chairman of the Centre for Generative Leadership where he works collaboratively with clients on large-scale organizational change and values-based leadership development.*

In this essay, Jaworski probes Greenleaf's ideas about a central issue of servant-leadership: how individuals and organizations go about discovering and fulfilling their unique purpose.

My first encounter with Robert Greenleaf's ideas on servant-leadership came just when I needed them. Greenleaf himself would have understood how that happens. "One gets what one is ready for, what one is open to receive," he once said by way of explaining a Robert Frost poem.[1]

Greenleaf's own introduction to the concept of servant-leadership occurred in just such a way, at just such a moment. As a consultant to a university racked by turmoil in the 1960s, Greenleaf felt a need to understand where the students were coming from. To do that, he decided to read what they were reading. That led him to Hermann Hesse, then one of the most popular authors on campus. He persevered through the bleakness of novel after novel until in 1970 he arrived at *Journey to the East*. This novel, with its powerful story of Leo, the archetypal servant-leader, permanently changed his view of leadership.

In my own life, I've become increasingly conscious of the way such "predictable miracles" operate in our lives: how doors open when we're ready to walk through them, how we encounter people or ideas at precisely the right moment. The closest I've come to finding a word to describe this phenomenon is *synchronicity,* which Carl Jung defines as "a meaningful coincidence of two or more events, where something other than the probability of chance is involved."[2]

I wrote about my personal experience with these predictable miracles in *Synchronicity: The Inner Path of Leadership.* The book was never intended to be an autobiography, even though I illustrate some of my ideas with events from my personal journey. All of us have pivotal events in our lives that leave us forever changed. For me, one of these was the national tragedy of Watergate, brought home to me because of my father's role as special prosecutor. And the second was the personal crisis of a divorce. In the aftermath of Watergate, I felt compelled to rethink everything I thought I knew about leadership. And my divorce prompted me to set out on a journey to discover my purpose in life—a journey, incidentally, that I think every leader must take.

In 1980, when I was just beginning to think deeply about these issues, a little pamphlet arrived in the mail—sent to me, I now think, by Vince Drucker, Peter Drucker's son. It was a copy of Robert Greenleaf's essay *The Servant as Leader,* which he had written after reading Hesse's *Journey to the East.* I was astounded at the extent to which our ideas converged. Greenleaf was saying what I felt but hadn't heard anyone say in quite the same way.

The framework Greenleaf set forth enabled me to understand the underlying dynamics of leadership. There are two essential dimensions to leadership, Greenleaf asserted. The first, and by far the best known, is the desire to serve others. The second is the desire to serve something beyond ourselves—a higher purpose. Greenleaf did not restrict himself to a single term in speaking of this transcendent reality. At one time or another, he spoke of it as the goal, the dream, the overarching purpose.

That guiding principle—that we must discover and serve our purpose—resonates powerfully with me. It also had a strong appeal for Greenleaf, who viewed it as "something to strive for, to move toward, or become."[3] Purpose is not the exclusive province of individuals. Those who would be servant-leaders must take the journey within to discover their personal purpose, but organizations that intend to endure and excel must also embark on a journey to discover the reason for their existence.

With Greenleaf, I have come to believe that if we are willing to take that most difficult journey toward self-discovery and lifelong learning, we will lead lives filled with meaning and adventure. Moreover, we will gain the capacity to create and shape the future for ourselves and our organizations in ways we can hardly imagine.

Because so much attention is often given to Greenleaf's ideas about serving others, I'd like to focus here on his ideas about the process through which individuals and organizations discover and serve their purpose, their destiny.

The Journey to Discover Our Personal Destiny

When I was just beginning my own journey of discovery, a friend sent me a copy of Hesse's *Demian* with a page turned down to this passage: "Each man has only one genuine vocation—to find the way to himself. His task is to discover his own destiny—not an arbitrary one—and live it out wholly and resolutely within himself."[4]

In the weeks after that, I committed myself to that journey of discovery. I decided to leave the law firm where I had been very successful and start a leadership program. Even today, I can still feel the incredible pain involved in leaving people who had been part of my life for 20 years. They didn't understand where I was going. And because I didn't understand it myself, I couldn't explain it to them. Later on, I would take comfort in Greenleaf's belief that it is enough to set out in the direction of your dreams. But at the time, all I knew was that I felt compelled to set out on that journey into the unknown.

Many others have written about this need to discover our destiny or purpose. Author-psychiatrist Viktor Frankl says that the most basic need for any human being is "the call of a potential meaning waiting to be fulfilled."[5] That call to meaning saved his life. When he arrived at Auschwitz, authorities confiscated a manuscript that he had devoted much of his life to preparing for publication. His desire to reconstruct the book enabled him to survive the horrors of the Nazi concentration camps. Frankl's experience led him to identify with Nietzche's insight that "he who has a *why* to live can bear almost any *how*."[6] What's important, Frankl came to believe, is not what we expect from life, but rather what life expects from us. That idea—that we are here for a reason—is strikingly similar to Martin Buber's idea that destiny stands in need of us.

I came across almost exactly the same thought in James Hillman's *The Soul's Code: In Search of Character and Calling*. Hillman believes that "each person enters the world called."[7] One of my favorite stories from the book concerns 16-year-old Ella Fitzgerald, who planned to make her debut as a dancer at the Harlem Opera House. But just as she was being announced, she changed her mind—or, as Hillman puts it, "she figured out her calling"—and decided to sing. That sense of personal calling, that belief that "there is a reason that I am alive" is at least as old as Plato's *The Republic*.

In his writings and in his PBS interview series with Bill Moyers, mythologist Joseph Campbell describes this search for calling or purpose as "following your bliss."[8] There are those who insist on interpreting his words as a call to "do your own thing." Nothing could have been further from

Campbell's thinking. He wasn't issuing an invitation to a hedonistic existence. He was calling us to take that journey to discover and serve our purpose, our destiny, or as he put it, "our vital design."

Most of us tend to avoid taking the journey to discover and serve our purpose. We refuse the call because deep down we know that to cooperate with fate brings not only great personal power, but great personal responsibility as well. When we do finally say yes to the call, we embark on a journey toward lifelong learning, meaning, and adventure.

In this process of continuous learning, growth, and development, we undergo three fundamental shifts of mind that set the stage for our becoming more capable of participating in our unfolding future. The first is a shift in the way we think about the world. Instead of seeing the universe as mechanistic, fixed, and determined, we begin to see it as open, dynamic, and alive. The second shift occurs when we come to understand that everything is connected to everything else and that relationship is the organizing principle of the universe. The third shift occurs in our understanding of commitment. It's not, as I once thought, doing whatever it takes to make things happen. It is, rather, a willingness to listen, yield, and respond to the inner voice that guides us toward our destiny.

When we follow our purpose and experience these fundamental shifts of mind, a sense of flow develops and we find ourselves in a coherent field of others who share our sense of purpose. We begin to see that with very small movements, at just the right time and place, all sorts of consequent actions are brought into being. We start to notice that the people who come to us are the very ones we need in relationship to our commitment and that doors seem to open for us in ways that we could hardly have imagined. Greenleaf spoke of this phenomenon in terms of encountering opportunities that he could not have anticipated. Campbell put it in terms of being helped by invisible hands.

My own experience is, I think, a good example of how this happens. One day, shortly after I had made the commitment to start the Leadership Forum, I was walking down a London street, wondering how I would ever find the experts and the money to launch such a venture. As I passed a newsstand, my eye was caught by a caption on the cover of *U.S. News & World Report.* "RX for Leadership in America," it said. I opened the magazine and found an article by Tom Cronin, a highly regarded presidential scholar which bore strong parallels to my own thoughts on leadership. I bought the magazine, tore the article out, and flew to the States. Within a couple of days, I was at Cronin's home in Colorado telling him about my dream. He listened intently as I explained what I wanted to do, then said, "You can count on me. Sign me up." He introduced me to John Gardner, the founder of the White House Fellows Program, the very model I had in mind for the Leadership Forum. Gardner introduced me to several thinkers and practitioners in the field who in turn introduced me to others. In a very short time, we had assembled a virtual Who's Who in the field of leadership development.

Then, in three short weeks, I was able to raise the very substantial amount of seed money needed for such a venture. I was experiencing the power of commitment to a higher purpose, discovering what the members of the Scottish Himalayan Expedition discovered—that "the moment one definitely commits oneself, then Providence moves too. . . . All sorts of things occur to help one that would otherwise never have occurred."[9]

Many of us, particularly business leaders with overcrowded agendas, avoid the difficult task of crossing the threshold to begin this inward journey. We may wrestle for years with fearfulness and denial before being able to transcend that fear. We tend to deny our destiny because of our insecurity, our dread of ostracism, our anxiety, and our lack of courage to risk what we have. The consequences of continuing to refuse to discover our purpose and act on it are clear. Abraham Maslow, my early guide through what was then unfamiliar terrain warns that if we deliberately plan to be less than we are capable of being, we run the risk of being deeply unhappy our whole lives.

The Corporate Journey to Discover Purpose

Greenleaf's ideas on the importance of corporate purpose grew out of his 36-year career at AT&T. He believed that under Theodore Vail's visionary leadership, AT&T had been "a great covenental company with a sense of enormous obligation for the nation's telephone service."[10] But somewhere along the way, that sense of purpose was lost, and with it the vision and spirit that had infused it.

Greenleaf had his own theories about why AT&T was broken up in 1984. Although he acknowledged that there could be many explanations, he consistently rejected the "official" reason: that the company had become too big and had a monopoly on the nation's telecommunications activity. His own explanation was that the company had lost its spirit, its great dream. If it had kept its original dream, or if it had been fortunate enough to have a visionary leader capable of creating a new one, he believed that AT&T might have been a leader instead of just another competitor in the telecommunications revolution.

So how do leaders discover the purpose—the destiny—of the organizations they lead? Very much as they discover their own. By embarking on a search to discover it. By asking: Why is this company here? What is its reason for existing? "Far too many of our contemporary institutions do not have an adequate dream, an imaginative concept that will raise people's sights close to where they have the potential to be," Greenleaf noted.[11] In a 1986 introduction to his earlier essay, "The Leadership Crisis," he made the somewhat startling assertion that the effectiveness of a company's leaders is directly proportional to the greatness of the company's dream.[12]

That idea—that a sense of purpose enlarges the capacity of leaders, and that the absence of a sense of purpose imposes limits—may be revolutionary, but my own experience tells me it is true. I have found that when the searches of an organization and its leaders run parallel and then converge, a great explosion of energy and creativity takes place. If organizations want that creative explosion, if they want the kind of performance that leads to truly exceptional results, their leaders have to be willing to take themselves and their organizations on a journey to discover and then act on their purpose.

In *Built to Last,* Jim Collins and Jerry Porras studied a number of "truly exceptional companies that have stood the test of time" and compared them with "another set of good companies that had the same shot in life, but didn't attain quite the same stature."[13]

Their study of exceptional companies led Collins and Porras to conclude that great company builders understand that "it is more important to know who you are than where you are going, for where you are going will change as the world around you changes."[14] The leaders of these great companies had a desire to create something enduring, something larger than themselves—an institution "rooted in a set of timeless core values, that exists for a purpose beyond just making money, and that stands the test of time by virtue of the ability to renew itself from within."[15]

For years, Peter Senge has been recommending Greenleaf's *Servant Leadership* as the single most important book on the subject of leadership. But as so often happens, the ideas and the influence flow both ways. In an introduction to a new edition written just a few years before his death, Greenleaf expressed his appreciation to Senge for the idea of "shared vision." Greenleaf believed that every person, regardless of his or her status in the organization, must be able to shape the dream and claim it as his or her own. This is especially true, he said, for "an old institution that has lost a great dream it once had and wants to get a new one."[16]

How can a company know if it has a big enough dream? "The test of greatness in a dream is that it has the energy to lift people out of their moribund ways to a level of being and relating from which the future can be faced with more hope than most of us can summon today," Greenleaf says.[17] I've heard a very similar idea expressed by Bill O'Brien, retired CEO of Hanover Insurance: "People have a burning need to feel that they are part of an ennobling mission."

Spirit and Being

Greenleaf often spoke of the importance of spirit. That has made some people question whether he was speaking in a religious sense that is somehow in conflict with the responsibilities of leaders of secular institutions.

I don't think so. Even when Greenleaf spoke of spiritual matters, it's clear that he was speaking in a very broad sense. He often turned to the root of the word—*religio,* "to rebind"—to explain his understanding of the purpose of religion: "to bridge the separation between persons and the cosmos, to heal the widespread alienation, and to reestablish men and women in the role of servants—*healers*—of society."[18] I see in his definition a great explanation of the servant-leader's responsibility to build common ground and to heal a fragmented society.

Greenleaf offers another explanation of the religious impulse, this one borrowed from Rabbi Abraham Joshua Heschel whose life and thinking he admired. "The root of religion is what to do with the feeling for the mystery of living, what to do with awe, wonder and amazement," Heschel said.[19] That idea is almost palpably present in the lives of those who exercise leadership in times of crisis. Shortly after Winston Churchill became prime minister of England during World War II, he shared his thoughts with some very close colleagues. "I felt as if I were walking with destiny," he said, "and all of my past life had been but a preparation for this hour and for this trial. I thought a good deal about it, and I was certain I would not fail."[20]

That sense of destiny enables leaders to help others cultivate optimism. It also gives them "a special obligation to act on what they believe." But this obligation is not to some external force. "I think of responsibility as beginning with a concern for self, to receive that inward growth that gives serenity of spirit without which someone cannot truly say, 'I am free,' " Greenleaf said.[21]

I have come to believe that leadership is much more about *being* than *doing*. It is about our orientation of character, our state of inner activity. I see the same emphasis in Greenleaf's writing. He does not say that we make the world a better place by our actions—though he worked hard to make leaders more effective. He believed that the world should "be a better place because of who one is and how one does one's work."[22]

Greenleaf's emphasis on *being* was not lost on Peter Drucker, who worked with him for 15 years. In the foreword to *On Becoming a Servant Leader*, a recently published collection of Greenleaf's private writings, Drucker recounts an incident that occurred at a corporate education session they were conducting together. When one of the participants approached with the question, "What do I do?" Greenleaf responded, "That comes later. First, what do you want to be?" Drucker, always the pragmatist, recalls that his own "What do you think will work?" elicited laughter from all three.[23]

Wholeness

Greenleaf was attracted to the notion of wholeness and to the leader's responsibility for helping individuals and organizations achieve it. In *My Debt to E. B. White,* he expressed his appreciation to the writer for his "ability to see things whole, or more whole than most."[24]

In 1980 I encountered this concept of wholeness in a very powerful way through the ideas of David Bohm, the great theoretical physicist. Bohm believed that everything in the universe is a part of one unbroken whole. He also believed that there is a level of reality—an implicate order—beyond our ordinary experience and perceptions. At this level of reality, everything, including the past, is enfolded in everything else.

Greenleaf may never have met David Bohm, but he had an intuitive understanding of the importance of wholeness. In probing the meaning of "Directive," one of Robert Frost's most enigmatic poems, Greenleaf concludes that we become whole through the difficult and sometimes mystifying journey of self-discovery. If we take that journey, we will become whole and we will gain the ability to "see things whole." The important thing, he says in words borrowed from Frost, is to live "in the light of your own inward experience." That inwardness and that wholeness are marks of the servant-leader.

From an early age, we're taught to deal with complexity by breaking things down into their separate parts. The flip side of this idea is that to see the big picture, we feel the need to put the pieces back together. I don't believe that Greenleaf, any more than David Bohm, felt that "seeing things whole" meant assembling pieces of reality into some kind of a mosaic whole. Seeing things whole is really about understanding the whole that already exists.

The Right Direction

One day in 1987, I was talking to a group of Forum fellows about the journey I had taken in creating the Leadership Forum. After the talk, Mary Ann Buchannan, director of our Oregon chapter, told me that my talk sounded as if it could have come directly from Joseph Campbell's *The Hero with a Thousand Faces*. Even though Joseph Campbell was very popular, I hadn't then heard of him. So she sent me the book. As I read it, I couldn't help thinking that in describing the hero's journey, he was describing the process people and organizations go through to discover their destiny. Not only did it bear a startling resemblance to the journey I had been taking for the past 15 years, but it tracked precisely with the ideas of Robert Greenleaf that had started me on that journey.

Those who would be servant-leaders, Greenleaf says, must "sooner or later—and in their own way—come to grips with who they are and where they are on the journey."[25] He believes that on this journey, our direction is far more important than our destination. "One often does not know the precise goal," he says, "but one must always be certain of one's direction. The goal will reveal itself in due course."[26]

Greenleaf, whose taste for the writings of Henry David Thoreau was an acquired one, encountered the same thought in *Walden:* "If one advances confidently in the direction of his dreams, and endeavors to live the life which he has imagined, he will meet with a success unexpected in common hours."[27]

The idea that life is a journey into the unknown is echoed in the words of the Spanish poet A. Machado, who tells us: "Wanderer, there is no path.

You lay a path in walking."[28] That's also been my experience. Direction is all we can really know. The path reveals itself as we walk along. Following the path requires us to be fully awake, filled with a sense of wonder, acutely aware of everything occurring around us, waiting expectantly for that "cubic centimeter of chance" to present itself. When it does, we must act with lightning speed and almost without conscious reasoning.

Creating the Future

The capacity for a different kind of consciousness is crucial to effective leadership. Greenleaf believed that leaders need to enlarge their capacity to "know the unknowable" and "foresee the unforeseeable." We do this, he explained, by increasing our ability to "intuit the gap" between what conscious rational thought tells us and what we need to know, between what is and what can be.[29]

The future, as Greenleaf saw it, is not something "out there," but something we create at every moment. "By our efforts," he said, "we bring the future into the present."[30] Greenleaf's views about creating the future are remarkably aligned with those of Bohm's implicate order—the unbroken wholeness out of which seemingly discrete events arise. All of us are part of that unbroken whole, which is continually unfolding from the implicate and making itself manifest in our explicate world. Greenleaf's and Bohm's ideas are very similar to those of Jonas Salk, who invented the vaccine that eventually wiped out polio. Salk believed that the universe unfolds kaleidoscopically according to a deeply ingrained order, and that people can develop the capacity to sense the way the future wants to unfold and guide that process by the choices they make.

I believe that we participate in creating the future, not by trying to impose our will on it, but by deepening our collective understanding of what wants to emerge in the world, and then having the courage to do what is required. This is the least understood and yet most crucial foundation of servant-leadership.

But how can we gain this sense of what wants to emerge and unfold in the world? We can begin by following Greenleaf's advice to "listen to signals." If we do, we will find, as Greenleaf did, that "prophetic voices are speaking all the time," pointing to a better way. We can heed his invitation to "develop a sensitivity to intimations from beyond the barrier that separates what we call reality from mystery."[31]

We can heighten this awareness in many ways. My deepest insights seem to come when I'm spending time in solitude, writing in my journal, going for a run, or sitting beside running water. Others find that they listen best when they're taking long walks, practicing yoga, or meditating. However we come by our insights, we should heed Greenleaf's advice to respond to each one as it is offered. That, he felt, was "the ticket of admission for receiving the next one."

By listening to signals we gain that sense of how the future is unfolding that enables us to cooperate with destiny. This brings us full circle to the responsibility of servant-leaders to discover and serve their own destiny and that of their organizations. It is a particularly optimistic thought. It opens us to a world of possibilities, a world of predictable miracles and synchronous events, a world in which we can create the future into which we are living.

PART FOUR

Servant-Leadership

*The servant-leader is servant first—as Leo was portrayed. It begins
with the natural feeling that one wants to serve, to serve first. Then
conscious choices brings one to aspire to lead. The difference manifests itself in the care taken by the servant-first to make sure that
other people's highest priority needs are being served. The best test is:
Do those served grow as persons? Do they, while being served, become
healthier, wiser, freer, more autonomous, more likely themselves to
become servants? And, what is the effect on the least privileged in society, will they benefit, or, at least, not be further deprived?*

Robert K. Greenleaf
Servant-Leadership

The words *service, stewardship, spirit,* and *servant-leadership* are each open
to numerous definitions and multiple interpretations. For many servant
leaders, each of these terms simply offers a different hue within a common
fabric that we choose to call "servant-leadership."

The essays contained within this final section offer a rich and diverse
understanding of servant-leadership and its relevance to modern society.

23

Servants, Egos, and Shoeshines: A World of Sacramental Possibility

John P. Schuster

John P. Schuster is principal of Schuster, Kane, & Stevenin, Inc., and coauthor of the recent book, The Power of Open-Book Management. *His articles have appeared in the* Washington Post, Training, *and* ASTD Journal, *and his first book,* Hum-Drum to Hot-Diggity, *was published in 1993. Schuster is both a certified management consultant and a certified speaking professional.*

In this essay, Schuster cites Robert Greenleaf's insights into the nature of sound leadership. He describes the delicate balance that a servant-leader must maintain between ego and the self and describes the best servant-leaders as having both healthy egos and grace of spirit. He concludes with a look at work as a daily sacrament.

Servus, Service, and Servant-Leadership

Years ago, when our firm was deepening its work in the customer service arena, my decades-old Latin lessons came in handy. The four years I plunged into the classics while at two different Catholic high schools brought to mind that the Latin word *servus,* or *slave,* was the root for the term *servile.* Servile labor was the lowest kind, the demeaning sort, subhuman even, that had little to do with using your head and everything to do with pushing a broom, or cleaning a toilet, or, as I learned later through the work of a budding servant-leader, shining shoes. *Servus* was also the root word for *service,* and, of course, *servant.*

Our clients were often surprised, and then enlightened by an explanation of the term *service,* where it had come from, its connection with the word *servile,* and the related observations that were easy to see in the workplace, like the two following, for instance:

1. The status in the corporation of the customer service department compared with strategic planning and other upper management functions. Marketing, finance, planning and a host of other business functions were, for as long as anyone can remember, more important and held higher status than customer service. The customer service folks were often the grunts, the people filling out orders and answering the 800 number. Upper management enjoyed the perks and the signs of privilege, of course, since they do the really important work.

2. The business schools turned out many business majors, none of which dealt primarily with customer service (though some are now offering majors in quality, of course).

The connection between the words *service* and *servile* and the historically low emphasis on the customer service function is also at the heart of Robert Greenleaf's insight into the nature of sound leadership. Servant-leadership is not about status in the sense of ego and perks and places in the corporate hierarchy. It is, instead, about the honor and privilege we enjoy as humans, to serve others. This kind of servant-based service comes from the sense of self, our true identity as persons and human beings, and not our ego, the functioning personality in the world with its titles and roles and human doings.

Greenleaf was among the first to raise the bar on the serious discussions of leadership. He, along with John Gardner and James MacGregor Burns, turned the corner for all students of leadership, describing how it is more than skills and situational know-how and is, instead and more fundamentally, a moral contract between leaders and followers to bring out the best in each other for the good of the whole. Greenleaf opened the door for Covey and Block and DePree and the others joining the conversation about a spirit-based, soul-based leadership. This follower-centered leadership stems from a well-developed selfhood that counters the ego-driven power moves of the corporate chieftains and politicos that make the headlines too regularly.

Balancing the Ego and the Self

One tricky part of servant/self-based leadership is that the ego never can be annihilated, and the juicy and energizing ego drives to compete, to win, to kick butt, to show off and strut your stuff—all these sources of passion and raw energy and creativity—can't just be shut off like water coming out of the shower spout. The human person is a combination of ego and self, and lopping off the ego leaves a wimpy, blissful pseudopersona that might be more than adequate for the Hare Krishna chanters (are there any of them left any more?) who don't have to get anything done in the world. (I am a fan, and erstwhile student, of the contemplative traditions, of course, and believe in the good they do. But what the contemplatives can afford to try, and some would argue with this—eradicating the ego—the rest of us can't.) For those of us with careers and kids and mortgages, an at-peace self, at one with the spirit world, will suffer if it can't tap the passionate sources of ego energy for accomplishing things in the world of enterprise and academics and government and nonprofits. The middle path for servant leaders is to avoid the extremes of either being driven by an out-of-control ego that has power and does harm—the usual pitfall for institutional leaders—or creating a blissful self that expresses peace and harmony but is ineffectual in the world.

Roberto Assagioli, the father of psychosynthesis, asks poignantly in his work (to paraphrase) "Why is it that the truly good people seem not to be powerful, and the truly powerful seem not to be good?"[1] A scary question worth asking.

The best servant-leaders are filled with the grace of the spirit/self, directing them to good, and are passionate warriors with strong egos that give them the drive to acquire and use power. This bimodal grace/ego reality leads to the internal war servant-leaders carry on within themselves, knowing that power and influence will accompany them on their journey, and that empowering others and distributing the capacity to influence is their charter.

One of the participants in a leadership development experience for managers at Sprint put together his thoughts for a "leadership credo," a closing exercise to have participants put an emotional and intellectual stake in the ground on their beliefs about leadership. Listen to how Uzair Siddiqui, a 24-year-old manager in the Washington, D.C. area, captured the essence of the ego/servant process:

> *I, Uzair Siddiqui, use my knowledge and passion to succeed to make my world a better place so that humanity can benefit from my existence, for I am nothing but a humble servant to humanity.*[2]

This statement came at the end of a three-day session on leadership, without a discussion of the ego/servant duality, but rather a discussion and set of experiences about influence, uses of power in the corporation, and value-based leadership. Uzair captures the ego's drive to succeed and places it in the service of a vision to serve others.

Without the charter to distribute the power and enable others, the ego is easily seduced by gratification and the shadow-side of ego-influence. Abuses of power emerge, at first as small and well-disguised intentions to help followers—"Well, I wouldn't normally be this commanding, but in this instance I better provide some strong direction"—and then often progressing, or rather *re*gressing, to serious forms of nonservant, followers-serve-me leadership.

The worst of these devolutions from serving a cause selflessly to using a cause and followers to achieve selfish ends can flame out in an occasional raging display of ego and passion. In my life I was privy to just such a display.

In our presentations on leadership I often ask the question: "I graduated from a Jesuit high school in 1966 in Cincinnati, Ohio. Can anyone tell me who my commencement speaker was?"

Usually I bring up the question at a time when we are discussing ethics, so you can see the active minds in the group groping for an answer related to morals and ethical behavior. Occasionally, someone will guess Pete Rose, a thoughtful conjecture that Cincinnati's local baseball superhero could have sent high-school seniors off to their inspiring futures some 20 years before he got caught in his addictive gambling problems. This is a grand guess, really, well placed in Cincinnati space and time, and anticipating the topic of how an ego flaw can ruin a career, or even a life of service. But, after rewarding the guess with a "Nice try!," I'll offer that Pete Rose did not give the speech and that business, not sports, is the source of the answer. This clue is to help those in the room (and it is the majority of participants or I won't ask the question for lack of relevance) who lived through the Boesky-Milkin era of unbridled ego-driven business leadership, infamous in the 1980s for greed and financial dealings.

After a bit of silence—no one has gotten the little riddle yet—I tell the group that our commencement speaker was none other than wheeler-dealer Charles Keating himself, jailed for his savings and loan mess and taking the life savings of thousands down with him in a series of bad deals. Even if Keating were never imprisoned, his legacy of ego and consumption would have been enough to qualify him for less than servant-based leadership. He was happily recorded in one 1980s documentary, while talking about the swim-up bar at his marbled and gilded Phoenician resort, raising the salary of a secretary to $100,000—"Would you like to be the first secretary to make more than a 100k?," he queries with a smile, surprising the secretary while they are being taped, while posing for the camera in obvious delight with the amount of money he could throw around as a sure sign of his success and power (and hubris).

But in 1966, in early June, Charles Keating was an upstanding civic and church leader, leading the citizen's fight against pornography and building a business network. And he was speaking to a senior class befuddled by the beginnings of Vietnam, stirred by Martin Luther King and social injustice, and eager to hear the words of someone who could stay the burgeoning cynicism and inspire us with idealism and credibility.

Only Charlie Keating knows the journey of his ego and his self during the two decades between the graduation speech and the jail sentence, or what has happened to his soul after serving time and, in the middle 1990s, being released. But, from the outside anyway, the ego seems to have gotten the upper hand during much of his career, and whatever ideals he had to serve the community got lost by the drive for power and money and showmanship.

Conversely, Nelson Mandela, on a world, not just an American stage, stands as a story of a leader with enough ego-will to take on a government and enough spiritual presence to live as a servant, inspiring the world with both his passion to fight injustice and his compassion for his enemies.

But on a much lesser stage, the invisible, not-in-the-press one where most of us live our lives, another young servant-leader taught me how the routines of a work world can hold servant and sacramental possibilities. This young man had the soul of a servant as taught to me in my Catholic upbringing.[3]

Work as Sacrament

I was raised Catholic. When I was a kid, I thought only Catholics knew about sacraments. It took me a long time to realize that lots of religions have a sacramental system, and that I have seen sacraments in the workplace.

How's that? Well, certainly not in the ordinary sense of the word. But in its root sense, there's no doubt. The best managers, leaders, and workers go about their work in a sacramental fashion. That takes some explaining, so let me take you back to what I learned very early about sacraments.

Every year, as Catholic kids, we had to study catechism. We would memorize a whole series of questions and answers. So I'll never forget the question, "What is a sacrament?" I can rattle off the answer to this day, without even thinking. And that, of course, is the problem. Most of us don't think about what sacrament is.

The answer went like this: A sacrament is an outward sign instituted by God to give grace.

I can remember being taught that baptism is a sacrament because, by pouring water on the person (or in some religions, by immersing the person), the water becomes an outward sign of the purification of that person's soul. That is, the soul is washed clean of original sin and made eligible for the Christian life.

There are all kinds of other Christian sacraments, of course, and all the other religions seem to have bunches of sacraments of their own. From the rites of the Jewish Seder to Christian communion, from the "laying on of hands" performed by fundamentalist Christians to the self-flagellation of some fundamentalist Muslims, many of us have determined that external signs can somehow symbolize an internal reality.

With all the talk of corporate culture these days, it would be well for managers to learn the power of these rituals. Many high-performance companies already have learned these lessons and—through the deliberate creation of a culture—they now better capture the total energy spectrum of their employees.

I remember an employee recognition dinner that I once attended for a midwestern manufacturer. The company pins attached to the lapel or blouse of every employee whose suggestions had helped make the company more productive were obvious external signs of internal employee commitment.

They were signs of recognition, pinned there with the same sense of cere-mony by which Christians are confirmed, and the grace of the company who had used employees' talents in the company's behalf.

But rituals need not be strictly solemn occasions. They also can play to the love we all share for humor. Employees can perform skits at corporate Christmas parties, and yet indulge the sacramental. They can even roast each other, with management's blessing, at dinners that spotlight—and spoof—employee quirks. Rituals like these do more than merely bestow grace, they permit employees and their managers to accept each other, faults and all. Such sacraments bless our highest intentions with laughter and loving tolerance.

On occasion, you will find a worker so aware of the significance of his or her work that all he or she does takes on the attributes of sacrament. Em-ployees like these grace everyone and everything around them.

My son and I were in Chicago's O'Hare airport. I had never had my shoes shined by anyone but myself, but I looked at my scuffed up shoes, re-alized I had a presentation the next day, and my son and I headed for the only place you can find a professional shoe shine in an airport: the men's restroom.

In the restroom we met a young man named David. David was, it turned out, an exceptional person. He greeted us cheerfully, asked us to sit down, and before long started asking my son some questions. "What grade are you in?" "What's your favorite subject?" "Do you think your Royals are gonna do any good this year? I'm about to give up on my White Sox." In what quickly became an engaging conversation, David was making us both feel very special. He didn't just quiz us about our lives, hopes, and so on. He shared himself with us—even pulled out a letter for our perusal, one that said he'd been accepted to work on his Ph.D. in educational psychology at Southern University. He was so proud, and happy, because his recently ac-quired master's degree was only part of what he wanted to achieve with his education.

It turned out David was working for his uncle who had the license to run the shoe shine concessions at O'Hare. When he started shining my shoes, I could see he took special care. And he explained the process as he went along, telling us why he chose water and polish and brush in the se-quence that he did. And as he talked and started to make those shoes shine like new dimes, it became apparent that he loved what he was doing.

Toward the end of his lecture and demonstration on the art of shining shoes, David pulled out his rag. If you've ever seen the magic of a good shoe shine professional, you've seen someone who knows how to make that rag pop with rhythm and syncopation that would make Scott Joplin proud.

And, as David got into his rhythm, popping that rag, talking and mak-ing those shoes shine like new armor, my son and I had something of a peak experience, in the men's bathroom at O'Hare airport.

Now remember, David is doing all this while working all summer in what you might call less than ideal working conditions. O'Hare's an okay airport, but its bathrooms, at least its men's bathrooms, are no better than the rest and worse than some others. And this guy's got a master's degree and has been accepted, already, in a Ph.D. program scheduled to begin that fall. He could just as easily have adopted an altogether different attitude. Instead, he chose to serve up his shoe shines in sacramental fashion, to create for my son and for me a very nice memory that will last us our whole lives. I mean, if he can do that in a men's room in O'Hare, what's your excuse?

David had tapped into a kind of grace. It's the kind of grace that all workers who bless their customers or coworkers with a sense of service have the power to bestow. Remember that definition of sacrament—an outward sign instituted by God to give grace? David had transformed the external act of shining shoes and communicating with customers into an act of internal significance. My son and I were in communion with a young black man whose spirit spilled over into his work and who will some day bless children and teachers alike with his knowledge of psychology and education.

And so it is that each of us have daily opportunity to bring our spirit into the workplace and make sacraments where before there may only have been sacrilege—or, if not sacrilege, a kind of humdrum working reality and ordinariness that kills the human spirit and forecloses the sacramental possibilities.

Some people in the world of work, of course, do not know about sacraments, or, if they do, they don't think work has anything to do with them. But the happiest managers and leaders and workers I know are the ones who understand, although they may put it in a different language, the sacramental dimensions of work. They get excited while doing jobs for people. They are thrilled at the opportunity to offer to their customers a quality of service that will truly improve their lives. Abraham Maslow, the great psychologist of motivation for this century, said an interesting thing about sacraments and miracles. He said that the people who look for great external miracles—outward signs and wonders—are looking at life all wrong. What they seem to fail to understand is that when you look at something closely enough and with the right eyes (sacramental eyes, I would say), then everything is miraculous.

Have you ever watched closely the altered-speed films on television of ordinary occurrences. A drop of milk falls into a bowl already half filled. In super slo-mo, the droplet explodes back upward while in the bowl beneath ripples move with the power of tidal waves; and what you observe in the ordinary fall of a drop of milk becomes a grand visual representation of symmetry. Or perhaps you've seen an arrow slash through an egg, with the help of high-speed photography, or Michael Jordan spinning a fingertip roll out of what started out as a slamming, jamming drive to the hoop. It's all miraculous.

Gerard Manley Hopkins, the priestly poet who lived 100 years ago, said the world is charged with the grandeur of God. But we don't notice this grandeur when we observe the world through the ordinary, everyday thinking patterns that treat a bowl of milk as simply a bowl of milk. Children, of course, find the grandeur everywhere. Their eyes see the miracles in every-thing because they have not yet been trained to do otherwise. All you have to do is watch the fascination of a two-year-old to witness Maslow's sense of everyday, miraculous nature of "ordinary" reality. So we need the right eyes at work. We need sacramental eyes that see the grace and the potential of the inner reality behind the external phenomena. Whether it's David at the air-port or a leader putting award pins on his hardworking staff, the world of work offers ample opportunity to explore the inner significance behind everything humans touch.

Oh, for the eyes to see. Oh, for the ears to hear. The sacraments and the grace and the miracles are there, but only for the beholder. Let's do our beholding with the eyes and ears of children. Then work can be not so much a daily drudgery, but a kind of daily saving grace.

24

Putting Servant-Leadership into Practice

Ken Melrose

Ken Melrose is chairman and CEO of The Toro Company, a Fortune 500 company. Melrose joined the company in 1970 and was named its president in 1981. In his recent book, Making the Grass Greener on Your Side: A CEO's Journey to Leading by Serving, *Melrose credits Robert Greenleaf with inspiring many of the organizational development changes that he has implemented at Toro.*

In this essay, Melrose recounts how the concept of leading by serving has helped to strengthen The Toro Company. He offers an insider's look at how servant-leadership principles have been implemented over time. Melrose concludes with an examination of six dynamic leadership attributes based on servant-leadership and shows how these attributes are lived out within the company.

At the end of fiscal year 1979, The Toro Company, manufacturer of lawn mowers and snow throwers, had reached a pinnacle of unparalleled expansion and development. Winters of blizzards and summer seasons of warm rainfalls had created a seemingly insatiable demand for Toro products. By 1981, however, when I became president of the company, everything seemed to be going wrong, including virtually no snowfall and the onset of a worldwide economic recession. At Toro, "Fiscal 1981" might have been termed "Fiasco 1981." The company lost more than $13 million—its first loss since 1945.

Today, Toro has repositioned itself as an outdoor environment care company, not merely a maker of lawn mowers and snow throwers. Toro's philosophy is to respond proactively to meet the preservation needs of outdoor landscapes with innovative products and earth-conscious strategies. Nearly everything made or sold by Toro preserves or enhances the outdoor environment in some way. In addition, Toro makes every effort to be an environmentally responsive manufacturer through improved waste management processes. In fiscal 1996 Toro posted record earnings of $22.2 million, with solid performance across all product lines—including snow throwers and lawn mowers.

This change did not happen overnight but has been the result of a long-term growth process stimulated by my desire to learn to practice servant-leadership. Toro's domain is the outdoor environment—planting, irrigating, fertilizing, mowing, recycling, composting, aerating, cutting, edging, trimming, and vacuuming all lawns, big and small. To have a healthy lawn, you must do all of this, as well as hope for warm seasons with sunshine and rainfall. I have learned that you grow a healthy organization the same way you grow grass:

Soil Preparation + Seeding
+ Sound Turf Management = Bountiful Harvest

These are the building blocks that lead to the desired results. Servant-leadership is the instrument that makes it happen.

Years ago, when I trained with 30 other adults to become a lay teacher of the Old and New Testaments in my church, our minister invited a Jewish rabbi to talk to our class one evening. As he was talking to us, the rabbi got onto the topic of the purpose of life. This was a rather esoteric subject, and most of us had fairly hazy views, if any, for our own selves. He pressed us by asking directly, "What's the purpose of your life? Why are you here?"

Some in the class described themselves as just taking one day at a time. Others felt life was too complex and hectic to warrant such consideration. Many hadn't even thought about their personal mission or purpose on this earth. And then there were those who felt they had no purpose, at least not that they could identify and put into words.

The rabbi said, "How many of you remember your grandfather? If you do, raise your hand." Almost everyone did and could cite a number of memories and characteristics about their grandfathers. Then he asked how many could recall their great-grandfather. Only a few raised their hands. Then the rabbi asked, "How many of you remember your great-great-grandfather?" Nobody, of course, did. "How many of you remember his name?" he asked. "The color of his eyes? Anything about his life?" We were all silent.

"All right," he said. "Now, let's move this forward. Suppose your grandchildren were in this room and they were your age, and I asked them the same questions about you. How many of them would remember you? Most of them would, of course. How about your great-grandchildren? Will they be able to remember you? Perhaps a few. And your great-great-grandchildren? Will they remember you? Will they remember your name, the color of your eyes, what you did?" The stark reality of it is that they won't. We will be gone years before they are born.

We realized that, of course, from our own experience. It is the way of the world. In four generations, our immediate families—those who are closest to us—will likely have forgotten all about us. In just four generations, we will cease even to be memories. Oh, there may be some traces of us they'll be able to find—letters, a memento, a fading photograph filed away in a drawer or on a shelf somewhere. Our great-great-grandchildren, however, will have absolutely no idea who we were. And if they don't remember, no one else will either.

"So what do you think about that?" the rabbi then asked. For me, it was a pretty sobering thought. It raised such questions in my mind as, "What *is* the purpose of my life? If I'll mean nothing at all to those just four generations ahead, why am I here today?"

The rabbi's answer was that we are all here to lead lives of purpose, and the purpose of life is to serve God and to serve humankind, however we choose to do so. He urged us to start some things of enduring value. Making long-term investments, such as protecting the environment, was probably worth our time and effort, he pointed out. No one is going to remember you as an individual in four generations, but they might well remember something you began, something you nurtured for someone else to foster, especially if our own families experience the benefits and results in their own lives.

At Toro today, we have established a definite momentum in the direction of long-term investment, but I still ponder the rabbi's question. Like blades of grass, 10 billion souls may occupy the world today, but who will be remembered in four generations? We grow and flourish like wild flowers; then the wind blows cold from the north, and the flowers are gone. Yet some of the wild flowers' seeds are scattered by that same wind, and some of them find soil that's ready to receive them, sun to warm them, and rain to nourish their growth.

At Toro, some of the seeds we've planted will come to fruition long after most of us are gone. Eventually, though, they'll bear fruit, and through generations there will still be people to benefit from our efforts. Plant a few seeds and a small crop will be harvested. Plant many seeds and you'll get a large crop. For most of us, it's the planting, not the harvesting, that's important, because in the planting we discover ourselves and our destiny as we move toward the future.

The First Step: Preparing the Soil

Preparation is essential before planting, whether it means readying the ground for seed or taking the time to build your own leadership model on a solid foundation of principles that can stand the test of time and weather the storms of the economy and the marketplace.

The process of building such a foundation begins by taking stock of where you are, assessing your vision and values, and grounding yourself in your principles. The next step is to become a self-starter, a principle-centered leader on your turf. The final step in building a solid foundation is to translate your principles to the rest of your management team, creating a vision and an organizational culture that reflects these principles and fosters deep-rooted growth.

In 1973 I began an important experience that gave shape to the kind of leader I wanted to be. I was 32 at the time and found myself in Litchfield, Michigan, a tiny town situated in the south-central and rural part of the state. I was the newly appointed president of Game Time, Inc., a recent acquisition by The Toro Company. Game Time manufactured and marketed playground equipment for the commercial and institutional market. The company had revenues of less than $10 million and about 200 employees, many of whom lived (and worked) on nearby farms. I was coming from a role in marketing lawn mowers and knew little or nothing about the business of playground equipment.

Different people had "helped" me build preconceptions about the Game Time company, its plant, and the small, rural town in which it was located. I presumed that the environment was not very sophisticated and that the company's culture and management practices were much simpler than those at Toro. The Game Time employees had their preconceptions about me, too. The head office at Toro had told them to expect a Princeton graduate with advanced degrees from MIT and the University of Chicago. I don't know who was more uncomfortable that first day—they or I.

Before I arrived, Game Time had been run by its founder, a man I would describe as a benevolent dictator (I'll call him Bill). I didn't know what my leadership style was or exactly what it would be a week after I arrived, but I knew one thing: Bill's leadership style and mine were worlds apart.

During Bill's tenure, the people at Game Time had learned that Bill made the decisions—all the decisions. He liked to be involved in every aspect of the business. There were reasons for this, of course. Game Time had been Bill's company. He started it and he knew everything there was to know about building playground equipment. Regardless of the question, Bill always had an answer. There was no doubt about it; Bill was the boss.

The problem was that Bill's management style had taught his people to wait for him to tell them what to do. As a result, they did not exhibit much initiative in their jobs. During my first few weeks with the company, employees would walk into my office and ask for advice. For example, I might have been asked, "How much steel should we purchase?" "Should I ship this order or that order first?" "In what magazines should we advertise?" I didn't know the answers to those questions, but I knew how to find them.

I turned the questions and decisions back to the employees and focused on teaching them the process of decision making, that is, gathering information, getting others involved, finding out what the requirements are, determining the impact, and then finally making the decision. As the people who had the knowledge, experience, and information began to solve problems and make their own decisions, they began to enjoy their work more. We made mistakes at first, but we learned together. People didn't get fired or chewed out; rather, they simply used the mistakes to learn and to get better. My fledgling leadership role created a learning environment. Together, we became more confident in our jobs and we developed more trust in each other. The bonds that formed allowed us to work as a team. We learned to accept and rely on our interdependence. We all grew in self-esteem and self-actualization, and through teaching others, I was the one who learned the most.

Lessons Learned at Game Time

Soon after my Game Time experience, I read *Servant Leadership* by Robert Greenleaf—a book about leading an organization by serving instead of by directing or controlling. Greenleaf's leadership model resonated with me as I reflected on my experience at Game Time. Bit by bit, I came to understand that leaders lead best by serving the needs of their people. The result of my leadership lessons at Game Time was that in three years Game Time became the most productive division of Toro with the best return on investment.

Everything I experienced and learned at Game Time became the basis for the development of our servant-leadership model at Toro and for the eventual creation of our culture, Pride in Excellence. The most important lessons I learned are the following:

- Everyone has the potential to be a strong contributor in an organization.
- Employees work best within a nurturing, valuing environment because that environment allows them to trust, risk, create, and measure up to the expectations of others, and thus become more valuable people.
- The driving forces behind continuous improvement are positive self-esteem and trust (not tools, techniques, and skills).
- Effective, long-lasting personal growth and learning are accomplished interactively on the job.
- Even though individuals may feel helpless at times and unable to exert enough influence to actually change an organization, we *can* in fact make a difference.

When I returned to Toro after Game Time was sold, I experienced how difficult it is to establish a culture from a subordinate position. As a division manager in Minneapolis, I went through the frustrating process of trying to create a new management environment within a top-down system that cared little for employee empowerment, employee involvement, or team psychology, and that did not view employees as the company's most important asset. I began to understand the power that the company head has in setting the operating tone and style of the organization.

Then, in the midst of the emerging recession in 1981, as the company's earnings were sinking along with morale, I became president of The Toro Company. All at once, it was my job to address questions of who we were, where we were going, and what we could achieve.

Building a Strong Foundation: Seed Not Sod

As leaders, do we go for the quick fix or for building a strong foundation slowly? Do we lay sod or do we plant seed to get growth? In a culture that's accustomed to quick results, "seed not sod" isn't an easy choice. Seeding takes time and quite a bit of care. Eventually, however, it results in a healthy and more resistant turf.

I believe the concept of *leading by serving* must be built on a strong foundation, what I call the "building blocks of leadership." The five blocks on which servant-leadership at Toro is built are (1) philosophy, (2) beliefs and values, (3) vision, (4) culture, and (5) leadership (see Figure 24.1).

Philosophy

Aspiring servant-leaders need to consciously think through their leadership philosophy and then articulate it as the foundation for their leadership style. Once a philosophy has been articulated, it can be translated into behaviors and expectations.

At the heart of Toro's philosophy is the concept that "Market leadership and financial success will best result from unleashing the potential of our people." It has been critically important for the entire Toro management team to visibly adopt this philosophy in their day-to-day work. But before

Figure 24.1
Building blocks of culture and leadership.

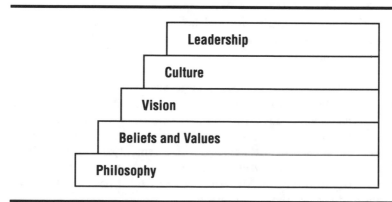

this philosophy could be adopted, it had to be translated into behaviors and expectations for the management team. My personal challenge has been to find a way for Toro management to lead by genuinely valuing others, to create a genuinely trusting and valuing organization.

Beliefs and Values

Beliefs and values are the core principles that direct a leader's actions and decisions. At Toro we have been very deliberate in defining the beliefs and values that drive our approach to leadership, as follows:

- Each individual has great potential.
- That potential is best achieved when individuals are allowed to perform.
- The best performance comes from those who are
  inspired, motivated, and encouraged;
  committed to the vision, goal, or task;
  empowered to execute the vision; and
  recognized for their part in completing the vision.
- The leader's role is to create an environment where employees can achieve their potential as they move the company toward its goals.

Vision

Once leadership philosophy is established and beliefs defined, they become the undergirding of a company's vision and culture. The vision gives goals and direction to the enterprise; it is the framework and the guide that leaders can use to bring others into the bigger picture.

The following words are etched in granite over the entrance to the main post office in St. Louis: "Where there is no vision, the people perish." This is a basic truth of human reality; history has demonstrated it decade after decade, society after society. Leaders have a responsibility to fashion and share a vision with their people, but what is a vision really? I believe it is *an overarching, guiding force that directs our efforts.*

In addition to our philosophy, beliefs, and values, Toro's vision includes our purpose, our mission, and a vivid description that helps our people to understand more specifically what we are trying to be and what it will look like when we get there. Following are descriptions of these key components of our vision:

Our Purpose is to help our customers beautify and preserve outdoor landscapes with environmentally responsible products of customer-valued quality and innovation.

Our Mission is to be the leading worldwide provider of outdoor landscaping products, support services, and integrated systems, as well as to explore new opportunities that build revenue growth and earnings sustainability using our core competencies to gain a leading market position.

Our Vivid Description paints a picture of what Toro will look like when we achieve our vision. This picture incorporates our customers' views of Toro, our products (whose innovativeness will be without precedent), and the level of our employees' contributions.

When we put all of these pieces together, starting with the philosophy of genuinely valuing others, we unleash the Toro organization to excel in delighting and satisfying customers. When we satisfy customers better than anyone else, this in turn leads to market leadership. Market leadership is the best way to achieve consistent and sustainable earnings growth. Then, coming full circle, our earnings allow us to invest more in our people, thus strengthening our trusting and valuing organization.

Culture

Year after year, research project after research project continues to report that what motivates or demotivates employees most and what has the greatest impact on individual performance and attitude is their supervisor or leader. Leaders set the tone; leaders create the environment for growth, development, and performance; and leaders get out of team members or staff (as employees perceive it) the effectiveness and the reinforcement that gives them the power to achieve. W. Edwards Deming, the late quality guru, is often quoted as saying, "Eighty-five percent of the problem with the lack of employee performance is management."

It is the culture that leaders create, nurture, and sustain that will most affect their people. Edward Lawler, director of the Center for Effective Organizations at the University of Southern California, says it this way:

> Corporate leaders will face two fundamental tasks: first, to develop and articulate exactly what the company is trying to accomplish, and second, to create an environment in which employees can figure out what needs to be done and then do it well.[1]

Culture tells people *how* to do *what* they do, and it determines *how well* they do it. A healthy people-oriented culture shapes the environment so that people perform to their potential while maximizing the performance of the company.

Pride in Excellence.   At Toro, we call our culture *Pride in Excellence,* or PIE. Pride in Excellence describes a culture based on mutual respect and recognition of the worth of each employee. Over the years, PIE has evolved two components: People Values (*how* we operate and interact with each other) and Performance Values (*what* needs to happen to achieve the Toro vision). These values blend together to direct us to do the right things right; they embody a quality culture that prizes both results and relationship, products and processes—quality in what we do and in how we do it. (See Figure 24.2.)

The six People Values are:

- Trust and respect for one another
- Teamwork and win-win partnerships
- Giving power away
- Coaching and serving
- Overtly recognizing small successes and good tries (recognition)
- Open, honest, clear communication

The six Performance Values are:

- Conformance to requirements and standards
- Customer responsiveness
- Sustainable growth and profit imperatives
- Preventing waste by anticipating outcomes and focusing on continuous improvement (prevention)
- Adding value through innovation and quality in product and process
- Bias for action

Figure 24.2
The Toro culture.

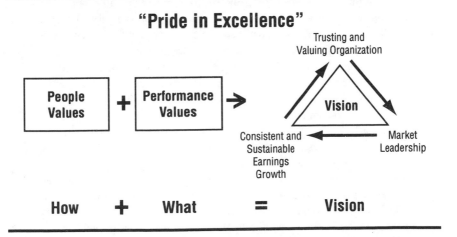

Both the People Values and the Performance Values were identified by the management group, about 70 officers and director-level managers, working in large-group meetings and small ad hoc teams to formulate our new culture over a six-month period. But, as we expected, Pride in Excellence did not become the Toro culture overnight. Few members of the management team embraced it wholeheartedly from the start; many paid it only lip service. Some thought it wouldn't work because it sounded soft and didn't seem results-oriented. Many saw no need for change.

My first task was to get the top management team to buy into PIE. If it was to become a way of life at Toro, they would need to lead. I expected them not only to embrace and espouse the values of PIE, but also to visibly live them as their own. Some immediately did as asked. Even so, they found it difficult to cultivate the culture within their groups and still keep focused on achieving our business goals. They simply couldn't see how to do seemingly contradictory things at the same time.

As we enlisted more managers in the task of creating the PIE culture, we came to expect each other to practice the principles every day. Some learned by example, some were coached by others, and some required outside help to modify their behaviors and style. Still, it wasn't easy. Now, a decade later, our managers know what is required of them. Most managers worked hard to realign their management style with our cultural values, but not all managers succeeded. After helping them make some noble attempts to change certain behaviors, we compassionately directed a few people out of the company. Those who have remained have accepted the PIE culture as Toro's way of life.

Taking Action.   Jim Seifert, assistant general counsel at Toro, tells a story about how he and his team, inspired by Toro's PIE culture, found new ways to think about a challenge resulting in a handsome payoff for Toro:

> Imagine that Toro is your company. You own it and you are responsible for your own survival. In other words, you are responsible for making a profit. As the owner, you know there are domestic and foreign competitors who want your markets and your customers, and who are willing to work extremely hard to obtain both. My suggestion is that if each of us viewed ourselves as the owner of Toro, we would see more clearly what we need to do in our individual jobs. More importantly, we would work passionately to eliminate waste.
>
> When I came to Toro in May of 1990, I was given the goal of doing whatever was necessary to reduce the company's product liability risk and costs associated with product liability, including attorneys' fees and insurance premiums. I approached the problem as if I were the sole owner of Toro. I asked myself, "What are the root causes of product liability risk? How does an insurance company view Toro's product liability risk? How does Toro defend itself? What processes are effective?"

After gathering information, the product liability team devised and executed a strategy designed to lower costs and long-term product liability risk. By July 1991 we had achieved results far beyond expectations. Because of our processes oriented toward preventing unnecessary costs, we were able to renegotiate our insurance contract, saving Toro $4.8 million, all because we used the total quality process to reengineer our work. No capital investment was needed; no jobs were eliminated; no additional costs were incurred. We simply thought about ourselves, our jobs, and our goals in a radically different way. Some examples are: We organized all work and decisions around reducing costs and reducing risks, which means we now do only work that is either required or makes a difference; we put decision making in the hands of those who have the most information to make a decision; we began using computers to accomplish a goal, not to do unnecessary work faster; we changed our work processes to reflect our respect for coworkers; we emphasized communication—telling those affected what we were going to do differently and why; and we acted as owners by embracing what is important about our jobs—executing our jobs with excellence—and letting go of everything else.[2]

Some other ways in which Toro has taken action to reinforce our Pride in Excellence culture include:

- *A Management-Plant Participation Program.* All the company officers work one day a year on the assembly line in most plants.
- *Redeployment.* Since our business is seasonal, we make every effort to assign other tasks or create new ones for employees threatened with layoff due to lack of work. Such times may be used for learning new skills or reinforcing old ones.
- *Communication.* When Toro began to feel the early effects of the 1991 recession, I initiated monthly recession update meetings with all employees to inform them of what was happening, what management was thinking, and what to expect. We have continued these meetings and now hold monthly or quarterly meetings with employees to keep them updated on the company's customer, quality, and financial status. Employees can make better decisions when they are better informed.

Our continuing goal at Toro is to ensure the PIE way of life for all our employees, including management. This requires intense, ongoing attention because we face a world so full of change: change in external environments, in peoples' needs and expectations, and in the industry. We live in a world of increased corporate complexity, which means that a corporate culture, a living organism, must either grow or die.

It takes time for an organization to develop a strong foundation, to embrace the vision, and to learn to work congruently within the culture. It will take even more time before positive results surface from leaders' efforts. Nonetheless, principles, beliefs and values, vision, and culture are essential building blocks, each of which plays a vital role in creating an environment that will yield long-term corporate growth, as well as provide personal growth for each employee. These are the seeds that a servant-leader plants and waters daily, in the hope that they will eventually bear fruit for the harvest.

Leadership: Managing and Maintaining the Turf

Leadership is the final building block in Toro's servant-leader model; it is supported by the other four. In many ways, the hardest test of leadership is not building but maintaining the new environment or the plan. Maintenance requires continuing the same work that built the foundation: walking the talk, resisting the quick fix, building trust, and exercising patience, perseverance, and courage. Constant nurturing and focus eventually lead the organization to the desired results, but it takes disciplined leaders to stay the course.

At Toro, our leadership model is based on a simple premise: If the leader (1) focuses on the needs of employees; (2) expects, encourages, and models results through valuing relationships; and (3) recognizes people for their contributions, the likely outcomes will be a greater sense of trust and accountability, leading to more risk taking, creativity, and innovation. This in turn will create a strong team that multiplies its ability to meet customer needs; it will also increase empowerment of individuals to solve problems at the grassroots level. The solutions will be better, there will be increased feelings of self-worth, and productivity will be higher.

To accomplish all of this, we developed roles and expectations for managers to assist them in learning, practicing, and adopting the new leadership skills. We created systems, processes, programs, and support structures to reinforce these leadership skills, mobilize the organization, and reward individuals who adopted our new model.

For example, Greg Kliner, then operations director of Toro's Irrigation Division, tells this story of how the PIE culture affected him and his team:

> A critical look at the Irrigation Division showed an inability to get products to market on time and within budget. As a result, Toro was losing market share and sales. So we formed a new Product Development Process Steering Committee to create a process that would make us more competitive. This was a great leap forward for us because our products must work, they must be on time, and we must make a profit. The goal of excellence in product development became a shared responsibility. To achieve that goal we improved the communication processes among customers, suppliers, and staff; we improved product cycle times, operating margins, and customer satisfaction by establishing benchmarks and measurable improvements in each product line; we set clear-cut guidelines that outline authority, responsibility, and role definitions; we trained team members to be-

come team players, knowledge resources, customer advocates, problem solvers, and decision makers with visibility throughout the division.

Our mission statement was to create an environment for product development that utilizes cross-functional involvement and results in the highest quality products developed in the shortest time frame that meets or exceeds customer requirements and the financial goals of Toro.

Steering committee members devoted about 500 hours per person to this cause. I was pleased to participate on this team because team members were very professional and able to debate issues without bruising feelings.[3]

When I teach the first module of our Building Better Leadership Skills development program at Toro, I try to give participants a new perspective, which can help to reorient their thinking. I divide the class in half and ask one group to list the words that come to mind when they see the word *supervision*. The second group lists the words they associate with *SuperVision*. The differences in their lists are illuminating. Here is a short sample of some of the words listed.

Supervision	SuperVision
Boss	Innovator
Instruction	Opportunities
Feedback	Foresight
Counseling	Dreams
Decision making	Big picture

Six Dynamic Leadership Attributes

Leadership, much like the preceding exercise, is also a matter of perspective. Leaders today have to be able to think out of the box, to expand their perspective and add new thinking. Our perspective on leadership at Toro is based on the five building blocks and on six dynamic leadership attributes. We ask that all leaders and employees at Toro incorporate these six attributes into their roles and interactions to ensure that our vision is achieved. I call them dynamic because I believe we never totally arrive at true leadership; we are always learning and becoming better leaders.

1. Anticipate and Respond to the Future

An insightful leader will have a sense for the unknowable, see the unforeseeable, and respond appropriately. He or she is able to paint a picture of the future and fashion a plan to move toward it opportunistically. For example, we purchased our major competitor as a result of anticipating how retailing patterns would change. Today, Toro is the only lawn mower manufacturer that has both a premium brand line in the mass merchant retail segment (Lawn-Boy) and a leading market position with both the Toro and Lawn-Boy brands in the service-dealer segment.

2. Live Your Vision, Communicate It, and Act It

It's not enough just to have a vision. It is also the leader's responsibility to articulate it clearly to those he or she leads. A leader must inspire others to embrace the vision, demonstrate his or her commitment to it, and incorporate it into the daily work setting. And most important, the leader must *live* the vision . . . each and every day. A vision is not just a statement on the walls of the lobby.

3. Give Power Away . . . Build Trust

As a leader exhibits a stronger coaching and empowering role, he or she will build trust, but this is a slow and difficult process. But it's worth it; individuals and teams will be much more inclined to take responsibility and be held accountable. Following are some ways to foster trust:

- Genuinely empower, don't just delegate.
- Involve employees early in the game.
- Honor commitments and be consistent.
- Develop real coaching skills.
- Foster risk taking (experimentation), innovation, and creativity by providing a "freedom-to-fail-with-learning" environment.

For example, at Toro, a group of employees worked long and hard to find a better method for producing a major part on one of our products. To make a long story short, the new process didn't work at high manufacturing volumes. Unfortunately, they learned this only after it had been implemented during the normal production process—well after the product had been introduced to the field and annual stock orders had been taken. Instead of giving them a reprimand, we celebrated. Word spread quickly; the message was: Good tries are encouraged and recognized. As a postscript to this story, and as is often the case, we were able to use their process later to assess the effectiveness of future designs.

4. Create an Environment for Personal Growth

An environment that encourages personal growth allows the company's most important assets to appreciate in value. To create such an environment, focus on:

- Visibly valuing the contributions of others, sincerely and frequently.
- Being receptive to learning from others.
- Encouraging others to own their responsibilities.
- Giving feedback frequently—both positive and negative.
- Creating win-win solutions.
- Practicing empathy, as Stephen Covey says, "Seek first to understand, then to be understood."

5. Champion Positive Change

Following are some ways to do it:

- Accept that ongoing change is a way of doing business in today's marketplace. At best, we operate today in managed chaos, with no letup in sight. Leaders must demonstrate their proactivity toward embracing, adopting, and even initiating change.
- Help employees to see change as an opportunity for

  professional growth,

  increased job satisfaction,

  contributing to the company's success, and

  making a difference in meeting customer needs and requirements.
- Recognize that some may be fearful of change; as a leader, help them move beyond their fear.

6. Integrate Results and Relationships

This is often the most difficult of all the leadership attributes. It seems so contradictory. While emphasizing the process via People Values (treating people in a valuing way), leaders must still honor Performance Values. That means leaders must expect and require excellence, positive results, and goal achievement. Accepting subpar performance is devaluing to those who are meeting requirements.

At Toro, these six leadership attributes are practiced under our culture umbrella, Pride in Excellence. We use a 360-degree evaluation process that measures leaders and managers against all of these values. For higher-level leaders (about 70 people), the evaluation process affects their annual compensation. It is a process we've been doing for 10 years now, and we keep fine-tuning it for greater effectiveness.

One fundamental goal in managing and maintaining the turf is ensuring that there will be harvests in the future as well as in the present. Practicing the six leadership attributes and cultivating awareness of the roles and responsibilities of leadership will not, alone, create servant leaders for our future. It is leaders who mentor, coach, and teach others, while serving, who will ultimately help to develop and empower future servant-leaders. Those individuals whose sense of purpose leads them to help unleash the potential of others, by creating valuing and caring environments, will make a positive difference in the lives of those they lead and ensure future harvests.

Bottom-Line and People-Oriented Results: The Harvest

Results are important, essential both in the short term and in the long run. Getting results is a key leadership requirement; a company must be financially viable to sustain itself. But not all results are financial. Several nonfinancial results directly generate a propensity for profits and returns. Still other results transcend economics. These are important, too; the longer a leader leads, the more important they become. These final results that go beyond the company's financial record may be the ultimate harvest that comes from servant-leadership, the leader attribute that ensures the future.

At Toro, we have many examples of bottom-line financial results as well as people-oriented results from the implementation of servant leadership.

- Our earnings and sales over the last 14 years have been consistently growing, except during the recession in the early 1990s. We recovered quickly from this period, and our earnings have been growing at a rate of 65 percent for the last three years.
- Our sales per employee lead the industry.
- Our turnover rate is 5.4 percent compared with the consumer durable goods industry average of 7 to 8 percent.
- We lead our industry in innovation, with over one-third of our worldwide sales from products less than three years old, year after year.
- We are recognized leaders in product safety and liability because we look at this issue as a human problem, not a legal problem.
- Shareholder value has increased tenfold since the turnaround in the early eighties.
- Through our employee stock ownership plan (ESOP), every employee is also an owner of the company.
- There is inordinate upward and cross-functional mobility among our employees at all levels.
- We operate everywhere with self-directed teams.
- Our culture today requires few symbols, speeches, and reminders because it has become a "way of life" for most of us.
- Each employee puts out 110 percent effort and still is having fun (for the most part!) or continues to be gratified.

- Many of us today recognize that the harvest occurs along the way, not only at the end of journey.
- Some of us are beginning to see that servant-leadership transcends the bottom line—that there is rich value beyond earnings per share.

How Do I Get Started?

I believe that leadership is not a position. It's a combination of something you are (your character) and some things you do (your skills and competence). In addition, I believe the best model for leadership is that of a servant-leader, who leads by serving the needs of people. A servant-leader doesn't do others' jobs for them, but rather enables others to learn and make progress toward mutual goals. When a leader creates an environment for personal growth, people rise to their potential and beyond.

In the hope that I have provoked in you an interest in pursuing the study and possible implementation of a servant-leadership model in your own life, I present the Personal Leadership Plan shown on page 296.

Conclusion

If you want to help create an organization dedicated to caring, valuing, and unleashing the potential of others, you can get started by executing your personal leadership plan. In a servant-leadership organization, everyone must act, everyone exerts influence, but if your organization is not there yet, starting the process is key.

You may be thinking this is something that can only be initiated at the top or that you don't have enough authority or control. I know that feeling because I have been there. When I came back to Toro after we sold Game Time in 1976, I was eager to replicate what I had learned in Michigan. It was difficult in a culture at odds with servant-leadership principles; it was frustrating and left me feeling, "What's the use?" Ultimately, I realized that what I lacked in authority was offset by the presence of a sphere of influence. I can see now that during that time I was planting seeds for our Pride in Excellence culture.

Remember, it's the planting of the seeds that is important, not the harvesting of them. Make the choice to sow some seeds today.

Personal Leadership Plan

I. Cultural Situation Analysis

1. To what degree are behaviors that value people (People Values) implemented and rewarded throughout your organization?

2. To what degree are behaviors that value performance (Performance Values) implemented and rewarded throughout your organization?

3. Are there areas or departments where servant-leadership values and actions are demonstrated consistently?

4. Are there areas or departments where more focused attention on leading by serving would benefit people and performance?

5. What strengths currently exist in your culture? What attributes describe your culture best?

II. Personal Situation Analysis

1. To what degree do you practice People Values and Performance Values when in a leadership position?

2. What are your leadership strengths?

III. Strategies and Actions for Personal Improvement

1. What are strategies and actions I can employ to do the following?
   - Demonstrate "walking my talk"
   - Improve the culture and leadership within my organization
   - Help effect change in systems and processes

2. How can I prioritize my actions?

3. What are my areas for personal improvement?

25

Servant-Leadership in a Christian Organization: The Sisters of St. Joseph Health System

John S. Lore

John S. Lore is president and CEO of the Sisters of St. Joseph (SSJ) Health System in Ann Arbor, Michigan. The SSJ Health System employs more than 22,000 people through dozens of hospitals, medical centers, and other health care facilities. It is now one of the largest organizations engaged in the daily practice of servant-leadership. John Lore has served the State of Michigan through appointed positions under three governors. He has served as board chair for the National Society of Fund Raising Executives and as a board member for the National Association for Community Leadership. John Lore was a keynote presenter at The Greenleaf Center's 1997 conference.

In this essay, Lore offers a firsthand, in-depth look at the practice of servant-leadership within the SSJ Health System. He examines how the SSJ System has integrated servant-leadership within its practice of "Leadership in a Christian Organization." Lore concludes that the strength of servant-leadership is to be found in its power to influence, rather than the power to control.

This is a report on a work in progress, one of the most exciting examples of servant-leadership in the nation.

Three things make the Sisters of St. Joseph (SSJ) Health System, with corporate offices in Ann Arbor, Michigan, a unique example of servant-leadership:

1. The fact that the ideal of servant-leadership is woven into the fabric and spiritual heritage of the parent organization, which was founded 107 years ago. This ideal has successfully been nurtured and carried

forward to this day, and servant-leadership is now one of the health system's five explicitly articulated values (the others being service to the neighbor, compassion, wisdom, and stewardship).

2. The fact that the organization that embraces these values—indeed, strives to *live* these values on a daily and an hourly basis—is also successfully fulfilling its mission in one of the most dynamic areas of today's society: health care.

3. Its very size. The Sisters of St. Joseph Health System today consists of about 30 sponsored and affiliated hospitals (ranging in size from about 60 to more than 600 beds), ambulatory care centers, outpatient surgery centers, nursing homes, substance abuse facilities, mental health programs, home health care agencies, and other facilities. This is an organization that has more than 20,000 employees, some separated from others by hundreds of miles. Yet it has grown from a seed sown more than a century ago.

"Go into the City and Serve the People in Need"

The Congregation of the Sisters of St. Joseph of Nazareth was founded in the late nineteenth century when a small band of sisters settled in Michigan. In Kalamazoo, they established a foundation and Borgess Hospital in 1889; in the region, they began a home for orphan boys and took charge of a school. Their mission was, and remains, to "go into the city and serve the people in need" with constant attention to compassionate, loving care, and a striving toward excellence.

The sisters were bold in pursuing that mission, and one can only say that they succeeded spectacularly. Although they faced significant resistance to the prevailing concept of hospital as an institution, their hands-on approach to caring for the sick in their homes gradually convinced families that the same personal and loving care would be provided in the new hospital. As the role of hospitals evolved, they extended their efforts into nontraditional areas that served emotional and social as well as physical needs.

The Sisters of St. Joseph were also practical in recognizing that their world was changing rapidly. They wanted to ensure that their work would be carried on into the next century and that their organization would continue to reflect the spirit in which it was established; thus, in the 1960s they began to broaden their governance by adding lay trustees, an unusual move in church-related organizations at that time.

In the 1970s the sisters began to add lay administrators to this mix. Again, there was opposition, based largely on concerns for the congregation's values of Christian compassion and service to others. Reorganization of the growing health system into regional holding companies began in 1979; the result is four affiliated systems—in southeastern Michigan (the

Detroit-Port Huron area), southwestern Michigan (centered around Kalamazoo), Genesee County (Flint area), and northeastern Lower Michigan (Tawas City-Oscoda). In 1982 governance was moved from the Sisters of St. Joseph of Nazareth into the new Sisters of St. Joseph Health System.

The next stage in this process was to hire lay leaders. Today, each region has a governance corporation whose chair and president-chief executive officer (CEO) are laypeople and whose vice president for sponsorship is a Sister of St. Joseph. The president-CEOs and the vice presidents for sponsorship are the officers of the Sisters of St. Joseph Health System governance corporation, whose chair is a Sister of St. Joseph and whose president-CEO is a layperson. The chair of the governance corporation also sits on the board of the parent member corporation, the Sisters of St. Joseph of Nazareth.

Two themes underlie this continuing evolution. One is a principle of local autonomy; each of the regional systems has a tradition of fulfilling its mission by fostering strong community ties and serving local needs. The other is the realization that, in the words of Sister Joyce DeShano, a senior vice president of the Sisters of St. Joseph Health System, "the health care mission does not belong to the sisters but to all people of good will."[1]

Sister Janet Fleischhacker, president of the Sisters of St. Joseph of Nazareth, the member corporation, sums up a lot of evolution in two sentences: "The way we have exercised sponsorship has changed significantly over the years. At first, sisters had direct responsibility for all aspects of what went on at each of the hospitals; but very early on the sisters began sharing both the work and then the leadership with others, bringing us to the arrangement we have today."[2]

Sister Joyce puts it succinctly: "We have a new understanding of the meaning of partnership, and we think Robert Greenleaf would agree that this approach and style is really servant-leadership."[3]

Sister Joyce has been instrumental in the past six years in shaping and guiding a process designed to ensure that the values that have sustained the Sisters of St. Joseph in their work for so many years become ingrained in the health system and the people who constitute it.

This fourth stage of development began in 1990, when a group consisting of the four regional CEOs and executive councils, plus three executives from the corporate office, began a series of conversations intended to help them define who they were, who they wanted to become, and what values and visions sustained them. They decided that they needed a clear statement of the values that would enable them to define Leadership in a Christian Organization and articulate how that would differ from, say, Christian Leadership (which would have excluded non-Christians) or leadership in the conventional corporate pyramid.

In fact, the phrase "Leadership in a Christian Organization" came to be known by its acronym: LICO.

The Leadership in a Christian Organization Initiative

This group expanded to include more members from around the system, then met, reflected, and struggled with the issues. They read widely, and they finally distilled their beliefs down to five values that resonated with all of them. One of these was servant-leadership, and the way in which this term and the others appeared—from the inside out, rather than as an imposed concept—is a hallmark of the LICO process. In other words, servant-leadership and the terms used to describe the other system values are, as Don M. Frick noted in his contribution to *Reflections on Leadership,* descriptive rather than dogmatic, anchored in the Christian Gospel but universally applicable.[4]

Servant-leadership is thus defined as "the use of gifts and talents on behalf of all of us in a way that models what we can be and empowers us to try," and it is rooted in the Scriptures: "You know that among the Gentiles those who exercise authority lord it over them; it cannot be like that with you. Any one among you who aspires to greatness must serve the rest," (Gospel of Mark).

The four other values are, of course, closely related to this. In fact, they can be seen as traits of the servant-leader:

1. Service to the neighbor: Unhesitating outreach to those in need, respecting the dignity of each person. "Which of these three, in your opinion, was neighbor to the one who fell in with robbers? The answer came, 'The one who treated him with compassion.' Jesus said, 'Then go and do the same' " (Gospel of Mark).

2. Compassion: The ability to enter into the deepest experiences of life and be present with one another in our need. "Jesus said, 'Go home to your people and tell them all that the Lord in compassion has done for you' " (Gospel of Mark).

3. Wisdom: The ability to appreciate the complexity of life and make sound judgments for the common good. "Because you have asked for yourself understanding to discern what is right . . . behold I give you a wise and discerning mind," (2 Kings).

4. Stewardship: Responsible, innovative use of human and material resources. "Then the one who had received the five talents came forward, bringing five more talents, saying, 'Master, you handed over to me five talents; see I have made five more talents.' The master said, 'Well done, good and trustworthy servant; you have been trustworthy in a few things; I will put you in charge of many things; enter into the joy of the master,' " (Gospel of Matthew).

These spiritual values constitute the core of the system's uniqueness in health care. The Sisters of St. Joseph Health System is committed to forming corporate cultures that are value based and to nurturing the development of leaders who are value centered. In this way the system integrates spiritual heritage with a contemporary excellence.

"The fact that these values could be isolated and identified indicates that they were there and operative before this effort began," Sister Janet says. "LICO did not change them in any way but simply allowed them to be articulated."[5]

That the values are more than abstract ideals is reflected in the LICO vision statement: "The values, in the form of values-based behaviors, processes, and structures, permeate every aspect of our organizational life. That presence is evident in the soulful way people are touched by it and is constantly reflected in the organizational climate, both in the form of motivating spirit and effective action. It is so deeply ingrained that the people in the health system cannot imagine the culture any other way."

Operationally, the values are apparent in the following:

- The priorities we set and the way we set them
- The services we provide and the reasons we provide them
- The decisions we make and the way we make them
- The way all of us relate with our visitors and with each other
- The ongoing collective support to improve individual and team integration of values and to have them reflected in our actions
- The constant attention toward maintaining a spiritual environment that draws its energy from the uniqueness of each of its members

The Sisters of St. Joseph Health System has a set of guiding principles for continuing the LICO process. Some of them clearly relate to the nature of the organization (or, organizations). For example:

- Create a critical mass of leadership in each region.
- Make LICO self-sustaining, over time, in each of our regions.
- Engage in long-term, methodical planning to close the gaps between what we have achieved and what we would like to achieve.
- Ensure that LICO is rooted in and driven by team synergy.
- Work for systemwide motivation, recognition, and support.

But some of the other principles read like a guidebook to servant-leadership:

- Executive management continues to promote and integrate a values-centered leadership style.

- Transformation is an inside-out process that depends on modeling and monitoring. The servant guide of the parable is really the leader of the expedition.
- LICO is experimental in nature—it touches the whole person.

And one principle bridges the gap, calling LICO a multidimensional process for cultural change that will involve personal and individual change, team development, the development of focused initiatives, and a redefined organizational architecture.

And how, exactly, does one effect a "redefined organizational architecture"?

An Acorn and a Process of Transformation

By 1992 the core group—the regional CEOs and executive councils, plus three executives from the corporate office—felt that it had defined its terms and goals well enough to present them to the next level of managers. The key here was, and remains, to communicate what LICO is all about and ensure acceptance of it as a natural, inside-out process in which each individual recognizes and takes ownership of the ideals. An ongoing series of retreats provides a context that is appropriate to this process.

Each retreat includes a showing of the short film *The Man Who Planted Trees*, the story of a shepherd, Elzeard Bouffier, who transformed a drought-ravaged land into a thriving landscape by diligently planting acorns. The trees grew into forests, and people prospered where before they had barely eked out a bitter living. The film, by Jean Giono, won the Academy Award for Best Animated Film in 1987.

The film shows the power of a patient, dedicated human being, and participants at the retreats each receive a wooden acorn, a reminder of the film and of the power of planting—in the Health System's case—values, one at a time, to nurture a corporate landscape in which the human spirit will thrive.

It is a process of transformation, and the material presented at these retreats, and the group sessions that are held at them, and the opportunities for individual reflection that are provided at them all lead to an understanding that real transformation begins with the individual and radiates outward, rather than the other way around. A value-based organization will occur naturally enough when the individuals within it are given an opportunity to consider their own values and behaviors and how those values and behaviors come together.

"We are all moving through a cycle of change," Sister Joyce says. "In the film, the man transformed his environment. We're trying to transform our corporate culture. As he planted acorns, we plant the seeds of value-based action."[6]

While the movement toward a value-based organization is stimulated and driven by events such as retreats, the real work occurs between events as individual participants and their peers work to deepen their ability to own the values and have them drive individual and collective behavior and choices.

A systemwide implementation structure was put in place in 1992, utilizing systemwide implementation teams. Regional teams were formed in 1993; in 1994 those teams sought and gained the support of regional trustees, ethics committees, and the sisters themselves for regional implementation.

In 1995 the process continued with the addition of audiences supportive of full implementation: public relations and communications staff, human resources specialists, managers, and, of course, physicians.

A series of concentric circles is used to illustrate how participants pass through levels of transformation. At the center—the very core of the process as well as of the diagram—is *individual transformation*, the process of becoming a servant-leader. This reinforces the reality that this is an inside-out process that has its roots in individual ownership of the values, and that the ownership must be complete before the process can be carried to the next person or group.

The next of the ever-widening circles is *work-group support*. Here, the values are shared with a specific work team, for example, or a group of cohorts in a department, unit, or other identifiable entity. It is worth noting that whenever the values are taken to a new level, the process pauses there to allow the new people to develop individual ownership before it moves on again. Furthermore, when the process expands to a new group, it does not move out of the consciousness of the previous group but remains there, changing focus to a deepening of one's personal understanding and ownership.

The third circle is *focused initiatives*, formal, identifiable efforts to accomplish organizational objectives. Since initiatives are the work of those who have assumed ownership of the core values, they will be founded on and imbued with those values.

The final circle is *organizational architecture*, which refers to the policies, procedures, and authority structures in the organization.

Executive councils . . . cycles of change . . . systemwide implementation structures . . . such terms might lead one to think that the Sisters of St. Joseph Health System has, like many another large organization, simply bought a management package off the shelf and has said, "This is our policy. Do it this way."

Implementation of LICO does not mandate anything, however, or even instill any values in anyone; it simply provides a context in which these values can come out. What happens in this system is that people are able to remove the layers of behavior that they have had to adopt to be acceptable in the conventional workplace. This lets them feel more congruent with the whole of their person—they feel more whole because the language used to describe servant-leadership gives people a sense of themselves—their selves—and their values. They are allowed and encouraged to bring to the workplace the same values of wisdom and stewardship that they often use in their own lives. Servant-leadership helps people bring forth more of who they are on a daily basis, while in some workplaces, people have to stifle who they are.

The LICO process seeks to help people close the gap while recognizing that the impulse to do this must come from within. People are not going to close the gap because one of their leaders or executives says they should close it; they will close it because it begins to make sense to them and it begins to pay off for them. Behavior must change policy, because the past clearly shows that changing policy does not change people or their behavior.

Incidentally, it's easy to see that the transition may be more difficult for management than for others. Many leaders in business, including those in health care, got where they are today through the traditional routes, after all, but it may no longer be sufficient for executives to follow the familiar steps: analyze a situation, decide on a course of action, then see that it is implemented. Now, the issue, the process, the intended result, and the implementation all must be viewed through the lens of servant-leadership and the system values.

Listen to Tom Thibault, vice president, organizational development, of the governance corporation:

> We continue to work very closely with all of the regional leadership toward full values implementation. The starting point of personal integration is often especially challenging to executives. The difficulty is not one of desire or ability, it is one of overcoming established patterns and the realities of their world. This is just plain hard to do when you are judged on your ability to get things accomplished through other people (not through focusing on personal change); when your success has been gained with behaviors that might not always be viewed as congruent with all the values; and when your normal workday is so packed that introspection about personal values integration is indeed a luxury.
>
> That's the bad news. The good news is that, to a person, they are struggling with those issues to develop a better, more consistent congruence between the values and daily behavior.[7]

Tom Thibault is an idealist—but he's also a realist, and he has a sense of humor. "It's easiest to be a values-based leader in fair weather," he says, "but when our backs are against the wall, we tend to revert to the old behaviors. It's like trying to stick to a new diet that would undo a lifetime of eating habits. Things go pretty well, but give me a frustrating enough day and a box of cookies looks pretty darn good!"[8]

Still, Thibault says, "We have come a long way, and we are in fact at the point in the process at which most organizations would stop and move on."[9]

The Sisters of St. Joseph Health System is not stopping.

What Does the Future Hold?

The business world in general and health care in particular are facing unprecedented challenges and opportunities in the foreseeable future. In the past few years, health care has begun to deal with the fundamental, quantum-leap type of change that none of us controls but every one of us has to respond to effectively. The Sisters of St. Joseph Health System, one of the largest health care delivery systems in one of the nation's most populous states, has hardly been immune to these pressures.

For example, many in health care cut their teeth in a cost-plus world of financing . . . then had to get used to the fact that the payer is going to determine the amount of payment through Medicare and Medicaid. Now they are faced with the fact that the whole way in which health care is conceived of and financed is again changing fundamentally, and there's no end in sight. Think of some of the changes—from an acute-care approach to preventive medicine, and from stand-alone organizations to integrated delivery systems, to name just two. These are not mere fluctuations but long-term, systemic change.

The Sisters of St. Joseph Health System is convinced that that knowledge itself presents a compelling argument for making a commitment to develop a values-based organization marked by a culture of servant-leadership. This way of thinking and being is not only consistent with Sisters of St. Joseph history, but it also nurtures relationships that are conducive to partnering, the critical human foundation best suited to facing the future.

For developing partnerships is a key feature of the new world of health care. To achieve the economies that are essential to its survival, the Sisters of St. Joseph Health System is forming linkages and partnerships with other organizations at a rate that would have seemed impossible a few years ago. The system's organizational chart shows hospitals, nursing homes, health centers, and clinics, all loosely bound into groups and forming an extended family that covers much of Michigan.

The organization has realized, in other words, that it must go beyond rethinking strategy and restructuring as an organization and must build an integrated system of organizations, which is a fundamentally different challenge. Among other things, this involves bringing together people from very different backgrounds so that they can work together in a congruent, integrated system.

For many health care organizations, this sort of partnering is something new, but not at the Sisters of St. Joseph Health System:

> *This system is designed to be decentralized, localized to meet local needs. In fact, our tradition of sharing authority at the regional level and throughout the system has roots in Sisters of St. Joseph history. The order's constitution makes it clear that authority in the congregation is a shared responsibility—of members to each other, of members to leaders, and of leaders to*

members. This preceded LICO, though they clearly have much in common;
LICO was a formalization of the older principle, a more tangible form of it.

The Sisters of St. Joseph came to this country in small groups and estab-
lished small local congregations. Today, there are 23 of those congregations
in the United States, each an independent organization with almost total
autonomy. That principle of local autonomy is very evident in the structure
of the Sisters of St. Joseph Health System.[10]

One manifestation of this is that the regional systems can respond
freely and effectively to their communities' needs in a way that a heavily cen-
tralized organization would find difficult to do. For example, the St. John
Detroit Health Center, which opened in 1993 and provides health care to an
underserved community on the city's east side, was an initiative of St. John
Health System but represented a collaboration between St. John, community-
based organizations, and local government—servant-leadership in action, if
you will.

Having a values-based system with servant-leadership as its linchpin
makes it relatively easy to respond to many of these pressures. If the executives and board members of the system and of the regional corporations—
and the middle managers, and the physicians, and the staff and employees—
have all recognized the same values in themselves and have taken ownership
of them and have created an organization of individuals whose lives reflect
those values, responding to outside forces is not as difficult as it might be for
other, more traditional kinds of organizations.

The Sisters of St. Joseph Health System has a presence in the marketplace. Its values-based approach is a source of strength and renewal that gives
it a competitive edge. One could say that the health system is unique among
organizations this size in the shared vision of its thousands of employees and
in their dedication to goals that permeate not only their work but all aspects
of their daily lives.

Conclusion

It is a challenge to make servant-leadership the management style of an organization, but the Sisters of St. Joseph Health System has an edge in this regard because servant-leadership has been the sisters' management style for a
long time. The Leadership in a Christian Organization initiative described in
this essay really seeks to re-create and perpetuate that environment and ensure its viability far into the future.

As the Sisters of St. Joseph Health System moves into its seventh year
of LICO, its executives continue to seek the guidance and support of national health care leaders such as Donald Brennan, president and CEO of the
Daughters of Charity National Health System, one of the largest national
health care systems in the United States. Other national leaders who have

been consulted include Patricia Cahill, president and CEO of Catholic Health Initiatives; Patricia Vandenberg, CSC, president and CEO of Holy Cross Health System; Patricia Siemen, OP, chair of the member corporation of Catholic Healthcare West; and David Lincoln, president and CEO of Covenant Health System and chair of the Catholic Health Association of the United States. These leaders have offered encouragement and support as the Sisters of St. Joseph Health System continues its pursuit of an entirely value-based organization.

Ultimately, however, the strongest voices come from within the system itself:

> *Servant-leadership is the power to influence rather than the power to control. We realize that when we choose to influence people rather than control them, it at first might seem like weakness, but it really calls forth an inner strength. We think it really serves to engage and develop the creativity, productivity, and vibrancy that already exist in the regions.*
>
> *It is a style that we feel will be effective in facing the challenges that are so critical in today's health care environment.*[11]

26

Bearing Witness

James A. Autry

James A. Autry is an author, poet, and consultant. Before taking early retirement in 1991 to pursue his present career, Autry was president of Meredith Corporation's Magazine Group, a $500 million operation with more than 900 employees. During his 32-year career, Autry served as a daily newspaper reporter, editor of a weekly newspaper, and editor and publisher of various books and magazines. He is the author of Love and Profit, Confessions of an Accidental Businessman, *and* Life and Work, *as well as two collections of poetry,* Nights Under a Tin Roof *and* Life After Mississippi. *Autry was a keynote speaker at The Greenleaf Center's 1995 conference.*

In this essay, which is adapted from a chapter in his most recent book, Confessions of an Accidental Businessman, *Autry draws on his own experiences as a leader who has sought to serve others. He reminds us of the need to be thankful for our work, for people, and for spirit.*

We may not be, as some suggest, "called" to work. We may indeed just start working to make money, to improve our status, to create a future, or just to stay off the dole, as they used to say.

I was very reluctant to get a job when I was a kid. I did not want to work. It seemed inconvenient, far too wasteful of my time. But we were poor. I did a little of everything—carried the morning newspaper on a regular route, then sold the afternoon paper on a corner to the businessmen who would stop in their cars on the way home from the office; chopped cotton and picked cotton on a farm; worked on a bread truck and on a construction crew, and, at various times, as a soda jerk, a waiter, a copy boy, a photographer's assistant, a teletype operator, a musician, a reporter, and a photographer—before I graduated from college. And this does not include my work scholarships as a university public relations writer, dark room technician, and—yes, I got paid to do it—drum major of the university marching band.

Not one of those jobs did I do for anything but money. Not for training or education, not for the advancement of a career, not to create a productive future, and certainly not for personal or spiritual growth. But for money (and occasionally for the chance to be around women, but that's another chapter).

My mother worked in degrading low-level jobs only because she had to make money, but I believe the reason that her learning to operate a comptometer machine, sort of a primitive calculator, meant so much was that it evidenced a skill, the mastery of something almost mystical that elevated her to another plain of achievement, in her mind something like a professional. And, of course, she credited God. She felt God had, as the old hymn said, planted her feet on higher ground.

Her belief that God had helped her did not stop there. God had helped her for a reason, and the reason was that she would now be in a better position to "witness for Jesus." This, in her view, was what we all were to do, those of us who called ourselves Christians.

"Jimmy," she would tell me, "you surely can use your paper route to witness for Jesus." Naturally I thought that to be impossible. What was I supposed to do, ask one of the people in the Linden Avenue mansions or in one of the low-income shotgun houses, "Have you accepted Jesus as your personal savior?" or "Would you like to go to church with me?" I remember once or twice trying to summon the courage to approach the subject with one of my customers, but I did not have Mother's confidence that the Lord would save me from ridicule and embarrassment.

And that is still my fear as I speak and write about the spirit of work, yet I know that the "liberation of the human spirit" in the context of the work we choose to do—even if we choose that work only for the money—is at the heart of the healing that must happen between management and employees if we are to save American business from a debilitating and destructive crisis of trust in the wake of all the downsizing of the past several years.

No, it's not the same as witnessing for Jesus, yet I do believe that our work gives us one of our best opportunities to look for the best—the Divine—in others and to manifest the best—the Divine—in ourselves. Indeed, I believe any good work we do for or with others is also God's work.

Just what is good work with others? It is any work, no matter how routine or menial, done with generosity, positive intention, a spirit of community, and a commitment to doing it well.

What is good work done for others? It is anything done with unselfishness and generosity, a putting aside (or overcoming) of ego, for the benefit of another person. But what if that other person is a jerk, a bad person, who doesn't give a damn for you or your good work? So much more the need for the courage I could not muster as paperboy and so much more the reason to try.

As Lao-tzu asks in the *Tao Te Ching*, "What is a good man but a bad man's teacher? What is a bad man but a good man's job?"[1]

In previous books, I have described my skepticism of companies that make much public hoo-ha about their claims to conduct their business according to Christian principles, then use those principles to try to prescribe and control behavior and to repress their employees rather than to liberate and enable them.

Yet I know of, and respect, business executives who do use their religious principles to guide them in liberating the human spirit and enabling and empowering their employees. I believe this is true of such American business leaders as Max DePree, author and former CEO of Herman Miller Inc.; his successor, Kermit Campbell; Peter and Jack Herschend of Silver Dollar City; Irv Hockaday of Hallmark; and Mike Moody of AT&T; among others.

Still, there is a certain uneasiness, a certain risk, in this whole subject. Some of the risk is put to rest, I believe, by concentrating on the spirit in work, the opportunity it gives us to find personal and spiritual growth, rather than focusing on a particular sectarian interpretation of that spirituality.

But what does *spiritual growth* mean? I don't have a simple answer, and perhaps not even a good answer, but I believe spiritual growth has a lot to do with opportunities we have to connect on a deeper level with one another. I want to believe that we find easy connection through our shared joys, but I know in my heart that the connections come most readily from shared loss and pain, and that is because in times of pain there is usually nothing to say to one another except the obvious, which leaves us searching for other expressions. Those expressions, if indeed we are open to the opportunities, may make appropriate the things we usually find difficult—a touch, even a hug, tears, a long walk, a note with a poem enclosed, the assurance that we will be thinking about our colleague or friend, or praying for them.

A lot of trivia drops away when someone says "I have cancer" or when someone's child is seriously ill or when a loved one dies. The only thing to do in those circumstances is show that you care.

I used to question the value of sympathy notes and flowers, but when my mother died, the first death of an immediate family member, I remember walking into that funeral home in Ripley, Mississippi, and being overwhelmed by the flowers from friends and coworkers. The same occurred when my father died and, six months later, my brother. The affection I felt expressed by the flowers and by the notes, as simple and obvious as those words were, was a revelation to me, and it awakened a recognition of connection that far transcended my previously held assessments of those relationships, professional and personal. In that recognition, I believe I experienced some inkling of the spiritual possibilities within everyday relationships.

This is not to say that those possibilities come only at times of pain. There simply is no denying something ineffable just in the very act of working together and in accomplishing together what we set out to accomplish. I believe we feel this something but often don't recognize it, much less understand how to express it. We can't even put labels on it. We say we "love" our jobs, we find them "challenging and rewarding," we are "motivated," we are "team players," we take "pride" in what we do.

Managers talk about *vision* and *excellence* and *quality* and *empowerment*. We coach and are coached; we mentor and are mentored. We seek continuous improvement. We want always to be learning. We talk about ethics and integrity, about health and healing. All of this language, but what does it literally say about that ineffable something we feel about what we have chosen to do? Very little. The same is true as we try to express those feeling through parties and celebrations and conferences, through pep rallies and retreats, through the simple act of an informal get-together after work.

But those who are willing to take a more metaphorical view will find that these superficial words and activities symbolize the most profound expressions of our deepest selves, and they will understand that we simply have not developed an adequate vocabulary for what we feel as we seek meaning and dignity and growth in the everydayness of our work and lives.

Among my regrets as a manager is that I did not develop a clear enough sense of this metaphorical view in earlier years and when I did, that I did not do more to help my colleagues and employees find that meaning.

Certainly I had no understanding about this as a young man, but I recognize now that several profound things were trying to make their way through in those years. One was a sense of worth and esteem I began to feel as a copy boy for the Associated Press. I would pronounce "The Associated Press" with an air of great importance, much the way Mother pronounced "comptometer." Later, I came to say "A.P." as if every boy in my high school should know what those initials stood for.

The sheer size of the organization, its dominant place in the world of news gathering, the energy of the office—reporters shouting, photographers rushing still-wet photographs from the dark room, the noise of the machines and the absolute miracle of them—and my place as a cog in this great wheel gave me feelings I had never had. Never. I was no longer this kid who had few clothes, little money, no car, and no time to play sports because he had to work. I was "with" the Associated Press, and the Associated Press needed what I could do.

Another dim understanding came in those moments when all of us— reporters, photographers, teletype operators, and I—had worked together and had beat the United Press with a story. We would stand at the teletype machine, watching it run as Harrell Alien or one of the expert teletype operators punched the tape, fed it into the transmitter, then with consummate skill punched the story fast enough to keep up—and even gain on—the tape as it clicked through the feeder, sending its signals that appeared magically on the machine. It was a particular spirit of celebration if our story ran on the "A" wire, the national news wire of the AP. I could not have used the words then, or understood the concept they represent, but I was participating in the community of work and feeling the spirit of it.

The community was made all the more real at Christmas, when on Christmas Eve the various AP bureaus around the country sent their elaborate Christmas greetings over the generally idle machines. There wasn't much news to transmit so the artists of the teletype were given the opportunity to exhibit their best work.

On my first Christmas, Harrell Alien asked, "Would you like to send your own Christmas greetings over the state wire?" I was overwhelmed. I was taking typing in high school in hopes of becoming a teletype operator but had never used the machines. Harrell set it up, and I carefully punched Xs into a simple pyramid design of a Christmas tree, and wrote, "Merry Christmas to all Tennessee AP staffers." I loved using words like *staffer*.

"How shall I sign it, Harrell? Memphis Bureau?"

"Just use your own initials, JA/MX."

I put the tape on the transmitter, then hit the toggle switch and watched the state wire come to life and print my message. I tore it from the machine, a two-inch strip of low-grade paper, took it home to show my mother, then kept it in a scrapbook for years. I realize now it was more than a memento.

I would not have said "more than a memento" in those days, however. For all the good feelings I was able to have in that clattering, carbon-smudged teletype room, it was to my mind still just a place I went to work to make some money, and making money—not the human spirit, not the enrichment of the inner life, not grace—was still how I identified the meaning of my work life.

The Air Force seemed so different that I assumed there could be no connection between life as a fighter pilot and a civilian working in an office. The camaraderie, the identity, the special bonds of risk and death surely could not be replicated in some damned office building while wearing a suit and tie.

Of course I questioned why some pilots got killed and I didn't, but the notion it might have something to do with grace never entered my consciousness. A part of all pilots wants to believe that we could handle any situation and would not have been killed as others were. But that was not true. We talked a lot about luck, but I found myself doing a lot more praying in those years, traditional praying in which we bring our wish list for consideration. I think I would now classify that as being scared back into religion, and I don't think it qualifies as enlightenment.

Back in civilian life I became immersed in what it took me a long time to realize was not unlike the fighter squadron after all, but to me it was still just a job. I've often wondered why it took so long to "get it," to realize what was really going on as my friends and colleagues and I turned to and busted our asses to do good work together, to get good results, to make our boss look good to his boss.

It was not until the early eighties when I was a senior corporate executive that I began to understand the power of the spirit in work, the need for community and connection among workers, the opportunity for growth of many kinds that work provides. Perhaps it was the influence of friends who began to lead me on more spiritual personal paths, perhaps it was the trauma of life in those days—divorce, sickness, death—perhaps it was the fabled midlife crisis, perhaps it was as simple as being brought face-to-face with my own mortality.

Whatever the reasons, I began to feel that the only choice in work and life is to find the balance and, in turn, to help others find that balance.

I began to understand the need to find meaning in the everyday things, to see the divine in others, to discover holiness in the most mundane of activities. I realized that burnout is not a matter of working too hard, it is a matter of finding no meaning in what we do. Not a problem of mental/physical energy but a problem of emotional energy. Not a crisis of time but a crisis of spirit. More and more I knew that what most of us need is not a getting away from the drudgery of work but a getting into the joy of work, not a separation of life and work but an integration of life and work.

To quote the Indian poet Rabindranath Tagore:

> I slept and dreamt that life was Joy;
> and then I awoke and realized
> that life was Duty.
> And then I went to work—and, lo
> and behold I discovered that
> Duty can be Joy.[2]

These understandings or realizations or moments of truth prescribed for me a path that was quite different from the one most often used in business, particularly by senior corporate executives. It was a path of leader not as boss but as servant.

So once again I found myself needing to come up with the courage to witness, and somehow it seemed more important than ever. Once I began, I found many fellow travelers. (Along the way I discovered Robert Greenleaf's writings and became familiar with the work of The Greenleaf Center for Servant-Leadership.)

I found that virtually everything I had learned from my newsboy days through the Air Force days and into senior management pointed incontrovertibly in the same direction: toward the inside, toward the inner life, toward the ineffable.

There are many lessons about the spirit of work, and three of the most important are these: We should be thankful for work itself, we should be thankful for the people we work with, and we should recognize and be thankful for the grace of our spiritual possibilities at work.

27

A Leverage Force:
Reflections on the Impact
of Servant-Leadership

Irving R. Stubbs

Irving R. Stubbs is chairman and CEO of Strategic Solutions. For more than 30 years Stubbs has provided consulting services for organization leaders in North America, Europe, and the Far East. His current work focuses on system optimization and values applications. He is the author of Make It Better *and* The Core Value of Applied Industrial Technologies. *Currently he is at work on a book with the working title* A Formula for CEO Effectiveness. *A longtime member of The Greenleaf Center, Stubbs is committed to the principles and practices of servant-leadership.*

In this essay, Stubbs discusses how Greenleaf's concept of servant-leadership provides a significant fulcrum for leveraging many kinds of institutions. Citing examples from his long career as an organizational consultant, Stubbs reminds us that servant-leadership demands much from its practitioners.

With the concept of servant-leadership, Robert Greenleaf tapped into a substratum of profound truth. He proclaimed his discovery to the world. The meaning and potential of that "discovery" took a while to be recognized by "the world." The many references to Greenleaf and his view of servant-leadership in current writings make it clear that the discovery is gaining endorsement.

The American Bar Association (ABA), in the September 1989 issue of *Legal Economics,* published my article, "The Attorney as Servant-Leader." Three stimuli prompted this article:

1. A business executive, now the chief executive officer of a Connecticut-based corporation, introduced me to Greenleaf's initial book.
2. A lawyer, with whose Virginia law firm I had worked beginning in the mid-1970s, expressed with some passion that he would like for

his firm to be a "caring law firm." By 1988 that firm included as part of its vision for the future a desire to exercise servant-leadership in the practice of law. The attorney with whom I had begun this work got me involved with the legal profession. Through the mid-1990s we coled three different ABA committees or task forces.

In the *Legal Economics* article, I attempted to translate Greenleaf's definition of servant-leadership for the legal profession. The servant-leader attorney is one who meets the highest priority needs of the client. As a result of that relationship, the client becomes wiser, freer, and more autonomous; rather than confused, more dependent and less confident.

3. In addition to the prompting of the business executive touched by Greenleaf's writings and the prodding of the attorney in search of the caring law firm is my own belief system. It is my conviction that human liberation is enabled by servant-leadership in an ultimate and pragmatic sense.

The business executive, the attorney, and my own belief system stimulated me to write the ABA article. I hoped that a few members of the legal profession might see a different way to practice law. The article attempted to show what this meant and how to do it. It dealt with concerns surfaced by Mark McCormick in his 1987 book, *The Terrible Truth about Lawyers.* It cited leaders in the profession who called for more pro bono work. It pointed to Lewis F. Powell Jr., retired U.S. Supreme Court Justice, as a role model for servant-leadership in the legal profession. Several years later The Greenleaf Center included the attorney demonstration of servant-leadership as a workshop in one of its annual meetings.

Many attorneys practice servant-leadership in a very genuine and effective way. But, on the basis of my experience, can I affirm that the legal profession is a benchmark profession in servant-leadership? I cannot. The effort to influence this group, however, encouraged me to continue to explore servant-leadership.

Community Change Leaders Energized by a Foot-Washing Pastor

The minister of a "high steeple" church in an affluent North Carolina community asked me for a special kind of consultant help. The elected leaders in his congregation were the power figures in his community. It was his view that the church did not adequately challenge these leaders to use their potential to work on significant changes in which the church had an interest. What would it take to get these established leaders to use their skills and influence to work for these changes?

A dramatic initiative occurred. At a meeting of these high-potential leaders, the minister, with appropriate preparation, washed their feet as a symbolic act of servant-leadership. He then asked them to participate in a retreat that would challenge them to use their leadership as servants. At the retreat, they identified several major needs of the community. The minister asked each of the leaders to be the "champion" to get that need met during the next year. Each accepted the challenge.

The group scheduled a midpoint review meeting. By the time of that meeting, 70 percent of the challenges were accomplished. Progress on the remainder of the challenges was well under way. The champions brought substantial energy, influence, inclusion, and resources to bear on these needs. They used their leadership to serve their community in new ways. In their own way, they had taken their symbolic towels, to serve their neighbors.

Out of this experience, I gained an insight into servant-leadership that caused me to look at this approach in a different way. Servant-leadership is a significant fulcrum for leverage. In this context, the leverage metaphor means that servant-leadership can be a force to cause something bigger to happen than appeared possible with the initial available resources. In the case of the church leaders, the project outcomes exceeded what would have happened without the intervention of the symbolic act and servant-leadership thinking. When an individual has less concern for the ego associations of leadership and more for the mission to serve by liberating and redirecting individual and institutional resources, potential expands. People do more than they had been doing because they feel freer to be more than previously they had felt it possible to be. As a result of the greater energy available through the more actualized individuals, there is more possibility for creative change in institutions.

To place an emphasis on the utilitarian value of servant-leadership can be dangerous. It would be wrong to think of it as a way to "use" people, even in a caring, enabling way, to achieve some self-interest directed purpose. On the other hand, many who affirm servant-leadership also affirm that we are stewards of the human and institutional resources entrusted to our care. Should we not celebrate the opportunities that we have to make what we view to be servant types of things happen? Should we not celebrate when we see people use their expanded potential to achieve what they affirm to be their high-priority needs? This is what I mean by seeing servant-leadership as a leverage force.

A Change in Corporate Culture
Energized by a Caring CEO

The chief executive officer of a Dallas-based corporation with several thousand employees desired to exercise a different kind of leadership. He had been in senior positions in other corporations. He had seen the ego, greed, and manipulation that is sometimes present at these levels. He wanted to use himself, including his position, to forge a different kind of culture for this institution. It was not easy to make his intent clear to many of his associates. He persisted. He invited me to help with this mission. We developed a culture-changing intervention. The purpose of this intervention was to provide a win-win-win partnership among shareholders, employees, and customers. This partnership is grounded in the keystone values: *care, honesty, integrity, and trust.*

A key principle was to free up resources to benefit the total partnership. The CEO challenged the other corporate leaders to be more than they had been. Resources were offered to support their growth. During 1995, 10 meetings were held in different parts of the corporation. The meetings began with dinner on one evening and continued through lunch the next day. At each meeting the CEO and I engaged in very open discussions with 20 to 25 employees.

He listened, he responded, he challenged, he changed. He was caring, honest, authentic. His genuine concern for all of the partners was real. They had new hope for the kind of company this would be. They had a new kind of trust in their new chief executive.

At this writing, the mission of this servant-leader has continued with consistent commitment. Substantial resources were required to support and sustain the effort. Progress is evident. The leverage force for change was this leader's commitment to serve his three key constituents by encouraging and enabling each to grow. There has been resistance. There has been pain. Tough love has been required. From an outside observer's point of view, however, the corporation and its key families are in much better health than before this executive launched his mission.

A Corporation's Systemic Optimization Energized by a Liberating CEO

The experience of the CEO of a Cleveland-based corporation with several thousand employees demonstrates a different kind of leverage and application of servant-leadership. His unique approach to corporate turnaround is through systemic transformation. He has led this corporation to view and manage itself as a system. This requires those in the organization to think and act beyond their functional "domains" and to work in an alignment similar to that required of players in a symphony orchestra. With the high degree of interdependence required to optimize such a system, serious attention is paid to open communication, collaboration, and the innovation required to achieve the aim of the system. A special effort is required to equip leaders to lead this kind of organization.

This CEO invited me to help with the transformation. A leadership model that evolved includes the following growth stages (see Figure 27.1):

Figure 27.1
The liberator process for system leadership.

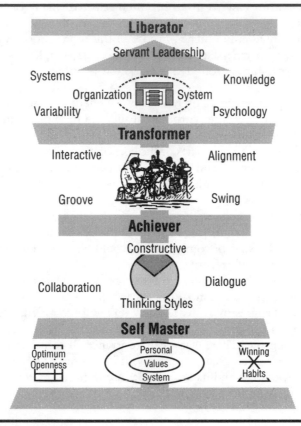

© 1996 Irving R. Stubbs.

1. First, the leader must achieve a high level of self-mastery. To accomplish this, the leader is encouraged to draw on the teachings of Joe Luft and Harry Ingham on communication and the teachings of Stephen Covey on habits that lead one from dependence through independence to a level of interdependence. This stage also requires a self-assessment of one's own personal system including the values that shape the individual's unique approach to leadership.

2. The second stage includes attention to a deeper level of communication labeled "dialogue" by David Bohm, a serious commitment to cooperation and behaviors congruent with the constructive thinking styles identified by Clay Lafferty in his Life Styles Inventory. At this level, the leader understands what it takes to be an achiever.

3. At the next level, the leader must practice transformational leadership. This dimension of leadership includes attention to releasing

human potential and high levels of interaction and alignment. A jazz ensemble is the metaphor for this level.

This model recognizes that something more than textbook leadership skills are required for competence to fully optimize an organization systemically. Learning from the *System of Profound Knowledge* by W. Edwards Deming and Peter Senge's *The Fifth Discipline,* leaders at this level must liberate their colleagues to go beyond the experience and knowledge base of any one talent source to be system thinkers and optimizers of a living system. This liberator level, described as the quintessential level for system optimization, includes servant-leadership as defined by Robert Greenleaf.

A set of core values, the systems approach, and servant-leadership have been key ingredients in the success of this process. Servant-leadership demonstrated by the CEO and other leaders has been the key source of energy and direction for this transformation.

Servant-leader characteristics observed include:

- Service to the customer is the keystone of the company's mission.
- Core values shape the culture and provide liberating support to associates.
- Value is placed on community service in the communities in which the corporation operates.
- The transformation is occurring in the context of a learning organization. Everyone is challenged to stretch toward their individual potential.
- Value is placed on the initiatives of associates to continuously improve the system.
- Emphasis is placed on teamwork and alignment. Leaders are reminded that the flight pattern of geese reduces the burden of their long range flights by 70 percent.
- From the CEO throughout the organization, importance is placed on walking the talk.

Servant-leadership is no longer manifest only in random acts. It appears in the experience of many in conscious, thoughtful, intentional "interventions." The essays in this book and others encouraged by The Greenleaf Center provide a continuing opportunity to reflect on the meaning and implication of these interventions.

Heavy Duty Change Requires Tough Caring

This essay focuses on the pragmatic implications of servant-leadership from the perspective of the for-profit business "institution." In the preceding experiences cited, we have underscored the leverage that servant-leadership makes possible. When leaders exercise their roles as servants and expand opportunities for people, win-win things happen:

- People stretch toward their potential and become more valuable assets.
- With more autonomy, they use their freedom to work smarter.
- They are encouraged to share in the recognition that shared loaves and fishes often multiply.
- Collaboration is encouraged, which becomes the opportunity for synergy.
- With all of the above, the cycle time for problem solving is reduced.
- Organization systems function more optimally.
- Services are rendered with greater value-added benefits for the customers.
- Better health is likely, which has an economic as well as humanitarian value.

From my work with the Connecticut, Texas, and Ohio chief executive officers, I have observed that it is not as easy to make this happen as some of us make it sound. The effort to achieve a win-win-win balance of interests among shareholders, customers, and employees rarely results in applause from each of these groups on the same issues.

When a plant or business is no longer competitive and profitable, the accountable servant-leader of the shareholders must take decisive action to eliminate that loss or insufficient profit contributor. Even when there is a fair and just process for pruning the non-fruit-bearing limb, those whose jobs and futures are impacted by such an initiative find it hard to see their interests served.

If a leader has pulled out all the stops to help someone stretch and grow to the potential needed for the required performance of a job, and that person cannot rise to that challenge, what must be done? Of course, within such decision making there is room for experimentation to help the individual close the gap between present and required performance. When these efforts have failed to accomplish that gap closing, however, a change in job or the person for the job may be required. The person who must change may find it hard to see the servant in the leader who calls for that change.

Words like *empowerment* and *teamwork* sound motivating. Those who would like greater autonomy and a family-type environment in which to work may have a view of what these words and concepts mean that is quite different from the view of their supervisors. At the point of implementing empowerment and teamwork, there may be a conflict of translation between the supervisor and the supervised. There may be constraints, requirements, and challenges in the job from the supervisor's point of view that were not anticipated by the supervised. The supervised may find it hard to see the servant-leader in the supervisor who has just poured cold water on their work expectations.

In situations such as the preceding, there is always the possibility that power is misused, that paternalism is present, or that the brand of servant-leadership practiced is a cosmetic cover for manipulation. For our purpose in this essay, however, let us make the assumption that the preceding examples are free of such distortions. Let us assume that the leaders in each of the three examples are genuine servant-leaders who must practice tough caring in the accountable fulfillment of their own jobs.

Who decides in such situations what is servant-leadership and what is bottom-line management? What help is there for those who must make those tough decisions? Where is the support group for those who attempt to make servant-leadership work in the competitive environment of present day corporate life? Servant-leadership as Robert Greenleaf spoke and wrote about it provides a significant fulcrum for leverage in many kinds of institutions.

28

Finding Your Voice

James M. Kouzes

James M. Kouzes is chairman of TPG/Learning Systems, a company in The Tom Peters Group. He has been conducting leadership development programs for corporations and nonprofit organizations since 1969. With Barry Z. Posner he has coauthored two best-selling books: The Leadership Challenge *and* Credibility: How Leaders Gain and Lose It, Why People Demand It.

In this essay, Kouzes reflects on the nature of leadership and addresses the question of whether leadership is something that can be learned. He compares leadership to art in describing three phases of the evolving leader as moving from the exterior, to the interior, and finally to the emergence of one's own unique voice as a leader.

One of the most persistent myths in our culture associates leadership with rank. But leadership isn't a position; it's a process.[1] It's an observable, understandable, learnable set of skills and practices available to everyone, anywhere in the organization.

I was making that case to a group of senior managers at a recent seminar when a hand shot up across the room. "I'd like to challenge that statement," said one participant. "I've been pondering this lately. Can anyone really learn to lead? If so, why do we seem to lack effective leadership these days?"

"Fair enough," I answered. "But let me respond by first asking you something: Can management be learned?"

"Yes," was the unanimous response from the group.

"Interesting, isn't it," I continued. "I've been asked in almost every seminar or workshop if leadership can be learned, but I've never been asked if management can be learned. Never!" I was screaming by this point.

That Special Leadership Something

Now why is that? What is it about management that allows us to assume that it can be learned, and what is it about leadership that constantly raises questions about our capacity to learn it? What is it about the concept of leadership that brings forth this question? Tell me, what is that unique something about leadership? What is the something else about leadership that can't be learned?

Here are a few representative responses to these questions from the workshop participants:

"Soul."

"Spirit."

"It's inside yourself."

"Managers do things right, leaders do the right things."

"Ethics."

"Value system."

Is there anything on this list that you cannot learn? Maybe some of these things can't be taught, but can you learn them? You may or may not agree with what others said, but think about it for a moment. Soul? Spirit? Ethics? Values? Can you learn your soul? Can you learn your spirit? Can you learn what is right? Can you learn what you hope the future to be? Can you learn what gives you passion? Not for everyone. Not for society. But for you?

I bet you can. But you won't find the answer in a workshop or a book, including the ones I've written. But you will, if you search, find your truth.

In his witty new book, *Management of the Absurd,* psychologist and CEO Richard Farson writes:

> In both parenthood and management, it's not so much what we do as what we are that counts. What parents do deliberately appears to make little difference in the most important outcomes—whether their children grow up to be happy or unhappy, successful or unsuccessful, good or evil. There is no question that parents can and should do worthwhile things for their children, but it's what they are that will really matter . . .
>
> The same dynamic occurs in management and leadership. People learn—and respond to—what we are.[2]

Farson has nailed it. All the techniques and all the tools that fill the pages of all the management and leadership books are not substitutes for who and what you are. In fact, they boomerang if thrown by some spinmeister who's mastered form but not substance.

My colleague Barry Posner and I have been collaborating on leadership research for nearly 15 years, and we keep learning the same thing over and over and over. We keep rediscovering that *credibility is the foundation of leadership*. It's been reinforced so often that we've come to refer to it as the "First Law of Leadership": People won't believe the message if they don't believe in the messenger. People don't follow your technique. They follow you—your message and your embodiment of that message.

In *Leadership Jazz,* Max DePree, former chairman and CEO of the Michigan furniture maker Herman Miller, tells a moving story about tending his prematurely born granddaughter during the first days of her fragile life. The nurse had advised DePree and his wife to touch as well as talk to the tiny infant, "because she has to be able to connect your voice to your touch." That message, says DePree, is "at the core of becoming a leader."[3]

Leadership credibility is about connecting voice and touch, about practicing what you preach, about doing what you say you will do. But as DePree makes quite clear, there's a prior task to connecting voice and touch. It's "finding one's voice in the first place."[4]

Soul Searching

Finding your voice is critical if you are to be an authentic leader. If you do not, you may find yourself with a vocabulary that belongs to someone else, mouthing words that were written by a speech writer who is nothing like you at all. If you doubt the importance of choosing your own vocabulary, consider these phrases from the speech by a banking manager we observed during the course of our research:

- "You've got to watch out for the headhunters."
- "Keep your capital, and keep it dry."
- "We'll act like SWAT teams."
- "We're going to beat their brains out."
- "We won't tolerate the building of fiefdoms."
- "There will be only a few survivors."

Contrast them with these phrases from The Body Shop founder, Anita Roddick:

- We communicate with passion—and passion persuades.
- I think all businesses practices would improve immeasurably if they were guided by 'feminine' principles, qualities like love and care and intuition.
- What we need is optimism, humanism, enthusiasm, intuition, curiosity, love, humour, magic, fun, and that secret ingredient euphoria.
- I believe that service whether it is serving the community or your family or the people you love or whatever, is fundamental to what life is about.[5]

What do these words communicate about the individuals speaking them—about their guiding beliefs and assumptions? Would any of these words be in your lexicon? Would you want them used in your organization?

Every artist knows that finding a voice is most definitely not a matter of technique. It's a matter of time and a matter of searching—soul searching.

I remember several years back attending a retrospective of painter Richard Diebenkorn's work with my wife and an artist friend. Toward the end of our gallery walk, our friend turned to us and made this observation: "There are really three periods in an artist's life. In the first we paint exterior landscapes. In the second, we paint interior landscapes. In the third they come together into an artist's unique style. In the third period we paint ourselves." I consider this the most important art appreciation lesson I've ever received. It applies just as well to the appreciation of the art of leadership.

When first learning to lead, we paint what we see outside ourselves, the exterior landscape. We read biographies and autobiographies of famous leaders, we read books by experienced executives and dedicated scholars, we attend speeches by famous military men, we buy tapes by motivational speakers, and we participate in training programs. We learn from others. We try things out.

We do all this to master the fundamentals, the tools, and the techniques. We're clumsy at first, failing more than succeeding, but pretty soon we can give a speech with ease, conduct a meeting with grace, and praise an employee with style. It's an essential period; an aspiring leader can no more skip the fundamentals than can an aspiring painter.

Then it happens. Somewhere along the way we notice how that last speech sounded mechanically rote, how that last meeting was a boring routine, and how that last encounter felt terribly sad and empty. We awaken to the frightening thought that the words aren't ours, that the technique is out of a text, not straight from the heart.

This is a truly terrifying moment. We've invested so much time and energy in learning to do all the right things, and we suddenly see that they are no longer serving us well. They seem hollow. We stare into the darkness of our inner territory, and we begin to wonder what lies inside.

For aspiring leaders, this awakening initiates a period of intense exploration. A period of going beyond technique, beyond training, beyond copying what the masters do, beyond taking the advice of others. And if you surrender to it, after exhausting experimentation and often painful suffering there emerges from all those abstract strokes on the canvas an expression of self that is truly your own.

So I'll have to amend what I said to the workshop participants a few weeks back. Yes, you can learn to lead, but don't confuse leadership with position and place. Don't confuse leadership with skills and systems. And don't confuse leadership with tools and techniques. They are not what earn you the respect and commitment of your constituents. What earns you their respect in the end is whether you are you. So just who are you, anyway?

29

The Inside-Out Proposition: Finding (and Keeping) Our Balance in Contemporary Organizations

Jeffrey N. McCollum

Jeffrey N. McCollum is director of organization development for Warner Lambert Consumer Healthcare, a global marketer and manufacturer of over-the-counter health products. He previously spent 25 years with AT&T, where he held executive positions in human resources, marketing, and sales. McCollum, who was a contributing author to Reflections on Leadership, *is a Greenleaf Center board trustee.*

In this essay, McCollum investigates how individuals and organizations can help to create a balance both within the workplace and between work and other areas of our lives. He makes the assertion that balance is something we must claim for ourselves. McCollum makes a major contribution to servant-leaders through his profiling of competency modeling, mentoring, communication, selection, reading-and-dialogue groups, and formal development programs as a means to growing in servant-leadership.

M ost of our lives are mitigated by institutions—the ones we work in, the ones we deal with, the ones that serve us, and the ones that don't. As one who works in a large organization and consults to others, I have experienced a common lament from members of contemporary organizations irrespective of whether they are for-profit or nonprofit organizations. It goes something like this, "I need/want/don't have balance in my life!"

This lament has found its way into the popular comic strip "Dilbert," perhaps the most widely quoted (and insightful) authority on the pathologies of organizational life in the 1990s. One strip begins with an employee complaining to her boss, "I can't keep working these long hours . . . I deserve a family life." To this the boss responds, "Alice! Alice! Alice! This isn't the 'me' generation of the 80s. This is the 'lifeless 90s.' I expect 178 hours of work from you each week." When Alice counters that a week only has 168 hours, the boss comments, "I expect your family to chip in a few hours."

Two things strike me about this strip. First, it resonates with what many people are experiencing in their organizations today. Second, it points the finger at management and ignores the question of whether or how the employee has colluded in the situation. When things are out of balance in our organizational life, where do we look? Whom do we blame? As members of an organization, how can we create balance for ourselves? As leaders, how can we help others find it for themselves?

Balance is an issue simply because so much more is being expected of us in an era of rising consumer expectations, rapid sociological and technical change, and global competitive forces. The rate of change is accelerating. At home and school, our children face choices and dilemmas that were not even on the scope when we were their age. At home and work, the amount of information available to us exceeds what we can absorb. The technologies available to us exceed our ability to understand and manage them. We have to increase our personal and organizational resources to cope with what's around us.

The first issue of balance is between the demands we face and the resources at our disposal in facing them. My thinking about balance rests on one fundamental assumption: *Balance is something that each individual must claim for himself or herself.* It cannot be given by the organization or the manager. What we, as leaders and managers, can do is claim balance for ourselves and create conditions that support others in staking their own claim to balance by helping them develop personal resources. In thinking about balance in our organization's lives, four questions come to mind:

1. What can I do, as an individual, to build my own resources?
2. What can I do, as an individual, to create opportunities to use my unique gifts?
3. What can I do, as a leader, to provide resources to help others learn to adapt to their demands?
4. What can I do, as a leader, to create systems, procedures, and organizational practices that draw out the potential and talents of those around me?

The answers to each of these questions can help create work organizations that are in balance. *Balance* has several dimensions that will be woven into my response to the four questions that I have posed. These dimensions of balance include balancing: our thoughts and feelings with our actions, objectivity with subjectivity, action with reflection, mind with soul, natural with synthetic, listening with advocacy, leadership with followership, and challenges with skills.

What Can I Do as an Individual
to Build My Own Resources?

Max DePree has described leadership as "serious meddling in other peoples' lives."[1] If we are going to seriously meddle, we should do so with a conscious and specific intent to serve. This idea of conscious intent is also embedded in one of Robert Greenleaf's most frequently cited observations on leadership:

> The servant-leader is servant first. . . . It begins with a natural feeling
> that one wants to serve, to serve first. Then conscious choice brings one
> to aspire to lead.[2]

As revealed in Greenleaf's words, becoming a servant-leader entails a process of learning to balance our thoughts, feelings, and values with our actions. The act of seeking this balance, which requires self-awareness, courage, and independence, is the crucible in which servant-leadership forms. When we find the balance, our ability to lead will be profoundly increased by what we, as leaders, model for those we seek to influence.

Embedded in this thought is the notion of continual learning through attention to our inner life. Paying attention to our feelings and trusting our intuition is the starting point, followed by a conscious decision to act on those feelings and intentions. When we are aware of our choices and are willing to act in the face of uncertain approval, we are leading—"going ahead and showing the way" in Greenleaf's terms. Making this choice demands what is described as strength by Greenleaf[3] and as courage by Peter Block.[4]

Leadership balances what's inside of us (our desire for meaning and purpose, our values and our aspirations) with what shows up on the outside—our actions. When our actions are balanced and in alignment with our thoughts and values, we are acting authentically. When we have learned to be authentic, we have increased our personal resources to lead and to manage change.

Poet David Whyte, who frequently consults to business, describes this process of inside-out influence as balancing our "soul" side with our "strategic" side. In his view, the soul is the seat of creativity, insight, playfulness, and spontaneity.[5] Greenleaf sees the soul as important to the choice of right aim for our actions. "What is *right* (Greenleaf's emphasis) for a particular individual in a particular situation? To some extent, it will be the fruit of a creative act. It is something that fits the occasion as nothing that has ever been codified would fit."[6] This indicates the need to rely on intuition as much as logical problem solving. It requires an awareness and understanding of our inner life.

Thomas Moore describes the reconciliation of our inner and outer lives as enchantment. "Spiritual values," he writes, "and a willingness to live a full life together create passion and vision. But, for some reason, we have kept passion and principle divided."[7] When we are leading lives rooted in personal passion and personal vision, concerns about balance tend to diminish. Therefore, it seems probable that the cry for balance is a lament for spiritual values and passion found missing in our work.

When we tap into the wellspring of personal passion, our work becomes inner-directed rather than outer-directed. When we are inner-directed versus outer-directed, we are at our most powerful and, as a consequence, more capable of staking our claim to balance.

Balance starts by building my own resources, which I do when:

1. I pay attention to my own spiritual life.
2. I reconcile my inner life with my outer life and seek to recover enchantment.
3. I am clear about what's important to me and use that as a basis for action.
4. I pay attention to my "soul" side as well as my "strategic" side by deepening my spiritual, emotional, and intellectual capacities.

Finding balance is an inside-out proposition. When I am paying attention to what's important to me, I increase the probability that I can discern what's important to those I lead or, failing that, can help them discover it for themselves. I must be doing my inner work to help others do their own work. When I know what's important to me and what's unique about me, I can turn my attention to finding outlets for my own giftedness.

What Can I Do, as an Individual, to Create Opportunities to Use My Unique Gifts?

It is estimated that, in any given situation, the human being is able to take in only about 15 percent of the data that are available. This fact sheds light on why personal vision is a powerful source of action in our personal repertoire. When I do the inner work discussed in the last section, I arm my perception with what biologists call a search image. When I am clear about what it is I seek to create and claim for myself, possibilities will present themselves.

I experienced this on a physical level during a recent trip to Montana. As part of a geology class, we visited a site known to gush with fossilized oysters, gryphaea, dating to the Jurassic period. We walked to the site through loose, granular gravel—or so I thought. Once I had been given a search image by being shown what the gryphaea looked like, I realized that the gravel underfoot was exactly what I was seeking. I didn't see them because I didn't know what I was looking for. It got me to thinking about the number of times that I had experienced events and circumstances as gravel underfoot rather than as opportunities to serve.

This experience serves as a metaphor for my quest for servant-leadership. I cannot escape the realization that opportunities to live from my personal vision abound in everyday life. In each moment, I face two choices: I can choose to cope with the gravel underfoot, or I can choose to find opportunities to serve. Choosing to see the rising demands of the environment in which we lead as an opportunity to create draws on the soul's desire. When I draw on that part of me, I can find and keep my balance.

The power of finding opportunities to serve in difficult circumstances emerges from Victor Frankl's wonderful book, *Man's Search for Meaning,* which documents Frankl's experience in a Nazi concentration camp during the Holocaust. I cannot imagine a set of circumstances where more human dignity and freedom were stripped away than in those camps. As a prisoner in the camps, Frankl observed that those who were confined seemed to take one of two approaches. Some put their energy and focus on surviving. Others found a way to put energy and focus to serving those who were confined with them. It was the latter group that survived while the former perished. The conclusion I draw is that, on the physical level as well as the spiritual, our viability hangs in the balance between service and self-interest.

This seems to be something that Greenleaf understood as well.

> The choices any of us can make, no matter how intolerable our lot, is to use what freedom and resources we possess to make others' lives more significant.[8]

I have seen this same choice played out in a contemporary organizational setting. A division president at AT&T, Ken Bertaccini, contracted a rare form of cancer. Faced with the disease, he chose to be a model to others and to devote much of his personal time counseling those in his organization who were dealing with the impact of cancer on their families. He did this without diminishing focus on his professional performance. In the context of leading an organization through a turbulent period of change, he found ways to make others lives more significant. He balanced service to others with his obligation to his organization.

In retirement, Ken continues his work by leading an organization that supports cancer victims. Avocation and vocation—in the sense of something calling us out—have merged.

Some answers present themselves to the question posed at the head of this section. I can create opportunities to use my unique gifts by:

1. Recognizing that I am unique and believing that I have something to offer.
2. Being clear about what's important to me.
3. Acting on the belief that every set of circumstances presents opportunities for choosing actions based on what's meaningful and important to me and by putting service ahead of self-interest.

4. Answering my soul's call.
5. Choosing to act, in this moment, from my values and ideals rather than from concerns for safety and security.
6. Asking myself, as a test in any set of circumstances, "How can I help?"

Our choices are crucial. Annie Dillard says, "How we spend our days is, of course, how we spend our lives. . . . There is no shortage of good days. It is good lives that are hard to come by."[9] Good lives, it can be argued, come from choosing service.

Dillard, as a writer, knows the creative process. She talks about how her gifts flow best when she has been exerting herself physically out of doors, which suggests another form of inside-out balance—balance between what we do indoors, like managing, meeting, writing, and reading, and what we do outdoors. Thomas Moore, too, relates being outdoors to discovering our soul.

> In nature, we become sensitive to our mortality and to the immensity of the life that is our matrix, and both of these sensations, mortality and immensity, offer the foundations for a spiritual life. . . . If we can allow ourselves to be stunned by nature's beauty, complexity and simplicity, devastating power, vast dimensions, and unexpected quirkiness, then lessons in spirituality will pour into us without effort on our part.[10]

Opportunities to use my unique gifts seem to begin with an understanding and valuing of my spirituality. There seems to be an ineffable connection between nature, moral development, and leadership. I cannot quite put words to it but the connection seems to work something like this. Nature reminds me of my place in the scheme of things. Knowing that, I learn that, in many ways, I am powerless. Learning that, I can approach the task of managing differently. Places of enormous natural beauty are places of inspiration, wonder, and reflection for me. I leave them with a peace that was absent when I entered them—a peace that helps me keep things in better perspective.

When I have things in perspective, my resilience increases and I am more effective as a leader and as a person.

What Can I Do, as a Leader, to Provide Resources to Help Others Learn to Adapt to Their Demands?

As discussed earlier, the level of demands placed on each of us is growing at an increasing rate. This demands that we grow and develop and help others do the same in the spirit of Greenleaf's oft-quoted "test" of leadership.

> The best test of a leader, and difficult to administer, [is] do those served grow as persons; do they, while being served, become healthier, wiser, freer, more autonomous, more likely themselves to become servants?[11]

According to Mihaly Csikszentmihalyi, optimum performance, what he calls "flow," results from a balance between the challenge that we face and the preparation, in the sense of skills and abilities, that we have for the challenge. Flow is a condition of maximum psychological involvement characterized by intense concentration and the loss of a sense of time. I can't imagine someone in flow worried about balance.[12]

The consequences of an imbalance between challenge and skills are significant organizationally and personally. According to Csikszentmihalyi, when the challenges overwhelm the skills, the individual performer is likely to suffer from anxiety and depression. When the skills are overmatched to the challenges, the consequences are boredom and low involvement.

As leaders, we have a responsibility to support our organization's goals and aims. As servant-leaders, we have a responsibility to support our colleagues in the development of the skills that are necessary for them to meet the challenges of the organization and for the organization to meet the challenges of its environment.

As the basis for organizational success shifts from financial to human resources, from capital to imagination, it's hard to imagine a successful organization peopled with an anxious, depressed, or bored workforce. As leaders, we must insist that people do their own work and that they develop the skills and abilities to deal with what they face.

Ronald Heifetz talks about this requirement of leadership in terms of the distinction between "developmental" and "technical" problems.[13] Developmental problems are ones that require learning and adaptation. Technical problems are those that have clear, definitive answers. I find this distinction useful in understanding the difference between bureaucratic "command and control" leadership and the developmental focus of servant-leadership.

Clearly, the heart of servant-leadership, as reflected in Greenleaf's test, is development. Do those led grow freer, more autonomous? Do they become more effective followers and do they develop the potential to exercise leadership in their own lives and in their organizations?

One way that we can provide resources to others is by refusing to rescue them from the difficulty of learning and growing. The bureaucratic form of management, which evolved during the Industrial Age, is based on the belief that it is management's responsibility to do most (if not all) of the thinking in our organizations and that the worker's role is to follow orders. This has institutionalized a parent-child relationship between worker and manager. Coupled with a reductionist view of job design (every job is broken down into small and discrete repetitive actions requiring little thought) and a growth in central staffs that reduced the worker's range of decision making even further, the "machine bureaucracy" breeds boredom and disaffection as unintended consequences of the industrialization of work.

This disaffection was apparent in the 1960s and 1970s when Greenleaf did much of his writing. Many of the efforts over the past 25 years—suggestion programs, quality circles, total quality management, natural work teams, and self-directed teams—have as a common aim bringing the worker to full participation in his or her work.

As leaders, we don't allow people to grow and learn if we take over for them in difficult times. There is an element of self-awareness here. We must understand where the urge to take over comes from. If it is rooted in the parent-child assumptions of the machine bureaucracy, it requires that we reframe the role of leader.

We live in most interesting times. We are working in a time when concepts of organization and leadership are in full ferment. The assumptions that led to the success of the bureaucratic model are disintegrating. A collective effort is under way to redefine how work is done and how our organizations are led. Organization design seems to be coming from the outside-in rather than from the top-down. This requires the full participation—physical, emotional, and intellectual—of all people in our organizations. Where they are stepping up to the challenge, we, as leaders, must stay out of their way. Where they are not, we, as leaders, must get in their face and insist that they learn and develop their skills. At the same time, we must be ready to admit that we, as leaders, don't have the answers!

Peter Vaill contends that most of us in today's organizations face "process frontiers," which he describes as:

> a new area of activity for the organization or a substantial modification in the way something has been done heretofore. It is probably not a one-shot affair but a new and continuing activity. Process frontiers involve new attitudes, abilities, and actions. People are feeling their way even if they cannot quite admit it to themselves.[14]

This dishes up a dicey set of circumstances. People in our organization will be working on process frontiers with which we, as leaders, have no direct experience. If we don't have the answers, what is our role?

Vaill offers some suggestions:

> [T]he leader to be needs to learn what that life [on a process frontier] is like, what kind of learning is needed on a process frontier, what kinds of help organizational members need in order to engage in that learning, and what his or her own role can best be to facilitate that learning.[15]

On the assumption that all of us, leader and led, are now on a process frontier, some actions suggest themselves to the question of how we, as leaders, can provide the resources to help others grow and learn.

By balancing the interests of all the stakeholders in our institutions, we provide a powerful model for others' actions. All of our stakeholders want our organization to be successful. They just measure in different terms. In for-profit organizations, profit is a measure of the organization's health and a way to share its success with those who have invested in it. The employees of those organizations want some sense of continuing employment and a way to derive meaning and purpose from their work. Customers want to have the sense that our organizations produce quality products and will be there to deal with them if, and when, problems occur. The communities in which we operate want a sense of mutual obligation to improving each other's lot and a sense that we will not recklessly or selfishly extract resources from the environment. The leader must balance all of these interests by constantly looking for the common ground and avoiding serving one stakeholder at the expense of another.

To help others learn, grow and adapt, I can:

1. Understand the difference between technical and developmental problems in order to choose an appropriate approach.
2. Require that people do their own learning, which in turn requires that we confront their wish for us to parent them and our own longing for control.
3. Be a personal example who acknowledges that I am doing my own learning and admits that I do not have the answers.
4. Create a climate that is conducive to learning and that welcomes challenge and question and is compassionate toward those who are on a process frontier.
5. Remain nonjudgmental and do what we can to make learning fun and an open exploration.
6. Insist that actions, ours and others, balances the interests of customers, community, colleagues, and financial contributors.

Joseph Campbell's metaphor of the spirit guide, one who, like Leo in *The Journey to the East,* helps others find their own way through life's journey approaches the leader's role in a time of constant ferment and change. We provide resources by balancing our actions between our own interest and theirs and by balancing the interests of all the stakeholders in our institutions.

What Can I Do, as a Leader, to Create Systems, Procedures, and Practices That Draw Out the Potential and Talents of Those Around Me?

This final question brings us to the matter of structure. Organizations, just as any other organism, require structure, in the form of practices, norms, processes, and procedures, to function. Assuming that our organizations will face ever-increasing challenges and that a key role of leadership is to develop people whose capacity is matched to the challenge, what are some of the structural elements with which we can work?

Several come to mind: competency modeling, mentoring, communication, selection, reading and dialogue groups and formal development programs.

Competency Modeling

Competency modeling is an important place to start for two reasons. First, it is a formal approach that has become commonplace in the 1990s, which reflects the shifting source of organizational advantage. No longer does the access to capital determine organizational success. Now it is the access to imagination, creativity, and skills—human capital. The second reason is that building competence, not just technical competence but also human competence, is the work of the leader.

Thomas Teal, writing in *Harvard Business Review*, a journal rarely noted for its spiritual content, argues that "great management is about character, not technique." In language that resonates with Greenleaf, he contends that great management in action "magnifies the social core of human nature, brings individual talents to fruition, creates value and combines those activities with enough passion to generate the greatest possible advantages for every player."[16]

In his article, Teal states that technical competence is not enough to qualify one as a great, or even competent, manager. Howard Gardner, another contemporary scholar of leadership, decries the rise of technical experts in the form of consultants and staff specialists as a mitigating factor against the formation of community and a factor in elevating self-interest ahead of service.

> Concomitant with the increasing need for technical expertise is an attenuation of the specialists' bonds to the rest of society. . . . The sense of identity of contemporary experts is less frequently rooted in their community or the nation, let alone in the wider world; nor is it, as seems to have been the case a century ago, linked to a moral tinged calling such as the law, medicine, the academy, or the clergy. Particularly because experts are so mobile and the institutions for which they work are so fluid, their bonds are chiefly to the few individuals who know what they know and, equally, to themselves.[17]

Gardner, Teal, and Vaill all argue for developing leader competencies. Further, they argue, leader competence is based on character rather than technique and on learning to learn more than learning a fixed body of knowledge. If our organizations are going to be based on competence, we must insist on leadership that develops through a focus on learning and being, rather than on techniques, steps, cookbooks, habits, or tools. The key to being is self-awareness and opening ourselves to others.

Communication

We open ourselves in communication by sharing information that otherwise would remain hidden and by opening ourselves to input from those we lead. Teal cites a number of examples where leaders, seeking to change from command and control to participative systems, fully disclosed corporate financial information while making themselves fully available to their employees. Sometimes the price for this openness and access has been catcalls, taunts, and attacks. They persisted, and they communicated in a powerful way.

What these leaders communicated, through word and deed, was that they were willing to give up authority[18] in order for employees to take back their power. One of the cases Teal cites is Ralph Stayer of Johnsonville Sausage. According to Teal, Stayer had to learn how he held onto power in ways he was not aware of and how to suppress his own need for control.

If managers have to learn to give up control, employees have to learn about taking responsibility. Many employees, offered an opportunity to participate in new ways in exchange for responsibility and risk, demur. To get them to step up, according to Teal, is "a continual exercise in learning, education and persuasion."[19]

The distinction between coercion, manipulation, and persuasion was one that Greenleaf thought and wrote about. In thinking about organizational change, he writes:

> *Persuasion* involves arriving at a feeling of rightness about a belief or action through one's own intuitive sense . . . [and] on critical issues, is a difficult, time-consuming process. It demands one of the most exacting of human skills.[20]

What seems common to Greenleaf, Gardner, Vaill, and Teal is a clear-cut moral and ethical basis to persuasion that serves the feeling of rightness that separates persuasion from manipulation.

Mentoring

One form of persuasive communication is mentoring. Greenleaf once described George Wythe's house as the "place where Thomas Jefferson was born" because so much of what Jefferson was to become as an intellectual force stemmed from Wythe's example and Wythe's person.

With growing recognition of the importance of character to successful leadership, mentoring, in the sense of helping someone learn how to "be" rather than what to "do," is coming back into vogue. In the height of the Industrial Age, mentoring had a machine and parental quality to it. Mentors were frequently described as "pulling strings," "greasing skids," or "putting wheels into motion" on behalf of others. In fact, most organizational mentoring programs involve pairing a senior manager, chosen for his or her power position in the organization, with a junior manager. (In my experience at AT&T, having a "godfather" was widely understood to be more important than performance in moving ahead in the organization.)

What's emerging now has a decidedly more spiritual quality to it. Mentoring is what Robert Bly describes as a "vertical" process—one in which young members of a society learn how to "be" in that society.[21] Bly's thesis is that the breakdown of these vertical relationships has created a sibling society—one in which the members live out a perpetual adolescence. His observation explains why it's sometimes so difficult to get employees to accept more responsibility for the organization and themselves.

Given the rising and rapidly changing demands placed on us, mentoring might now also involve demonstrating how to learn on process frontiers. Beyond the confines of our organizations, mentoring has broad social implications that go to preserving civilization. The servant-leader can be a mentor to kids at risk and to others among the least-privileged in society.

Clearly, mentoring is about the use of personal example and not about the use of organizational power. Teal observes, "Great managers also bring forth other great managers." This is the essence of Greenleaf's famous "test." Jefferson, whom Greenleaf so admired, is an example. Having been mentored by Wythe, Jefferson became mentor to Meriwether Lewis, who coled the remarkable expedition that mapped the Louisiana Purchase and greatly advanced our scientific knowledge.

Teaching, learning, and persuading—by example—is a structure that builds resources in the organization.

Building Followership

The combination of building business literacy in our organizations, modeling the values and beliefs that we espouse, relinquishing authority to our employees in exchange for their responsibility in building our organizations and teaching and persuading creates what Robert Kelley has defined as *exemplary followership*.[22]

Kelley looks at followership along two continua. One runs from uncritical, dependent thinking to critical independent thinking. The other runs from passive engagement to active engagement. Those who are high on both scales are exemplary followers. Active engagement and independent critical thinking are the qualities that we will require in our organizations if we are to meet the growing demands posed by today's environment. People need to learn, and our organizations need to create systems that support both.

Selection

If we seek active engagement and critical independent thinking, we need to select for those qualities in our hiring and in our firing. Assessment centers, a concept that Greenleaf pioneered in AT&T, are generally regarded as the most effective way to select. They are coming into broader use as developmental tools. The behavioral event interview, although not as effective as assessment centers, is growing in use as a hiring tool and helping organizations base selection decisions on competencies.

The harder side of selection is firing. If we want active engagement and critical independent thinking in our organizations, we must insist on it, provide people with the tools to develop it, and, if they choose not to learn, we must ask them to leave.

Dialogue

One skill that builds critical and independent thinking, openness, and insight is dialogue. It is growing in popularity. Reading and dialogue groups have sprouted up in many organizations. Dialogue is difficult and, for many of us in organizations, counterintuitive. It is about discovery rather than problem solving. It is about insight as the source of action. It is based on the premise, "go slow in order to go fast"—a premise that confronts a world that seems rarely to have time for reflection but always time to do things twice. Dialogue requires that I reveal my logic and hold up my assumptions and beliefs, rather than my arguments, for public scrutiny. It can be uncomfortable. And it can be a crucible for learning.

Development

It is important to formalize "development" as part of an organization's culture and to formalize it as a shared responsibility between the individual colleague and the organization. Development, which can take many forms, starts with an awareness of what I don't know and what I don't do well. Feedback is the foundation of developmental efforts.

Once the performer is aware of where his or her developmental needs lie, it is up to the performer and supervisor to craft jointly a development plan that will build the missing capacity. These plans can include: formal training, on-the-job training, mentoring, assignment to new responsibilities, task force assignments and special projects. The idea is to create challenging jobs that focus on learning. Using the actual job design to enhance learning is more powerful than using formal training. There is no transference problem. Using actual job experiences as learning events builds the capability to handle developmental problems. Here the performer may need support, in the form of time or money, from the organization.

As leaders, we face three fundamental tasks: creating strategies to adapt our organization to its environment, building a structure that is capable of implementing our strategy, and building the capacity of the members of our organization.

In this section, I have looked at some of the structures that we as leaders can use to draw out the talents and capacity of those in the organization:

1. Building a competency-based strategy and organization
2. Creating open, two-way communication
3. Installing a mentoring program
4. Selecting exemplary followers
5. Firing those who choose not to be exemplary followers
6. Building dialogue into the organization's communications repertoire
7. Committing resources to development

Leadership, in the context of today's organization, is about communicating in words and actions what's important and building structures that support the growth and development of those employed by the organization.

Conclusion

The conditions of modern organizational life require a lot from its leaders and its members. Growing demands from a variety of stakeholders raise the pressure felt by organizational members who cry out for balance and, in many cases, look to their organization or their manager for the solution. Leadership is increasingly about balancing a set of demands coming from customers, community, colleagues, and financial contributors and about balancing internal organization capacity against the external environment.

Growing demands require that the organization do a better job of helping the individual develop the capacity to deal with an ever-increasing set of demands. This can be done when leaders at all levels set a powerful personal example by modeling the qualities sought in the organization and by creating structures that foster growth in organization members.

Balance is something that each member of the organization must claim for himself or herself. Successful organizations require exemplary followership characterized by individuals who are capable of independent critical thinking and who stay actively engaged in the business by contributing energy, innovation, and imagination.

Balance, if it is to be found and kept, starts inside out with a knowledge of what is personally important and what is right. Leaders whose lives are in balance create organizations in which others can find, for themselves, balance and meaning and success.

There is no magic—only the hard work of learning more about myself and improving how I use my knowledge, skills, and abilities in service to my organization and others.

30

What Is Our Work?

Margaret J. Wheatley

Margaret J. Wheatley is a writer, speaker, and teacher. She is the author of the best-selling book Leadership and the New Science *(1992), and coauthor with Myron Kellner-Rogers of* A Simpler Way *(1996). Meg Wheatley was a keynote speaker at The Greenleaf Center's 1995 conference. She lives in the mountains of Utah. Meg expresses her deep gratitude to her partner, Myron Kellner-Rogers, for his many insights that are woven throughout this essay and all her work.*

In this essay, Margaret Wheatley challenges each of us to proclaim the "new story" of organizational change throughout our culture. The old hierarchical, mechanistic model of organizations is fast disappearing and is being replaced by a model based on self-organizing systems, servant-leadership, and life itself. This new paradigm for the twenty-first century will lift up both spirit and creativity in our institutions.

I believe our work is changing. The world is calling us to share our knowledge about servant-leadership, even as the countervailing voices of domineering leadership grow louder. This call adds a new dimension to our work. Not only must we continue to explore the ideas and practice of servant-leaders, we now must become clarion voices, broadcasting our message to as many people as we can reach, moving into arenas we ignored or avoided.

I meet too many people who falter in expressing their voice because others have told them that their ideas about leaders, organizations, and people are crazy. It is time to change this definition of craziness. We, in fact, represent the new sanity—the ideas and values and practices that can create a future worth wanting. In our spirits and in our experience we hold a new story, and it is time to share it with everyone we meet.

Those who carry a new story and who risk speaking it abroad have played a crucial role in times of historic shifts. Before a new era can come into form, there must be a new story. The playwright Arthur Miller noted that we know an era has ended when its basic illusions have been exhausted. I would add that these basic illusions not only are exhausted but also have become exhausting. As they fail to produce the results we want, we just repeat them with greater desperation, plummeting ourselves into cynicism and despair as we lock into these cycles of failure.

The New Story's Role

I was introduced to the critical nature of the teller-of-new-stories role in reading the work of physicist and author Brian Swimme. Brian has spent the past several years developing a new story of the universe, based on his belief that creating a new cosmic story is the most important work of our times because it will usher in a new era of human and planetary health.[1]

Lest you believe that cosmic stories can only be told by physicists or theologians, Brian's idea of a cosmic story is one that answers such questions as: What's going on? Where did everything come from? Why are you doing what you do?

For me, it is important to label this as *story* because it helps call attention to the realization that all of our activities and beliefs spring from stories. Science tells a particular story, so do all religions. As individuals telling our stories to one another, we create an interpretation of our lives, their purpose and significance. And through shared stories, we see patterns emerge that unite our separating experiences into shared meanings.

I believe that you and I have an important theme to contribute to this new cosmic story. As students and believers in servant-leadership, we tell a story that is quite different from the dominant one of our times. I would like to contrast in some detail the new and the old stories. My hope is that in seeing the great polarities between these two, you will feel even more strongly called to give voice to the new.

For at least 300 years, Western culture has been developing the old story. I would characterize it as a story of dominion and control and all-encompassing materialism. This story began with a dream that it was within humankind's province to understand the workings of the universe and to gain complete mastery over physical matter. This dream embraced the image of the universe as a grand, clockwork machine. As with any machine, we would understand it by minute dissection, we would engineer it to do what we saw fit, and we would fix it through our engineering brilliance. This hypnotic image of powers beyond previous human imagination gradually was applied to everything we looked at: Our bodies were seen as the ultimate machines; our organizations had all the parts and specifications to ensure well-oiled performance; and in science, where it had all begun, many scientists confused metaphor with reality and believed life *was* a machine.

This dream still has immense hypnotic power over us. For every problem, we quickly leap to technical solutions, even if technology is the cause of the initial problem. Science will still save us, no matter the earthly mess we've created. In our bodies, we long to believe the promises of genetic engineering. Our greatest ills, perhaps even death, will vanish once we identify the troubling gene. We need only invest more in technology to yield unsurpassed benefits in health and longevity, and all because we are such smart engineers of the human body.

In most of our endeavors—in science, health, organizational management, self-help—the focus is on creating better functioning machines. We replace the faulty part, reengineer the organization, install a new behavior or attitude, create a better fit, recharge our batteries. The language and thinking is all machines. And we give this image such hegemony over our lives because it seems our only hope for combatting life's cyclical nature, our only hope of escape from life's incessant demands for creation and destruction.

When we created this story of complete dominion over matter, we also brought in control's unwelcome partner, fear. Once we are intent on controlling something, we can only interpret its resistance to our control as fearsome. Since nothing is as controllable as we hope, we soon become entangled in a cycle of exerting control, failing to control, exerting harsher control, failing again. The fear that arises from this cycle is notable in many of us, especially in our leaders. Things aren't working as they had hoped, but none of us knows of any other way to proceed. The world becomes scarier and scarier as we realize the depths of our ignorance and confront our true powerlessness. It is from this place, from an acknowledgment of our ignorance and lack of power, that the call goes out for a new story.

But the old story has some further dimensions worth noticing. This story has had a particularly pernicious effect on how we think about one another and how we approach the task of organizing any human endeavor.

When we conceived of ourselves as machines, we gave up most of what is essential to being human. We created ourselves devoid of spirit, will, passion, compassion, even intelligence. Machines have none of these characteristics innately, and none of them can be built into its specifications. The imagery is so foreign to what we know and feel to be true about ourselves that it seems strange that we ever adopted this as an accurate description of being human. But we did, and we do. A colleague of mine, as he was about to work with a group of oil company engineers, was warned that they had "heads of cement." He cheerfully remarked that it didn't matter, because they all had hearts, didn't they? "Well," they replied, "we call it a pump."

The engineering image we carry of ourselves has led to organizational lives together where we believe we can ignore the deep realities of human existence. We can ignore that people carry spiritual questions and quests into their work; we can ignore that people need love and acknowledgment; we can pretend that emotions are not part of our work lives; we can pretend we don't have families, or health crises, or deep worries. In essence, we take the complexity of human life and organize it away. It is not part of the story we want to believe. We want a story of simple dimensions: People can be viewed as machines and controlled to perform with the same efficiency and predictability.

It is important to recognize that in our experience, people *never* behave like machines. When given directions, we insist on putting our unique spin on them. When told to follow orders, we resist in obvious or subtle ways. When told to accept someone else's solution, or to institute a program created elsewhere, we deny that it has sufficient value.

As leaders, when we meet with such nonmechanical responses, we've had two different options. We could criticize our own leadership, or we could blame our followers. If we the leader were the problem, perhaps we had poor communication skills; perhaps we weren't visionary enough; maybe we'd chosen the wrong sales technique. If our people were the problem, they lacked motivation, or a clear sense of responsibility, or it could be that this time we'd just been cursed with an obstinate and rebellious group. With so much blame looking for targets, we haven't taken time to stop and question our basic beliefs about each other. Are expectations of machinelike obedience and regularity even appropriate when working together?

Trying to be an effective leader in this machine story is especially exhausting. He or she (but in this story it's primarily he) is leading a group of lifeless, empty automatons who are just waiting to be filled with vision and direction and intelligence. The leader is responsible for providing everything: the organizational mission and values, the organizational structure, the plans, the supervision. The leader must also figure out, through clever use of incentives or coercives, how to pump energy into this lifeless mass. Once the pump is primed, he or she must then rush hither and yon to make sure that everyone is clanking along in the same direction, at the established speed, with no diversions. It is the role of the leader to provide the organizing energy for a system that is believed to have no internal capacities for self-creation, self-organization, or self-correction.

As I reflect on the awful demands placed on leaders by the old story, I wonder how anyone could survive in that job. Yet the mechanistic story has created roles for all of us that are equally deadly. It has led us to believe that we, with our unpredictable behaviors, our passions, our independence, our creativity, our consciousness—that we are the problem rather than the blessing. While the rest of nature follows obediently in the great mechanistic parade of progress, we humans show up as rebellious and untrustworthy. Our problematic natures are the very reason we need to create organizations as we do. How else could we structure such recalcitrance into vehicles of efficient production?

In this story, such key human traits as uniqueness, free will, and creativity pose enormous problems. Machines are built to do repetitive functions that require no thought and minimal adjustment. Conformity and compliance are part of the expectations of this story. Creativity is unwanted, because it is always surprising and therefore uncontrollable. If we tolerate creative expressions, we find ourselves with unmanageable levels of diversity. A machine world is willing to sacrifice exploration for prediction. Guaranteed levels of performance are preferable to surprising breakthroughs. In our machine-organizations, we try to extinguish individuality in order to reach our goal of certainty. We trade uniqueness for control and barter our humanness for petty performance measures.

It is one of the great ironies of our age that we created organizations to constrain our problematic human natures, and now the only thing that can save these organizations is a full appreciation of the expansive capacities of us humans.

The New Story as a Tale of Life

So it is time for the new story. Our old one, with its alienating myths, is eating away at us from the inside, rotting from its core. Fewer of us can tell it with any conviction. Many more of us are beginning to understand that our experience and our beliefs tell a story that celebrates life rather than denying it. We can see these in the pronounced increase in conversations and writings about destiny, purpose, soul, spirit, love, legacy, courage, integrity, meaning. The new story is being born in these conversations. We are learning to give voice to a different and fuller sense of who we really are.

I would like to characterize the new story as a tale of life. Setting aside our machine glasses, we observe a world that exhibits life's ebullient creativity and life's great need for other life. We observe a world where creative self-expression and embracing systems of relationships are the organizing energies, where there is no such thing as a separate individual, and no need for a leader to do it all.

As I develop some of the major themes of this new story of life, I will be drawing on the work of modern science. However, I know that science is only lending its voice to a story that in fact is very ancient. We can find this story in early primal wisdom traditions, in modern indigenous tribes, in most spiritual thought, and in poets old and new. It is a story that has never been forgotten by any of us and that has been held for us continually by many peoples and cultures. Yet for those of us emerging from our exhaustion with the old mechanistic tale, it feels new. And it certainly opens us to new discoveries about who we are as people, as organizations, and as leaders.

For me, one of the most wonderful contrasts of the old and new stories came from thinking about a passage I read in Kevin Kelly's book, *Out of Control*. As he reached for language to describe life, he moved into sheer exuberance. (I always pay attention when a scientist uses poetry or exuberant language—I know that something has touched him or her at a level of awareness that I don't want to ignore.) Kelly was trying to describe the ceaseless creativity that characterizes life. He said that life gives to itself this great freedom, the freedom to become. Then he asked, "Becoming what?" and went on to answer:

> Becoming becoming. Life is on its way to further complications, further deepness and mystery, further processes of becoming and change. Life is circles of becoming, an autocatalytic set, inflaming itself with its own sparks, breeding upon itself more life and more wildness and more "be-

comingness." Life has no conditions, no moments that are not instantly becoming something more than life itself.[2]

Kelly's passionate descriptions of processes that inflame, breed more life and wildness, create more deepness and mystery, stand in stark contrast to the expectations we have held for one another. I like to contemplate Kelly's description of life with the lives we describe when we design an organizational chart. The contrast between the two is both funny and sobering. Could we even begin to tolerate such levels of passion and creativity in our organizations? But can we survive without them?

In the 1960s, the great American poet A. R. Ammons told the same story in different and precise language:

Don't establish the
    boundaries
    first
    the squares, triangles,
    boxes
    of preconceived
    possibility,
    and then
    pour
    life into them, trimming
off left-over edges,
ending potential:
    let centers
    proliferate
    from
self-justifying motions![3]

In both recent science and poetry we are remembering a story about life that has creativity and connectedness as its essential themes. As we use this new story to look into our organizational lives, it offers us images of organizations and leaders that are both startling and enticing. It offers us ways of being together where our diversity—our uniqueness—is essential and revered. It offers us an arena big enough to embrace the full expression of our infinitely creative human natures. And for the first time in a long time, it offers us the recognition that we humans are, in the words of physicist Ilya Prigogine, "the most striking realization of the laws of nature."[4] We can use ourselves and what we know about ourselves to understand the universe. By observing with new eyes the processes of creation in us, we can understand the forces that create galaxies, move continents, and give birth to stars. No longer intent on describing ourselves as the machines we thought the universe to be, we are encouraged now to describe the universe through the life we know we are.

As we look at life through the lens of human nature and human desire, we are presented with some wonderful realizations. Our own desire for autonomy and creativity is reflected in all life. Life appears as boundlessly creative, searching for new possibilities and new capacities wherever it can. Observing the diversity of life forms has become a humbling experience for many biologists. At this point, no one knows how many different species there are, or where the next forms of life will appear, except that now we even expect them to appear elsewhere in our solar system.

Life is born from this unquenchable need to be. One of the most interesting definitions of life in modern biology is that something is considered alive if it has the capacity to create itself. The term for this is *autopoiesis*—self-creation—from the same root as poetry. At the very heart of our ideas about life is this definition, that life begins from the desire to create something original, to bring a new being into form.

As I have read about and observed more consciously the incredible diversity of life, I have felt witness to a level of creativity that has little to do with the survival struggles that we thought explained everything. Newness appears not for simple utilitarian purposes, but just because it is possible to be inventive. Life gives to itself the freedom to become, as Kevin Kelly noted, because life is about discovering new possibilities, new forms of expression. Two Chilean biologists, Francisco Varela and Humberto Maturana, observe that life responds not to "survival of the fittest," but to the greater space of experimentation of "survival of the fit."[5] Many designs, many adaptations are possible, and organisms enjoy far more freedom to experiment than we humans, with our insane demand to "Get it right the first time."

The freedom to experiment, to tinker oneself into a form of being that can live and reproduce, leads to diversity that has no bounds. In my own telling of a new cosmic story, I believe that the great forces of creation are focused on exploring newness, that newness is a primary value embraced by all life, a primary force that encourages life into new discoveries. The need and ability to create one's self is a force we see quite clearly in human experience, but which we have greatly misunderstood in our organizations.

The second great force I would like to add to this new story is that life needs to link with other life, to form systems of relationships where all individuals are better supported by the system they have created. It is impossible to look into the natural world and find an individual. As an African proverb states: "Alone, I have seen many marvelous things, none of which were true." Biologist Lynn Margulis expresses a similar realization when she comments that independence is not a biological concept, it is a political concept.[6] Everywhere we look, we see complex, tangled, messy webs of relationships. From these relationships, life creates systems that offer greater stability and support than life lived alone. Organisms shape themselves in response to their neighbors and their environments. All respond to one another, co-evolving and cocreating the complex systems of organization that we see in nature. Life is systems-seeking. It seeks organization. Organization is a naturally occurring phenomenon. Self-organization is a powerful force that creates the systems we observe and that testifies to a world that knows how to organize from the inside out.

Self-organizing systems have the capacity to create for themselves the aspects of organization that we thought we, as leaders, had to provide. Self-organizing systems create structures and pathways, networks of communication, values and meaning, behaviors and norms. In essence, they do for themselves most of what we believed we had to do for them. Rather than thinking of organization as an imposed structure, plan, design, or role, it is clear that in life, organization arises from the interactions and needs of individuals who have decided to come together. We see the results of these relationships in the forms that arise; but it is important, especially because we are so easily seduced by material forms, to look past these manifestations to the desires for relationship that gave birth to the forms.

It is easy to observe the clash of the old and new stories in many places, but one arena where it is painfully visible is in organizations that were created to fulfill some special purpose, some important call. People came together in response to the call; they joined because they knew that more was possible by organizing together than by staying alone. Their dream of contribution required an organization to move forward. These human desires—to find meaning in one's life, to bring more good into the world, to seek out others—are part of the new story.

But the clash with old beliefs and images occurs as soon as we embark on the task of creating an organization. We move back to machine ideas about structures, roles, designs, leaders. We create organizations from the outside, imposing these limiting designs on the rich desires of those who have come together. Over time, the organization that was created in response to some deep call becomes a rigid structure that impedes fulfilling that call. People come to resent the organization they created, because now it is a major impediment to their creativity, to their faith, to their purposeful dreams.

The new story holds out different images of organization—it teaches us that we, when we join together, are capable of giving birth to the form of the organization, to the plans, to the values, to the vision. All of life is self-organizing and so are we. But the new story also details a process for organizing that stands in shocking contrast to the images of well-planned, well-orchestrated, well-supervised organizing. I can summarize the organizing processes of life quite simply: Life seeks organization, but it uses messes to get there. Organization is a process, not a structure. Simultaneously, and in ways difficult to chart, the process of organizing involves creating relationships around a shared sense of purpose, exchanging and creating information, learning constantly, paying attention to the results of our efforts, co-adapting, coevolving, developing wisdom as we learn, staying clear about our purpose, being alert to changes from all directions. Living systems give form to their organization, and evolve those forms into new ones, because of exquisite capacities to create meaning together, to communicate, and to notice what's going on in the moment. These are the capacities that give any organization its true liveliness, that support self-organization.

In the new story, we enter a world where life gives birth to itself in response to powerful forces. These forces are the imperative to create one's self as an exploration of newness and the need to reach out for relationships with others to create systems. I could similarly describe them as the forces of creativity and freedom and the need to join with others for purposes that enrich both the individual and the system. These forces do not disappear from life, whatever approach we take to leadership, organizing, or relating. Even if we deny them, we never extinguish them. They are always active, even in the most repressive human organizations. Life can never stop asserting its need to create itself, and life never stops searching for connections. Because we misperceive life, we create responses in others that we then rail against. We then use their difficult behaviors to justify a controlling style of leadership. Many of the failures and discontents in today's organizations can be understood as the result of this denial of life's forces, and the pushing back of life against a story that excludes them.

As an example of these competing forces, think about how many times you have engaged in conversations about resistance to change. I have participated in far too many of these, and in the old days, when I still thought that it was me who was "managing" change, my colleagues and I always were thoughtful enough to plan a campaign to overcome this resistance. Contrast this view of human resistance to change with Kelly's images of life as "further processes of becoming and change . . . circles of becoming, inflaming itself with its own sparks, breeding upon itself more life and more wildness."[7] Who's telling the right story? Do we, as a species, dig in our heels while the rest of life is engaged in this awesome dance of creation? Are we the only problem, whereas the rest of life participates in something wild and wonderful?

The old story asserts that resistance to change is a fact of life. Having created a world image that sought stability and control, change has always been undesired and difficult. But the new story explains resistance not as a fact of life, but as evidence of an act against life. Life is in motion, constantly creating, exploring, discovering. Newness is its desire. Nothing alive, including us, resists these great creative motions. But all of life resists control. All of life pushes back against any process that inhibits its freedom to create itself.

In organizations of the old story, plans and designs are constantly being imposed. People are told what to do all the time. As a final insult, we go outside the organization to look for answers, returning with benchmarks that we offer up as great gifts. Yet those in the organization can only see these packaged solutions as insults. Their creativity has been dismissed, their opportunity to discover something new for the organization has been denied. When we deny life's need to create, life pushes back. We label it resistance and invent strategies to overcome it. But we could change the story and honor the resident creativity of those in our organization by figuring out how to invite them in. We need to work with these insistent creative forces or they will be provoked to work against us. Life isn't life unless it is free to create itself.

And most organizations deny the systems-seeking, self-organizing forces that are always present, the forces that, in fact, are responsible for uncharted levels of contribution and innovation. These fail to get reported because they occur outside "the boxes of preconceived possibility." There is no better indicator of the daily but unrecognized contributions made by people than when a municipal union decides to "work to rule." Cities cease running, civil functions stop—even though the rule books and policy manuals were designed to create productive employees. No organization can function on the planned contributions of its members. Without acknowledging it, we rely intensely on individuals going beyond the rules and roles. We rely on them to figure out what needs to be done, to solve an unexpected problem, to contribute in a crisis situation. But we seldom take this experience and use it to question our beliefs about structure, leadership, or motivation.

We also deny these system-seeking forces when we narrow people to self-serving work, when we pit colleagues against one another to improve performance, when we believe people are most strongly motivated by promises of personal gain. When we deny people's great need for relationships, for systems of support, for work that connects to a larger purpose, they push back. They may respond first by embracing competition, but then lose interest in the incentives. Performance falls back to precontest levels. In organizations driven by greed, people push back by distrusting and despising their leaders. In organizations that try to substitute monetary rewards for a true purpose, people respond with apathy and disaffection.

It is possible to look at the negative and troubling behaviors in organizations today as the clash between the forces of life and the forces of domination, between the new story and the old. Once we realize that we cannot ever extinguish these creative forces, that it is impossible to deny the life that lives in our organizations, we can begin to search for new ways of being together. Robert Greenleaf seemed well tuned to these forces. In expressing the need for servants to be leaders, and leaders to serve, he knew that the energy, desire, and talent for organizing comes from people. And though he drew from traditions other than science to explore his ideas about leadership, I feel a strong connection to his work through the understandings about organization that I have gleaned from the sciences. We act in service to the great creative desires that each of us carries. We serve one another because it is the nature of life to move toward one another. It is the nature of life to want to serve.

In many different places, the new story is emerging. It is, in its essence, a story about the human spirit. This realization is surfacing in many different disciplines and people. For those who have focused on organizations, I find it delightful to note that W. Edwards Deming, the great voice for quality in organizations, and Robert Greenleaf both focused on the human spirit in their final writings. Deming concluded his long years of work by stating simply that quality was about the human spirit. As we grew to understand that spirit, we would create organizations of quality. Greenleaf understood that we stood as servants to the human spirit, that it was our responsibility to nurture that spirit.

Following different paths, they arrived at the same centering place. We can create the lives and organizations we desire only by understanding the enlivening spirit in us that always is seeking to express itself. Servant-leaders help us understand ourselves differently by the way they lead. They trust our humanness; they welcome the surprises we bring to them; they are curious about our differences; they delight in our inventiveness. They trust that we can create wisely and well, that we seek the best interests of our organization and our community, that we want to bring more good into the world.

The Hope of the New Story

This new story gives us hope because it reveals some of life's beauty. In *The Soul's Code,* James Hillman comments that beauty is an essential need. Our human hearts long for beauty. "A theory of life," he notes, "must have a base in beauty if it would explain the beauty that life seeks."[8] The stories that we tell one another and the societies we create must allow us to see one another's beauty. Otherwise, we cannot love what we see.

We who hold this story feel both its beauty and its promise. What might we create if we lived our lives closer to the human spirit? What might our organizations accomplish if they trusted and called on that spirit? I want us to be telling this story in health care organizations, in schools, in religious denominations, in corporations. I want us to stop being quiet in the presence of businesspeople who sit on our boards and in our executive offices. As they offer *their* story as the standard, I want our voices to emerge with what *we* know to be true. I want business logic to stop being the only story; I want business imperatives to stop moving us away from the deeper realities we know. The old story has failed abysmally even in the for-profit sectors where it still dominates. Why would we continue to let such thinking move unchallenged into other kinds of organizations?

I would like to end by returning to the historic importance of the teller of new stories. When it is time for a new story to emerge, holding onto the past only intensifies our dilemma. We experience our ineffectiveness daily, and if we fail to find anything new, we descend more deeply into a profound sense of lost.

What we ask of the tellers of the new story is their voice and their courage. We do not need them to create a massive training program, a globalwide approach, a dramatic style. We only need them to speak to us when we are with them. We need them to break their silence and share their ideas of the world as they have come to know it.

If you carry this story within you, it is time to tell it, wherever you are, to whomever you meet. Brian Swimme compares our role with that of the early Christians. They had nothing but "a profound revelatory experience. They did nothing—nothing but wander about telling a new story."[9] As with these early believers, Brian encourages us to become wanderers, telling this new story. Through our simple wanderings, we will "ignite the transformation of humanity."

And he leaves us with a promise:

> What will happen when the storytellers emerge? What will happen when "the primal mind" sings of our common origin, our stupendous journey, our immense good fortune? We will become Earthlings. We will have evoked out of the depths of the human psyche those qualities enabling our transformation from disease to health. They will sing our epic of being, and stirring up from our roots will be a vast awe, an enduring gratitude, the astonishment of communion experiences, and the realization of cosmic adventure.[10]

What a wonderful promise. I invite you into the telling.

AFTERWORD

Understanding Robert K. Greenleaf and Servant-Leadership

Don M. Frick

Don M. Frick has worked with The Greenleaf Center since 1992. With Larry Spears, he is coeditor of On Becoming a Servant-Leader *(1996), and he has contributed essays and articles on servant-leadership to* Reflections on Leadership *(1995),* The Servant Leader *newsletter, and other publications. Don also writes and produces documentary, training, and promotional materials for national and local clients. He is a speaker and consultant on management and communication issues. Don is presently at work on a biography of Robert K. Greenleaf.*

In the afterword, Don Frick provides a fitting coda to this collection with his insider's look at Bob Greenleaf, the man. He provides us with insights into Greenleaf's own life evolution from a conservative "organization man" to the seeker of truth and meaning, which eventually found its strongest expression in his idea of "the servant as leader."

"Could you give me a quick, easy way to explain servant-leadership?" asked a university student involved in a campus servant-leadership program. "The biggest problem is explaining it to faculty. I started to answer one teacher by saying servant-leadership tends to result in a more flat organizational structure. He jumped in and said, 'Oh, the Japanese model. I'm already familiar with that,' and walked away."

The student did not begin his response by focusing on the core values of servant-leadership, but the faculty member's snap judgment and desire for an easy answer precluded further discussion. One is reminded of a conclusion Robert Greenleaf reached during a talk by his friend, psychotherapist William Wolf, "Once we judge, we have erected a wall against understanding."[1]

Many people would like a quick explanation of servant-leadership, but that may not be possible. Even though it is simple at its core—"a force of nature" as Stephen Covey observed—it is not easy to explain.[2] Nor is it easy to practice. That's because it describes a process of inner growth and outer consequences that, though based on some universal principles, must necessarily take unique expression within particular individuals and institutions. Organizations that embrace servant-leadership develop strikingly different organizational charts (which often more resemble maps), and individuals who seek to integrate its lessons express servant-leadership through their endless personality styles.

One could try for an easy answer by summarizing Greenleaf's own ideas, which we might summarize with the following statements: The servant-leader is one who is servant first and acts with integrity, foresight, intuition, a dedication to consensus, and a sense of history. Organizations can also be servants, as well as the trustees who hold organizations "in trust." Our entire society could be transformed by serving institutions deciding to become distinguished, using available resources. This short summary leaves out much of the richness of Greenleaf's writings but is still a messy answer to a simple question. Most of us would rather have the box defined, the categories outlined. We would rather squeeze out spirit and replace it with structure.

Alas for us, because, like most seminal thinkers, Greenleaf and his writings are generally more subtle than explicit. In fact, the word *servant* is one that Greenleaf chose in 1969 because he felt the word *spirit* was not communicating his message to people in organizations, especially universities.[3] Any synonym for *spirit* is bound to be messy!

In our efforts to understand servant-leadership, we constantly work within the tensions of its inherent paradoxes, which we naturally wish to resolve for our own comfort. To use Greenleaf's terms, we generally react as operationalizers rather than conceptualizers who accept a certain amount of ambiguity.[4] As a result, servant-leadership runs the risk of being misunderstood through reductionism that makes it "easy." That could happen in several ways.

First, if servant-leadership is reduced to a collection of admirable qualities and learned skills that are displayed in organizational settings, it is all too easy to forget that servant-leadership is, first, about deep identity. In his foreword to *On Becoming a Servant Leader*, Peter Drucker recalls an experience at the Bell System Advanced Management School in Asbury Park, New Jersey. A senior participant approached both Greenleaf and Drucker with a problem and asked, "What do I do?" Greenleaf immediately answered, "That comes later. First, what do you want to be?"[5] Greenleaf was a home-grown mystic in many ways, but a practical one who saw doing and being as inseparable. For him, servant-leadership begins with an enlargement of identity, followed by behaviors. The reverse order—enlarging behaviors to mask identity—is false, and people know it.

In his biographical notes Greenleaf tells how he learned this lesson, initially from his father, and later from his first foreman at AT&T. After a rigorous day digging postholes in a swamp near Akron, Ohio, Greenleaf's foreman waxed philosophical and told his young worker, "You know, if a fellow is an

S.O.B., deep down inside, he had just better go ahead and be one, because if he tries to be something else he will likely be seen as both a hypocrite and an S.O.B., and that's worse!"[6] In some of his later writings, Greenleaf delivers his own opinion that some people just aren't cut out to operate in the ways of a servant-leader and would do everyone a favor by simply being who they are.

There's another problem with turning servant-leadership into an easy, manageable checklist. We open the way to feeling guilt and frustration for not living up to this latest set of ideal standards and are tempted to project them on others, expecting them to be what we cannot. There has been a lot of projecting onto organizational types in the last few years: Lee Iacocca as a heroic John Wayne, the tough, strategic CEO as Atilla the Hun, even Jesus as a kindly manager who claims his anima. While projections are not all bad, and while we need to reclaim honest heroes (Greenleaf is one of mine), we can never lose sight that servant-leadership "starts in here, in the servant, not out there" with projections.[7]

In most Greenleaf Center workshops, at least one participant will mutter a comment like, "This sounds great, but my boss is the one who needs to hear it." That's another way of saying, "If I began to live these ideas myself I don't believe I could make a difference; so I'm going to make it easy by putting the responsibility on someone else." The good news about servant-leadership is that one person, acting with integrity, rooted in right motives, can make a difference. Defining an acceptable "difference" is the rub. If, by serving, one seeks attention or greater status or universal admiration, the flame is out. If, on the other hand, an acceptable difference is a perceptible change in the work environment—warming of trust, increased expressions of honesty, more honest attempts at power sharing—then the flame increases. Here's how Greenleaf put it in his journal in 1941:

> What does it take to make a rich life out of what one has in hand now? It means an end to daydreaming, speculation on ships coming in, promotions, salary increases, meeting influential people. Focus the mind on what is achievable with the materials and abilities in hand and dream about what is reachable by extending the hand from where one now stands. The reach of tomorrow will be gauged from where one stands tomorrow.
>
> This is somewhat the antithesis of "Hitch your wagon to a star," (or) "Ah, that a man's reach should exceed his grasp." Mountains are not moved this way nor are empires created nor great fortunes amassed. But a full life? Yes, I shall risk it.[8]

And risk it he did. Greenleaf consistently turned down promotions in order to make a difference in his own way at AT&T.

Newcomb Greenleaf, Robert's son, says his father came home one day and asked, "If you had a good idea and you wanted people to know about it, what would you do?"

Newcomb, a vital teenager at the time, replied, "I'd make a speech or put up posters. Make sure everyone heard about it."

"That would be one way to go about it," said his father. "But maybe you could just not say anything and start acting on your idea. Pretty soon people would notice and ask you about it and you could spread the idea that way."[9]

Newcomb was startled and thought this was a pretty dumb idea. Maybe it is, in some cases. But it is what Robert Greenleaf did. A few years before his death, speaking with Diane Cory and Fred Myers of AT&T, Greenleaf cautioned against having too much missionary zeal or being too open about any new principles that might shake up the organization. His counsel was to live it first.[10] That's something all of us can do, provided our own ego and grandiosity gets out of the way.

A second area where some seek to simplify the complexity of servant-leadership is by turning Greenleaf himself into a kindly, gentle dreamer who might have had few hard edges but nearly always got it right. The truth, as described by people who worked with him, is much more interesting.

In midcareer, Greenleaf met a manager at AT&T who helped young people extend their learning by putting them in situations that had a built-in failure factor. The failures were never devastating but could be constructive tools for learning as long as the young person carried that attitude.[11] Greenleaf admired this approach provided it was used sparingly, with the right people and the right motives. Dr. Joseph DiStefano, a colleague and protégé of Greenleaf's, has remembered that Greenleaf's assignments to his people sometimes bordered on the diabolical, but there was purpose and learning in the tasks, even when they were impossible.

Greenleaf was not always conciliatory, either. He could chase the money changers from the temple (a biblical event he questioned because of its use of coercive power) with righteous indignation. Sitting in on a high-level AT&T meeting one day, Greenleaf became suspicious of a presentation being made to the company. It was a multimillion-dollar proposal to provide economic education for all employees whether they needed it or not. During a break, Greenleaf went to a phone and asked his staff to do some quick investigation on the people offering the proposal. By lunchtime they had developed a dossier that would make the CIA proud, revealing that the two protagonists had shady histories.

In the afternoon when it became clear the group was ready to accept the proposal, Greenleaf revealed his information and then blew up. "Where is your thinking? Where is your intuition?" he demanded. He finished the tirade by declaring, "I think I'll sell all my stock in this company!" The board quickly backed down.[12]

Always gentle? No, but Greenleaf seemed to be consistently caring in his motives.

Greenleaf had his shadows, and they were no easier for him to face than for any of us. Always an avid learner, he spent two years in the late 1950s keeping track of his dreams and discussing them with Jungian therapists Ira Progoff and Martha Jaeger. His dream journal during these years, as well as other contemporary writings, reveal that he had some regrets about the time his work had stolen from his children, concerns about the organization-man persona he presented to the world (part of the problem was that it often fit too well), and a concern about a certain severity that lingered, in spite of the influence of his wife, Esther, an accomplished artist, an intellectual equal, and probably his greatest teacher about intuition. So, at the age of 56, Greenleaf was accomplished, admired, and frustrated. Somehow his destiny had not yet unfolded; his inner "call," which the Romans named the *genius* and the Greeks the *daimon,* was not fully answered. A shadow was blocking the fullest expression of his life's meaning. What was it?

Seeking answers, he talked with a pesky squirrel. Not a real squirrel, a dream squirrel. In his dream the squirrel nestled in Greenleaf's arms, digging sharp claws deep into his flesh, demanding attention. Greenleaf removed the squirrel, but its symbolism would not go away after he awoke. Having learned the art of engagement with dream images through his Jungian therapy, Greenleaf later had an imaginary conversation with the squirrel.

> So I talked with the squirrel. And he said that the part of me that doesn't trust myself is my capacity for great things. The untrusted part is my concern with possessions: thinking about possessions, protecting the future in terms of possessions. The capacity for greatness in me doesn't trust this and apparently will not materialize until this aspect of me is in check or transmuted.

If Greenleaf could face this block, the squirrel promised a great work would flow from him, as long as he did not write anything cute but wrote for all seekers, worldwide and universal. Pointing out that his family had suffered, the squirrel told Greenleaf, "When you get your great work underway, love and gentleness will follow."[13]

Greenleaf didn't know what to make of this experience. Was it simply ego or wishful thinking? Didn't his promised "great work" sound a little grandiose? In the end, he seemed to draw strength from the encounter, precisely because it helped him understand ways in which he was imperfect.

In Nikos Kazantzakis's novel *The Last Temptation of Christ,* Jesus' last temptation was the urge to be normal, to have a family, children, and a house in the suburbs. Greenleaf answered his own version of the last temptation by quitting his job at the age of 60 and going on to create a very unorthodox second career, writing on the servant theme, and bringing a powerful and positive influence to thousands of leaders and organizations.

Greenleaf wasn't perfect, and he wasn't always right. It remains to be seen whether his ideas about seminaries assuming the leavening role for a serving society are possible. Not all of his notions about organizational structures and board-staff relationships have worked well when they have been tried literally. That would be fine with Greenleaf, of course. His was a work in progress. He gave it his best shot, took the risk, and did something that was not easy.

If we wish to idealize anything about the person Robert Greenleaf, perhaps it should be his unwillingness to take the easy route: intellectually, personally, ethically, or in his inner life. In his essay "Uniqueness, Paradox and Choice," Greenleaf outlines ways in which servant-leadership is hard. For openers he warns us that these "achievements" may be misleading indicators of true growth: status or material success, social success, doing all that is expected of me, family success, relative peace and quiet, and compulsive busyness.

By contrast, those possessed of *entheos,* which is the power actuating one who is inspired, are likely to live with two paradoxes: a concurrent satisfaction and dissatisfaction with the status quo, and a concurrent feeling of broadening responsibilities and of centering down. He offers some practical tests for genuine growth, like the good use of time, an emerging sense of unity, and a developing view of people.[14]

In this and many other writings, Greenleaf observes that rewarding, challenging, risky growth is often uncomfortable and seldom neat. Servant-leadership simply is not easy. Most meaningful things seldom are.

ACKNOWLEDGMENTS

I am particularly indebted to my colleagues at the Greenleaf Center—Tamyra Freeman, Don Frick, Nancy Larner, Michele Lawrence, Isabel Lopez, Geneva Loudd, Jim Robinson, and Richard Smith, for their friendship, encouragement, and support. My own journey in servant-leadership has also been enriched through my partnership with the following past and present Greenleaf Center Trustees: Bill Bottum, Linda Chezem, Diane Cory, Sister Joyce DeShano, Joe DiStefano, Harley Flack, Newcomb Greenleaf, Bill Guillory, Carole Hamm, Jack Lowe Jr., Jeff McCollum, Ann McGee-Cooper, Andy Morikawa, Jim Morris, Paul Olson, Bob Payton, Sister Joel Read, Sister Sharon Richardt, Judith Sturnick, and Jim Tatum.

I am most grateful to two institutions—the W. K. Kellogg Foundation (especially Larraine Matusak, John Burkhardt, and Stephanie Clohessey) and Lilly Endowment Inc. (particularly Willis Bright and Craig Dykstra) for their unwavering support of servant-leadership and The Greenleaf Center.

My special thanks go to the staff of Impressions, Monika Jain, Sasha Kintzler, Laurie McGee, Ruth Mills, and Diane Worden, and especially to the many authors whose contributions make up the content of this book: James Autry, Susana Barciela, Joe Batten, Thomas Bausch, Ken Blanchard, Peter Block, Bill Bottum, James Conley, Diane Cory, Stephen Covey, Diane Fassel, Don Frick, John J. Gardiner, Jill Graham, Robert K. Greenleaf, Joe Jaworski, Elizabeth Jeffries, Robert Kelley, Jim Kouzes, Larry Lad, Dorothy Lenz, John Lore, Jack Lowe Jr., David Luechauer, Jeff McCollum, Ann McGee-Cooper, Ken Melrose, Richard Nielsen, Parker Palmer, John Schuster, Irving Stubbs, Judith Sturnick, Fraya Wagner-Marsh, Margaret Wheatley, and Christine Wicker.

I want to thank my family and friends for their love and encouragement, especially my wife, Beth Lafferty; my sons, James and Matthew Spears; and my parents, Bertha and L.C. Spears. I would also like to thank the following people and institutions for their encouragement and support along the way: James Autry, Walter Brogan, Dick Broholm, Steve Brooks, Max Case, the Central Committee for Conscientious Objectors, the Childbirth Education Association of Greater Philadelphia, Donna Davis, Roberta and Robert DeHaan, Vinton Deming, DePauw University, Max DePree, Karen Farmer, Anne Fraker, Friends Journal, Friends Select School, Joe and Laurie Goss, Cathy Gray, the Great Lakes Colleges Association's Philadelphia Center, the Greater Philadelphia Philosophy Consortium, Robert K. Greenleaf, John and Mary Gummere, John Haynes, Todd and Ellen Daniels-Howell,

Frank and Marian Killian, Michael Krausz, Eva and Richard Krebs, John and Aline Lafferty, Roger and Verona Lafferty, Jon Landau, Diane Lisco, Isabel Lopez, John Nason, Marcia Newman, Keith Opdahl, Lou Outlaw, M. Scott Peck, Mike and Nancy Revnes, Olcutt Sanders, Karen Shultz, Peter Senge, Alice Simpson, Elissa Sklaroff, Debra Spears, Lucian and Chassie Spears, Debra Thomas, Kelly Tobe, Wendell Walls, and Signe Wilkinson.

Finally, I wish to express my deep appreciation to the many servant-leaders working within countless institutions around the world. Your efforts at building spirit in the workplace truly inspire others to servant-leadership.

ABOUT THE EDITOR AND THE GREENLEAF CENTER FOR SERVANT-LEADERSHIP

Larry Spears is a prolific writer and editor. He is a contributing author to Leadership in a New Era *(New Leaders Press, 1994). He is also the editor of a book of essays,* Reflections on Leadership, *published by John Wiley & Sons in 1995 and now in its fourth printing. Spears has co-edited two books of previously unpublished works by Robert Greenleaf,* On Becoming a Servant-Leader *and* Seeker and Servant, *both published in 1996 by Jossey-Bass. Since 1970, Spears has also published over 300 articles, essays, and book reviews, including many for in-house publications. Among his more recent articles are: "Servant-Leadership: Quest for Caring Leadership" and "Merging Competition and Compassion." He writes and edits the Greenleaf Center's quarterly newsletter,* The Servant-Leader, *as well.*

Spears was named Executive Director of the Robert K. Greenleaf Center for Servant-Leadership in February 1990. Under his leadership, The Greenleaf Center has experienced tremendous growth and influence. As a manager and leader, Spears has been noted for his successes in applying entrepreneurial methodologies to nonprofit organizations. He has also frequently spoken on the topic of servant-leadership. The titles of some of his addresses include "Servant-Leadership and the Honoring of Excellence" and "Greenleaf's Influence on Trusteeship."

In addition to his involvement with the Center, Spears is a member of the National Society of Fund Raising Executives, the World Futures Society, and the American Society of Association Executives. Spears serves as a board trustee for the Quaker magazine Friends Journal *and chairs its advancement committee.*

The Greenleaf Center for Servant-Leadership in Indianapolis, Indiana, is an international nonprofit educational organization that seeks to encourage the understanding and practice of servant-leadership. The Center's mission is to improve the caring and quality of all institutions through a new approach to leadership, structure, and decision making.

The Greenleaf Center's programs include the worldwide sale of books, essays, and videotapes on servant-leadership and the preparation and presentation of workshops, seminars, institutes, retreats, an annual international conference, a partnership program, and consultation.

Through the dissemination of Robert Greenleaf's ideas about servant-leadership, a number of institutions and individuals have been changed. Servant-leadership is now used as an institutional model, as the basis for educating and training nonprofit trustees and community leaders, as the foundation of college and university courses and corporate training programs, and as a vehicle for personal growth and transformation.

For further information about the resources for study and programming available from the Center, contact:

The Greenleaf Center for Servant-Leadership
921 East Eighty-Sixth Street, Suite 200
Indianapolis, IN 46240
phone (317) 259-1241; fax (317) 259-0560
e-mail: greenleaf@iquest.net
visit us at http://www.greenleaf.org

NOTES

Foreword

1. Helen Gardner, *Composition of "Four Quartets,"* (London: Faber, 1978), p. 242.

Introduction

1. Robert K. Greenleaf, *The Servant as Leader* (Indianapolis: The Robert Greenleaf Center, 1970).
2. Ibid., p. 7.
3. Ibid., p. 27.
4. Ibid., p. 20.
5. Peter Block, *Stewardship: Choosing Service Over Self-Interest* (San Francisco: Berrett-Koehler, 1993) and *The Empowered Manager* (San Francisco: Jossey-Bass, 1987).
6. Greenleaf, *The Servant as Leader,* p. 30.
7. Robert Levering and Milton Moskowitz, *The 100 Best Companies to Work for in America* (New York: Doubleday/Currency, 1993), p. 443.
8. Max DePree, *Leadership Is an Art* (New York: Dell Trade Paperback, Bantam, Doubleday, 1989) and *Leadership Jazz* (New York: Dell, 1992).
9. Peter Senge, *The Fifth Discipline* (New York: Doubleday, 1990).
10. Robert K. Greenleaf, *Trustees as Servants,* (Indianapolis: The Robert Greenleaf Center, 1991).
11. Scott Peck, *A World Waiting to Be Born: Civility Rediscovered* (New York: Simon & Schuster, 1993), p. 366.
12. Juana Bordas, "Pluralistic Reflection on Servant-Leadership," in *The Servant-Leader* (newsletter of The Greenleaf Center), Summer 1993.
13. Patsy Sampson, *The Leader as Servant* (Indianapolis: The Robert Greenleaf Center, 1989), p. 3.

Chapter 1

1. Albert Camus, *Create Dangerously.*
2. Hermann Hesse, *Journey to the East* (New York: Noonday Press/Farrar Straus and Giroux, 1956).

Chapter 2

1. Ken Blanchard, John Carlos, and Alan Randolph, *Enpowerment Takes More Than a Minute* (San Francisco: Berrett-Koehler Publishers Inc., 1996).
2. Don Shula and Ken Blanchard, *Everyone's a Coach* (New York and Grand Rapids, Mich.: Harper Business and Zondervan Publishing House, 1995).

Chapter 3

1. Robert K. Greenleaf, *Servant Leadership* (New York: Paulist Press, 1977), p. 13.

2. Ibid., p. 14.
3. Robert Greenleaf, "Life's Choices and Markers" (commencement speech given at Alverno College, Milwaukee, Wisconsin, Spring 1984). Published in *Reflections on Leadership* (New York, John Wiley & Sons, 1995), p. 17.
4. Greenleaf, *Servant Leadership*.
5. Michael Novak, *Business as a Calling: Work and the Examined Life* (New York: The Free Press, 1996).
6. Greenleaf, *Servant Leadership,* p. 7.
7. Greenleaf, "Life's Choices and Markers."
8. Ibid.
9. Frederick Buechner, *Wishful Thinking: A Theological ABC* (San Francisco: HarperCollins, 1973).
10. Richard Bolles, *How to Find Your Mission in Life* (Berkeley: Ten Speed Press, 1991).
11. Stephen Covey, *The Seven Habits of Highly Effective People* (New York: Simon & Schuster, 1989).
12. Greenleaf, "Life's Choices and Markers."
13. Michael Novak, *Business as a Calling*.
14. Ibid.
15. Edward Hoffman, *The Right to Be Human: A Biography of Abraham Maslow* (Los Angeles: Jeremy P. Tarcher, Inc., 1988).
16. Greenleaf, *Servant Leadership*.
17. Peter Block, 1994 Keynote Address, International Conference on Servant Leadership, The Greenleaf Center for Servant Leadership, 1994, Indianapolis.

Chapter 4

1. Warren Bennis and Burt Nanus, *Leaders* (New York: Harper & Row, 1985).
2. Rosabeth Moss Kantor, *The Change Masters,* (London: Routledge, 1983).
3. Robert Schuller, *The Be (Happy) Attitudes,* (New York: Bantam Books, 1987).
4. Joe Batten, *Building a Total Quality Culture* (Menlo Park, Calif.: Crisp Publications, 1992).

Chapter 5

1. Mary Morrison, "In Praise of Paradox."
2. Peter Block, *The Empowered Manager* (San Francisco: Jossey-Bass, 1987).
3. Ibid.

Chapter 6

1. Stephen Covey, *First Things First* (New York: Fireside/Simon & Schuster, 1994), p. 203.
2. Robert Levering and Milton Moskowitz, *The 100 Best Companies to Work for in America* (New York: Currency/Doubleday, 1993).

Chapter 7

1. Robert Greenleaf, *The Servant as Leader* (Indianapolis: The Greenleaf Center, 1970), p. 13.
2. Peter Senge, *The Fifth Discipline* (New York: Doubleday, 1990).
3. Viktor Frankl, *Man's Search for Meaning* (New York: Simon and Schuster, 1959).
4. Greenleaf, *The Servant as Leader,* p. 7.

Chapter 8

1. Robert Putnam, "Bowling Alone," *Journal of Democracy*.

Chapter 10

1. Robert K. Greenleaf, *The Servant as Leader* (Indianapolis: The Robert K. Greenleaf Center, 1991), p. 1.
2. David Bohm, *Wholeness and the Implicate Order* (London: Ark Paperbacks, 1980), p. 3.
3. Vaclav Havel in Parker J. Palmer, "Leadership from Within: Reflections on Spirituality and Leadership," Madison, Wisconsin, October, 1990, p. 2.
4. Charlene Spretnak, *States of Grace* (New York: HarperCollins, 1991), p. 188.
5. David Bohm, quoted in Joseph Jaworski, *Synchronicity: The Inner Path of Leadership* (San Francisco: Berrett-Koehler Publishers, 1996), p. 80.
6. Thich Nhat Hanh, *The Heart of Understanding* (Berkeley, Calif.: Parallax Press, 1988), p. 4.
7. Mahatma Gandhi, *All Men Are Brothers* (New York: Continuum, 1990), p. 71.
8. Hermann Hesse, *Siddhartha* (New York: Bantam, Books, 1951).
9. Ralph Waldo Emerson, *Self Reliance* (New York: Bell Tower, 1991), p. 34.
10. Gandhi, *All Men*, p. 63.
11. Teilhard de Chardin, quoted in Stephen R. Covey, *The Seven Habits of Highly Effective People* (New York: Simon & Schuster, 1989), p. 319.
12. Emerson, *Self-Reliance*, p. 32.
13. Robert H. Waterman Jr., *The Renewal Factor* (Toronto: Bantam Books, 1987), p. 10.
14. Kevin W. Kelley, *The Home Planet* (Reading, Mass.: Addison-Wesley, 1988), p. 12.
15. Ibid., p. 196.
16. Ibid., p. 121.
17. Ibid., p. 126.
18. Spretnak, *States*, p. 188.
19. Stephen J. Bergman and Janet Surrey, "The Changing Nature of Relationships on Campus: Impasses and Possibilities," *Educational Record* 74 (Winter 1993): 14.
20. Fritjof Capra, *The Web of Life* (New York: Doubleday, 1996), p. 295.
21. Robert Gilman, "The Next Great Turning," *In Context 33* (Winter 1993): 11–12.
22. Capra, *The Web*, p. 7.
23. Bohm, quoted in Jaworski, *Synchronicity*, pp. 80–81.
24. William Blake, quoted in Wayne W. Dyer, *Your Sacred Self* (New York: HarperCollins, 1991), p. 58.
25. Covey, *Seven Habits of Highly Effective People*, pp. 46–63.
26. Bohm, *Wholeness*, pp. 1–26.
27. Ibid., p. 23.
28. Robert Fritz, *The Path of Least Resistance* (New York: Fawcett Columbine, 1984), p. 3.
29. Ibid., pp. 4–5.
30. James MacGregor Burns, *Leadership* (New York: Harper and Row, 1978).
31. Robert K. Greenleaf, *Servant Leadership* (New York: Paulist Press, 1977).
32. Robert K. Greenleaf, *Old Age: The Ultimate Test of the Spirit* (Indianapolis: The Robert K. Greenleaf Center, 1987), p. 2.
33. Kate Steichen, "Natural Leadership," in *Leadership in a New Era*, ed. John Renesch (San Francisco: New Leaders Press, 1994), pp. 118–19.
34. John Ruysbroeck, quoted in T. C. McLuhan, *Cathedrals of the Spirit* (New York: HarperCollins, 1996), p. 262.
35. Howard Gardner, *Leading Minds: An Anatomy of Leadership* (New York: HarperCollins, 1995), p. 278.
36. Paul Roland, *Revelations: The Wisdom of the Ages* (London: Carlton Books Limited, 1995), pp. 90–91.
37. Greenleaf, *Old Age*, p. 8.
38. Ibid., pp. 14–15.
39. Ibid., p. 25.
40. Deepak Chopra, *Ageless Body, Timeless Mind* (New York: Harmony Books, 1993), p. 314.
41. Francisco Varela, quoted in Jaworski, *Synchronicity*, pp. 179–80.
42. Jaworski, *Synchronicity*, p. 91.
43. Sperry Andrews, "Promoting a Sense of Connectedness among Individuals by Scientifically Demonstrating the Existence of a Planetary Consciousness," *Alternative Therapies* 2 (May 1996): 39–45.
44. Paul Hawken, *The Magic of Findhorn* (New York: Harper and Row, 1975), pp. 314, 325.

45. Jaworski, *Synchronicity.*
46. Robert K. Greenleaf, *The Servant as Leader* (Indianapolis: The Robert K. Greenleaf Center, 1988), p. 19.
47. Diana L. Eck, *Encountering God* (Boston, Mass.: Beacon Press, 1993), p. 158.
48. Duane Elgin, "Awakening to the Species Mind," *Noetic Sciences Review* 40 (Winter 1996): 19.
49. Krishnamurti, *You Are the World* (New York: Harper & Row Publishers, 1972), p. 117.
50. W. B. Yeats, "Mindfulness."
51. Other essays in area: John J. Gardiner, "Interdisciplinary Groups and Leadership Teams," *European Journal of Engineering Education* 16 (1991): 269–72; John J. Gardiner, "Beyond Leader and Community: Creating New Metaphors," Proceedings of the Association of Management 13th Annual International Conference 13 (August 1995), pp. 56–62; John J. Gardiner, "Building Leadership Teams," in *Leaders for a New Era,* ed. Madeleine F. Green (New York: American Council on Education/Macmillan, 1988), pp. 137–53; John J. Gardiner, "Excellence in Research: Restructuring Higher Education for the 1990s," *Educational Record* 71 (Spring 1990): 51–53.

Chapter 11

1. Information about Robert Greenleaf's work came from his articles and book and my personal interviews with him. His numbers concerning black manager employment levels within AT&T are the same as those in the Wharton School Industrial Research Unit study by Northup and Larson (see the following note 8). I met Robert Greenleaf and learned of his work in the Religious Society of Friends, of which we are both members.
   Parts of this article first appeared in my following two journal articles and book. Permission to use this material is gratefully acknowledged:
   " 'I Am We' Consciousness and Dialog as Organizational Ethics Method," *Journal of Business Ethics* 10 (1991): 649–63. Copyright 1991 by Kluwer Academic Publishers.
   "Woolman's 'I Am We' Triple-Loop Action-Learning: Origin and Application in Organization Ethics," *Journal of Applied Behavioral Science* 29, no. 1 (1993): 117–38. Copyright 1993 by NTL Institute, Inc., and Sage Publications, Inc.
   The Politics of Ethics: Methods for Acting, Learning, and Sometimes Fighting with Others in Addressing Ethics Problems in Organizational Life (New York: Oxford University Press). Copyright 1996 by Oxford University Press.
2. Robert Greenleaf, *Servant Leadership* (New York: Paulist Press, 1977).
3. Richard P. Nielsen, " 'I Am We' Consciousness and Dialog"; "Woolman's 'I Am We' Triple-Loop Action-Learning"; *The Politics of Ethics.*
4. John Woolman, *The Works of John Woolman in Two Parts,* 5th ed. (Philadelphia: Benjamin & Thomas Kite, 1774/1818); Paul H. Emden, *Quakers in Commerce* (London: Sampson Low, Marston & Co., 1939); Rufus M. Jones, "Our Day in the German Gestapo," *Friends Intelligencer,* 2 August 1947; Frederick B. Tolles, *Meeting House and Counting House: The Quaker Merchants of Colonial Philadelphia 1682–1763* (New York: Norton, 1948); Robert Greenleaf, *Servant Leadership;* Robert Greenleaf, "Overcome Evil with Good," *Friends Journal,* 15 May 1977, pp. 292–96.
5. Nielsen, "Woolman's 'I Am We' Triple-Loop Action-Learning"; *The Politics of Ethics.*
6. Nielsen, " 'I Am We' Consciousness and Dialog."
7. Nielsen, "Woolman's 'I Am We' Triple-Loop Action-Learning"; *The Politics of Ethics.*
8. Herbert R. Northrup and James A. Larson, *The Impact of the AT&T-EEO Consent Decree* (Philadelphia: University of Pennsylvania, Industrial Research Unit, The Wharton School, 1979).
9. Woolman, *The Works of John Woolman;* Anne Gummere, *The Journal and Essays of John Woolman* (London: Macmillan, 1922). Nielsen, "Woolman's 'I Am We' Triple-Loop Action-Learning"; *The Politics of Ethics.*
10. Gummere, *The Journal and Essays of John Woolman;* Frederick B. Tolles, *Meeting House and Counting House;* Sydney V. James, *A People among Peoples: Quaker Benevolence in Eighteenth-Century America* (Cambridge: Harvard University Press, 1963).
11. George B. Nash and John R. Soderland, *Freedom by Degrees: Emanicipation in Pennsylvania and Its Aftermath* (New York: Oxford University Press, 1991).
12. Greenleaf, *Servant Leadership,* pp. 29–30.

13. Woolman, *The Works of John Woolman*, p. 39.
14. Ibid., p. 45.
15. Ibid., p. 54.
16. Ibid., p. 59.
17. Ibid., pp. 50–51.
18. Gummere, *The Journal and Essays of John Woolman;* Nash and Soderland, *Freedom by Degrees*.
19. Woolman, *The Works of John Woolman*, p. 460.
20. Ibid., p. 54.
21. Ibid.
22. James Kouzes and Barry Z. Posner, *The Leadership Challenge* (San Francisco: Jossey-Bass, 1995).
23. Howard Gardner, *Leading Minds: An Anatomy of Leadership* (New York: Basic Books, 1995).
24. George Fox, *The Journal of George Fox*, ed. John L. Nickalls (Cambridge: Cambridge University Press, 1952).
25. Paul Ricoeur, *From Text to Action: Essays in Hermeneutics* (Evanston, Ill.: Northwestern University Press, 1991), p. 334.
26. Jones, "Our Day in the German Gestapo."
27. Ibid, appendix 3, p. 1.
28. Ibid.
29. Ibid., appendix 1, pp. 1–2.
30. Ibid., appendix 3, p. 2.
31. Elizabeth Gray Vining, *Friend of Life: The Biography of Rufus M. Jones* (Philadelphia: Lippincott, 1958).
32. Chris Argyris, *Overcoming Organizational Defenses: Facilitation Organizational Learning* (Boston: Allyn and Bacon, 1990).
33. Woolman, *The Works of John Woolman*, p. 380.

Chapter 12

1. Kenneth Andrews' pioneering work on corporate strategy (*The Concept of Corporate Strategy*, 3d ed. [Homewood, Ill.: Irwin, 1987, originally published in 1971]) included an explicit discussion of values, but that perspective was not widely shared in the early years of strategy research. Only within the last decade has a body of work developed that focuses on the ethical underpinnings of strategy; for example, see R. Edward Freeman and Daniel R. Gilbert, *Corporate Strategy and the Search for Ethics* (Engelwood Cliffs, N.J.: Prentice-Hall, 1988); R. Edward Freeman, Daniel R. Gilbert, and Edwin Hartman, "Values and the Foundations of Strategic Management," *Journal of Business Ethics* 7 (1988): 821–34; Daniel R. Gilbert, "Corporate Strategy and Ethics," *Journal of Business Ethics* 5 (1986): 137–50 and *The Twilight of Corporate Strategy: A Comparative Ethical Critique* (New York: Oxford University Press, 1992); Larue Tone Hosmer, "Strategic Planning as If Ethics Mattered," *Strategic Management Journal* 15 (1994): 17–34; Martin Meznar, James J. Chrisman, and Archie B. Carroll, "Social Responsibility and Strategic Management: Toward an Enterprise Strategy Classification," *Academy of Management Best Papers Proceedings*, (1990); 332–36; and Edwin A. Murray, "Ethics and Corporate Strategy," in *Corporations and the Common Good*, ed. Robert B. Dickie and Leroy S. Rouner (Notre Dame, Ind.: University of Notre Dame Press, 1986).
2. Andrews, *The Concept of Corporate Strategy*, p. 13.
3. Igor Ansoff, "The Changing Shape of the Strategic Problem," in *Strategic Management*, ed. Dan E. Schendel and Charles W. Hofer (Boston, Mass.: Little Brown, 1979).
4. R. Edward Freeman, *Strategic Management: A Stakeholder Approach* (Boston: Pitman, 1984), p. 89.
5. Meznar, Chrisman, and Carroll, "Social Responsibility and Strategic Management," p. 333.
6. Freeman and Gilbert, *Corporate Strategy and the Search for Ethics*, pp. 70–71.
7. Ibid., p. 73.
8. Ibid. pp. 75–76.
9. Ibid. p. 80.

10. Robert Greenleaf, *Servant Leadership: A Journey into the Nature of Legitimate Power and Greatness* (New York: Paulist Press, 1977).

11. James MacGregor Burns, *Leadership* (New York: Harper & Row, 1978).

12. Jill W. Graham, "Servant-Leadership in Organizations: Inspirational and Moral," *Leadership Quarterly* 2, no. 2 (1991): 105–19.

13. Jill W. Graham, "Leadership, Moral Development, and Citizenship Behavior," *Business Ethics Quarterly* 5, no. 1 (1995): 43–54.

14. Lawrence Kohlberg, "Moral Stages and Moralization: The Cognitive-Developmental Approach, in *Moral Development and Behavior,* ed. Thomas Lickona (New York: Holt, Rinehart & Winston, 1976).

15. Carol Gilligan, *In a Different Voice: Psychological Theory and Women's Development* (New York: Oxford University Press, 1982).

16. Irving L. Janis, *Victims of Groupthink: A Psychological Study of Foreign-Policy Decisions and Fiascoes* (Boston: Houghton Mifflin, 1972).

17. Gilligan, *In a Different Voice.*

18. Burns, *Leadership.*

19. John Rawls, *A Theory of Justice* (Cambridge, Mass.: Harvard University Press, 1971).

20. Ronald A. Heifetz, *Leadership without Easy Answers* (Cambridge, Mass.: Harvard University Press, 1994), p. 3.

21. Burns, *Leadership,* p. 20.

22. Ibid., p. 42.

23. Heifetz, *Leadership without Easy Answers,* p. 2.

Chapter 13

1. See W. Edwards Deming, Mary Walton, *The Deming Management Method* (New York Perisee/Rotnam, 1986); Thomas J. Peters and Robert H. Waterman, *In Search of Excellence* (New York: Harper & Row, 1982); Stephen R. Covey, *The Seven Habits of Highly Effective People* (New York: Simon & Schuster, 1989).

2. Chester Barnard, *The Functions of the Executive* (Cambridge Mass.: Harvard Univ. Press, 1938).

3. Douglas McGregor, *The Human Side of Enterprise* (New York: McGraw-Hill, 1960).

4. Robert Greenleaf, *The Servant as Leader* (Newton Center, Mass.: Robert K. Greenleaf Center, 1970), p. 7.

5. Robert K. Greenleaf, *Servant Leadership* (New York: Paulist Press, 1977), pp. 63–72.

6. George San Facon, personal interview, August 1996.

7. Paul Ray, "The Integral Culture Survey," Fetzer Institute and Institute of Noetic Sciences (Paul Ray, 1995).

Chapter 14

1. This chapter builds on and adapts material from two sources: Robert E. Kelley, *How to Be a Star at Work: the Breakthrough Strategies That Help Ordinary People Become Extraordinary Performers* (New York: Times Books, in press) and Robert E. Kelley, *The Power of Followership* (New York: Doubleday, 1992).

2. Arnold "Red" Auerbach, "Misleading Followers," *Harvard Business Review* (January–February 1989): 152.

3. John Huey, "Secrets of Great Second Bananas," *Fortune,* 6 May 1991, 64–76.

4. Chester I. Barnard, *The Functions of the Executive* (Cambridge, Mass.: Harvard University Press, 1938).

5. William Frederick and James Weber, "The Values of Corporate Managers and Their Critics: An Empirical Description and Normative Implications," in *Business Ethics: Research Issues and Empirical Studies,* ed. William Frederick and Lee Preston (Greenwich, Conn.: 1990).

6. Rick Wartzman, "Nature or Nurture? Study Blames Ethical Lapses on Corporate Goals," *Wall Street Journal,* 9 October 1987, p. 27.

7. Harvey Hornstein, *Managerial Courage* (New York: John Wiley & Sons, 1986).

8. John Huey, "Nothing is Impossible," *Fortune,* 23 September 1991, pp. 135–40.

Chapter 15

1. Matthew Fox, *The Reinvention of Work: A New Vision or Livelihood for Our Time* (Harper-SanFrancisco, San Francisco: 1995), 127.
2. Walter Wink, "The Spirits of Institutions," a paper prepared for the Institutional Vocation Exploration at the Fetzer Institute, December 11–13, 1996.
3. Parker Palmer, "Leading from Within," *Noetic Sciences Review* (Winter 1996): 35.

Chapter 16

1. The original version of this chapter appeared as a pamphlet based on a speech entitled "Leading from Within: Reflections on Spirituality and Leadership," published by the Indiana Office for Campus Ministries in Indianapolis with support from the Lilly Endowment, 1990. My thanks to Sharon Palmer, and to Barbara McNeill of the Institute of Noetic Sciences, who offered helpful editorial advice for this revision.
2. Vaclav Havel, "The Revolution Has Just Begun," *Time,* March 5, 1990, pp. 14–15.
3. Annie Dillard, *Teaching a Stone to Talk* (New York: Harper & Row, 1982), pp. 94–95.
4. Rainer Maria Rilke, *Letters to a Young Poet* (New York: Vintage Books, 1987), p. 78.

Chapter 17

1. J. Ruth Gendler, *The Book of Qualities* (New York: Harper Perennial, 1988).
2. John Heider, *The Tao of Leadership* (New York: Bantam Books, 1986).
3. Benjamin Hoff, *The Tao of Pooh* (New York: Penguin Books, 1983).

Chapter 18

1. Charles Handy, *The Age of Paradox* (Cambridge: Harvard Business School Press, 1994), p. 28.
2. John O'Neil, *The Paradox of Success* (New York: G. P. Putnam's Sons, 1994), p. 128.
3. Ian Morrison, *The Second Curve* (New York: Ballantine, 1996), p. 7.
4. O'Neil, *The Paradox of Success,* p. 123.
5. Peter Gomes, "The New Liberation Theology," *Harvard Magazine,* Nov.–Dec. 1996.
6. Juliet Schorr, *The Overworked American* (New York: Basic Books, 1992), p. 21.
7. Erik Erikson, reported by Doris Kearns Goodwin of a seminar given by Erikson on the critical importance of finding balance in life.
8. Elsa Walsh, *Divided Lives: The Public and Private Struggles of Three Accomplished Women* (New York: Simon & Schuster, 1995), p. 18.
9. Helen Nearing and Scott Nearing, *Living the Good Life: How to Live Simply and Sanely in a Troubled World* (New York: Schocken Books, 1987), p. 36.
10. Robert Greenleaf, untitled, undated book manuscript, p. 54.
11. Ibid.
12. Margaret Wheatley and Myron Kellner-Rodgers, *A Simpler Way* (San Francisco: Berrett-Koehler, 1996), p. 13.
13. Robert Greenleaf, *The Servant as Leader* (Indianapolis: The Robert K. Greenleaf Center, 1991), p. 34.
14. Greenleaf, *The Servant as Leader,* p. 12.
15. Paulanne Balch, private correspondence, 1996.
16. Adrienne Rich, ed., *The Best American Poetry 1996* (New York: Scribner, 1996), p. 23.

Chapter 19

1. Gerard Manley Hopkins, "Inversnaid," *Poems of Gerard Manley Hopkins,* 3d ed. (New York and London: Oxford University Press, 1948), p. 95.
2. Charles Handy, *The Age of Unreason* (Boston: Harvard Business Review Press, 1989).

3. Charles Handy, "Unimagined Futures," in Francis Hesselbein, Marshall Goldsmith, and Richard Beckhard, *The Organization of the Future* (San Francisco, Jossey-Bass, 1997), pp. 377–83.

4. Ibid, p. 378.

5. Ibid, p. 379.

6. Robert K. Greenleaf, *Servant Leadership* (New York: Paulist Press, 1977), p. 4.

7. Stephen R. Covey, *The Seven Habits of Highly Effective People* (New York: Simon & Schuster, Fireside Edition, 1990).

8. Francis Fukayama, *Trust: The Social Virtues and the Creation of Prosperity* (New York: Freedom Press, 1995).

9. Handy, "Unimagined Futures," p. 381.

10. Ibid.

11. Peter Drucker, "Introduction: Toward the New Organization," in *The Organization of the Future,* ed. Frances Hesselbein, et al., (San Francisco: Jossey-Bass, 1997).

12. Greenleaf, *Servant-Leadership,* pp. 29–34.

13. Tom Wolfe, *Bonfire of the Vanities* (New York: Farrar Straus Giroux, 1989).

14. Dennis P. McCann, "'If Life Hands You a Lemmon . . .': Business Ethics from *The Apartment* to *Glengary Glenn Ross,"* Notre Dame Center for Ethics and Religious Values in Business, September 30, 1996.

15. Max DePree, *Leadership Is an Art* (New York: Dell Trade Paperback, Bantam Doubleday Dell, 1989), p. 129.

16. Studs Terkel, *Working* (New York: Pantheon Books, 1972), p. 104.

17. For a very incisive work on business managers who lose their jobs and the turmoil that is caused in personal lives, I recommend the work of William Byron.

18. Lee Tavis, *The Multinational Firm and Developmental Responsibility* (South Bend, Ind.: University of Notre Dame Press, 1997). If there is any situation calling for the servant-leader in business, it is the management of the multinational in the third world. Tavis analyzes the problems and appropriate responses. The book includes a number of cases where one is forced to ask, what difference could the servant-leader make?

19. Greenleaf, *Servant-Leadership,* p. 14.

20. Edwin O'Connor, *The Last Hurrah* (Boston: Little, Brown, 1956).

21. John Haughey, "The Growing Dilemma of Loyalty to the Firm," Business Vocation Conference, Georgetown University, Washington, D.C., 1993, p. 8.

22. The lack of meaning most executives find in their work has been researched by Thomas McMahon. The results were published in "Religion and Business: Concepts and Data," *Chicago Studies,* 28, no. 1 (April 1989).

23. Anyone interested in this company should read the case, "Starbucks: Taking the Espresso Lane to Profits," by Melissa A. Schilling, in C. W. L. Hill, and R. J. Jones, *Strategic Management An Integrated Approach,* 3d ed., (Boston: Houghton Mifflin, 1995), pp. C19–C38.

24. Derek F. Abel, *Defining the Business: The Starting Point of Strategic Planning* (Englewood Cliffs, N.J.: Prentice-Hall, 1980), p. 17.

25. Michael Novak, *The Catholic Ethic and the Spirit of Capitalism* (New York: Free Press, Macmillan, 1993), p. 85.

26. Pope John Paul II, *Centesimus Annus* (Washington, D.C.: United States Catholic Conference, 1991), #32.

27. Ibid., #37.

28. Ibid., #43.

29. Michael J. Naughton, *An Organizational Work Ethic Based on the Papal Social Tradition,* Ph.D. diss., Marquette University, 1991.

30. Michael Stebbins can be contacted at The Woodstock Center, Georgetown University, Washington, D.C. for his working papers on the subject.

31. Greenleaf, *Servant Leadership,* p. 14.

32. Ibid., p. 15.

33. Ibid.

34. Ibid.

Chapter 20

Quotes in this chapter were obtained through personal interviews.

Chapter 21

1. "Body Shop Questions Hurt Socially Aware Investing," *Detroit Free Press,* 17 September 1994, p. 9A.
2. Dan R. Dalton, Michael B. Metzger, and John W. Hill, "The 'New' U.S. Sentencing Commission Guidelines: A Wake-up Call for Corporate America," *Academy of Management Executive* 8, no. 1 (1994), pp. 7–13.
3. Lynn S. Paine, "Managing for Organizational Integrity," *Harvard Business Review* (March/April 1994): 106–17.
4. Norman Bowie, "The Firm as a Moral Community," in *Morality, Rationality, and Efficiency: New Perspectives on Socio-Economics,* ed. Richard M. Coughlin (New York: M. E. Sharpe, Inc., 1991).
5. Kenneth E. Aupperle, Archie B. Carroll, and John D. Hartfield, "An Empirical Examination of the Relationship between Corporate Social Responsibility and Profitability," *Academy of Management Journal* 28 (1985): 446–63.
6. "Social Responsibility and the Bottom Line," *Business Ethics* (July/August 1994): 11.
7. John Kohls, Christi Chapman, and Casey Mathieu, "Ethics Training Programs in the Fortune 500," *Business & Professional Ethics Journal* 8, no. 2 (1989): 55–72.
8. Robert Kennedy, "Virtue and Corporate Culture: The Ethical Formation of Baby Wolverines," *Review of Business* (Winter 1995/1996): 10–15.
9. Edward Ottensmeyer and Gerald D. McCarthy, *Ethics in the Workplace* (New York: McGraw-Hill, 1996).
10. Patrick E. Murphy, "Creating Ethical Corporate Structures," *Sloan Management Review* 30, no. 2 (Winter 1989): 81–87.
11. Kohls et al., "Ethics Training Programs."
12. Susan J. Harrington, "What Corporate America Is Teaching about Ethics," *Academy of Management Executive* 5, no. 1 (1991): 21–30.
13. Murphy, "Creating Ethical Corporate Structures."
14. Harrington, "What Corporate America Is Teaching about Ethics."
15. Kennedy, "Virtue and Corporate Culture."
16. Chris Lee and Ron Zemke, "The Search for Spirit in the Workplace, *Training,* June 1993, pp. 21–28.
17. Jay Conger, *Spirit at Work: Discovering the Spirituality in Leadership* (San Francisco: Jossey-Bass, 1994); Max DePree, *Leadership Jazz* (New York: Dell, 1992); Tom Chappell, *The Soul of a Business* (New York: Bantam, 1993); Peter Block, *Stewardship: Choosing Service Over Self-Interest* (San Francisco: Berrett-Koehler, 1993); Kendrick Melrose, *Making the Grass Greener on Your Side: A CEO's Journey to Leading by Serving* (San Francisco: Berrett-Koehler, 1995).
18. Lee and Zemke, "The Search for Spirit,"; Ellen Brandt, "Corporate Pioneers Explore Spirituality," *HRMagazine,* April 1996, pp. 82–87; Michele Galen and Karen West, "Companies Hit the Road Less Traveled," *Business Week,* June 5, 1995, pp. 82–84.
19. "Merging Spirituality with Work," *Business Ethics,* July/August 1994, p. 27.
20. *The Trusteed Corporation: A Case Study of the Townsend & Bottum Family of Companies* (New York: Carl Rieser, 1987).
21. "Interview—Tom Chappell," *Business Ethics,* January/February 1994, pp. 16–18.
22. Beverly Geber, "Herman Miller: Where Profits and Participation Meet," *Training,* November 1987, pp. 62–66.
23. "People Are the Chemistry at Lancaster Laboratories," Annual Report, 1991.
24. Ronald Henkoff, "Piety, Profits, and Productivity," *Fortune,* June 29, 1992, pp. 84–85.
25. Galen and West, "Companies Hit the Road Less Traveled."
26. Ian I. Mitroff, Richard O. Mason, and Christine M. Pearson, "Radical Surgery: What Will Tomorrow's Organizations Look Like?" *Academy of Management Executive* 8, no. 2 (1994): 11–21.
27. Lee and Zemke, "The Search for Spirit."
28. Block, *Stewardship.*
29. DePree, *Leadership Jazz.*
30. Ibid.
31. Stephen R. Covey, *The Seven Habits of Highly Effective People* (New York: Simon & Schuster, 1989).
32. Ibid., p. 35.

33. M. Scott Peck, *The Road Less Traveled* (New York: Simon & Schuster, 1978) and *A World Waiting to Be Born* (New York: Simon & Schuster, 1993).
34. "Interview—M. Scott Peck," *Business Ethics,* March/April 1994, pp. 17–19.
35. Mitroff et al., "Radical Surgery."
36. "Interview—M. Scott Peck."
37. Larry Spears, ed., *Reflections on Leadership* (New York: John Wiley & Sons, 1995).
38. James Kouzes and Barry Pozner, *Credibility: How Leaders Gain and Lose It, Why People Demand It* (San Francisco: Jossey-Bass, 1993).
39. John H. Dobbs, "The Empowerment Environment," *Training and Development* 47, no. 2 (1993): 55–57.
40. Earl Hess, personal interview between Earl Hess and James Conley, August 1995.
41. Ibid.
42. Marie Bothé, personal interview between Marie E. Bothé and James Conley, August 1995.
43. "Interview with Bill George: In Care of the Company Soul," *Business Ethics,* November/December 1993, pp. 17–19.
44. Ibid.
45. Richard Osborne, "Company with a Soul, *IW,* May 1, 1995, pp. 21–26.
46. Walter Kiechel, "The Leader as Servant," *Fortune,* May 4, 1992, pp. 121–22.

Chapter 22

1. Robert Greenleaf, "An Inward Journey," *Servant Leadership* (New York: Paulist Press, 1977), p. 816.
2. C. G. Jung, "Synchronicity: An Acausal Connecting Principle," in *The Structure and Dynamics of the Psyche,* Vol. 8 of *The Collected Works of C. G. Jung,* trans. R.F.C. Hull (Princeton: Princeton University Press, 1960), p. 520.
3. Greenleaf, "The Servant as Leader," *Servant Leadership,* p. 16.
4. Hermann Hesse, *Demian: The Story of Emil Sinclair's Youth,* trans. M. Roloff and M. Lebeck (New York: Bantam Books, 1965), p. 108.
5. Viktor Frankl, *Man's Search for Meaning* (New York: Washington Square Press, 1959, 1984), p. 127.
6. Friedrich Nietzche, quoted in *Man's Search for Meaning,* p. 97.
7. James Hillman, *The Soul's Code: In Search of Character and Calling* (New York: Random House, 1996), p. 7.
8. Joseph Campbell with Bill Moyers, *The Power of Myth,* ed. Betty S. Flowers (New York: Doubleday, 1988), p. 120.
9. W. N. Murray, *The Scottish Himalayan Expedition,* quoted in *Synchronicity: The Inner Path of Leadership* by Joseph Jaworski (San Francisco: Berrett-Koehler, 1996), p. 137.
10. Robert K. Greenleaf, *On Becoming a Servant Leader, ed. Don M. Frick and Larry C. Spears (San Francisco: Jossey-Bass Publishers, 1996), pp. 241–42.
11. Robert K. Greenleaf, *The Leadership Crisis: A Message for College and University Faculty* (Indianapolis: The Robert K. Greenleaf Center for Servant-Leadership, 1985), p. 8.
12. Ibid., 1986, Introduction.
13. James C. Collins and Jerry I. Porras, *Built to Last: Successful Habits of Visionary Companies* (New York: HarperBusiness, a division of HarperCollins, 1997), p. xxiii.
14. Collins and Porras, "Building Your Company's Vision," *Harvard Business Review* (September–October 1996): 66.
15. Collins and Porras, *Built to Last,* p. xiii.
16. Greenleaf, "The Leadership Crisis," 1986, Introduction.
17. Ibid.
18. Robert K. Greenleaf, "On Being a Seeker in the Late Twentieth Century," *Friends Journal: Quaker Thought and Life Today,* September 15, 1975, p. 25.
19. Ibid., p.20.
20. Winston Churchill, *Second World War,* Vol. 1 (Boston: Houghton Mifflin, 1948), p. 526.
21. Greenleaf, "Servant Responsibility in a Bureaucratic Society," *Servant Leadership,* p. 293.
22. Greenleaf, "Preface to the Ethic of Strength," *On Becoming a Servant Leader,* p. 14.
23. Peter F. Drucker, Foreword to *On Becoming a Servant Leader,* p. xii.
24. Greenleaf, *My Debt to E. B. White* (Indianapolis: The Robert K. Greenleaf Center for Servant-Leadership, 1987), p. 1.

25. Ibid.
26. Ibid., p. 22.
27. Henry David Thoreau, quoted in *My Debt to E. B. White,* pp. 6–7.
28. A. Machado, quoted in *Synchronicity* by Joseph Jaworski, p. 134.
29. Greenleaf, "Leadership and Foresight," *On Becoming a Servant Leader,* p. 319.
30. Greenleaf, "The Future Is Now," *On Becoming a Servant Leader,* p. 75.
31. Greenleaf, *Old Age: The Ultimate Test of Spirit (An Essay on Preparation)* (Indianapolis: The Robert K. Greenleaf Center for Servant-Leadership, 1987), p. 15.

Chapter 23

1. Roberto Assagioli, *Psychosynthesis* (New York: Penguin Books, 1965).
2. Uzair Siddiqui's quote is printed with permission.
3. The following excerpt is printed with permission from Steadfast Publishing, the publishers of *Hum-Drum to Hot Diggity,* 1993, a book of essays on the human spirit written by the author.

Chapter 24

1. Edward Lawler, "The New-Post Heroic Leadership," *Fortune,* February 21, 1994.
2. Ken Melrose, *Making the Grass Greener on Your Side* (San Francisco: Barrett-Koehler, 1995).
3. Ibid.

Chapter 25

1. Interview with Sister Joyce DeShano, Senior Vice President, Sponsorship, Sisters of St. Joseph Health System.
2. Interview with Sister Janet Fleischhacker, President, Sisters of St. Joseph of Nazareth.
3. Deshano.
4. Don M. Frick, *Reflections on Leadership; From Acorns to Forests: The Sisters of St. Joseph Health System and Leadership in a Christian Organization,* 1995.
5. Fleischhacker.
6. DeShano.
7. Interview with Tom Thibault, Vice President, Organizational Development, Sisters of St. Joseph Health System.
8. Ibid.
9. Ibid.
10. Fleischhacker.
11. DeShano.

Chapter 26

1. Lao-tzu, *Tao Te Ching,* A new English version, with foreword and notes, by Stephen Mitchell (New York: HarperCollins Publishers, 1988).
2. Rabindranath Tagore. *Collected Poems and Plays,* 1973.

Chapter 28

1. Portions of this article are adapted from *The Leadership Challenge: How to Keep Getting Extraordinary Things Done in Organizations* by James M. Kouzes and Barry Z. Posner (San Francisco: Jossey-Bass, 1995).
2. Richard Farson, *Management of the Absurd: Paradoxes of Leadership* (New York: Simon & Schuster, 1996), p. 34.

3. Max DePree. *Leadership Jazz* (New York: Currency Doubleday, 1992), pp. 1–3.
4. Ibid., p. 5.
5. Anita Roddick, *Body and Soul: Profits with Principles—The Amazing Story of Anita Roddick and the Body Shop* (New York: Crown Publishers, 1991), pp. 17, 21, 25, 117.

Chapter 29

1. Max DePree, *Leadership Jazz* (New York: Doubleday, 1992).
2. Robert Greenleaf, *The Servant Leader* (Indianapolis, Ind: The Robert K. Greenleaf Center, 1991), p. 7.
3. Robert Greenleaf, *On Becoming a Servant Leader* (San Francisco: Jossey-Bass, 1996).
4. Peter Block, *The Empowered Manager* (San Francisco: Jossey-Bass, 1987), p. 178.
5. David Whyte, personal communication during AT&T training programs.
6. Greenleaf, *On Becoming a Servant Leader*.
7. Thomas Moore, *The Re-Enchantment of Everyday Life* (New York: HarperCollins, 1996), p. 280.
8. Robert Greenleaf, *Servant and Seeker* (San Francisco: Jossey-Bass, 1996), p. 163.
9. Annie Dillard, *The Writing Life* (New York: Harper & Row, 1989), p. 32.
10. Moore, *The Re-Enchantment of Everyday Life*.
11. Greenleaf, *The Servant Leader*.
12. Milhaly Csikszentmihalyi, *Flow: The Psychology of Optimal Experience* (New York: Harper & Row, 1990).
13. Ronald Heifetz, *Leadership without Easy Answers* (Cambridge, Mass.: The Belknap Press of Harvard University Press, 1994).
14. Peter Vaill, *Learning as a Way of Being* (San Francisco: Jossey-Bass, 1996), p. 135.
15. Ibid., p. 136.
16. Thomas Teal, "The Human Side of Management," *Harvard Business Review* 74, no. 6 (1996): 35.
17. Howard Gardner, *Leading Minds* (Cambridge, Mass.: The Belknap Press of Harvard University Press, 1995).
18. Here I am using Ronald Heifetz's definition of authority as "power conferred in exchange." This thought explains how the machine bureaucracy functions—through a series of relationships in which individuals give up their power to those in authority.
19. Teal, "The Human Side of Management."
20. Greenleaf, *On Becoming a Servant Leader*, p. 129.
21. Robert Bly, *The Sibling Society* (Reading, Mass.: Addison-Wesley, 1996).
22. Robert Kelley, *The Power of Followership* (New York: Doubleday Currency, 1992).

Chapter 30

1. Brian Swimme and Thomas Berry, *The Universe Story* (San Francisco: HarperSanFrancisco, 1992).
2. Kevin Kelly, *Out of Control* (Reading, Mass.: Addison-Wesley, 1994).
3. A.R. Ammons, *Tape for the Turn of the Year* (New York: W.W. Norton, 1965).
4. Ilya Prigogine, "The Philosophy of Instability," *Futures* (August 1989): 396–400.
5. Francisco Varela and Humberto Maturana, *The Tree of Knowledge* (Boston, Mass.: Shambala, 1992).
6. Lynn Margulis, private correspondence.
7. Kelly, *Out of Control*.
8. James Hillman, *The Soul's Code* (New York: Random House, 1996).
9. Swimme, *The Universe Story*.
10. Ibid.

Afterword

1. "Notes on talks by Dr. William Wolf, psychotherapist, 1960–1971." Robert K. Greenleaf Archives.

2. Stephen Covey, from his presentation at the International Conference on Servant-Leadership, October 1995.
3. Letter from Robert Greenleaf to Bob Lynn, October 15, 1983. Robert K. Greenleaf Archives.
4. Robert Greenleaf, "The Operator verses the Conceptualizer." *On Becoming a Servant Leader,* (San Francisco: Jossey-Bass, 1996), pp. 217–20.
5. Greenleaf, *On Becoming a Servant Leader,* Foreword, p. xii.
6. "Autobiography Miscellaneous Notes." Robert K. Greenleaf Archives.
7. Robert Greenleaf, *Servant-Leadership* (New York: Paulist Press, 1976), p. 44.
8. Robert Greenleaf, "Journal, 1940–1943," 6 September 1941, Robert K. Greenleaf Archives.
9. Greenleaf, Newcomb. Closing remarks to International Conference on Servant-Leadership, October 1995.
10. Videotaped interview with Robert Greenleaf, conducted by Fred Meyer and Diane Cory, December 1986. Robert K. Greenleaf Archives.
11. Robert Greenleaf, "Being Who You Are," *Seeker and Servant* (San Francisco: Jossey-Bass, 1996), pp. 163–65.
12. Letter from Robert Greenleaf to Bob Lynn, October 15, 1983. Robert K. Greenleaf Archives.
13. Robert Greenleaf, "Dreams, c. 1958–1962," Robert K. Greenleaf Archives.
14. Robert Greenleaf, "Uniqueness, Paradox, and Choice. Notes on a Strategy for Potentially Successful People," Robert K. Greenleaf Archives.

PERMISSIONS AND COPYRIGHTS

Chapter 9, "Dharamshala Dreaming: A Traveler's Search for the Meaning of Work," is an original essay by Susana Barciela. Copyright © 1997 Susana Barciela. Printed with permission of the author.

Chapter 10, "Quiet Presence: The Holy Ground of Leadership," is an original essay created for this collection by John J. Gardiner. Copyright © 1997 John J. Gardiner. Printed with permission of the author.

Chapter 11, "Quaker Foundations for Greenleaf's Servant-Leadership and "Friendly Disentangling" Method," is an original essay created for this collection by Richard P. Nielsen. Copyright © 1997 Richard P. Nielsen. Printed with permission of the author.

Chapter 12, "Servant-Leadership and Enterprise Strategy," is an original essay created for this collection by Jill W. Graham. Copyright © 1997 Jill W. Graham. Printed with permission of the author.

Chapter 13, "Within Our Reach: Servant-Leadership for the Twenty-first Century," is an original essay created for this collection by Bill Bottum with Dorothy Lenz. Copyright © 1997 Bill Bottum. Printed with permission of the author.

Chapter 14, "Followership in a Leadership World," is an original essay created for this collection by Robert E. Kelley. Copyright © 1997 Robert E. Kelley and Consultants to Executives and Organizations, Ltd. All rights reserved. Printed with permission of the author.

Chapter 15, "Healing Leadership," is an original essay created for this collection by Judith A. Sturnick. Copyright © 1997 Judith A. Sturnick. Printed with permission of the author.

Chapter 16, "Leading from Within," by Parker J. Palmer is adapted from a pamphlet based on a speech entitled "Leading from Within: Reflections on Spirituality and Leadership," published by the Indiana Office for Campus Ministries in Indianapolis, Indiana. Copyright © 1997 Parker J. Palmer. Printed with permission of the author.

Chapter 17, "The Killing Fields: Institutions and the Death of Our Spirits," is an original essay created for this collection by Diane Cory. Copyright © 1997 Diane Cory. Printed with the permission of the author.

Chapter 18, "Lives in the Balance: The Challenge of Servant-Leaders in a Workaholic Society," is an original essay created for this collection by Diane Fassel. Copyright © 1997 Diane Fassel. Printed with permission of the author.

Chapter 19, "Servant-Leaders Making Human New Models of Work and Organization," is an original essay created for this collection by Thomas A. Bausch. Copyright © 1997 Thomas A. Bausch. Printed with permission of the author.

Chapter 20, "Seeking the Soul of Business," by Christine Wicker originally appeared as an article in *The Dallas Morning News*. Copyright © 1995. *The Dallas Morning News,* Dallas, Texas. All rights reserved. Reprinted by permission of *The Dallas Morning News*.

RECOMMENDED READING

Autry, James A. *Confessions of an Accidental Businessman*. San Francisco: Berrett-Koehler, 1996.

Blanchard, Ken, and Michael O'Connor. *Managing by Values*. San Francisco: Berrett-Koehler, 1997.

Block, Peter. *Stewardship*. San Francisco: Berrett-Koehler, 1993.

Broholm, Richard, and Douglas Johnson. *A Balcony Perspective: Clarifying the Trustee Role*. Indianapolis: The Greenleaf Center, 1993.

Chaleef, Ira. *The Courageous Follower: Standing Up To and For Our Leaders*. San Francisco: Berrett-Koehler, 1995.

Cheshire, Ashley. *A Partnership of the Spirit*. Dallas: TDIndustries, 1987.

Covey, Stephen. *First Things First*. New York: Fireside/Simon & Schuster, 1994.

Daloz, Laurent A. Parks, Cheryl H. Keen, James P. Keen, and Sharon Daloz Parks. *Common Fire: Lives of Commitment in a Complex World*. Boston: Beacon Press, 1996.

DePree, Max. *Leadership Is an Art*. New York: Doubleday, 1989.

———. *Leadership Jazz*. New York: Dell Publishing, 1992.

Fassel, Diane. *Working Ourselves To Death*. San Francisco: HarperCollins, 1990.

Greenleaf, Robert K. *The Institution as Servant*. Indianapolis: The Greenleaf Center, 1976.

———. *Servant Leadership*. New York: Paulist Press, 1977.

———. *The Leadership Crisis*. Indianapolis: The Greenleaf Center, 1978.

———. *Servant: Retrospect and Prospect*. Indianapolis: The Greenleaf Center, 1980.

———. *The Servant as Religious Leader*. Indianapolis: The Greenleaf Center, 1982.

———. *Seminary as Servant*. Indianapolis: The Greenleaf Center, 1983.

———. *Life's Choices and Markers*. Indianapolis: The Greenleaf Center, 1986.

———. *My Debt to E. B. White*. Indianapolis: The Greenleaf Center, 1987.

———. *Old Age: The Ultimate Test of Spirit*. Indianapolis: The Greenleaf Center, 1987.

———. *Teacher as Servant: A Parable*. Indianapolis: The Greenleaf Center, 1987.

———. *Education and Maturity*. Indianapolis: The Greenleaf Center, 1988.

————. *Have You a Dream Deferred*. Indianapolis: The Greenleaf Center, 1988.

————. *Spirituality as Leadership*. Indianapolis: The Greenleaf Center, 1988.

————. *Trustees as Servants*. Indianapolis: The Greenleaf Center, 1990.

————. *Advices to Servants*. Indianapolis: The Greenleaf Center, 1991.

————. *The Servant as Leader*. Indianapolis: The Greenleaf Center, 1991.

————. *On Becoming a Servant Leader*. San Francisco: Jossey-Bass, 1996.

————. *Seeker and Servant*. San Francisco: Jossey-Bass, 1996.

Hennessy, James E., and Suki Robins, editors. *Managing Toward the Millenium*. New York: Fordham University Press, 1991.

Hesse, Hermann. *The Journey to the East*. New York: The Noonday Press, 1992.

Jaworski, Joseph. *Synchronicity: The Inner Path of Leadership*. San Francisco: Berrett-Koehler, 1996.

Jeffries, Elizabeth. *The Heart of Leadership: Influencing by Design*. Dubuque: Kendall/Hunt, 1993.

Kelley, Robert. *The Power of Followership: How to Create Leaders People Want to Follow . . . And Followers Who Lead Themselves*. New York: Doubleday/Currency, 1992.

Kouzes, James M., and Barry Z. Posner. *Credibility: How Leaders Gain and Lose It, Why People Demand It*. San Francisco: Jossey-Bass Publishers, 1993.

Levering, Robert, and Milton Morkowitz. *100 Best Companies To Work for in America*. New York: Currency/Doubleday, 1993.

Liebig, James E. *Business Ethics: Profiles in Civic Virtue*. Golden, Co.: Fulcrum Publishing, 1991.

Marcic, Dorothy. *Managing with the Wisdom of Love*. San Francisco: Jossey-Bass, 1997.

Matusak, Larraine R. *Finding Your Voice*. San Francisco: Jossey-Bass, 1997.

McGee-Cooper, Ann, Duane Trammell, and Barbara Lau. *You Don't Have to Go Home from Work Exhausted!* New York: Bantam Books, 1992.

Melrose, Ken. *Making the Grass Greener on Your Side: A CEO's Journey to Leading by Serving*. San Francisco: Berrett-Koehler, 1995.

Nielsen, Richard P. *The Politics of Ethics*. New York: Oxford University Press, 1996.

Palmer, Parker J. *The Active Life: A Spirituality of Work, Creativity, and Caring*. San Francisco: Harper & Row, 1990.

Peck, M. Scott. *The Road Less Traveled*. New York: Simon & Schuster, 1978.

————. *A World Waiting to Be Born: Civility Rediscovered*. New York: Bantam, 1993.

Renesch, John, editor. *New Traditions in Business: Spirit and Leadership in the 21st Century*. San Francisco: Berrett-Koehler Publishers, 1992.

————. *Leadership in a New Era*. San Francisco: New Leaders Press, 1994.

Rieser, Carl. *The Trusteed Corporation: A Case Study of the Townsend & Bottum Family of Companies*. Indianapolis: The Robert K. Greenleaf Center, 1988.

Schuster, John P., Jill Carpenter, and M. Patricia Kane. *The Power of Open Book Management*. New York: John Wiley & Sons, 1996.

Senge, Peter M. *The Fifth Discipline: The Art and Practice of the Learning Organization*. New York: Doubleday/Currency, 1990.

Spears, Larry C., editor. *Reflections on Leadership: How Robert K. Greenleaf's Theory of Servant-Leadership Influenced Today's Top Management Thinkers*. New York: John Wiley & Sons, 1995.

Vaill, Peter. *Learning as a Way of Being*. San Francisco: Jossey-Bass, 1996.

Wheatley, Margaret J. *Leadership and the New Science: Learning about Organization from an Orderly Universe*. San Francisco: Berrett-Koehler, 1992.

Williams, Lea E. *Servants of the People: The 1960s Legacy of African American Leadership*. New York: St. Martin's Press, 1996.

INDEX

Page numbers in **boldface** designate **biographical sketches** of contributors; in *italics, figures*. The letter t after page numbers refers to tables.